Read the original

Russell

Gwen Byrne

"The greatest love story ever told"
Michael Roll - Researcher and Author
www.cfpf.org.uk

"A moving book...a joy to read"
Chloris Morgan - Writer and Researcher

"very interesting...a wealth of survival evidence"
Robin Foy - Author & Researcher
www.physicalmediumship4u.ning.com

Available to buy online...

The Russell Connection

Reuniting Parents with their Children in the Spirit World through Physical & Trance Mediumship

by
Gwen Byrne

Psychic Book Club Publishing UK

www.psychicbookclub.com

The Russell Connection -
Reuniting Parents with their Children in the Spirit World
through Physical & Trance Mediumship

by Gwen Byrne

Published in Great Britain
by Psychic Book Club Publishing

on September 21st 2014
~ Russell Byrne's birthday ~

www.psychicbookclub.com

© Copyright K Jackson-Barnes 2014
(except chapters 8, 10, 14, 21 & 23
where copyright remains with the respective authors)
Front cover image - courtesy & copyright of Christine Brisley Z

All rights reserved. No part of this work may be
reproduced, stored in a retrieval system, or transmitted in any
form or by any means, electronically, mechanically, photocopied,
or otherwise without prior permission of the copyright holder,
nor be otherwise circulated in any form other than which it is published.

Any lyrics or amended lyrics are included herein for purely education and research
purposes. No copyright infringement is intended.
Since every effort has been made to contact relevant copyright holders,
the publisher regrets any unwilling copyright infringements -
but would be pleased to hear from any current copyright holders.

A catalogue record for this book is available from the British Library.
Copies also legally deposited with Cambridge University Library,
the National Library of Wales, the National Library of Scotland,
the Library of Trinity College Dublin and the Bodleian Libraries
of the University of Oxford.

ISBN: 978-0-9575007-2-3

Dedication...

In Loving Memory of Sharon Byrne 1957 - 2003

My second book, is dedicated to the seven men in my Earthly life.

*To my husband Alf for his wonderful support
and his love and devotion through it all.*

*Also to my sons, Kevin and Gary, now two fine men
and of course the four lights of my life,
my Grandsons - Graeme, Jon, Russell and Brett.*

I hope that this Truth stays with them, all through their lives.

~ Gwen Byrne

Contents

A Father's Letter

The Meeting

Foreword

Introduction
...or how the Pink Panther Society began !

One
Mother's Day

Two
The Agony & the Ecstasy

Three
A Motorway Adventure

Four
Automatic Writing & Puzzles

Five
Grail Haven

Six
A Time For More Learning...

Seven
Recorded Trance Mediumship Session

Eight
My Son Steven...by Gill Smith

Nine
America I Love You !

Ten
Two Little Sisters...by Shirley Gifford

Eleven
Angel of Music

Twelve
I'm A Music Man !

Thirteen
Hello...? It's Time !

Fourteen
What I Think About My Daughter's Death...by D.Wheatley

Fifteen
I'm Nine & Three Quarters, So There !

Sixteen
Bridging Two Worlds

Seventeen
A Magical Mystery Tour ?

Eighteen
Summerland Tape Three

Nineteen
Gossamer Nets

Twenty
The Great Master

Twenty One
Margaret Prentice's Story

Twenty Two
Poetry By Another Bridge

Twenty Three
Alan Brown's Story - by Frankie Brown

Twenty Four
My Field Of Dreams

Twenty Five
When A Child Is Born

Twenty Six
Reincarnation - The Cycle of Souls

Twenty Seven
A Chapter Of Mysteries To Solve !

Twenty Eight
Sunrise, Sunset

Twenty Nine
The Heart Is Slow To Learn...

Thirty
Here Comes The Millennium !

Postscript
...& Russell Vernon Byrne Has The Last Word.

A Father's Letter...

July 6th 2010

Dear Mrs Byrne,

I have been meaning to write for some time, but have been involved in other distractions.

Nevertheless, here I am finally writing to warm-heartedly thank you from the depth of my soul, for the profound effect your first book 'Russell' has had upon me - and the seismic shift it has had on my way of thinking.

After losing my daughter to suicide in 2006 I became caught up in a vortex of guilt, anger, frustration and gut-wrenching sadness. It was as if I was drowning in an endlessly deep ocean, but on reading your book I could swim to the surface and breath again. Words cannot and shall never describe my sense of relief and joy enabling me to once again smile and laugh.

I am fairly well read, but other books pale into insignificance compared to your book. It has given me gave me a reason to live.

Please, please fully understand and comprehend the importance of your work and how desperately it is needed by millions of others who need reassurance and need to know of the Spiritual World's eternal love and compassion.

Keep up the good work. It is much needed and loved.

Your sincerely,

Mr. A.G.

The Meeting

'Come gently now' my dear child said,
'For I know more than you.
Arise now, let me take you from your bed,
To a beautiful land that's new,

Come let me show you wonderful skies,
Teach you all I have learned in this land,'
Then he held my face and I dried my eyes,
And we floated off, hand in hand,

With joy in our hearts, and love in our souls,
Together we did entwine,
So I'm here at last - I am part of the whole,
I was his - this was love - he was mine.

We went up towards the Golden Light,
We were together, forever - at last,
Then with a chuckle he said, 'I told you it'd be alright'
All your sadness is now in the past,

'Dear child' I said, 'you have not changed'
He said, 'no Mum, nor have you,'
And with another embrace, we both held hands,
And we flew and we flew and we flew...

~ received through the Mediumship
of Frankie Brown.

Foreword

by K. Jackson-Barnes

I met Gwen Byrne when she was in her 85th year and I found her as bright as a button. Her mind is as agile today as when she was a child and her interest in the mysteries of life continue. At the time, I already had a copy of her first book, *'Russell'* but I hadn't read it. I'd imagined Gwen's story would be one of tragic loss and like many others, were followed by a comforting collection of Spirit messages from Mediums. I couldn't have been more mistaken.

So who is Russell and what's the connection ?

I learned that Russell Vernon Byrne had passed away just before his tenth birthday. It was 1963 and his parents and brothers felt his loss like nothing on Earth. His mother was not content that he had gone for good and it soon became clear, that Russell was not content to stay silent either...

Six months after his 'death' Russell had inspired the famous Psychic artist Frank Leah, to draw his picture for his parents. Gwen had also started to visit various Spirit Mediums and kept meticulous notes from all her sittings. Over time, it became clear that Russell had more than just comforting words to share - he seemed to have a mission of his own.

The evolving soul of Russell Byrne soon explained that he had decided to help other Spirit children, so they could reach their own parents on Earth !

Years later, a miracle came when Russell's father Alfie, received the kind of phone call that all bereaved parents dream of...

It appeared that Russell had managed to materialise in a Leicester séance room and he had a simple message for the small group assembled. He told them that he wanted to reunite with his parents - and he even supplied the correct telephone number to call. Once again, Gwen and Alfie's world was turned upside down.

Gwen told me, that over the next seven years Russell would regularly materialise at these séances, where he shared his wisdom, his songs and his dreams. Then one Christmas, he brought a toy Pink Panther into the séance room as a gift for his parents. Then he asked his mother to form a special self-help group called 'Russell's Pink Panther Society.' He wanted her to help other bereaved parents, so they could share their burdens of loss, but they also began to exchange stories of experiences of Spirit contact with their own children...

Eventually, Gwen began corresponding with dozens of other bereaved mothers and fathers and together they helped each other. This book contains the true stories from some of those who have re-connected with their beloved children after death. There are also detailed transcripts included, taken from various séance recordings, where Russell chats away quite naturally with those present. These have never been published before and stand as a testament to the power of the Spirit World when working with such a dedicated Medium as Rita Goold.

Yet aside from Gwen's own adventures and discoveries, this book details a family's journey together - beyond receiving simple messages of comfort - and moves into deeper realms of understanding.

Now, after 50 years of study and the publication of her first book, one could say that Gwen Byrne's second volume is a labour of love. Yet all the Mums, their partners, families and their children in the Spirit World have played their part. Even I could not have taken on the task of helping to publish this work properly and not be affected by it. I have learned so much - especially about the power of music. Gwen Byrne is almost like a 'walking music box' herself, because she has an amazing recall of tunes, songs and their lyrics. Like his mother, Russell uses songs throughout this book, to get his message across and for inspiration. So when Russell Byrne is around, you can expect a song and dance !

It is wrong to think that anyone is bigger or better than another, but I do believe that Russell Vernon Byrne is a very special boy from the Spirit World. His legacy grows and his work continues and if ever you feel a tune come to mind and you just don't know where it came from, check the lyrics, because there may be a message there for you - from someone in the Spirit World who loves you !

The connection is right here..

> *'Wherever the love light shines, there is hope.*
> *Wherever a bond exists, there is continuation.*
> *Whenever the mind is open, there is communication.'*

Introduction

...or how the Pink Panther Society began !

by Russell Vernon Byrne

'Well, I was working in the Children's Realms
with my new pal called Al Brown,
I said, 'Look at all the sad little faces Al'
- for each of them held a frown.

They're sad because they miss their Mums and Dads,
then I came up with this idea.
'I'll form a contact club' I said,
'to prove that we are here.'

'You see Al, I've already contacted my dear Mum.'
'How do you do that ?' he said.
'It's easy Al, just form a thought
and put it in their head.'

'I'll show you how' and so I did,
then he went off to contact his Mum,
'Good luck' I said, 'I'll see you later.'
and off went my old chum.

I sat there pondering, deep in thought,
when out of a clear blue sky,
stood Helen and Raymond in front of me,
with a twinkle in their eye...

'Russell, we have a job for you,
we need a little clown.
Someone to make others laugh' they said,
'to lift them when they feel down.'

'You see, we're going to materialise on Earth through a circle where,
the energy is rare but True,
and we need a clown to lift the vibrations.
Come on, we'll show you what to do.'

'Then through your Mum & Dad, you can form your club,
we'll give you our support.
'What's the name of your club ?' they asked.
'Don't know yet, I said, 'I'll think of an apport.'

Now I've always liked the Pink Panther,
so I'll send one to my Mum !
Oh that will make her laugh I know,
and stop her feeling glum.

The day was set and time was near,
I felt electrified - my parents sitting there,
'Hello Mum, hello Dad,' says I,
It's me, it's Russell here.'

Time went by, the contact got stronger,
then on one Christmas dawn,
I apported my Pink Panther,
and the RPPS was born.

I looked around for my first child
and saw a boy who looked like he was waiting for the dentist.
'What's your name?' I said 'You look so forlorn.'
He replied, 'I'm Richard Prentice!'

'Cheer up' I said.
'There's no need to look so glum,
I've formed a club and you're the first
to be reunited with your Mum.'

And now the club's spread far and wide,
(Parents, all you have to do is search and look.)
and here's a few successful stories,
written down for you, in my Mum's second book.

Please parents, search for the Truth.
and you <u>will</u> find your daughter or son.
Please help us reunite with you,
so we can all feel that we've <u>won</u>.'

~ *through the Mediumship of Frankie Brown*

*I don't want to die with cancer,
but if I do and there is an Afterlife,
I want to come back
as a butterfly...*

~ Jamie Bowen (aged 11)

One

Mother's Day

13th March 1994

*'Children are true connoisseurs,
what is precious to them has no price, only value'*

~ Bel Kaufman

It's six in the morning on a lovely Spring day and the birds are singing their hearts out as I awake.

I lay there so cosy, thinking about this particular day and whether its meaning is really understood in this crazy world. Of course, my thoughts go to my own lovely mother and after so many years, I think of how I still miss her. I think too, of my husband Alfie's mother Kathleen and how I wish I had known her in life.

Sleepily, my thoughts go to the Spirit World and I'm aware of their closeness, as I am every morning. If I'm rushed or restless, I feel my son Russell draw close and as usual, I hear him singing to me. It's always something with a deep meaning in the lyrics. Today it's a lovely song entitled *'You Needed Me'* by Randy Godrum.

Sometimes Russell changes the lyrics to suit the occasion - I think they speak for themselves...

*'You cried a tear, I wiped it dry,
You were confused, I cleared your mind,
I gave you hope, when you were at the end...*

*...I gave you strength, to stand alone again,
To face the world, out on your own again,*

*You put me high, upon a pedestal...
...You needed me, you needed me.'*

I hope Mr Godrum will understand the changes in the lyrics under the circumstances !

Over the last couple of years I have developed a Clairaudient 'gift' - but mostly for songs. They come fast and furious at times and very interesting too. Their lyrics can say so much and all set to music. I've been making notes over the last few years, and it's amazing just how many meaningful words one can scribble onto scraps of paper. The biggest task is when you come to gather it all together and now is no exception, so here goes... Hopefully, it won't take me another 30 years as it did for the first book - for I don't have that long !

Our son Russell 'died' in 1963, just before his tenth birthday. In April 1989 his father Alfie and I, were privileged to speak with Russell as a man. This was to be our *last* time at a physical phenomena séance. Russell had promised me then, that he would provide me with the words for the end of my first book *'Russell'*. At a later date, we did receive poems from him through the Mediumship of my good friend Frankie Brown, one of the RPPS mothers. In 1990 he gave us the poem, *'By Hook or by Crook, I'll be Last in the Book.'* I include some poems by Russell in a later chapter.

This second book shares some of those mother's stories. Stories of their own loss and pain and how they found their truths *and* their children - whom they thought were 'lost forever.' I have chosen to include the stories of five 'Mums' here. They are all dear friends and I will endeavour to entwine my 'adventures' along with their experiences. Adventures has to be the operative word, for once again Russell shows his superb skills as a communicator. Everything is dated so that readers can fully understand all the links involved. Indeed, some of the adventures are so amazing that some readers may choose not to believe them - but then, there were always witnesses. Thank goodness we all made notes, otherwise we wouldn't be able to join it all together !

There are about 50 mothers in the RPPS at the moment and we try and help each other through the bad times. Those whose wonderful stories are included here, are written quite openly and painfully, of their beloved children. There are tales of fights against dreadful illnesses or even horrendous murder and they open their hearts and share their pain with you. I truly believe this is therapy in itself.
Apart from an attempt to help other parents in the same position, they write of their children in a way that suggests, that they know they have only gone on ahead. They write openly of visits to Mediums - something that no one dared even mention 30 or more years ago ! Some of the RPPS Mums have even formed their own self-help groups. There are so many ways to help and each has to find their own pathway.

One brave soul, the mother of a young lad named Tim, who was killed by the Warrington bombings in 1993, wrote to me saying how she simply 'misses doing his washing'. We all find these small things so hard to bear, yet to talk of them, poignant though it is, somehow it makes it easier.

As the five stories included here unfold, so will the reasons we have been brought together and become such pals. Whilst I don't wish to dwell so much on the pain and grief of it all, I want to speak of some of my observations from the past five years. Things that set the mind thinking or the 'why' and the 'how' of it all. It's so difficult to write of the pain, in a book like this, but there have been such wonderful happenings too. It is not all sadness, just wait and see !

Also, all the mothers here sought comfort in 'orthodoxy' - but it was not forthcoming, which seems to be the norm, so to speak. Of course, I do realise that there are some who find their needs *are* fulfilled by orthodox religion.

* * *

Many who have read the first book *'Russell'* have asked me what I was like as a child, so I will try and write something of the child 'Gwen.' For in thinking on the answer, I find it does have a bearing on this book - although now, those days do seem like centuries ago !

I was an odd child at home and could be very quiet, yet when I was allowed, I could be quite the extrovert who was always full of questions. As I think now, I realise certain things stand out clearly in my mind - even faces become clearer when I think of my childhood.

I was one of a group of friends, six little girls who played 'whip & top' and skipped for hours with any old length of rope that was handy. Then, we could go miles on our old roller skates - and we did, all thinking we were *'Sonja Henie'* the famous ice skater. Although we only knew of her via the radio, or a trip to the 'flicks'. In those days, the once a week treat with our Mums, was a trip to the cinema. None of us could have been more than five or six. Or maybe we'd go off to our sixpence tap dancing class - all wearing our pink outfits and bows. We really thought we were great and perhaps we were, for now I understand the phrase *'as we think, we are.'*

Together, we were Gwen, Pat, Joyce, Pamela, Joan and Doreen. I have no idea *why* this particular gang, but somehow we all stuck together like glue and each of us wanted to be the boss !

At that time the movies were full of musicals, black and white of course. But oh the bliss - sitting on a hard seat, sucking on an ice-cream with the place full of cigarette smoke ! None of us seemed to mind though, just as long as we had our 'flicks'.

We watched things like '*King Kong*' or '*Donald Duck*'. We never seemed to mind what was on, we just sat there ! There was Shirley Temple. Oh, she was wonderful ! We would sit there agog at her tap dancing and singing and there was a young Judy Garland - this was before she became the wonderful '*Dorothy of the Red Shoes*' in '*The Wizard of Oz.*' Then there was the wonderful actress and dancer Jessie Matthews, with legs that seemed to go on forever. At the time her dancing had a little Gwen speechless with wonder - to say nothing of her amazing vibrato singing voice - which was a revelation to me. Soon enough, I found that I could actually imitate her voice and when I thought I'd nailed it, didn't I think I was clever ?

So when us girls had our weekly 'concerts up the alley' which we held up the side of my friend Pat's house - all of us dressed up in crepe paper and pins - I was allowed to be 'boss'. Of course this was only because I could imitate Jessie, Judy and Shirley ! So there I was, ordering everyone around and generally being producer, director - the lot ! We even managed to acquire a proper lipstick, so we didn't have to sink to only using a red liquorice comfit ! Black boot polish came in very handy for our eyes or black faces whenever we tried to be Al Jolson. Although this was always a bit tricky since we were all girls.

However, we had such fun and I think at the time, I thought I *was* Jessie Matthews. What wonderful fantasies a child can weave at that age. We would all try and outdo one another, but that was all part of the fun. I can't for the life of me remember what Pat, Joan, Pamela or Joyce did, but Doreen could sing like an angel - which of course made us both act like two proper little prima donna's ! It never really mattered though.

Our 'concerts up the alley' were always attended by gangs of neighbour's kids, who all paid a penny to come 'up the alley' - and if they didn't have a penny, they weren't allowed. We really used to pack the kids in and these concerts only ended when mothers would come to drag our 'audience' away to bed, usually against their will !

Once, it was arranged for our entire tap dancing class to go on a 'magic trip' - well it was for me anyway ! I'd never been to a real theatre and certainly never on a coach. To top it all, we were going to London. Now this *was* a big deal. London ! I really hadn't got a clue where we were going, just those two words were enough, 'Theatre' and 'London' !

So there we were, about fifty of us little girls, all dressed in our pink outfits and lined up outside The Elm Park Hotel, waiting excitedly for our coach. My little singing pal Doreen was with me and in a photograph taken at the time, I've got a huge bow on the top of my curls. Oh, I recall the agony of the night before, having to sleep with rags tied into my hair, just so that I could have ringlets !

I can't remember the journey at all, but into the world of theatre we went. I really did think it was all a dream, especially when the great comedy actor, Lupino Lane came onto the stage singing, *'Doing the Lambeth Walk'* I was utterly amazed by it all in fact. I remember they had a job finding me afterwards, when it was time to go to tea.

We all headed off to the famous Lyons Corner House. Wow ! We had tea and sandwiches cut so thinly, that I wondered how they even managed to cut them like that. I can remember that I'd never seen so much salad in my life ! There was all sorts and I stared at it all in wonder. Then there were the waitresses, who trotted around all over the place in their black and white uniforms. I was told that they were called 'Nippies' although no one could tell me why.

When I think that this was the only trip to anywhere that *ever* happened during my childhood - it was no wonder I was totally hooked !

Our dance teacher had named our tap group the 'Spitfire Babes' and I still often wonder if there any of us left from those days ? After all, 1938 is a long time ago. Also, Spitfire aircraft must have been around before the war began, otherwise just *where* did she get the name from ?

The Spitfire Babes - 1938
I'm hiding in the middle, on the back row

Even in 1938 there was a lot of talk of war. I must have been a very curious child, for I knew all the chat that went on between my parents ! Those dark clouds of war were hovering over us for a long time. Even at such a tender age, I recall us all waiting for Mr Chamberlain to return home from Germany, with a promise of peace after visiting Hitler. Soon afterwards however, war broke out and the air raid sirens began. I can still vividly remember thinking at the time, how my beloved Dad had told me a lie. You see he'd always said to me, *'there won't be a war, girl.'*
Of course, he was just being protective and reassuring to his children.

Whilst all this darkness began to gather around us, somehow my little gang of friends became even more stage struck - especially after our theatre trip to London. Except of course, when the family would gather round our little radio at home, to listen to the BBC News, when solemn voices told us that it was bad news.
As small children we knew war was coming, but we never knew the terrible reality of it all. How could we ? We were too busy anyway, pretending to be someone else ! Children are experts at putting things out of their minds, aren't they ? When our concerts 'up the alley' abruptly ended, the cinema took over. The 'flicks' were a real escape from the reality of war for everyone.

Looking back, it isn't difficult to recall how night after night, there were seven of us cramped into our tiny air raid shelter. We had all helped to build it and suddenly we were all sitting in it, looking at each other. I remember seeing poor old Dad, always in his tin hat outside the shelter and we always seemed scared, always hungry. Though we were always happy to clamber out of this 'dug-out' in the morning - never knowing whether the house would still be standing. Then we'd rush into the house each morning at about six or seven, to get ready for school - only to have the wretched air raid siren go off again and we'd find ourselves in yet another shelter ! Most of us were too scared to even remotely think of learning anything. Our main purpose was to stay alive...

We all had to carry our dreaded gas masks with us everywhere we went. They were kept in little square boxes of brown cardboard and how we hated them ! I remember we always tried to leave them behind, thinking hopefully, that we'd never really need them.

As war took hold, all our childish games promptly ended. Now our main preoccupation was to see who could find the biggest lump of shrapnel ! We roamed around the sites of bombed-out buildings looking for it. By today's standards, it would seem like a very odd game, but we gained an awful lot of satisfaction from it.

Sometimes at home, if the siren went, we'd dive into the cupboard under the stairs. It's quite amazing how resilient children are really.

My two younger sisters were evacuated out of Essex to Birmingham. It was supposed to take them away from the bombs. I was too old to qualify for the trip, but I wasn't really sorry, because it meant more room in the dug-out for the rest of us ! However, within a few months, my sisters were back home. I'd been told they were unhappy, although I didn't understand why, because they were away from bombs, with no fear and no black out. They'd been sleeping in a real bed too, all warm and cosy - not in a shelter like us. In my innocence, I also thought we'd have more food without them. I didn't realise that they'd have to take their ration books with them. I do recall being miffed when I heard that they were coming back home so soon, because they, *'didn't like Birmingham.'*

I don't recall missing them, but I do remember how my brother Hector and me once had to rush for cover in the the dug-out. A German fighter plane was machine gunning us and the plane swooped so low that I actually recall seeing the pilot's face. I'm happy to say of course, that he missed us ! Though looking around afterwards, we discovered that the dustbins were now full of holes and most of everything else was too, then we just went round and picked up the bullets. As children, we kind of just accepted it all, then promptly argued about which bullets were mine or his ! What odd little children we must have seemed then, we didn't have a lot, but we just played and played quite happily.

I have such a lot of memories to look back on, but as usual, lovely things have to come to an end and roughly at around the age of seven, they did.

* * *

First, I recall our little singing friend Doreen contracted an illness and to our great distress she died.

We all watched her funeral procession, yet we were all so shocked that we had to pretend it hadn't happened. I remember her distraught mother. I was sent to her house with flowers for her to take to Doreen's grave. The door opened when I knocked, to reveal a sad, old looking woman.

But as fast as that had happened, we began to play again. We were without Doreen's lovely voice and songs like *'I know why and so do you.'* Things weren't the same without her.

Nothing was *ever* the same again, for shortly after this our other little friend Pamela, was brutally murdered. She was just nine years old.

It was January 19th, 1939 when her body was found in a ditch, in Wood Lane near Hornchurch Aerodrome. I know this because my Uncle Jack, who was on his way to the Aerodrome where he worked as a batman, had seen a bundle of clothes. It was about six in the morning and still dark. He'd shone a torch into the darkness and to his horror saw that it was the body of Pamela. She had been brutally assaulted and strangled.

In my childish innocence, I recall that my biggest worry at the time had been, who would play Scarlet O'Hara in our version of '*Gone with the Wind*' - but with the awful reality of Pam's murder, I soon forgot all about that. Even today, over seventy years later, whenever I see *'Gone with the Wind'* on TV, I still recall the horror that came that day in January 1939.

I can clearly remember that lunchtime, as I was hurrying home to tell my mother that the police had been to school, to tell us that Pam was missing from home. I arrived to find my mother trying to calm my Uncle Jack. He and my Auntie Rose were living with us at that time, whilst waiting for their own home - it was utter chaos.

The day Pam had vanished, she had gone over the hill to her home for lunch, as we all did. The rest of us, Pat, Joyce and I, had all gone the other way. Pamela was never seen alive again.

The area we lived in Elm Park, was alive with police. People were searching for clues and every male in the district was fingerprinted, including my own Dad and brother. It was all very frightening. Our parents were afraid to let us out of their sight. To this day, dear Pam's murder has never been solved.

Even at a tender age, a child can be shocked and shocked we were. We whispered amongst ourselves, as we stood silently with 2,000 other people, as Pam's funeral procession went slowly along Coronation Avenue. We wept into our little hankies with everyone else. All this I recall clearly and the 'grown-ups' whispered about it for weeks, especially when they thought little ears were not listening. Although I would sit by myself at the top of the stairs, straining my ears to hear them talking. I was in misery, but so curious. I said to my mother, '*but Mum, what's Pam's mother going to do ? What about her poor Mum ?'*

Of course, as always there was no answer to this eternal question. I longed to go to Pam's home with flowers, but my mother had forbidden it. I never saw Pam's mother again.

After keeping on and on at my mother, she eventually took me to Barking Cemetery so I could take flowers to Pamela's grave. I remember seeing another lady's name on the gravestone and I was certain that it was Pam's mother. Now this may not be true and I apologise to any of Pamela's family reading this if I'm wrong, but I do recall hearing that Pamela's mother had taken her own life.

Our own little gang of friends were so devastated at the loss of both Doreen and Pamela, that we never bothered to even try and play. All we did was whisper and wait. We had all been waiting that lunchtime for Pam to come over the hill to meet us - but of course, she never came. Our little concerts came to an end and our friend Pat, the eldest of our group, had to go to court to give evidence. I was too young to testify, so Pat had to go.

It seemed to be one long round of funerals then. Although they were never relatives, they were still very painful for us - and always the poor mothers were left devastated and always so young. As children, we find it hard to understand young people's funerals, because we think you don't die unless you are old. How wrong can we be !

At the house next to ours lived a dear lady, Mrs G. She had lost her young husband and within a few weeks her son Ronald died. He was just fourteen years old. So there were another two sad processions that went by. I remember sitting on the upstairs window sill at home, peeping out from the edge of the curtains. I watched this lady with a strange interest and I really have no idea why.
I really only wanted to know *'what she was going to do ?'*

Death really seemed commonplace at the time and this question of 'what will they do ?' always seemed to be on my lips. It was many years later however, when I found my own answer to that question.

By September 3rd 1939, the country was at war - and since we lived near Hornchurch Aerodrome, of course night after night it was bombs and more bombs. Each evening we'd go down into the shelter, with my Dad standing there in his tin hat. He was furious back then because at thirty-eight, he was too old to join the army. I remember us dodging bombs, shrapnel and fires. Once we were machine-gunned whilst running for the shelter - and me with a cat under each arm, rushing across Dad's precious vegetable garden ! How quickly our lives had changed.

My father was a very quiet man, gentle and kind. However he gradually became angry and we saw the change in him, as he feared for our lives each day. He worked in the Albert Docks, which of course were bombed. Often on the way home from work, he would help in trying to rescue people trapped after nearby bombing. He would often come home soaked in blood. During these terrible bombing raids he saw such horrors.

Yet how resilient children are. We soon got used to the wartime routine, we had to and we remained cheerful. I remember when Mum worked all day in the munitions factory, so we would come home from school and try to light the fire ourselves. We used matches, sticks, paper and paraffin, but how we didn't burn the house down, I'll never know !

When in May 1940 the Battle of Dunkirk came, again my Dad was angry, because *'they'* - whoever *'they'* were - would not let him go. He had a family and that was reason enough *'they'* said. Poor Mum always did her best with food shortages. She would hide the sugar and tea rations in the lid of the piano. As if we didn't know where to find them ! Bless her dear heart. What a struggle our parents went through and how little we realised it then.

I do have one vivid memory from those days, of a young soldier rushing along the road we lived in. He was blood stained and ill-looking, so I called my mother. We watched this poor young man, who apparently had been through the hell of Dunkirk. He'd jumped off a lorry that had brought soldiers back to this country. Lord knows how he got to where he was, but he was clearly going home at all costs. It seemed grossly unfair to hear later, that he had been Court Martialled for desertion. To a ten year old me, this seemed very unfair. *War !*

Of course we did have nicer times, even if we were a bit naughty. My sister Doreen and myself were often up to mischief. Sometimes, we'd go to school in the morning, then come home for lunch, but we would follow our mother to the bus stop. Mum would always get on the number 152 to go to work, then us two naughty girls would hop on another bus which took us to the cinema. We'd happily sit through anything while bombs could be dropping over Romford, but were never bothered. We were just totally lost in whatever was on the screen. Looking back, I think now it was an escape from the horrors around us.

The only film I can remember from back then, was *'Sanders of the River'* starring Paul Robeson. Why I can only recall this particular film, I have no idea. Perhaps it was his glorious singing voice ? Maybe the continuous explosions outside just made me forget all the others, but my preoccupation with death was not so apparent during the bombing. I guess because it was all around us - though nothing like the isolated case that was soon to come to a ten year old Gwen...

One Spring morning in 1941, I was alone in the house - which was quite uncommon then, for there were always various neighbours coming and going. I was trying to light the fire with matches and a few bits of wood, then holding a sheet of newspaper up to the front of the fireplace, in an effort to make the flames flare - when there was a knock at the door. There seemed to be a sense of urgency about it, so I left what I was doing and went to the door. Standing on the doorstep was my Great Aunt Rose, my father's mother's sister. As I opened the door wider, she literally just fell inside. I was so amazed at the sight of our usually elegant Aunt, who was now quite dishevelled and distraught.

As she wept uncontrollably I had no idea what to do, but here was job for me nonetheless. Then Aunt Rose began to whisper,
'I've lost my boy, my Russell', over and over again. I remember these words because they stand out even now, after all these years. Aunt Rose's son was my cousin Russell, who was a Battle of Britain pilot who'd been reported missing in action. Aunt Rose was a very favourite Auntie of mine so I sat holding her hand as she wept. Then I made her a cup of tea, but I felt so useless ! Thankfully, my mother came in shortly afterwards and took over.

It was odd that over twenty years later, that same Aunt Rose arrived at my own door, bearing a wreath with the words *'Goodbye Russell'* for my own son's funeral. I remember she said to me,
'I never expected to write those words for a memorial again.'

Little did Aunt Rose know or expect that this same young pilot, my cousin Russell, would later communicate to me through a Medium. He told me how he'd died and asked me to please tell his mother, *'not to keep going to the cemetery, where a stone had been laid in his memory.'*

As time passed, I watched this special Auntie begin to look sadder and sadder. I was very curious and again I heard whispers like, *'she sat in the cemetery every day - Winter and Summer.'* This was made worse for Aunt Rose, because soon after Russell's passing, his fiancée was also killed - by a flying bomb. Poor Auntie Rose just sat there staring at the words carved in stone *'Olive, now with Russell.'*

How sad and empty for her, to never know what happened to her gorgeous son. Also, to think that at the time, she still had another son fighting in the Deserts of Tobruk. She became very quiet and her husband, my Uncle Jack, became just a shadow of himself. All this I watched, and years later I tried to tell her of my own Truths - but she would not listen. As far as I knew, no one ever spoke of *'life after death'* back then and no one ever seemed to even wonder about it - except this strange quiet child, called Gwen.

The war went on and one Saturday I went with my mother on a visit to East Ham. There we were, just about to start our shopping, when the air raid siren sounds off again. So we dived into a nearby greengrocer's shop and into their underground cellar. Just as we got inside, an almighty explosion came out of nowhere. We eventually crept out of the shelter to find that the whole of East Ham's Woolworth's store was completely flattened. We realised there had been a great loss of life, but we just had to get on with things. Meanwhile, my Dad was rushing up and down the High Street searching for us both, thinking that we'd both been caught in the blast. Poor old Dad !

Why is it that most of us who recall memories from our childhood, always remember the nice bits. Yet at that time of war, there weren't that many nice bits. What loomed at us was fear, hunger and loneliness, yet now only fragments of it remain in the mind. Such is memory and thankfully so.

I wonder how we children ever learned to read and write, for most of our school days were spent in large air raid shelters, which were fitted out with makeshift desks. Our classrooms were literally next door to Hornchurch Aerodrome - which was really asking for trouble !

One afternoon, after the bombing raids had ceased, we all lined up and walked back to our classrooms. We soon settled in and continued with our lessons. There wasn't always the sound of a siren to warn us of incoming enemy planes. Instead, on this particular afternoon, we all heard the *sound* of a plane - which seemed to be in trouble. Because the engine was making such odd sounds, we all pricked our ears up. Of course we were quite sensitive to the sounds of aircraft by then, having heard so many before. We jumped up and rushed to the classroom windows, where we saw a low flying Spitfire, which was struggling to make it to the nearby airfield.

As we watched in horror we saw the plane lift up over the Infants School, about 200 yards away from us. It flew over the gardens and lawns, where some boys were having a lesson on growing vegetables and flowers - we saw them lay down flat after a warning from their teacher. Then we realised that this Spitfire was heading straight for us and our classroom.

'UNDER YOUR DESKS' our teacher screamed at us. As we dived under our desks, the Spitfire crashed straight into our classroom.

Then there was a great panic, as we came out from hiding covered in dust and debris. Our classroom was wrecked, the teachers were in hysterics and the plane was at a standstill. One of its wings had come straight through our classroom roof.

Apparently, the plane had tried to swerve to miss the school altogether, but the pilot kept heading down and down. Until he'd missed the Infants

School and the boys outside - but ended up coming through our classroom roof. How none of us were killed I'll never know. Unfortunately the pilot was not so lucky. As we all looked up at the Spitfire, which now hung through the ceiling, we could see the young pilot. I remember his face to this day. He was red haired and had a moustache, but was dead. Yet in his bravery and skill, he had saved all our lives.

Of course, more panic followed, as parents came rushing to the school demanding to be let in, to find their children. We were all terrified and shocked, but mostly unscathed by the incident.

I later learned that this brave young pilot was an American named Raimund Sanders-Draper and he had a famous family. His Aunt was the actress Ruth Draper and one day his mother came to the school to lay a memorial stone in the wall outside. I remember that she was a glamorous and tragic figure and I wonder to this day, what happened to her after that. Many years later I discovered that our old school was renamed after him, in his honour.

By 1945, the end of the war came and we adjusted to a different way of life. There were no more air raids, no shelters or bombs, and no ration books or gas masks to constantly carry around with us ! And at last we had things to eat - like bananas and fish - that we hadn't seen for six long years. It was such bliss when we could finally feed our faces ! Yet the war had made us children grow up too quickly, but not in the way modern children do today. We were just happy to play and the memories of all the horrors of the war began to fade, thank God...

* * *

Now I was really growing up and turning into a teenager. One day I was surprised to be reunited with my old school friend Marion, who had all but vanished from my life for a time. What I didn't know was that she had been very ill with a TB infection, which in those days of no antibiotics, was very serious indeed.

However, here we were meeting on a train to London. We were both going off to begin work at the Bank of England, to printing Pound Notes - and us barely fourteen years old ! Oh, didn't we think we were the 'cats whiskers' with our high heels and lipstick ? Marion and I drifted in and out of each others lives over the years, but always seemed to meet up again. Neither of us had ever had the chance to learn a trade, so it was a question of finding work wherever and whenever you could. We lost touch yet again, almost up until we both married. It was now 1948 and Marion was courting a handsome man named Terry and I was courting another fella, just as handsome, named Alf. Then after our respective weddings, again we lost touch and after I'd had my first baby we moved into different worlds.

Years passed and I was a young mother now myself. Kevin was our first child, who was just seven months old when Alfie and I moved into our brand new council house. We had very little money, but we were very happy. We had our own baby, a garden and lovely neighbours.

It seems to me now, that in my life I'd seen a lot of grieving mothers over a short space of around ten years. Maybe as children we are not aware of all of that's going on, but on reflection I think I knew even then, that I would join this unique club, later in life. Somehow I just knew.

One night I awoke at about three in the morning screaming the place down - and oh how I could scream ! Alf's hair stood on end as I screamed out, *'he's dead, he's dead'* over and over again. I threw myself on baby Kevin, frantically clutching him to me. Poor Alf and the neighbours, who were awoken by my screams. To say nothing of the poor, bewildered baby. Good job he was only seven months old at the time ! I'm sure it didn't have any adverse effects. But did I know then ?

Did I know that I would lose a child even then - before our next baby was even born ? Of course I did. I just got the timing wrong. Kevin was absolutely fine, but what was hidden away in my subconscious mind, even before our Russell was born, thirteen months later ?

* * *

All the mothers who have written their own stories for this book, have said to me, *'Gwennie, I'm not a writer !'* So I said the same thing to them all, *'just write the Truth and let it come freely from the heart.'* It's my job to link them all together and each story becomes entwined as we go along.

Now all these years later I find it ironic that I'm the one actually writing about the Spirit World. That place that I yearned to know of years ago, yet no one could enlighten me. Perhaps it's that thing of timing again ?
I had to find out myself, *by* myself. I had to lose my son Russell, to know the truth !

Now it's 1995 and to know that much can be explained by Physics and in a scientific manner, really makes sense to me - even if I will never understand it all ! I don't really wish or need to. I just know that the Spirit World may be in the same place that your invisible TV and radio signals are. Plus, now we have the knowledge of *'subatomic phenomena'* although it's beyond me, so I'll leave that subject to the scientists right now !

I have experienced many wonderful Spiritual happenings and along with those of other mothers, they are written about in this book. Some of these incidents have taken place either with or without a Medium being present. One sometimes wonders how the Spirit people can accomplish such wonders ? Perhaps there *is* a Medium around at those times, somewhere - but I can't answer that and be sure.

It seems to me that many people *are* Mediums, but without even being aware of it - which is a pity and something I say with sadness. For I do know that true Mediumship takes *love* in its purest and loveliest forms.

Two

The Agony and the Ecstasy

20th September 1994

*'And the streets of God's city
shall be full of boys and girls playing in it's streets...'*

~ Zechariah 8:5

Whilst my intention was not to write too much on the agony of the *loss* of a child in this second book, since forming the RPPS I've been amazed by the letters I have received from many bereaved parents. Through them, I have learned so much more on the subject of grief and of the different ways of coping.

I was going to leave this subject to the end of the book, but somehow it feels better to 'chat' about it earlier on, before the other mothers tell their own stories. After all, it is truly a beginning and an adventure - but only if we search, as others have searched.

The death of a child is a complete reversal of the order of things. The same thought comes to every bereaved parent, and I too thought I would die from the pain. These thoughts come from the shock and despair. You actually tremble with shock. You can't even hold a tea cup. It's a kind of madness that comes over you. Anger takes a hold of you and we'd all agree that however lovely prayers can be - at that particular time, the words can't possibly be of use, can they ? I recall at one séance Russell said to me, *'I can speak to your thoughts Mum.'* I understand that now.

Before I go on, I want to say I'm so afraid of frills and exaggeration in this book. We must have absolute Truth ! I also am aware that so many researchers and indeed many ordinary people will say, what a load of rubbish and that it's all hallucinations, etc. Well, let them say exactly whatever pleases them. They may keep wearing their blinkers ! For me, it is these very people who are the ones prone to illusion.

I don't envy anyone who can be unmoved by the honesty of a mother, or of a dying child. Even after the panic in the eyes of the doctor, who has to pass on the devastating news.

It takes just one word to open the door of *memory*. Although some prefer to keep their memories firmly locked away. Yet sad or bad memories must come out somewhere, they cannot be suppressed forever. Tragedy reveals us all for what we are. It takes away all pretence and we cannot be artificial. We can all remember exactly, even years later, the moment when you are given the dreaded news. It is then that we learn how complex we all really are, for that moment is imprinted indelibly in the mind.

When we learn the truth of survival and how simple God is, we also learn that in the loss of a child, one never really recovers. There is always underlying sorrow and this great loss gives us a different approach when handling other problems. We all learn the *'one day at a time'* theory - and you hope like hell that you can do it.

A child's love is so completely unconditional. Your child will love you whether you yell at them *or* worship them. Truly, it is only that love that can pierce the veil between Spirit and the physical world. Nobody grieves in a text-book fashion, you have to train yourself *not* to feel, even when you want to scream ! There is that awful state of 'nothingness' which we all recognise - when we seem to be without hope and religion has no magic pill. Doctors also know that they too, don't have any pills that can numb the agonising ache of loss.

It's become clear to us Mums, that in books lies hope. So arm yourself with the *right* books, for within them lies that hope, it really does ! As you begin to read of the Truth of survival, with the turmoil that is going on inside you, you think to yourself, *'can this I am reading, really be true'* ? It can help your sense of reality too.

Of course there are stages at this time, like denial ! That dark place where you don't cry - either because you don't want to, or you can't. Then comes all sorts of physical pains, which cannot be numbed. Showing your feelings is okay and trying to live in a normal fashion can help, but pain can harden your heart, for sure.

Every marriage or partnership has to find its own way of coping. The death of a child is the greatest test any marriage can endure. Some couples lean on each other, but there are some who cannot accept the truth. This is very common with fathers, I have found. It is so easy to become cynical, and very, very sad. We learn to savour any joy we can find and usually that joy is found in the simple things in life. The death of a child can teach us the transitory nature of life. We are told we must *'grin and bear it'* - which is an old fashioned phrase. Yet for me, all these years later, I have learned instead to actually *'sing and bear it'* ! Of course, this is not for everyone.

We all think our child is a gift and sometimes you wonder why you gave birth in pain and tears. We ask so many questions like,
'why ? what if ? why didn't I ? why did I ? Or if.'
You hope to find an answer, but of course you don't, so these words always haunt you and are forever popping in and out of your mind.

When you read the mother's own stories later in this book, you will see how they express themselves. You will read of their pain and their feelings of triumph - after learning about the *Truth* of survival after death. They tell how they found their own Truth and I can assure you that these stories are quite moving and fascinating too. Many people will think that these stories are made up - but I defy anyone to prove otherwise.

* * *

At this point, I am wondering how in the world I am ever going to entwine all these stories together, but I will. For it is clear to me, that we are all inexplicably entwined with each other. All the mothers have found it so painful to write of their agonies, but they have all 'had a go' so to speak. They tell such wonderful tales of love and devotion. As I write, one dear mother has lost a second son, so how she will ultimately tell her story, I just don't know at present. Yet tell it she will, just as soon as she can collect her thoughts.

I hope readers can bear with me as I occasionally rewind or fast-forward, as in the first book. I have also dated each chapter, so you may note how superb the Spirit World are at making things happen on special dates.

Many of those who have read *'Russell'* speak of their own coincidences in their lives and Russell's own splendid explanation from the book says,
'coincidence, is God's way of performing a miracle anonymously !'
He didn't tell me who originally said these words, but I do know that I've lost count of just how many miracles have I been blessed with.

The more letters I receive from mothers and fathers, the more I realise the bravery of our children. Whilst writing of parents' courage, one is apt to forget their children's bravery. Way back in 68-70 A.D. the early Jewish-Roman scholar Josephus said, *'so far did the strength of a brave young spirit prevail over the weakness of their little bodies'* And how many of us ladies have said, *'oh, men are just like little boys'* - but how many of these little boys are like men ? Having had all sons and grandsons myself, I see that very clearly now.

Parents know too, that children can look you straight in the eye. They sometimes seem to know so much and their love is so intense, it hurts. To those who have lost a child I say, they must remain a part of your life. Even at times when it seems that your emotions have been stolen - keep at it. Speak *to* them and speak *of* them.

At the séances with Russell, I learned that humour can come from despair. Russell was our clown on Earth, as is often the case with the second or middle child. Without that humour in the home, it can seem like a morgue. Yet the strength to cope with it all, ebbs and flows. Even while writing this now, it still comes flooding back, but now I can cope. I even feel happiness in a very overwhelming way - such are memories !

I don't believe that time is a healer, but it *is* a great adjuster, especially when we learn to disguise the scars which remain for a lifetime. It is indeed a life sentence. So let your children become a household name and let them stay - for are they not *more alive* than ever ?

There can be no preparation for this loss, the gap always remains. You might watch similar events on TV and back it all comes, like a big echo. Yet every letter I receive is like an echo too. I think the RPPS is a therapy, so *'to those with ears, let them hear and to those with eyes, let them see.'*

I recall chatting to Russell at a séance once, about the fact he had got to know Dr Albert Schweitzer very well. He told me that he often worked with him in the Spirit World and why not ? In life Schweitzer said, *'the tragedy of life is not that we die, but is rather, it is what dies inside us while we live.'*

We all know that truth is elusive and no one with an ounce of wisdom, will leap too quickly to conclusions.

Today as I write, it is the 28th anniversary of the 1966 coal hill disaster in Aberfan, Wales. I had spoken to Russell about this at a séance in the mid 1980s and he told us that he had been there himself at the time. He went to help to bring over some of the 116 children who had 'died' on that awful day, when their world turned black. The great grief and sadness of that tragedy still hangs over that little Welsh community. Yet science is reputed to say that there is no such thing as a broken heart. Those scientists should try and tell that to the people of Aberfan, who still mourn their beautiful children. A generation was swept away by that awful black colliery waste. I've often wondered if any of those dear parents ever learned the Truth of life after death. I recall reading some time ago how the community was still racked with problems of depression.

I wonder how many of these brave parents know that their beloved children live on, and have even grown up in the Spirit World. I hope and pray that they did find this Truth - for it would have given them back their sanity. There is a wonderful old proverb which says, *'say not in grief that he is no more, but live in thankfulness that he was.'*

These are wonderful words, but in my understanding, I think perhaps the last two words should read *'he is'*, rather than *'he was.'*

In the earlier years, after having dealt with so many heartbreaking letters from parents, I was asked again and again whether I suffer from 'Compassion Fatigue' (there seems to be a name for everything these days !) Well yes, I have suffered from it, but how could I not, when dealing so often with such deep and affecting sorrow, from so many bereaved parents, but I coped because I know the Truth !

I *know* I am helped over every hurdle and as these stories unfold, readers will understand exactly what I mean. I really did not intend to write so much on this subject because one *can* write forever. Yet still I find there are no words to cope with the devastating reality of it all. I guess the subject will come up again later in the book, but so too will *Love* and *Joy* shine through, by the time we reach the last chapter.

Three

A Motorway Adventure

21st September 1989

*'Where is she, who I close my eyes to see,
will I ever know the sweet 'hello' that's meant only for me ?'*

~ from Lionel Bart's musical 'Oliver!'

1989 was a strange year for me. We knew that the physical phenomena séances were now over and once again we had said goodbye to Russell - at least from the séance room. We realised how we had been given so much, indeed we had been very privileged people. We were under no illusions however, but I cannot explain what I felt. Oh, the emotions ! One moment I felt the wonder of it all and yet, it seemed as though a second bereavement had come upon us. It was like an emotional see-saw that year. Just how do you find someone who's been in a similar position ?

Fortunately, my mind was occupied at least, since I had found myself a little job - I was selling 'undies' at a market ! Now I know and have said, that there are reasons for everything. Yet try as I may, I couldn't see the purpose to things at this time. Even though I had learned so much from that particular experience.

I truly believe that when we come to this Earth we know exactly what we are in for. Is it Karma ? For me, I think this is the only thing that helped make sense of the situation. Plus, if we know what we are in for, then what is the point of resisting ? I knew mine was a 'Karmic' experience and after the *'Russell'* book I received many letters on the subject. I knew that many would not agree with me, so my response to this was simply to say, that this *'was my reasoning.'* I truly believe that we are bound up in our past lives and Karmic dramas and this was one of mine. It was such an enormous situation for me to deal with and being at low ebb, didn't help. My deepest inner 'me' knew that there had to be a reason.

The new friends I'd made at work did not understand my dark times, indeed how could they ? If it is possible to go through a second bereavement for the same child - then I did just that. During the night if I awoke, I was suddenly aware something was wrong, but on fully waking, I soon knew what it was. So once again, I shed more tears in the darkness. They are always there, under the surface. It's like a lake really, but one that you can never reach the bottom of.

When we feel this depth of sadness, we tell ourselves all sorts of *crazy* things to ease the ache and fill the void. It's only when we can tell ourselves that the pain is the price we pay for loving. Although this usually comes years later, for you *can* discover yourself in later years.

* * *

Now, when beginning your *'Big Search'* into evidence for survival after death, sometimes it's easy to doubt your own sanity - and that of others ! So instead of yielding to the explanations of others, use your common sense - plus, you'll know by the way you *feel*. <u>Always</u> remember that !

Whilst nearly all members of the RPPS are mothers, I do write to a few fathers. I learned very quickly that many men protect themselves emotionally, when presented with things they don't wish to know. Not all of course, but they do handle their pain in a different way to mothers. Also, it seems to me that many men are confirmed sceptics. If comparing notes after a wonderful séance experience, you can be met with responses like, *'well I didn't see anything'* or *'I don't want to be told what I saw.'*

Yet you're thinking, *'well I'm having problems believing it myself, mate !'*

Then they say, *'I don't want to discuss this matter with you again.'*

I've learned that this reaction is simply their way of *'protecting themselves emotionally.'* It was the great Oglala Sioux 'Black Elk' who said those words - which explain my point beautifully. Maybe some men can switch their feelings off at times. Is it because they are taught as children that they mustn't cry ?

Then on the other hand, some fathers have bared their very souls to me, in their letters about their lost children. It would be wrong of me to assume that all fathers are disinterested in survival evidence. They seek in their own specific way and sometimes, a mistake can teach you more than a right move. Each loss is unique ! A brother can do no more than miss the presence of the other child, what else can they do ? They watch the scenes of despair unfolding all around them and they too can be emotionally damaged. At the time perhaps we can't always see it - but it comes later.

Learning to find the edge of where self pity ends and grief begins, is an invaluable lesson. Sleep may still be fragmented and unreal and of course,

will you *ever* be able to smile again ? That's always another 'biggie' and one we all agree on. Sometimes though, you just can't win, because if you try to smile and appear happy and natural, people say, *'well it didn't take her long to get over it.'*
Or if you are unable to crack your face into a smile - because it feels like it's set in cement - you hear, *'oh leave her alone, she's miserable.'*
This I know to be true, because it happened to me.

It does seem that the death of a child is still very much taboo and where, oh where, can you possibly find someone who understands ? Thankfully, although slowly, attitudes do seem to be changing these days. Of course, a lot of these things happen out of sheer embarrassment and are not because others have an uncaring attitude. Many parents who face others who are grieving their child, only respond from fear - the fear that it could happen to them !

After Russell's passing, I often tried to express how I felt, although not very successfully I'm afraid. It was a desperate nightmare and I don't think I will ever forget it. I'd heard about 'personal growth' and I think I did plenty of that, but always the small voice inside of me asked, *'why ?'* and, *'what is it all about ?'* At times it seemed so much like a dream, sometimes I didn't even feel that I was a part of this planet.

I did a <u>lot</u> of thinking and a lot of growing - *soul growth* they call it. I never really did expect an answer to all those eternal questions. Yet the deep thinking I did about reincarnation and Karma helped so much, for it gave me something to 'chew on' so to speak. It made sense and it appealed to my logic. Years later during the séances, Russell himself told me, *'it had to be Mum.'*
Then when the RPPS began to take off I began to see more clearly. Other mothers began to write to me via Michael Roll, the author of the thesis, *'The Scientific Proof of Survival After Death.'*

Without Michael's help, they would never have found me. I quickly realised that my experiences could help other mothers come to terms with their loss. At the time I didn't realise how much I was helping, until certain incidents began to happen. Was there a pattern unfolding ? Well I began to see a little of that through the RPPS.

Now, as in 1964 when I began my work, I always focus on Truth. I am true to myself and that's all that matters. I don't worry now, I just write. Yet so many years later, I still hadn't been given the ending for the *'Russell'* book. I knew my son in Spirit wouldn't break his promise of providing me with the final chapter. Many times I would look at a poster on my wall at home, which had on it the words of Rudyard Kipling's poem *'IF'*.

I had underlined the very words that Russell had asserted to me, when during a séance in the 80s, he recited the whole poem. The line, *'if you can wait, and not tire of waiting...'* is very dear to me. I knew I had to wait, but just wondered how and where ? At the time I made the excuse that I'm *'only human'* !

Even now in 2014, I find I am waiting. Waiting for the completion of this second book, waiting for my new grandchild and waiting to take the final journey of my Earthly life...

However, once a mother tells you that she *knows* something, then you can be sure *she knows it* ! It was the same when I *knew* that Russell was to have just a short incarnation. At the time I didn't know how I knew and when I asked my brother-in-law Ron, the ex-priest, his explanation was, *'it comes from the womb Gwen.'* I accepted that back in 1963, but now I realise that I understood it on a very deep, etheric level.

* * *

In September of 1989 my friend Rose Hebenaar came over for a week's holiday, from her home in Holland. Those who have read *'Russell'* may remember that she is the mother of young Ronald. Rose had experienced talking to her son and her own mother in the Spirit World, in fluent Dutch at many séances.

Rose and I have a great deal in common and we are close friends. We both enjoy our music played at full blast and we both love to shop until we drop ! Rose is partially sighted, but she has a wonderful sensitivity which makes her amazing at finding her way around. How she does it, one can only watch in wonder. I knew she was well aware that she was helped by those in Spirit.

We both accept each other's darker times and we remain friends still. After the loss of her boy, Rose also feels a void - you simply can't ignore it. We talk naturally of both Ronald and Russell, so of course these two boys, who are now men in Spirit, are the basis of a real friendship.

Through the anguish of our Earthly experiences we can talk way into the night and really 'dig deep' into our feelings. We never have to search for a subject, even in our quiet times and since we share the same sense of humour, we have many, many laughs too. However, the chats and the shopping has to stop eventually and on one glorious day, we set off to visit my sister Doreen...

Today was September 21st and Russell's 39th Birthday and as I drove,

I wondered what he was up to today. I had only passed my driving test around a year earlier and never really felt terribly confident with a passenger in my old 'banger' of a car. However on our way I kept thinking, *'what am I doing wrong ?'* and for some reason Rose had gone very quiet on me.

Now, since I have no notes for this story, I have to recall the details from memory, as though I could ever forget them ! Yet I am conscious of how easy it is to exaggerate, which is always a constant anxiety when writing.

However, the trip was going great and we were sailing along the A127 towards Hornchurch. There were no traffic jams, no road works, just a straight run. I'd checked for petrol and knew we had plenty for the trip there and back. Though knowing Rose so well, I was aware of how silent she had become and I felt concerned. She had recently had an operation on her eyes and was wearing dark glasses, so I couldn't tell from her face what might be bothering her.

Rose had met my sister Doreen before, yet after we'd safely arrived at her home, for some reason we only stayed for a short time. I could tell Rose was definitely not her usual chatty self and that she wanted to go. *'Crumbs !'* I thought, *'was my driving that bad ?'*

Now I didn't feel confident driving back home to Rayleigh. Rose's very stillness made me feel nervous, though every time I asked if she was okay, she simply replied, *'yes Gwennie,'* but I knew she wasn't. It was as though she knew something, but wasn't saying.

Collecting my thoughts, I told myself to *'concentrate on the road !'* The traffic was now building up and although the trip home is short one, you still need your wits about you.

After driving through Basildon, I realised I was not too familiar with this stretch of motorway, but I needed to watch out for a particular turn-off. I moved over into the left-hand lane to prepare to leave the motorway, when suddenly a huge lorry came out of nowhere and was completely blocking my view. I ended up having to follow him and then hoped like mad that he was going my direction. I was wrong, he wasn't, so now we were lost !

Now it seemed like there were so many traffic islands and round and round we went. All the signs I should have recognised seemed to have vanished ! I began to feel very fraught and was now panicking over the petrol gauge. *'Oh dear'* I thought *'am I going to be stranded on the motorway without enough fuel to get home ?'*

Then I remembered the advice my son Gary had given me, *'Mother, when the gauge is on red you still have one gallon left. Remember that.'*

Finally I started to relax a little, as we end up back at the Chelmsford turn-off and somewhere I actually recognised, *'phew !'* We should be home in a few minutes...

Pausing at a red light, I changed gear and waited. Then green means go, so down on the accelerator my foot went, but then nothing. Not even a flicker ! The car had stalled. Frantically I tried the ignition, again and again and even banged my foot on the pedal, but there was still no signs of life. *Had* I run out of petrol ?

So there we were, two 'gals' stuck at the lights, with impatient drivers all around us, who were now tooting their horns. I even think I heard a few swear words too, as they looked as us through their windows. I'm sure these men were thinking 'silly women' - so I got out of the car and just stood there, looking just like a complete 'silly woman !' In fact this was not difficult, for what I knew about cars you could write on the back of a postage stamp. Fortunately, the car directly behind us contained a gentleman. He was a short, sturdy, dark-haired young man, who got out of his vehicle and walked towards us.

'Can I help you love ?' He said.

'Well, I don't know what's wrong with my car,' I replied, though I needn't have said anything, for he could plainly see that.

'I'll get <u>her</u> going for you love.' he said, as he kindly got into the drivers seat and twiddled with the ignition. Why *do* men call cars 'her' I wonder ?

By now, all the other cars I'd held up, were flying past us as if there were a siege on - of course it was rush hour ! Now I don't mind looking a fool, but this was now becoming totally ridiculous. The young man suggested, *'we'd better get this car off the road. You get behind the steering wheel and I'll push.'*

Rosie was out of the car by now and standing well out of the way. She waited by a roadside fence, where all around her, long grass and pink and white clover was growing. She hung onto a small carrier bag containing all her bits and pieces, including a little gift given to her by my sister.

There was nobody else around to help, so between myself steering and this young man pushing, we managed to move the car onto the grass verge. Yet no sooner had the wheels touched the grass, there came such a WALLOP and a BANG ! I leapt out of the car and found my drivers side wheel had hit an open drain, where some idiot had left the cover off. Now we were in worse state...

'Looks like your tyre's had it !' said the young man. *'We'll never get that*

wheel out of there,'

The poor chap was becoming flustered himself by now, I mean what else could go wrong ? My heart was pounding in panic and inside my head I was yelling, *'Help ! Help !'* in a kind of silent, hysterical fashion.

Then out of the blue, a voice said,
'can I help you ? Looks like a big problem.'

Turning around, I realised that we'd been joined by another young man. He was very tall, dark and handsome and wearing a brown leather jacket. I quickly thanked him and explained what had happened, but couldn't understand where he had come from, on this busy motorway.

'Well, we'll all just have to lift it won't we ? Came the voice of Rosie as she stepped in to join us. *'I can help, I'm very strong.'*

So then we were four. Two ladies and two men all standing in a line, as we bent down to try to and lift my car, with all our strength, out of this open drain.

Thankfully the wheel came out surprisingly easily, but the car rolled backwards a little, ending in a thud - just as Rosie went to take a step forward. *'Stop !'* the second young man said, as he quickly reached out and grabbed her.

It's such a good job that he did, because Rosie, who couldn't see too well at all, would have fallen straight down into this large open drain. The young man held on to my friend saying, *'if you had fallen down there my dear, you would have never come up again.'*

This awful drain seemed bottomless, black and dirty as I looked from Rosie's face and gazed down into it. *'Oh my God,'* I said, then felt quite ill and weak as a kitten.

On examination and to my amazement, we saw that the car was quite intact. Rosie was now thanking this fine, tall, young man profusely and I was so grateful for the rescue and that the car was in one piece, the next few minutes are a blank. With all the traffic whizzing past, I didn't see where the second young man went. He just waved and disappeared. I didn't even ask his name <u>and</u> he saved Rosie too. *'Crumbs !'*

The first young man who'd helped, now offered to take us to the petrol station for fuel, so off we went in his car. He told us his name was Chris and after even more thanks, he just said *'that's okay love.'* Eventually we got back to my car with some petrol, but still not a flicker came from the engine. I was beginning to think Chris was getting a bit 'cheesed off.'
'Oh well,' he said, *'you'll just have to leave her there love and I'll drive you*

both home.'

We agreed, saying that he really was a 'knight of the road.' All the way back, I noticed that Rosie was even quieter than before, but we were glad to finally be on our way.

Alfie made me drink a small brandy once we'd got back, as I was quite shaky. My son Gary towed my car home and later said to us,
'blimey that drain - how did you manage it Mother ?' Then he said,
'if you'd have fallen in Rosie, the mind boggles !

* * *

Later that evening after we'd rested and had a meal, we felt a lot better. Even Rosie, who wasn't her usual chatty self, cheered up later on. It was creeping towards midnight and Alfie had already gone to bed. I began to tell Rosie about a wonderful old book I'd been given as a gift. I had admired it through a shop window, whilst away on a Spiritual seminar with the Lynwood Fellowship. My friends there had heard me talk about how the price had put me off buying it, but how beautiful I thought it was. To my great joy, some of my dear seminar friends had bought it for me as a gift !

I took this huge book out of my cupboard to show Rosie, who could only vaguely see to read it, even with the help of her magnifying glass. It was Dante's *'Purgatory & Paradiso'* and to me, was really a work of great art and wonder. As we studied it between us, my friend Rosie who is an excellent Medium, suddenly said the strangest thing.
'Gwennie, can you see his sandals down by my feet ?'

'What ?' I replied. No, of course I couldn't see any 'sandals' - no matter how hard I looked and I said so. Then out of nowhere, the room suddenly went icy cold - and I mean *icy*. Yet this was the 21st September and Autumn. The weather had cooled, but it wasn't *that* cold. I quickly realised something was happening.

Rosie then told me how she could *'see'* a tall man - a soldier of some sort. He was standing beside her and she was Clairaudiently listening to what he was saying ! *'Quick Gwennie, please get me a pen from my bag.'*

I raced into the kitchen to fetch Rosie's carrier bag with all her bits and pieces inside it. She reached inside and pulled out a pen, I was agog to what she said next.
'This was was his book and he wants to sign his signature.'

She opened the book just inside the cover but then said,
'no, he doesn't want to sign the book. Could you get me a piece of paper

Gwennie, quick?'
Returning, I watched in fascination as the pen, held softly by Rosie, began to move across the surface of the paper, spelling out...

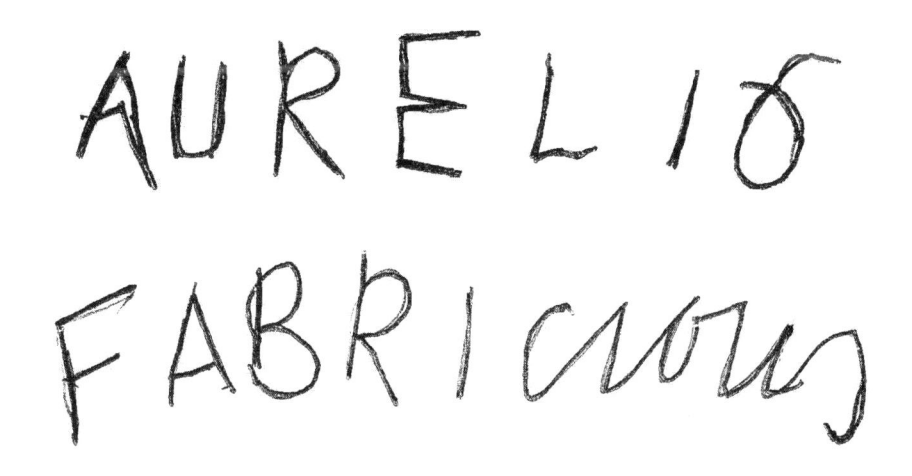

AURELIO FABRICIOUS

(AURELIO FABRICIOUS)

Rosie then said thank you to this 'soldier' and explained to me that his mother called him Aurelio. She said that my book had once belonged to him and that he was very happy it had now found a good home. Rosie went on saying *'when he owned it, people were arrested for keeping such books. That's why there's no signature inside it.'*

Then he was gone.

The room was still cold, in fact it was colder than before. Now Rosie had kept her carrier bag with her throughout our motorway experience, earlier in the day. After we'd arrived back, we were so shattered, so she'd just hung it on the back of a chair in my kitchen.

Now, she put her hand into the bag and neatly pulled out two clumps of pink and white clover - with the soil still attached ! I remember seeing some around Rosie's feet in the place where she'd waited, when we began to have car trouble. Now this clover must have come from that motorway verge, yet we were both amazed, because Rosie said she knew nothing about it. We thought that someone in Spirit must have put it into her bag, although I had no idea who and if Rosie did, she wasn't saying.

We looked back at the book and once more I saw her Mediumship at work. She put her hand into the carrier bag, which had soil in the bottom of it, and fished out her magnifying glass.

'What page ?' she said, out loud. 'I can't find the page.'

Rosie wasn't talking to me at this point. Then she said, *'it's all in Italian with Roman numerals for page numbers.'*

Instantly she opened the book to find the page she'd been guided to. Now I knew some Italian to sing and Rosie knew a few words, but looking through her magnifying glass she read out the words she'd found, *'behold and ye shall be guarded and loved by two angels.'*

    I was stunned by these beautiful words. This seemed exactly what had happened to us out on the motorway, with our gentleman rescuers. For me this was a wonderful ending to an extraordinary day. As my clock struck twelve, it was exactly 24 hours after Russell had been born 36 years earlier. The timing was wonderful. I took some of Rosie's clover flowers and pressed them into this big book of Aurelio's and Rosie took hers back with her to Holland.

    The climax to my story of the car incident and the clovers, wasn't revealed to us for another 18 months...and at the time we had no idea there would be more to come. Even when I visited Rosie in Holland a month or so later, we only briefly spoke of what had happened. Rosie seemed to just clam up whenever I mentioned it, but her Mediumship *was* extraordinary.

    To see the artwork that she produced, at night whilst in Trance *and in the dark* - was indeed a sight to behold. During my visit, through her Mediumship, Rosie gave me a beautiful coloured pencil drawing of two butterflies. In the drawing, they seemed to be struggling to reach each other. One was purple and one was white, this was very symbolic for me !

    One morning during my visit, I awoke to the strong smell of oil paint. We could both smell it and while eating breakfast my eyes beheld, on the top of the dresser, a most gorgeous oil painting. I just dropped my spoon in amazement ! Rosie *was* a talented painter, but only during the Trance state. Seeing the painting, she looked almost as amazed as I did. Looking back at us was a beautiful oil painting of Chinese roses coloured the palest pink. They were on a background of pale blue and sitting in a deep blue Chinese vase. Having a closer look, I saw something written on the back. It said, *'To Gwennie.'*

    Now the paint was still wet, yet somehow I managed to it get through customs at the airport without smudging it. The painting hangs on my lounge wall today. It is such a treasure and admired by many. If only they knew how it was created and would they believe me anyway ? It doesn't matter. It happened and I know how.

On another day of my stay, Rosie gave me one of her black and white pencil drawings, it was of such delicacy. It showed a fragile butterfly with dark speckles, which was sitting on top of a lovely clover flower. As Rosie handed me the drawing, she said, *'they say it's to go on the cover of book number two. When it is coloured, then it will be time.'*

I have kept this drawing since that visit in Autumn 1989, but only recently felt inclined to colour it. I know my Spirit friends sent it to me for a purpose. You can see a copy of it now, on the back this book.

For me, the clover flower symbolises my friendship with Rosie Hebenaar. She is another of the very special RPPS mothers. The flower itself brings me memories of some very special days and the image of the white butterfly, later turned out to symbolise another brave young Mum - but more of her later.

My visit to Holland was truly amazing, but what Rosie had said was news to me. What second book ?

Four

Automatic Writing and Puzzles

1990-1991

'We know what we are, but know not what we may be...'
~ William Shakespeare

At a séance we were discussing Automatic Writing, when Russell said to me, *'Mum, you could sit there all day, but it won't go !'*

Russell meant the pencil and he's right I still can't do it - or should I say, it just won't work for me ! However, my friend of a lifetime Marion, became quite adept at it. We would always sit regularly and keep to the same time and day - always Friday evenings at 8.30 and we would continue until it just stopped. Often we ended up with pages and pages of writing when we'd finished and it was always extremely interesting, to say the least.

During 1990s our automatic writing proved to contain a lot of cryptic clues about future happenings, which at the time of course, we didn't realise. The Spirit communicator who worked through Marion's hand, gave his name as *James Denver, Security.* Well we laughed at this, for we felt it really was a only a pseudonym, yet whoever he was - he was smart !

It all began when Alfie and I were at the end of our seven and a half years span of the Pink Panther séances. I was still aware of some sadness because of it and maybe this is why the writing began, but I really don't think it was Russell. My suspicions lay at the feet of my Spirit friend Norman, otherwise known as *'Ray-of-Light'* or Raymond Lodge - the son of the Edwardian scientist Sir Oliver Lodge.

I could fill an entire book of the automatic writing that I've kept over the years, so I cannot go through it all here. Yet often, when coming out of a dark and troubled time, something wonderful happens and for Marion and me, it was just like that. As a result of this, what we discovered proved to me that once again, it was all meant to be. I'm very pleased that I kept notes from this time, but then I'm a compulsive note keeper, whereas Marion is the complete reverse !

We began, slowly and laboriously at first and we never took it lightly or 'played' at it. It was too precious for that. With Marion being something of a poet, we'd sometimes get delightful little poems come through the writing. Yet whenever Marion said, *'Oh Gwen, it's my mind,'* the poems would just stop. Often, we had a little girl come through to write, who said, *'I'm Gwen's helper and my name is Margaret. Gwen will know me when she hears me singing children's songs. Just wait and see !"*

Margaret came through frequently, along with 'James Denver, Security' yet to me, they really seemed to be an odd pair. James Denver, Security would urge us to hurry and get the *'Russell'* book published, no matter what. He'd say, *'hurry up and get it on the shelves Gwen !'*

This plea came regularly and *very* seriously too ! Sometimes he seemed like a real clown of sorts, for these times were full of laughter. I did suspect it was Russell of course, but once when I asked him, the answer came back, *'just say I'm from the local circus.'* Enough said !

* * *

During the 1990s Alfie worked every possible hour he could, even though we knew the company he worked for would soon fold. I remember that the Christmas of 1990 was freezing and we had deep snow and ice, yet Alfie always seemed to be working. However we had no choice, so it just had to be.

Around about this time poor Alfie had picked up a dose of flu, and as is usual with couples, he'd caught it from me. I'd spent most of Christmas in bed feeling very ill indeed, but Alfie was left with a pain which seemed like a very bad headache. Although at first he thought he may have simply pulled a muscle whilst training, he still worked around the clock. After consulting a doctor, he was prescribed some painkillers which he took for quite a long time indeed.

Then came February 1991, which was an awful time for our family. I remember it all too well...

One Saturday we learned that our nephew's little son Sean, was killed by a car. There was a family wedding in Dublin and Sean's parents, Richard and Pam, were attending. While they were away, their children - including Sean - were being cared for by Pam's sister. It was Pam's first visit to Ireland and the first time she and Richard had ever left their children at all. On the Friday evening they flew off to Dublin, in time for the wedding the following Saturday.

Both Alfie and I felt most peculiar all day on that Saturday, with a sort of sick feeling. Then at about 6.30 that evening, we received a phone call from the police. They were calling from Dublin and asked if we knew where the wedding had taken place. Thank goodness I remembered it was in a place called Crumlin, but I thought that couldn't be a lot of help.

The police did finally find Richard and Pam and had the painful job of telling them that their son had been hit by a car. Richard's mother was with Sean in the hospital, while the little chap was on life support. His parents flew home instantly, but it was almost over. There was little anyone could do at the time, although I think somehow that we did eventually help them.

Pam told me that while she and Richard had been flying over to Dublin for the wedding, she had somehow 'seen' Sean, all in a green mask. In fact I felt she was seeing what was to come, before it happened. Later they both told us how on that Saturday, they had been shopping in Dublin. They were looking for gifts for their children, but explained how they couldn't find anything suitable for Sean. I told them how Alfie and I had a similar experience back in 1963, before Russell passed away (see Chapter 2 of 'Russell.')

After Sean's funeral service, we presumed that Pam and Richard wouldn't want us all back at the house. Although we later found out that we'd been mistaken, I knew that we were right to have left them for a while. For his family, the shock was so intense. It was so, so sad and it was all too agonising to watch them suffer. I prayed fervently that I would be able to comfort them in some way and I hope I did. It was a very sad situation, but we kept in touch.

Before Alfie and I had attended little Sean's funeral, my friend Marion and I'd had a message through the automatic writing, which said, *'Gwen do not wear black at the funeral. You know better. What about a dusky lilac? Not all black, enough to frighten a child. But do pass on your knowledge Gwen, please. They have to grieve and they will come to you.'*

Later, Marion and I were questioning this tragedy when via the writing, we were told, *'Gwen, we know what has happened, yet it had to be...'*
Of course we all felt that there was *no* real answer for this awful tragedy.

* * *

By mid-March 1991, Alfie and I had decided to go on a week-long Spiritual seminar in Scarborough. A week before, the now very friendly Spirit communicator, 'Mr James Denver, Security' came through once

again. This time he told us,
'the little girl Margaret sends the scent of roses...Gwen there will be a 'happening' at your seminar. Be aware won't you?'
I recall just murmuring a simple, *'okay friend.'*

Then little Margaret herself wrote through Marion's hand saying,
'I hope you haven't forgotten to listen for my songs. I do love blue Gwen, don't you?'
I replied with a simple *'yes'* then realised that I hadn't heard any children's songs up to this point, but promised to pay attention to any that did pop up. However, I didn't have a clue about the 'blue' bit!

Although Alfie continued to experience his head pain, he took his painkillers regularly. His two tablets every four hours kept it at bay, so we stuck to our plans and travelled to the Cober Hill Hotel in Scarborough, for the first week of the Lynwood Fellowship seminars.

It was Spring but still very cold and damp, so naturally we took warm clothes for our stay. Alfie had with him his lovely blue-coloured leather jacket, which would come in handy if we wanted to go out for a walk. We arrived at the hotel on Monday and were given the key to our room, after parking the car in the hotel car park.

'This is excellent,' I thought to myself, as I began to unpack our suitcases in the cosy little room we'd been given. I quickly put everything into the wardrobe - all neat and tidy. So now we could go and greet our friends who we knew would be gathering by the main entrance. They were such lovely warm friends too - but just then, came a bang on the door. It was Don Galloway, our host for the week. He said,
'Gwen, there's been a mistake, I'm so sorry. You're in the wrong room!'

Not being especially pleased, but knowing mistakes can happen, I took everything out of the wardrobe and haphazardly piled them back into our cases. We went back to the car which was just outside and Alf drove us the few brief minutes away, to find our other room in another part of the hotel grounds. Apparently the room we had been mistakenly allocated, was meant for one of the visiting Mediums.

Shortly afterwards Alfie asked me if I'd seen his blue leather jacket.
'No. Where was it?' I replied.
'In the other room, where we were before,' Alfie said, *'and when we changed rooms, I assumed you had taken it.'*
Well I hadn't seen it at all, so we went back to search the previous room. In

fact Alfie, myself and various people, all searched the room and I even spoke to the manager about it, but he looked about as vague as I did ! I mean how could a gorgeous blue leather jacket just vanish completely ?

It wasn't an easy thing to lose, but I went back a second time and searched the wardrobe, under the bed, all the drawers and just about everywhere - but still no blue leather jacket. By now of course, everyone at the seminar had heard about it's disappearance and I was becoming cross because it was very expensive, for it had been made especially for Alfie.

The next day however, I'd forgotten about being cross and we began to have a lovely week with our friends. During the day I suddenly recalled what the automatic writing had said,
'there will be a 'happening' at your seminar...' and there had been a mention of the colour blue too. So I wondered...

By the Friday morning, our seminar had come to an end and we'd a great week. Everyone was gathered in the entrance hall for our farewells, as we hugged and laughed with each other. Just then, in walked the Medium - the one who'd been booked to stay in our room - and her face was pale. Guess what she was carrying over her arm ? One *blue leather jacket* ! She told us how she had just returned to the room to collect her things and there on the rug, in the middle of the floor, was Alfie's jacket. Well we were delighted, in fact everyone cheered ! For me, this was the 'happening' that I'd been promised !

Now we already knew how Russell was an expert at de-materialising things, then materialising them back again. He'd explained enough about these things during the séances. One time, I'd asked him where he keeps all these things while he has them. Typically, a humorous answer came back, *'well Mum, I've got a great big fridge in the sky.'*

Of course, he knows me well enough that it's no good trying to explain the science of these things to me. I only know that things 'went' and 'came back' - and often at home too. Yet Alfie's jacket was, more or less, taken in front of us *and* brought back before the end of the week. There were at least 65 witnesses who heard all about it. Now I don't pretend to know how he does it, but he does !

This happening really had me puzzled. Why his Dad's jacket ? I mean, it's quite heavy and large, but I wondered just *how* did he do it ? Mostly I just wondered why ? I mean, there had to be a reason.

Later, back at home, Marion and I asked the question and the automatic writing gave us this answer,

'Your son just wanted to show his Dad and Mum what he can do.'
So that was that !

* * *

It's strange how friends come and go out of our lives. Back in 1988 I was the 'cabaret' when I sang at the first Lynwood Fellowship's Dinner Dance (which was held at The Russell Hotel in Russell Square, London !) After the dinner and my singing, from the far end of our table coming towards me, I saw the face of a friend I hadn't seen since the mid 1970s.

It was none other than Rachael Hunt, the Medium. At that time I wasn't aware that she'd been to the USA many times or even that she'd been married there. Her new husband was Keith High, so she had now become Rachael Hunt-High. We were delighted to meet again, after what had seemed like centuries. We hugged and hugged each other like mad ! Unfortunately she needed to leave, so she gave me her card with her details. What I noticed on the card was the symbol of a lighthouse and the intriguing name of 'Grail Haven'. *'You must come and see us'* Rachael urged, then she hugged Alfie and was gone.

Rachael lived in Somerset, which is at the very heart of 'Camelot' country and the land of King Arthur, Queen Guinevere and all those myths and legends ! Yet it wasn't until Easter time 1991, that we planned a short visit. A couple of weeks had passed since the incident at the hotel with Alfie's blue leather jacket, but now we were looking forward to finally catching up with Rachael at Grail Haven.

We grew to love this beautiful home of Rachael's, because it was so beautiful and restful. In fact, we travelled there many times that year. Rachael and I were able to resume a wonderful friendship and once we'd arrived, Alfie and I were amazed to be treated to a lovely Ruby Wedding Anniversary party - what a surprise for us both !

In fun, Rachael refused to call Alfie '*Alf*,' so instead he became known as King Arthur and she renamed me Queen Guinevere - so we became *'Their Royal Majesties of Grail Haven'* ! We had such a lot of fun together. One Christmas I remember Rachael had lots of guests over for a 'fancy dress' party. They were all dressed as either Sir Lancelot, Sir Galahad or Ladies of King Arthur's Court. Alfie was dressed as King Arthur, all in green velvet with a crown and sword for Excalibur, while I went floating around the place dressed as Queen Guinevere, in pink chiffon and a huge crown ! It's amazing how daft grown ups can be when they're all dressed up, but then I guess it's easier to play the fool when you're rigged out in a crazy costumes. I mean, even Rachael's dogs wore frills round their necks ! Those were the days for us, which now seem like something lost through the 'mists of Avalon' itself.

Our Easter visit to see Rachael coincided with Alfie's very first week of retirement from work. We had hoped that this would help Alfie's head pains, but they persisted - even though he continued taking his pain killers. But then I guess that pain is really a signal that something is wrong. Little did we know what was coming...

* * *

The automatic writing had come through very strongly before our visit to Grail Haven. My friend Marion and I had many puzzles to try and solve - for at the time we just couldn't understand any of it. For example...

Mr Security: *'Gwen, watch on the motorway for The Barn. Don't ask questions please ladies. Does someone have their bedroom slippers ready ? And their dressing gown ?'*

Gwen/Marion: 'Who are you talking about ?'

Mr Security: *'As I was saying - who has a problem with their glasses ? Oh, it's the lenses. And the wheel of the child's pushchair has broken...!'*

Gwen/Marion: 'can you tell us ?'

Mr Security: *'No. Listen ladies, please. Gwen, please watch for The Barn, five lattice windows and a cracked windscreen. Be careful with your right ankle, because that's your support - don't fall. It's all very green, with lovely smells too. You won't need a doctor Gwen and you'll learn of many weird and wonderful things - be aware.'*

It was no use us questioning who this was, and we never obtained a satisfactory answer anyway. I thought the part about the doctor was very strange, but why was it mostly about me ? Marion seemed to be invisible, although on occasions she *was* sometimes asked to *'concentrate Marion !'*

After reading what 'Mr Security' had said about the barn, I found myself watching out for it everywhere we went ! I began to get a bit paranoid in the end, so I stopped looking, yet it was always at the back of my mind. Then one evening Mr Security said to us,
'your Majesty - Gwen - watch out for the soldier and remember the wooden horse !'

No amount of asking would give us a clearer answer, so in the end I just said, *'okay friend, I'll do my best !'*

Like a couple of nuts, Marion and me tried our best to think of everything we could associate with a soldier, a wooden horse or a barn, but we still came up with nothing ! Now our Spirit friends always come through with love and even though we were really puzzled, there was still more to come...

My philosophy for a few years now has been, *'one day at a time Gwen !'* I think that was how I got through the next six months. Though what did come, completely solved the mysteries we'd been given in the automatic writing. Every single cryptic clue was there, as clear as it could be and so, so clever. There was only one remaining puzzle. It was a message we always received at the end of any automatic writing and it was always the same.

Mr Security: *'Gwen, you and Russell have always had the same eyes !'*
I would ask, *'what do you mean ?'* But we always had the same answer.
Mr Security: *'Remember - in other lives you and Russell have been together and you have always had the same eyes, in colour and shape.'*

Well this would mystify most people, but I knew enough of automatic writing by now to understand there had to be a reason for this emphasised remark. It was few years before the 'penny' finally dropped, so to speak, but you can read more of this particular mystery later in the book. It has been said that I will write a third volume - my goodness, I am going to be busy and old too !

Ah well, we must press on...

Five

Grail Haven

March-September 1991

'Who, being loved, is poor?'
~ Oscar Wilde

We arrived at my friend Rachael's home of Grail Haven, for a three day break. After the freezing Winter, thankfully now we had some wonderful signs of Spring around us and Somerset seemed the place to be somehow - it just felt right. We arrived on Easter Sunday and it was so very quiet. Rachael, Alfie and I just sat chatting - there was so much news to catch up on - but that's the way it is with real friends, you can just be yourself.

Although we had only come away for three days, it seemed that fate had other plans. We *may* have planned to stay for three days, but it was to be *September* before we went home again to Rayleigh !

One Sunday evening, Rachael was to be the demonstrating Medium at a Spiritualist Church near Bath. So together, Rachael and I set off in good time to be there by around six, with the demonstration due to start at seven. After it was over, we drove back rather silently and it was a curious kind of silence, just like the quiet before the storm. We both felt a quiet sense of urgency, so we were hurrying but not speeding. When a car pulled over in front of us, our eyes caught the letters on the registration plate, which were K.W.I.K. We both felt this seemed to be telling us something, so Rachael put her foot down on the accelerator. Now we really were being 'KWIK' ! and both agreed that we felt something was wrong back at the house. Once there, we quickly rushed inside and found there was an empty armchair, but no Alfie !

We could hear Rachael's dear old dog Pepsi and she was upstairs, whimpering. Following the sound, we found that poor Alfie was stretched out on the bed, he had been very sick and was almost unconscious. We only needed to look at him to see that he was very ill indeed, so we

instantly called for a doctor. We'd made Alfie a little more comfortable by the time the doctor arrived and he gave Alfie a thorough examination. He then wrote a prescription for some medication, so Rachael went chasing off to find a pharmacy. As the doctor left he told me, *'call me anytime and I'll come back.'*
However, by midnight there was a further development so we called the doctor, who returned as promised. He needed to give an injection to Alfie, who then fell into a very fitful sleep.

The room that Rachael had given Alfie and I was decorated in a lovely soft green and had twin beds - but I hardly dared to sleep. I lay there all night only dozing with just one eye shut, so to speak.

In the quiet of the night, I became aware of the sweet and clear voice of a child - but it was not Russell. I heard them singing, *'Jesus bids us shine, with a clear blue light. Like a little candle shining in the night. In this world of darkness, so we must shine. You in your small corner, and I in mine.'*

I thought back to the automatic writing, and realised that this must be the little girl Margaret, who had promised she would sing for me. I lay there and drifted in and out of sleep, and when Alfie showed signs of distress, I put pillows on the floor and sat beside his bed.
Yet still she sang on, *'when I grow up in a year, or two, or three - I'll be as happy as can be, like the birds upon the tree.'*

Alfie slept on and off for four days and the dear doctor came in during the day to check on him, then again around midnight each night. On the fourth evening I noticed another change in Alfie's condition, but in my rush to get to the phone I panicked. With the sudden thought of, *'oh my God, he's going to die'* - I fell down three stairs and twisted my ankle ! As I fell I heard the words, *'that's the thought that made you fall Gwennie. Alf is your support and the right ankle is on your male side.'*

I didn't really understand what was meant by these words, but this was no time to be puzzled. I had the doctor on the phone and he was quite definite that Alfie would have to be admitted to hospital by the morning. Now since we had only come to Rachael's for the weekend, Alfie had neither *slippers* or *dressing gown* with him - which was something else the automatic writing had said.

However, as I came limping down the stairs with my twisted ankle, there was the most amazing smell of *roses* in the room. I commented on it to Rachael, not realising that the doctor who had arrived, was still on the phone to the hospital. Rachael put her finger to her lips and smiled at me. I don't know if the doctor had noticed the lovely scent, but it was like the room was full of roses.

For me that night was a nightmare, but yet again it was broken by that sweet child's singing voice. *'Lavender blue, dilly dilly, lavender green. I'll be your king, dilly dilly, if you'll be my queen.'*

I caught a Clairvoyant glimpse of the dear little girl. She was so pretty with brown, curly hair and was about 8 to 9 years old. She kept me going through the night as I lay and listened to her, despite the frightening circumstances.

She really helped to calm my rising panic - for the doctor had also told us that because of industrial action, there would be no ambulances. We would have to get Alfie to the hospital alone ! Yet as ill as Alfie was, we didn't even know how we'd get him from the room and down *two* flights of stairs. As Alfie had described himself afterwards, he was like 'an old knitted teddy bear' - he couldn't even stand, so we had a real problem on our hands. I lay on the bed that night, not daring to go to sleep, just drifting and waiting for the dawn.

Rachael had gone out that evening to post some letters and walk her dog. I'd heard her come back a while later, then go to bed. So there I lay listening to every sound from the corner of where Alfie lay. Then once again my night was broken by this delightful child singing to me, *'there'll be blue birds over, the white cliffs of Dover. Tomorrow just you wait and see.'*

It was Margaret again, bless her ! Still she sang some more - *'I'm as beautiful as a butterfly and as proud as a queen, is pretty little Polly Perkins of Paddington Green.'* This was followed by the hymn, *'What a friend we have in Jesus...'*

Morning eventually came and at about five-thirty I hobbled down the stairs to the kitchen. The morning was cold with a chill in the air. My mind was in turmoil by now as I switched on the kettle and stood by the sink. I stared out of the window with such mixed feelings and can honestly say I felt 'sheer misery.' Suddenly I heard a deep, male voice say to me, *'out of weakness, she was made strong.'*

The sheer beauty of this voice comforted me and later, when all the havoc was over, I began to wonder exactly who it was - although I didn't need to wait long before I found out. Now having literally brought myself to the Bible, I recognised these words were from Hebrews, in the New Testament. They gave me comfort and lifted my spirits. I made some tea and I sat down, but then began to worry again. I wondered how on Earth we would get poor Alfie down all those stairs. Then to my utter astonishment I heard Russell's voice, exactly as it was at the Pink Panther séances. He was singing, *'do you think I would leave you dying, when there's room on my horse for two ? Climb up here Dad we'll soon be flying, I can go just as fast with two.'*

These are lyrics from the 1960s song 'Two Little Boys' - which refer to a *wooden horse* !

With just these four lines I stood there transfixed, rooted to the spot with my cup of tea in hand. I *knew* it was Russell. Now my spirits were truly lifted and was it any wonder ? My son was there with me.

I heard movement from Rachael and Pepsi, who were coming down the stairs and again I felt a sense of urgency. Dear, dear Rachael. In her hand she had blankets at the ready to wrap round Alfie for his journey to the hospital. She must have seen the look on my face, because she said, *'it's ok Gwennie. I met a friend last night when I took the dog out. He's an ex-soldier who's over six feet tall and he's coming round this morning to carry Alfie down the stairs !'*

Oh, the blessed relief I felt at that moment. Clearly, this soldier friend of Rachael's had been sent to us. By now, Rachael should have been in the USA for a conference, but she was so kind that she cancelled her trip to stay with us. She is a real friend, the rare kind not often found in a lifetime. Indeed, no mother could have even done more for me.

When Rachael's soldier friend arrived on the doorstep, I could see he was tall and strong, just as she had said. Then, as if he was only lifting a child, he carried a very sick Alfie down the stairs and into the car. The passenger seat had been pushed back to lay almost flat, so the soldier gently laid Alfie down and tucked him up with Rachael's blankets. After our thanks for the kindness of this man, we were off.

We took a careful journey all round the back roads, so as not to upset our patient. Alfie lay there looking so ill, he even seemed to me to have lost weight at a fast speed. On we went, until we finally arrived at The Royal Marsden Hospital in Bath. Dear Alfie was found a comfortable bed on a ward and surrounded by caring nurses. They told us there was nothing more we could do, except leave him in their very capable hands, so Rachael drove me away from the hospital. We were both very relieved, but quite exhausted.

Soon Rachael and I found ourselves in the city of Bath. This was the very first time I had been. *'Come on'* said Rachael, *'I'm taking you to the Pump Room restaurant for tea and cakes !'*

This was to be another new experience for me and I discovered that it was sheer bliss ! We fed our faces with gorgeous cream cakes, as the waiters almost waltzed about the place. We had silver teapots and there was music too. We sat chatting and I told Rachael about the songs from the Spirit girl Margaret and everything that had happened. She smiled saying, *'It's alright Gwennie, Alfie will be fine. He is very sick but with care and treatment, he will be well again.'*

I guessed Russell was with us because I saw that Rachael was also conversing with Spirit. The week's events had all come so suddenly and I admit that I was scared - but Rachael's message reassured me.

As we sat there, we saw some musicians step onto a stage at one end of the restaurant. They were a wonderful trio of piano, violin and cello and they played beautifully. After a few minutes they began to play a selection of tunes from the musical 'Oliver!' and I was amazed ! Those who may have read my first book *'Russell'* will know, that the first song Russell sang to me at a séance, was *'Where is Love ?'* from 'Oliver!' So listening to this music now with Rachael, I think I must have had my mouth wide open. I know I had tears pouring down my face - not quite the thing to do in a posh restaurant !

I had already been in touch with my family regarding their Dad's situation and Rachael and I were expecting my son Kevin and his family, to arrive the next day. After a rest and numerous pots of tea, we left the Pump Room Restaurant and Rachael said, *'now Gwennie, I want to take you somewhere else.'*

Before I knew it I was literally in 'Oliver-land.' I'd had no idea that parts of the 1968 musical had been filmed in Bath. Again I was amazed, for it seemed to me that Russell was everywhere ! We visited a gallery and lots of interesting shops. In the window of one, we saw two wooden horses and Rachael bought both - one for each of us. At that moment I could hear the lines, *'two little boys had two little toys, each had a wooden horse'*

'Okay Russell' I thought out loud, *'I know you're here. Thank you so much.'*

We went back to Rachael's that Friday, exhausted. After placing our two wooden horses on the shelf, I phoned the hospital. Thankfully, they told me that Alfie was comfortable, which meant that night I had a glorious sleep. I had mixed dreams, but *no* songs ! Next morning however, I was woken to the tune of, *'the King is in the altogether, the altogether - he's altogether as naked as the day that he was born.'*

I had to smile to myself - thanks for cheering me up Russell !

Russell's brother Kevin was due at Grail Haven that day, with his wife Chris and their two young sons, Graeme and Jon. After a long journey, they arrived and with his big brother visiting, I heard Russell's voice once again, he was singing, *'and I think it's that I remember, when we were two little boys.'* !

We all headed off to the hospital to see Alfie, but we had a very disgruntled ten year old on our hands. I remember that for my grandson Graeme it was a big day. This was Cup Final day and for him it was very, very important ! My daughter-in-law Chris had kindly gone into Bath to buy my Alfie a personal stereo for the duration of his hospital stay. She told me that while there, to my little grandson Jon's delight, there were buskers, street artists and fire-eaters everywhere. I think that at eight years old, little Jon would have stayed there all day, but I know that feeling well, because to me Bath is a magical city.

Kevin, Chris and the boys stayed overnight at Grail Haven and left on the Sunday. After we said our goodbyes and promised to tell them any news of their Dad and Grandad, I realised I felt like a wreck. My hair was a mess and so was my face, yet I'd come to Grail Haven for a weekend and a rest. I only had enough clothes for a few days, so had begun to wear some Rachael's, but they were a wee bit big for me at the time. I remember looking in the mirror and thinking, *'oh what a mess !'* Just then I heard the Jerome Kern song, *'You were never lovelier, you were never so fair, you were never lovelier, pardon me if I stare.'*

Russell was doing his stuff again - and changing the words. Ha, ha, very funny Russell.

The next morning one of the lenses fell out of my glasses, so just as the automatic writing had said, I was having a problem with them. Now this meant a trek to the opticians, so off we went. There was Rachael and me and we were joined by her daughter Ann and her grandson Jordan. However it seemed the little one's pushchair was clearly broken ! Luckily we had one ourselves in the boot of Alfie's car, but by now I had noticed that almost all of the clues from the automatic writing were there. I was not consciously looking for them, they were simply happening naturally, as we went along...

Rachael's home of Grail Haven is in a beautiful part of the countryside, but you have to be a very good driver, since the house is along a very narrow road. One occasion we were heading out at the top of this road, when I noticed the local pub, which has been there for years. As soon as I saw the name I laughed. It was called *'The Barn,'* plus it had *five lattice windows* at the front. Now *all* the automatic writing clues were there - except perhaps the *'many wonderful things'* I was supposed to learn, though maybe they would come later ?

By mid-September we were *still* at Grail Haven. Alfie was with me, after being discharged from the hospital and he was much better. Rachael had finally been able to take her trip to the USA and Alfie and I felt very grateful to her. She had done so much to help us during that darker period earlier in the year. Knowing she was due home on a certain day, Alfie and I both decided that we'd have the house 'spick and span' to welcome her back. We were like a couple of Snow White's as we busied ourselves with the vacuum cleaner - and the polish went everywhere !

Rachael arrived from the airport jet lagged, but pleased to be home and she was delighted to see Alfie looking so well. After opening her suitcase in the hall, she walked over to a large dresser in the lounge. She placed a pile of new books there, that she'd bought in America. Then she went back to her case in the hall and continued to unpack. I asked her where all the books were, that she'd brought back with her.
'Just a minute' she replied, *'I'll go and get them for you.'*

Rachael went back to the dresser to get the books, when I suddenly heard a sort of loud *'whoopee'* from Rachael. We rushed into the lounge to find her hugging a small box and saying, *'thank you Russell, thank you. I've always wanted a bit of phenomena. Thank you, thank you.'*

Alfie and I just looked at each other as an ecstatic Rachael explained what had happened. The little box she was holding contained a tiny hair-slide, consisting of two tiny bluebirds. She told us that this hair-slide had been hers since she was four years old, but it was always kept in a box, in another box, then in a cupboard in her bedroom upstairs. It hadn't been on the shelf earlier, so *she* knew and *we* both knew that it had been apported from the bedroom into the lounge. We all agreed that it was a sort of homecoming gift and perhaps a 'thank you' from Russell.

That evening, Rachael gave me a photograph of an American bluebird. It was one that she had actually touched and stroked whilst there. She also gave me a lovely blue feather as a souvenir. For me it was a souvenir of one amazing year !

Six

A Time for More Learning...

'My heart leaps up, when I behold a rainbow in the sky...'
~ William Wordsworth

It's true that we never know what lies around the corner. When confronted with unexpected traumas we can really be shaken and we wonder how we might cope. I know I was guided to Grail Haven with Alfie, during his illness. Otherwise I would have been at home, alone and without support. Rachael was *more* than a tower of strength for me and our friendship became deeper and deeper, if that is possible. We had seemed to be permanently exhausted. For me, the whole experience had been quite frightening and it took me a while to settle down.

While we were there, my youngest son Gary and his wife Sharon had also visited us. They had brought their young son Russell with them, who was a very grown up eight year old and a real 'chatter-box.' I remember, as they arrived, once again hearing my Russell sing, *'I think it's that I remember, when we were two little boys.'*

They went to see Alfie in the hospital that weekend, while we were still waiting for an explanation of his illness. He had been moved from one ward to another and seen by so many doctors. Finally, he was diagnosed with a virus which had caused a serious infection, and now he was on a ton of antibiotics. Each day Rachael and I took the long drive to the hospital and we talked a lot. On these journeys I seemed to learn so much from her. One time she tried to explain numerology to me. Rachael had studied it herself for years in the 1970s and it totally intrigued me!

I had only ever managed to understand something called the 'Divine Triangle' - but after that, I was lost. As we drove along, Rachael pointed out a car registration. It had the three numbers 942. Rachael told me that using numerology, this translated to 'RVB' - which are Russell's initials. Now this wasn't difficult for me to comprehend. In fact, many times a car

with this number 'jumped' out at us, when we were usually frantically searching for a parking place !
I'm not suggesting that Russell Vernon Byrne is a car park attendant - but a car with 942 on its plate would often either lead us to a parking place or would be just coming out of a space we wanted. One afternoon, we even saw a lorry in front of us with *'MYSON942'* on the back of it !

I was often staggered at all these amazing happenings, but I know just how clever our Spirit friends are at making us notice things. Once, when Rachael and I went into a second hand shop, Rachael walked straight to the book shelf and right in the middle next to a huge Bible, was the book *'The Wooden Horse'* - was it just another coincidence ?

While at Grail Haven, I was serenaded every night by the gorgeous little Spirit girl Margaret, who by now I had seen Clairvoyantly. So not only was I hearing songs sung to me by Spirit, but I was finally *becoming* Clairvoyant - much to my surprise and delight. What a fascinating time it was for me !

One glorious incident that I *know* was engineered by Spirit, was while I was very stressed during the time Alfie was sick. Rachael had said,
'I know what you need Gwennie, a good old sing.'

Well that was the last thing I felt like doing myself, but of course she was right. So after visiting Alfie in the hospital, we decided to go to Bath Spiritualist Church to attend a demonstration of Mediumship. The church was quite full as we sat at the front, as usual. Now I don't remember who the Medium was, but she spoke to a young man in the audience. A piece of the message she gave him, was something about a 'music case' with the letter 'J' on it - to which said he recognised.

After the service, the young man approached Rachael, with a smile. He clearly knew her and as they chatted, Rachael beckoned me over to meet him. She introduced him to me as Mr Jon Moxham and told him, *'this is our Gwennie, we call her Queen Genevieve,'* then explained that 'King Arthur' was in hospital - which of course brought a very quizzical look to Jon's face ! Rachael then explained that I was a singer too, but I wondered what she meant by *'too'* ?

Well it appeared that Mr Moxham was a student at the Bath College of Music and he was a tenor. *'Oh, a real tenor,'* I said, *'how wonderful.'*

Jon then said to me, *'would you like to come to the College one evening, then we can sing together ?'* Now was I hearing right ? Oh yes I was !

'Bring your music,' he said, *'and I'll be your piano accompanist.'*

What could I say to an invitation like that except, *'wow !'*

We drove to the College, and to my delight there was my tenor for the evening. Of course he had to be renamed, so I called him *'Sir Lancelot'* just for the occasion ! Then when he began to sing, his voice was glorious ! I remember we joined forces for *'All I Ask of You'* from Andrew Lloyd-Webber's *'Phantom of the Opera'* and at first Rachael and her dog Pepsi were the only *seen* audience. We both later agreed that we could also feel an *'unseen'* audience of Spirit friends, all around us. The emotion we felt with the music made Rachael cry, for it was such a release for her. It was the same for me, as I was really able to 'let rip.' It was both therapeutic and delightful.

We sang duets the whole evening and all accompanied by this fine young pianist and tenor. We sang everything from Pop to Grand Opera and as the evening went on, other students came in to join us. Eventually we'd gathered a small audience, so at the end I said, *'come on all of you, join us around the piano.'* Then one by one they did and together we had a glorious sing-along. We ended with a choral version of *'Climb Every Mountain'* from Rodgers and Hammerstein's *'Sound of Music'* - it was bliss. Finally we said our grateful *thank you's* to Jon and his friends and we all agreed that it had been such a magical evening !

Back at Grail Haven, my Spirit friends continued to wake me each morning with lyrics like *'in the shadows, let me come and sing to you,'* from *'The Shadow Waltz'* or the Rogers and Hart tune *'With a song in my heart (I behold your adorable face)'*
Although I certainly didn't feel adorable first thing in the morning, it was so lovely to be woken in this way !

That Summer I learnt so many wondrous things. I discovered how Rachael had married a Native American gentleman and had learned so much of their way of life. We would talk into the early hours, until we both just fell asleep ! Then in the morning we'd awaken with songs in our heads, so we would swap songs, so to speak. More than once we'd both awaken to the same one. *'Over the Rainbow'* was one of them. This familiar tune has a particular importance with what was to come next - the meeting of one special friend - and while all the drama was taking place at Grail Haven, I had no idea that Russell had been making plans...

* * *

Now all my RPPS 'Mums' are very special to me, for we share an unbreakable bond - our connection to our children in the Spirit World. I had already met and befriended Rosie Hebenaar, Margaret Prentice, Frankie Brown, Shirley Gifford, Dorothy Wheatley, Gill Smith, Marion Proby, Marie from Ireland, and Mary from the United States. Yet there was one little lady who was different, she was another 'Mum' but she was also a Trance Medium ! Since she has chosen to remain anonymous, from now on I will refer to her simply as B-.

We met at Melksham Spiritualist Church, in Wiltshire and at the time, I only knew that she was the mother of a child in Spirit. Little did I know it then, but Russell had *already* made a delightful friendship with her...

As usual, I sat at the front for Rachael's demonstration. Over on my right, on the far side of the church, was a young woman with a small boy of about four years old. I was drawn to the boy, because he sat so quietly and actually seemed to be listening to what was being said !

During the demonstration, Rachael pointed to this woman from the platform and gave her a message from the Spirit World. It seemed that she had lost a daughter through cot death syndrome. As the Spirit link became more established, in came my Russell as young man - with a beautiful baby girl of about three years old, perched on his shoulder !

After the demonstration the young woman came over to speak to Rachael. As part of her Spirit message, Rachael had given her the symbol of a white butterfly and explained how it linked with Russell and his own symbol of the Red Admiral butterfly. She introduced herself as B- to Rachael and myself and we chatted about Russell's Pink Panther Society. Before we left, we promised to keep in touch. At the time I was in the middle of such drama with Alfie and I only wanted to get him well and back home to Rayleigh. Once we were home and settled, I did correspond with B- and I learned that she was going through some very tough life experiences indeed. Perhaps we were destined to meet ?

B- told me that she had a Spirit friend and helper named John, who had told her that a new Spirit communicator was going to be working with her. I'm sure that on her first meeting she must have been very surprised when he arrived - for it was my Russell !

B- explained that, *'he told me his name was Russell Vernon Byrne. 'Vernon' as in the name of the Football Pools.'*

She told me how he was, *'tall and dark haired, with hair that went in different directions.'*

'Well that's Russell' I said.

'He has an amazing smile,' B- said, *'and dark blue eyes that light up when*

he smiles.' B- then told me how she had seen him wearing a soft brown leather jacket with a purple silk shirt and highly polished shoes.

'That's just like his father,' I told her.

I imagined that she had expected to see a little boy of nine and three quarters, so it must have been a shock to be confronted by a tall, handsome grown up ! B- told me that Russell had explained how he could be any age he wanted and that his Mother *knew* he was now a man. Now B- had known of her Spirit friend John since she was a girl. She recognised his energy, but Russell's energy was different. She said it was sparkling and very, very quick. B- said that he'd appeared 'childlike' when he first asked if he could work with her. However, they agreed to give it a go.

Although B- and Russell had to work at getting their vibrations right, to find a balance because of Russell's speed, I know Russell's arrival for B- was a joy. Then of course he just *had* to sing to her ! One song he gave her was '*Love and Marriage*,' but as usual he changed the words, this time to *'Ghosts and Mediums...go together like a horse and carriage..!'*

B- had also noticed Russell's dark blue eyes and commented on them being so like mine. Russell told B-, *'that's because she is my Mother.'*

So Russell and B- have become good pals, but then so have B- and Alfie and I too. What a powerful link we all have, as we share a bond of love for our children in Spirit. I have also learned how Russell cares for B-'s little daughter in Spirit. This is the beautiful child he brought with him on his shoulder, during Rachael's demonstration. I have been lucky enough to see her myself once - though only briefly. Seeing her, I can now understand how Russell shares such a love for this child. Once I heard him sing these words to me, from the Rodgers & Hammerstein musical, *'Carousel.'*
'My little girl, soft and pink as peaches and cream can be, and my little girl is half again as bright, as girls are meant to be.'

What a comforting thought to know, that our children in Spirit can be loved and cared for - even 'adopted' into a loving relationship in the Spirit World.

B- told me of nothing of Russell that surprised me, but she delighted me when she told me how he often came dressed for every occasion. I already knew that he did this through other Mediums, for he had been seen before in full Indian head-dress and even a soldiers Busby ! It seems he also is a great fan of Fred Astaire and Gene Kelly for I was highly amused, when once she told me how he liked to impersonate these dancers. I think Russell has entertained B- many times this way. She told me it was like living with a *'cabaret act'* !

Yet Russell is so much like his father with his gentleness, quick wit and humour. Although Alfie doesn't have Russell's fine tenor voice. He gets his musical talents from me. He shares my serious mind too, but it was my curiosity that led to him to give me such amazing answers, throughout all through the years that have passed. I once wrote to B- telling her about how the Pink Panther physical séances ended. I told her of my sadness and how this was the price I had to pay for all the wonders I had witnessed. Some of these are described in later chapters.

With her Mediumistic gifts, B- took Russell, his father and me, into her heart and I will be eternally grateful to her for the long hours she put in. I know Russell loves B- or his 'Dutch' as he calls her !

* * *

It was the Summer of 1991 when B- had come into our lives and what a glorious Summer it was too. By August, Alfie was well enough for us to make the most of it and we got into the car and visited various places. I'd heard that Somerset was beautiful, but also that it was so interesting. There seemed to be places of myth and legend everywhere we went.

Alfie and I had the thrill of visiting Avebury village in Wiltshire and what a fascinating place that is ! Plus, it was Crop Circle season so we went miles up into the hills searching for them. We saw many formations and were totally mystified and entranced by them - but who wouldn't be, sitting there in the middle of a monster-sized formation ?

Now unfortunately my Clairvoyance seemed to have vanished, but not so my Clairaudience. I still heard songs and usually in the morning. Two good examples I remember from that year, show how clever our Spirit friends can be at using songs, with lyrics that contain a message...

Song number one came on the morning of my birthday in May. I awoke to these lyrics from the old Arthur Tracy song,
'To Mother with love, I'm sending this lovely bouquet...a rose or two, some violets blue...to Mother with love...'

Sure enough, I did receive some flowers, from a lovely lady who came to my surprise party. She said to me, *'I'm sure your son wanted me to pick these for you. I felt very impressed to buy them.'* When I saw them I *knew* that he did, so I told her about the song. There were red and yellow roses and some blue daisy-like flowers - not violets, for it was a bit late for those, but they were close !

Song number two came on August 14th, the anniversary of Russell's passing, yet this one really puzzled me - especially on this day. The words I heard were, *'And did those feet in ancient time, walk upon England's mountains green, and was the Holy Lamb of God, on England's pleasant pastures seen...'*

but they really led me on a journey of discovery. I could vaguely recall hearing them from my school days, but I could honestly say that I had no idea. I had certainly never considered their meaning. I repeated the words to Alfie and he told me they were originally written as a poem by William Blake over 200 years ago. Like me, Alfie had no idea what they meant, but we were to find out.

Now the automatic writing had promised that I would learn some *weird and wonderful things* - although what is weird to one, might be wonderful to another and vice-versa - but on another excursion with Alfie, we went off to Glastonbury and visited the glorious Chalice Well. It's difficult to describe the atmosphere of this place, so I won't try - but I was enchanted. It was so interesting, I could have stayed there all day ! There were people meditating in the gardens and there were butterflies everywhere. In the tiny bookshop there, I found a book all about the hymn *'And did those feet...'* Now I just *had* to know more.

I don't know why this song intrigued me so. Maybe it was because Russell had sung it to me on the anniversary of his passing, but in deciding to examine all the evidence, I found the most extraordinary tale. It all begins with William Blake and his poem, which was the inspiration for the hymn known as *'Jerusalem.'*

I think it would take a strange heart, not to be moved by the 'legend' of this beautiful hymn and the more I read about it, the more I wanted to know. Was it simply a beautiful legend or did it have any foundation in truth ? I had my book from the Chalice Well bookshop, but then a friend in America sent me a 1985 edition of the magazine *'Heart'* containing an article called, *'Did Jesus go to High School in Britain ?'*

So was it a more than just story ? *Did* the boy Jesus actually come to Britain and *'walk upon England's mountains green ?'* If the written records of the first 500 years of the Christian age are entirely blank, then where do we look ? Well in one book I found, called *'Did Our Lord visit Britain, As They Say in Cornwall and Somerset ?'* the Reverend Cyril Dobson recounts four separate traditions telling how Jesus came to Britain in his youth. The first is from *'A Book Of Cornwall,'* by S. Baring-Gould. It tells an old Cornish story of Joseph of Arimathea coming to Cornwall in a boat and he brings the child Jesus with him. It tells how Joseph was a merchant who taught the young Jesus the method of separating tin from wolfram !

The second tradition describes how Joseph and Jesus came to Somerset - or as it was known then 'Summerland.' They supposedly arrived on a ship from Tarshish and stayed in a place called 'Paradise' - a traditional place name commonly used around the areas of Burnham and Glastonbury.

The third tradition says that Jesus and Joseph stayed in the mining village of Priddy, north of Glastonbury, near the Mendip Hills - where an old Priddy saying goes, *'as sure as our Lord was at Priddy.'*

The fourth tradition puts Jesus and Joseph in Glastonbury itself. A trade in tin existed between Cornwall and the Mediterranean then, so Joseph took the young Jesus with him.

I discovered in another book some writings from the sixth century that suggested Jesus visited Glastonbury. For around 550 A.D the Welsh poet and Druid, Prince Taliesin wrote, *'Christ, the Word from the beginning, was from the beginning, our teacher and we never lost His teachings.'*

So if Jesus did come to England, what did he do here ? Perhaps he studied under Joseph's care or learned the ways of the native English ? The Bible says that he studied somewhere, but not in his native synagogue. St. John 7:15 says, *'and the Jews marvelled saying 'How knoweth this man letters, having never learned ?'*

Just imagine Jesus as a boy, travelling to Glastonbury by ship. Picture him on board, with the fresh wind and the fine sea spray - his mind *must* have been excited by the adventure ahead of him. With the Roman empire far behind him, he would have been safe in Britain and free to study, plan his life and realise his mission - which was just over the horizon.

I know I've digressed here, but I personally find this story so enchanting. Perhaps it takes a childlike heart to understand it, yet it seems to be devastatingly simple to grasp - and if it takes a childlike mind and not a *childish* one, then I'll stay that way ! Anyway, it proved to be wonderful reading for our last weeks at Grail Haven.

In the third week of September I had a call from B- who asked to visit us while we were still there. I'd felt inspired to buy some flowers for her arrival - though more as a gift from her baby in Spirit. So I went wandering around the shops in Shepton Mallet and was drawn to a lovely bunch of peach and pink rose buds. I didn't have a clue why, they just seemed right ! Back at the house I made them into a beautiful posy, with the aid of a silver doily, some foil and two pink ribbons I just 'happened' to buy.

It was all ready for B- when she arrived. She had also bought me some flowers, but when she gazed at the posy, she was amazed. She explained that it was an excellent replica of the posy of flowers she had placed on her baby daughter's grave, even down to the pink ribbons.

Talking later, we were both doubly amazed when we discovered that her baby and my Russell, both share the same birthday of 20th September. So now we had even more to chat about ! Was it just coincidence ? Well I don't believe in them. For me there has to be a deeper reason...

At this point I didn't know that B- was a Trance Medium, she just never spoke of it, but we'd had a good time and now she was leaving. As we said goodnight I couldn't help noticing that her car had a *cracked windscreen* - yet another 'clue' from the automatic writing, from almost 6 months earlier !

Just before Alfie and I left Grail Haven to go back home, I visited the town of Frome. I was in a charity shop and as usual went straight to the book shelf. I seemed to be led to find a dear little book called *'The Cedar Box'* by John Oxenham. Now it only cost me a few pennies, but this small book is such a treasure for me. Inside is a beautiful illustration of the boy Jesus handing a gift to his mother Mary - a box made from Cedar wood. They are standing together in his father's workshop and Mary is accepting the gift. Beneath are the words, *'For thee Mother' he said, 'and I made it with my own hands, all for thee.'* Now this little book stays beside my bed and I read it over and over again. After all, it's only a legend, yet certain legends do seem to contain an element of *Truth* within them, don't they ?

I have already mentioned how Russell had said, *'By Hook or by Crook, I'll be Last in the Book'* and of course, he *did* have the last word in the first book. Although at the time I had no idea how he would do it, but I knew he'd keep his promise to me. That final chapter which beautifully describes Russell's journey to the Spirit World, was actually a transcript from an audio recording - created through the Trance Mediumship of my new friend B-. It was the first 'Summerland Tape' entitled 'Coming Home' and since then, there have been more. I actually found their title quite intriguing, especially after discovering that 'Summerland' was the ancient name for Somerset, where Alfie and I had spent so much time.

So the next chapter is a transcript of another Summerland Tape which I think you will agree, is full of interest and typically 'Russell' !

Seven

Recorded Trance Mediumship Session

Summerland Tape 1
February/March 1992

'Whither thou goest I will go, and where thou lodge, I will lodge,
Thy people shall be my people, and Thy God shall be my God.'

~ Ruth 1:16

Russell: *'Hello Mum ! Hello Dad ! Can you hear me ? Do you know who this is ? I hope you do ! It's been a very long time since you heard my voice, but through this lady I can speak to you. You understand it's Trance work, but that doesn't mean it can't be as effective as other forms of work ! Working with a 'Light Trance' Medium is just different.*

When one approaches Mediumship with sincerity and integrity and humility, anything is possible ! The trouble lies in people using their Mediumistic skills for their own glorification, to fulfil a power need within themselves - and when the person starts to do that, then it destroys the purity of the work and will destroy the purity of the Mediumship ! The only way that a person can become a pure vessel of light, is with kind humility and understanding of our fellow human beings.

I was very disturbed Mum, to learn why you had to wait for the end of the first book. Mediumship doesn't have to be like that. Mediums don't have to behave like that, but some do.

We are constantly worried about the standard of Mediumship which is exhibited in this country at the moment, and we are more worried about the standard of Mediumship in the USA. Spirit can only work as well as the person that works with them. The majority of Mediums do not have a pure channel, because they haven't got a pure insight into the power of

Love and they haven't got a pure insight into the world of Life itself. So you find the purity of Mediumship is lost.

It's very good of B- to do this work - which she has done on her own for years. It isn't very easy and depends upon her ability to allow me to slip in and out of her body very quickly. Because of that she can't really open up and be a pure channel - for half the time she is listening out for her baby daughter. I do appreciate it, but she is very busy and we don't get much time to do this kind of work.

It is very important that you know, that the Mediumship you've seen so far, is perhaps secondary to that which you'll see in the future. I am new to Trance work but B- is not, for she has done this work before with Spirit members of the 'White Brotherhood.' I really feel Mum and Dad, that there was a need to give you some tangible proof that we are as worried as you are, about the standards of Mediumship that you have seen.

It is not our way to use that Greater Love - which you use to combine both worlds - and have that Great Love used against you. To an extent, I think that's what has happened in the past. Though B- can tell you what I've said when we've talked together. We wanted to try and do this because you'd then have a tape of me speaking to you and you could refer to it and I think that's important.

You probably wonder how or when or why I started to work with B-, but it's quite easy to explain really. As you know, during my time in Spirit I've tried to learn about all ways of communication with the Earth plane. I started out learning about ways of communication through my Love for you and Dad. I wanted you to know - and know very profoundly - that I hadn't died and I hadn't left. So I began to learn all the various practices that Spirit have to learn in order to communicate with people on the Earth.

It's been a very long learning process, but I don't regret it. But the more you find out, the more you want to know and so though my wish to communicate with you and Dad, I began to study. I began to realise what a valuable thing this was and how it could benefit, not only you and Dad, but also many others on the Earth plane, who feel they have lost their children.

If I put it into Earth terms, you will understand that to begin with, you have to learn the basics of communication - the ABC. Then there's your 'O' levels and 'A' levels, then your PhD's ! Halfway through my training I was promised that if I worked hard and studied hard, then the day would come when I'd meet a Medium who was able to relay the messages accurately *and truthfully, with humility and lit by a great deal of Love.*

Now I waited a long time for this Medium and I must admit that I've tried and worked with others, but some - and I stress the word some - are very prejudiced and not at all humble. If a Medium's own channel is blocked with their own preconceptions, then it's very difficult to get the great concept of Spirit through to them. Because no matter how hard you try, preconceived ideas affect the translation of the message and this is very frustrating. Some Mediums I've tried to work with, instead of giving you the pure message I want to get through, they add bits or leave bits out. Although I understand it's very difficult for them, but the moment you start adding to a message, it gets altered then the message loses its purity of understanding, so it is very frustrating for us.

I was told a few years ago, that there was a Medium on Earth who had studied long and hard and gone through a lot of trials. Then she began 'reaching out to Spirit' for guidance. She was also a lady educated in communication skills with the 'White Brotherhood' and they were very, very anxious that during her tutorial learning stage, if you like, that she would only deal with the 'White Brotherhood.' So you see, my channel of communication at that time, wasn't as open as I would have liked. I couldn't work with her - but I don't regret it, as now I think perhaps we were probably not ready.

However, there came a time when it was essential, that in order for this communication to take place, it was necessary to arrange for your paths to cross. It was ideal Mum, that the first person to cross your path should be Rachael Hunt-High. So what happened?

As you know, B- went to Melksham Spiritualist Church and heard Rachael speak and her words touched her soul. Then she had a message from Rachael at a time when she needed it very badly - so the link had been established. During that meeting, Rachael mentioned you Mum and the book and the butterflies - so the foundation was laid. But at that time, B- was going through a great deal and really had 'enough on her plate' - without needing me to come in and try to form a relationship to work with her. So, again that contact was put on hold.

Then one day it was decided that you should be introduced to B- and through Rachael and you, B- learned of the RPPS. Then the lines of communication became open between all of us and from that moment on, the foundation of that relationship could begin to form.

Now I didn't come in immediately to work with B-, I observed her from a distance. Because this lady is capable of communication from Spirit of a very high level, she is very particular about who she worked with. In fact she refuses to work in any other way. This made it very important to introduce you gradually, so she became aware of you and no cross lines were established.

For a while I would just listen to her talk and simply watch her live - so I could get used to the vibratory level that she worked at. At first I was a bit apprehensive of what I might find - because Mum, in our voyage of discovery for a Medium, we have found some extremely odd channel's haven't we ?

Yet what I found in B- was something completely different to anything that I'd found before. I discovered someone who was down to Earth and very, very realistic. She lived her life very much in this world, but her soul was very much stretching towards communication with ours. It was a great surprise to find someone who wasn't pretentious about their ability, and who didn't even really believe that they <u>had</u> the ability. I've worked with some Mediums who believed in their abilities so much, that they sort of flaunted it at you. Some just can't wait to tell you how good they are or how wonderful and clever they are !

Meeting B- was an entirely different thing, because she didn't really believe that she was that capable or could communicate at such a level - or even that her work could help a great deal in the world. So then I was placed in the extraordinary position of having to encourage her and try to help establish her faith in herself and her skills. Because of that, we were able to form quite a close working relationship and it's because of the complexities of such relationships, that bring people closer together.

I feel very much in awe of her - well, not really ! Although I did sometimes have to encourage her. I was almost a teacher in a way, as well as a practitioner. I'd never been in that position before and it was very interesting. Now although I say I was teaching, I couldn't really teach this lady about Great Philosophical Truths, because she already understood the teachings of the 'White Brotherhood' - which has always guarded and guided her. Yet together, we actually learned more about the ability to communicate between worlds. So Mum, you're our guinea pig in a way !

Between us, we are constantly learning to perfect the skills of communication in Mediumship. She helps me to control the Psychic energy that comes through me, because at this point I am very new to Trance, so it may all seem a bit disjointed. I am finding it very hard to use her voice box to actually use words again, because it's been a long time for me. I know you and Dad have heard my voice through Physical Phenomena, but you've never heard my voice directly through a Medium.

It's very hard for me to slow down my vibratory level, especially with the thought that I am actually talking to you and Dad, but B- encourages me to channel the energy just by being there.

You probably wonder why it's taken me so long to find this avenue of communication ? The fact is Mum, that I hadn't learnt enough and B- hadn't got to the place in her studies, for this level of communication to take place. I hope you can understand. I think you will. I'm very excited about it and you know what I'm like when I get excited - I get fidgety and tend to put too much energy through. I'm trying very hard but I don't always find it easy.

Now, I think it would be a good time for us to try an experiment. We will now try to have both of us talking, through the same body, so to speak. B- and I will try to have a conversation together on this tape - so you can actually hear us both. It's a tricky process, but I will now step back and let B- explain it.'

B-: Hello Gwennie. I'm back, it's me ! I think what Russell would like to do, is to show you how the actual process of communication takes place in Trance work. I don't know why he wants to do this, but he feels he'd like to try. So I want you to imagine me sitting at my dining room table. We are sitting in the light, but without daylight. Now, Russell has worked through me and he is on my left hand side. Now he is going to change over to my right hand side, so we are going to attempt a conversation with one another through one body.

I don't know if it's going to work, but Russell will come half way in and I have to go half way out. So for a time, we have two influencing the body of one. Now, I've only ever done this with the White Brotherhood, we have practised and it does work, although we've never done this on tape before, so we'll see what happens.
So Russell will come in. I will count him in. It will be nice for you.
...1...2...3...4...5...

Russell: '6...7...8...9...10...and I'm in ! That's how this Trance works. Now, I'm going to move out to the right and B- is going to come back from the left and we're going to attempt a conversation with one another.'

B-: It's me again. Russell, I know your Mum would like to know why I can communicate with you on a one to one basis and she can't - would you explain ?

Russell: 'Yes. Mum, what you need to remember is that B- has studied and *lived the Philosophy of the White Brotherhood for almost forty years - yet she never knew what it was. Her abilities of Clairvoyance, Clairaudience and Clairsentience have never been switched off for her. During her childhood she perfected the art of listening. She has understood the value of silence. She has listened and because she is capable of communicating at a very high level, she has learned a great deal of the Philosophy of Life itself - and in doing that she has evolved. She has also led a very full life, with many events which have overtaken her, but with the benefit of the Philosophy, she has learned to come through and to understand.*

For many years B- has studied the growth and development of life and the soul, therefore she is an open channel to Spirit and the way they communicate. You Mum, have tremendous ability and during the next five years you'll find that ability awakening within you. Remember there is no doubt about it, you cannot have contact with a high Spiritual vibration, without it stretching and procuring your own growth. It touches your own soul. So what I am trying to say to you Mum, is have patience and you will develop. Unfortunately, the way forward for you has been hampered by the mediocrity you have met in some Mediums, during your quest for Truth.'

B-: Gwen, I hope that helps you? I must say here that although I can speak with and see Russell very clearly, I have very little contact with my own daughter in Spirit. Perhaps in a way that is quite valuable, because we are so emotionally involved with our children. It could affect us quite profoundly if we had a very close Spiritual contact with them here on Earth. We all have our own destiny to fulfil, so sometimes I think it's easier to have an intermediary.

Russell: *'Yes Mum, it is easier for you to have an intermediary, even though you might not believe it. This is because it would take very little perhaps, for you to just give up on life. I know your life has held such great disappointments for you, but you are not in the world of Spirit because you still have a great deal of work to do. I do not wish to distract you from that work, before you do join me.*

So for you, it is better that there is an intermediary. Though having said that, the more you open up to the power of the White Brotherhood, then the more your soul will stretch and grow and the more you'll become involved.

It is wrong to evoke Spirit, which is one of the principles of the White Brotherhood. Because each have their own destiny to fulfill in the Spirit World - just as the people on the Earth have their own destiny to fulfill. It's very important to remember that a certain separateness must be maintained, just until you have grown enough Spiritually. You and I are very emotionally involved, but B- and I are not. So it's easier for me to work through B-.

However, B- is very emotionally involved with her own daughter in Spirit, so I think it would be harder for them to work together in the same way. But then B-'s daughter, whom we have given the Spirit name of Rainbow, is still very young.

B-: Russell, Rachael Hunt-High told me that you had taken responsibility for my baby, she said you had become her adopted Spirit Dad !

Russell: 'Yes that's right. I have taken responsibility for her. Because I passed to Spirit as young as I was, I was never able to learn about parenting. It is possible to adopt a child here in Spirit. I mean it's a little different to the Earth plane but yes, we can take special responsibility for a child and learn the complexities of parenthood. I did that because I wanted to. There was a time link, since we were born on the same day and there was a tremendous link of sorrow, that I saw around you B- and my Mother. We seemed to have so much in common that I felt it was the right thing to do and my elders in the Spirit World agreed with me, and so I have undertaken Spiritual responsibility for her.

So Mum and Dad, Rainbow is your adopted granddaughter and my adopted daughter too. This does not detract from the fact that B- is her mother and we wouldn't want it any other way. Rainbow is very proud of her mother and so am I.'

B-: Russell, it does make me cross when a Medium sometimes says that a child in Spirit who comes through, is for themselves or any person other than the child's own parents.

Russell: 'There is a tremendous bond of love between a parent and their child. So it makes me very sad and even cross, when a Medium does not get the message right or decides to adopt that tremendous love for themselves. This has happened to us hasn't it Mum, but I am *your* son and I'm very proud to be *your* son - I don't want any other parents ! You are my parents and always will be...

B-: A lot of things have been promised to your Mum and Dad, Russell. For April is to be a beginning. I believe they are sitting in a circle.

Russell: 'Yes. It's wonderful. I'm so pleased that Mum and Dad are so secure in their knowledge of Spirit, that they can sit in a home circle. They have a tremendous amount of knowledge and an understanding of the philosophy - Mum has definitely opened herself up to it. What I would say is keep going. Meet in love and harmony and with accord and union, then tremendous things will take place. This tape will bring them a lot of Spiritual Energy and well being.'

B-: Has there ever been a moment Russell, when your Mum has mourned for you, that you haven't heard her ?

Russell: *'No, no. Every tear that my Mother and Father have cried for me, I have known about. I have felt them soul deep. There's never been a moment since my passing, that I haven't known of the tremendous love that they have for me. It was that love that inspired me to learn more about the possibility of communication between the two worlds. Dear Mum and Dad, your amazing love has lit up the pathway that now I travel.*

It was your love which guided me to find a way to communicate and tell you of that Great Truth - that I hadn't died and that I hadn't gone through a bad experience. I'd just made a transition from one life to another. That was all. I'd never left them and I'm always here. Dear Mum, I know when you talk to my photo in the bedroom. I know all the time and it's wonderful. I keep an eye on all that is going on in your life and I know when you are hurting. I'm here, though I know you can't quite pick me up yet - but you will - I am so close to you both.

I'm so thrilled that the RPPS has started. It's going to attract attention and the inspiration you derive from it all, will enable you to write the second book. Mum, I said that you'd write about this - and the work of compassion, love and understanding that you give to other mothers in the same position. We know that they haven't really 'lost' their children at all.

Dear Mum and Dad, I know that you are going through a time of change in your lives at the moment, but don't worry. Everything will be resolved, for you are being watched over and protected at every turn you make. The reason your lives have now changed course, is because this is the next step in your progression. For you are developing and you will go forward. The only way that any of us can progress, the only way anyone can grow soul deep, is in service and that is wonderful and of enormous value.'

B-: Now Russell wants to sing through me ! He can sing, but I can't. This really is new ground for me in Trance Mediumship. Russell is very musical and he has a tremendous love of music. I guess he gets that from you Gwen, but it seems that no recording would be complete for you, without some music.
I don't play an instrument and I can't sing, but Russell wants to do it. The song is '*Camelot*' and I know it has a special significance to you. Gwen, I know you are a trained singer, so this may be painful for you - but believe me, I'm doing my best ! It's one of the longest songs that one can sing, but I'll try.

Russell: *'I'm here Mum and Dad and I want to sing you the song 'Camelot' but B- is quite appalled ! Never mind, I'll have to jolly her along...I am very insistent on having the correct lyrics and I want you to know that this part of the country is steeped in the Camelot mythology. So do listen to it, absorb it and have a think about it...*

'Oh, do look around you friends,
we have the most equable climate in all of England.
It's True ! It's True !
The Crown has made it clear,
the climate must be perfect for the year.
A law was passed a distant moon ago here,
July and August cannot be too hot !
And there's a legal limit to the snow here,
in Camelot ! Camelot !

The Winter is forbidden till December,
and exits March the 2nd - on the dot !
by order, Summer lingers to September,
in Camelot ! Camelot !

That's how conditions are -
the rain may never fall till after sundown,
By 8, the morning fog must disappear,
In short there's simply not, a more congenial spot
For 'happily ever after'-ing, than here, in Camelot.

I suppose the Autumn leaves will fall into neat little piles,
Oh no, B- they blow away at night of course !
in Camelot ! Camelot !

I know it gives a person pause,
but in Camelot ! Camelot !
Those are the legal laws,
the snow may never slush against the hillside,
By 9 p.m. the moonlight must appear.
In short there's simply not, a more congenial spot,
for 'happily ever after'-ing than here, in Camelot.

Each evening from December to December,
before you drift to sleep upon your cot,
Think back on all the tales that you remember,
of Camelot.

Ask every person if he's heard the story,
and tell it strong and clear if he has not,
that once there was a fleeting wisp of glory,
called Camelot ! Camelot !

Where once it never rained till after sundown,
by 8 a.m. the morning fog had flown,
Don't let it be forgot - that once there was a spot ,
For one brief shining moment,
that was known as Camelot'

~ Lyrics by Alan Jay Lerner & Frederick Leowe

Rainbow: (who comes in very quietly.)
'All things bright and beautiful, all creatures great and small,
All things wise and wonderful, the Lord God made them all,
Each little flower that opens, each little bird that sings,
He made their glowing colours, He made their tiny wings...'

Russell: *'All things bright and beautiful, all creatures great and small...'*
Rainbow: *'All things wise and wonderful, the Lord God made them all.'*

B-: Well I'm back after a short a break and I've just listened to the tape. I am amazed and thrilled, this really is a first. Russell brought little Rainbow in very quickly at the end there.

Russell: *'B- was appalled that I wanted to sing on tape to you, so I had to break it to her gently ! Before we made this tape I told her, 'it's time music came back into your life, we ought to sing together !'*
So at first we practised together with nursery rhymes, but the only words she knew were from 'Sing a Song of Sixpence' ! But we practised it and perfected it. After the nursery rhymes we tried some pub songs which we enjoyed, but she won't let me put them on this tape !'

'She'll be coming round the mountain when she comes,
Singing aye, aye, yippee, yippee aye !'

'Dance, Dance, wherever you may be,
I am the Lord of the Dance said he,
I'll live in you, if you live in me,
I am the Lord of the Dance said he...'

'Mum, all this singing and jollity is for you and it's no coincidence that you'll receive it in time for Mother's Day. Chin up Mum and Happy

Mother's Day.'

B-: This *is* a long tape Gwennie, but I hope it helps...

Russell: *'Mum and Dad, there is someone else who is standing by to speak to you, so I will step aside...'*

John: *'Blessings be upon you my children - to you and your families and your homes. I have come but briefly, to speak to you tonight. My name is John and I wish to give you the Blessings of the White Brotherhood of the Light - and say to you, that the path you follow may not always be easy, but it is a good path and it will guide you always unto the light.*

Beloved of the Brotherhood are Gwen and Alfred. We wish to tell you Alfred, that your work as a healer on the Earth plane will begin when you undergo a training programme - within the next six months. Do not be alarmed or overawed by it. You have the power of the Brotherhood with you. The light walks with you and no harm will come.

My daughter Gwen. You fret and fume for growth, yet you are growing mightily as we speak. As you sit and listen and learn, you grow and the more your knowledge grows, so will your abilities grow likewise. It is very important that your book be written. It will take time to gather the material, but at all times and at every turn, ask for guidance and it will be given to you. In fact, there is very little that will not be given to you - you only have to ask.

Sometimes the way forward is hard, but the way can also be lit by many who share your philosophy and your belief. So I give you the Blessings of the White Brotherhood and I truly believe what the Brotherhood has said unto you,
'that when people meet in harmony and accord and humility, and truly ask the Divine Light to guide, guard and protect them and to enrich them by the knowledge of their Law - truly anything is possible.'

This is only the beginning. Blessings to you Gwen and Alfred – children of the light - and to your family. A special blessing goes to your grandson Russell - named after your own son Russell, who joined us in spirit at a very early age. Your grandson is a gifted boy, a lovely boy. He is an old soul, brought to the Earth to achieve things in the power of light and love of the Spirit. Nothing will dim the light of that soul.

I hope that tonight you have seen something of what is possible between one Earth soul and one of the Spirit. You and your son and B- have worked hard to prove that communication between two worlds is possible. The more they work together, I'm sure the greater that communication will be. Now I will leave you and give you the blessings and peace of the

Brotherhood, so that wherever you walk, may it always be in the light.'

B-: I didn't know John was coming in ! I'm glad he did. I hope it makes up for your disappointments in the past. It's midnight now, so goodnight to you both, Gwen and Alfie. God Bless, until we speak again.

* * *

Well, after first listening to this recording of my son Russell speaking through B-, I scribbled so many notes ! Then as I put away my paper and pens and feeling somewhat weary, in came the familiar voice of Russell singing to me down my ear,

> *In the morning of my life I will look to the sunlight,*
> *In the evening of my life when the day is through,*
> *And the question I will ask - only you can answer,*
> *Was I brave and strong and true ?* **Like you, Like you,**
> *Did I fill the world with Love my whole life through ?*
> *Did I fill the world with Love my whole life through ?*
>
> ~ Leslie Bricusse from 'Goodbye, Mr Chips.'

Then mentally I talk with him,
'yes my son. I think you're doing your very best in that direction. I promise I'll do exactly the same'
Whatever he asks of me, I will do.

On this tape Russell speaks of meeting B- and waiting to work with her. There are the songs, which I feel may have a deeper meaning for me to discover in the future. Then April is mentioned as an important time for us - in fact, it was then that Alfie and I made the quick decision *not* to move home, but to stay here in Rayleigh.

Also in April, I was at another Lynwood Seminar and I had a sitting with the Medium, Shirley West. Here is word for word, what she said to me...

Medium: *'Gwen, I know you have a son in Spirit, but he is saying that you now know that he comes back as a man.'*

Gwen: *'Yes.'*

Medium: *'You have a gold key round your neck. He will open doors for you. I also have to say Russell is under tuition from one of the Masters. He works with them. You have been given April for confirmation of this.'*

Gwen: 'Yes, April.'

Medium: *'You are going to the USA. Get ready for this. Russell brings with him a beautiful little girl of about 4 years old. She is* *blonde with the initial R. He is teaching her and he loves her.'*

Gwen: 'Yes, I know who this little girl is.'

Medium: *'There is a tall man here wearing sandals. He thanks you for taking care of his book.'* (see Chapter 3.) *Do you know that you have strong Jewish links, but not from this life ? Also a strong Egyptian link.'*

Gwen: 'I think so, yes.'

Medium: *'This little girl is showing me a rainbow.'*

Gwen: 'Yes !'

Medium: *'Russell is saying, 'we are twin souls Mum' '*

(I nod here, for I have been told this so many times before.)

Medium: *'There is a little red haired boy here, about 9 years old. He says his name is Sean-ie.'*

Gwen: 'Yes, my nephew's son.' (see Chapter 4.)

Medium: *'I also have an Alan, Steven and Ronald.'*

Gwen: 'Yes.'

Medium: *'Are these three of the RPPS gang ?'*

Gwen: 'Yes.'

Medium: *'and a Dutch influence ?'*

Gwen: 'Yes, that's Ronald.'

Medium: *'This is around you with the letter 'K' that is giving you aggro ! They think they know it all.* (I nod here.)
Gwen, are you receiving poems from someone ?'

Gwen: 'Yes.' (see Chapter 22).

Medium: *'One will be about doves and one about Egypt.'*

Well I'd been hoping for confirmation and as usual, it came when I least expected it ! What Shirley had given me was 100% correct, although I've only shared some of it here.

Now at this point, I didn't yet have the beautiful ending for *'Russell'* - so for me this had been an excellent sitting. Shirley had mentioned the names Alan and Steven, and their mothers both tell their stories later in the book, yet some of Shirley's information was news to me then. This shows me the faultless efficiency of the Spirit World and how we really should pay attention to every word !

Eight

My Son Steven

by Gill Smith

*'He was beautiful, beautiful to my eyes,
from the moment I saw him
the sun filled the sky...'*

~ from Cavatina, by Stanley Miles & Cleo Laine

My name is Gill Smith and I lost my beautiful son Steven, on 7th February 1988. He had simply decided to take an overdose. He was 22 years old.

When a two year relationship ended, he just could not handle the emotions. He was hurt so deeply because he loved Joanne so very much, but when she broke off their relationship he went into a state of deep depression. He could not get a suitable job, then became even more depressed when he couldn't continue his degree in Physics. Yet he was a very bright young man, which showed by his school work, having obtained eight 'O' levels and five 'A' levels.

Steven didn't get on with his father and after an argument, Steven left home. He moved into a flat to be on his own, but did come home three or four times a week for meals. Apart from being very quiet, he didn't seem any different. Although perhaps he was good at putting on an act, I don't know. You see, Steven had always been a quiet lad. He thought nothing of staying in his room alone saying, *'Mum, I have to do my revision.'* Of course, I realise now that he liked his own company.

It's easy to say this now, but he was always so gentle, so loving and would never hurt anyone. The only time he made a noise was when he played his guitar - but he could play it very well and loved his music. I could often hear him practising for hours in his room.

During Christmas 1987 Steven came home, but he was even more quiet than usual. He would just sit and watch television rather a lot. We did have a few games of cards, but his quietness disturbed me. Indeed it worried me, for this was a very different kind of silence. His father Ray, took him back to his flat just before the New Year bells, but they returned about and half an hour later. Ray said that Steven had been very, very upset and said that he badly needed help.

I tried all ways to get that much needed help, but because it was New Year, everything was closed. I phoned our family doctor and told him how bad a state Steven was in, but all he could do was put me in touch with the Health Centre at the top of our road. I was desperate. There were nurses there and one even promised to come after the New Year, but ten minutes before the appointed time, he phoned to say he couldn't make it. I was so angry. In fact, I was furious.

The nurse promised us another appointment, but he didn't keep to that one either. So yet again I phoned him and it was the following week when he finally arrived. I was at work that day and Steven's father came home early, arriving just as the male nurse was leaving. He told Ray that he'd talked with Steven to try and find out what was troubling him so badly. Then he said he wanted to talk it all over with a colleague, but we never heard from him again. It seemed to us that he really didn't care.

The following Friday I took Steven to see a doctor named Taylor, who after a long discussion, said he would send a consultant to see Steven. When I saw Steven on the Sunday he asked, *'Mum, when is the consultant coming ?'* I could only answer *'I don't know Steven'* and I really didn't know. I do know though that by now Steven was desperate, not knowing which way to turn. On the Monday the consultant finally came.

We knew that Steven had been smoking very heavily and had gone off for a long walk. I became more and more anxious and I talked to the consultant for thirty minutes trying to explain the situation. At the same time I was scared that he might leave before Steven returned. As it was, he was just on the point of leaving when Steven returned. Steven seemed pleased to see the consultant and I guess he thought help had come at last. They shook hands then they both went into the living room. I made them a drink and left, thinking it best to leave them alone to talk it out. I wish so much now that I'd stayed with them - for I knew the state my son was in. I had previously told the consultant of Steven's problems, so thought I was doing the right thing. I waited anxiously outside the door wondering whatever was going on inside - and still wishing I had been in there with my son. I was sure that help had arrived at last.

How wrong can one be ? After a further 30 minutes they came out of the living room. Of course, my first question was,
'what can you do to help my son ?'

He answered, *'Mrs Smith, you have a fine healthy lad here.'*
That was that and he went.

Steven knew then, at that moment, that he was not going to receive any help. I think it was actually then, that he made up his mind what he was going to do next. On the following Wednesday, he went to visit his grandmother, my husband's mother. Whilst he was there, he stole some very strong tablets. He must have kept them and made his plans. On the Saturday he just said that he was going back to his flat. He did, and there he took all the tablets, and quietly left this world alone.

Only those who have had a child take their own life can know how we both felt. Devastated is not a strong enough word. I also wanted to die. I felt that Steven had just slipped through my fingers. I felt so angry, for I'd tried everything I could to get him help, but somehow it eluded me. With the anger, came guilt. Guilt that I hadn't done more than I did. We were totally and utterly destroyed by the whole thing.

When Steven's funeral was over, I just became numb. I couldn't feel anything. When I wasn't numb, I felt bitter. I was so lost and confused and I missed Steven so much that it hurt - almost in a physical way. It is hard to explain. One has to experience it to know.

The shock was too much to bear and in the weeks that followed, I felt so weak from weeping - both physically and mentally. My mind was going over and over those last few weeks until I thought I was going completely mad. I didn't want to do anything except lay down and cry. Yet I knew I had to cook meals for my two other sons, who were suffering too. They missed their brother so much and were stunned by what had happened. Poor lads, they were finding it so hard to cope too.

I started to encourage them to go out, even if it was just to play a game of pool. I didn't care about myself, but I knew that I had to keep them going. When I was alone I tried to watch television, but my mind and heart wasn't there. There were times when I was at my lowest ebb, that I seemed to smell tobacco smoke. I wondered whether it was Steven trying to tell me he was alright. He was the only one of my sons that smoked, and this was when he became depressed.

Around that time my sister had given me some books by Doris Stokes, the Medium. I began going to bed early so I could read them and I became so interested in these wonderfully comforting books. What a wonderful lady she was. This gentle, homely Medium with the power to comfort the broken-hearted and those poor people who had the life crushed out of them by circumstances in their lives. It was around that time that I began to 'sense' someone standing in the corner of my bedroom. Now I thought I really was going out of my mind.

As time went on I read all I could on the subject of life after death. I visited a Medium, who told me that I'd sensed someone standing in the corner of my bedroom. The Medium said it was Steven trying to let me know that he was around. By now I was getting very, very interested.

My other sister had been talking to a friend at a club who had lost a daughter. They said they had found great comfort from the Spiritualist Church and said *'was I interested?'* Was I? How could I not be by now! So they kindly said they would pick me up and take me with them to the Church. From this point I became more and more intrigued and I began to find some peace in my heart. At the Church, I was asked if I'd like to sit in a 'development circle.' The Medium told me,
'there is a young man with you every time I see you.'
I was very drawn to this Medium, who started to give me small but true messages from this 'young man.' At the time I thought, *'oh, someone must have told her,'* but I wasn't sure.

By 1989 I'd started to read a newspaper called the *'Psychic News.'* I waited eagerly for it every week and read it over and over again. I was beginning to learn, and to hope too. In one issue there was an article by Michael Roll on 'Physical Mediumship' - regarding Spirit materialisation. I wrote to him immediately, because I longed to know more on this intriguing subject. He kindly wrote back straight away, telling me that at that time, he didn't know of any suitable 'Physical Mediums.'

However, he did send me the name and address of Gwen Byrne. Her son Russell, had materialised to her many times and they had been reunited on hundreds of occasions. She'd even held his hands. Although her own search had lasted 20 years, Gwen helped me so much. She has helped a lot of other mothers, who have 'lost' their children and all feel the same awful pain.
Gwen knew another mother who had the ability to draw Spirit people. I didn't know her, but once Gwen sent me a drawing of Steven. She'd had the drawing long before I'd even got in touch with her, so for me this proves that we were meant to meet. The portrait is certainly a very good likeness of my Steven, but since Gwen already had it amongst a pile of drawings created by her friend Frankie Brown, that in itself was wonderful evidence for me.

Clear in my mind is one incident from 1991. I had been busy doing some gardening, then came into the house to cook the family meal. I called my son Andrew in for his tea, but when he reached the living room door I couldn't take my eyes off him. I watched as he put his hands into a drawer and as I stared at his hands, I realised they were Steven's hands. I looked up and to my astonishment, for a few moments I saw Steven's face ! Later I learned that this was Steven *'transfiguring'* over his brother. Now this spurred me on.

In 1992 I joined 'The Noah's Ark Society' for Physical Phenomena. I went to Warrington for a séance, where the Medium was Stewart Alexander. Mr Alexander's child Spirit control was named Christopher, and during the séance he asked, *'is there a Mrs Smith in the room ?'* His little piping voice was coming through the séance trumpet, not the Medium. Then he said, *'a young man wants to talk to his Mum.'*

Now I couldn't hear too well as I was near the back of the room, but someone in the circle kindly offered to relay the message to me. It was Steven and he said, *'Mum, please stop the tears.'*

He told me that he loved me very much and he was so very emotional when he came through, but of course, so was I.

Now I sit in two of these 'Physical Circles' and I hope and pray that one day I'll see my son or hear him speak to me clearly. I only know that I must keep on searching - because one day I will see him again.

It's nice belonging to Gwen's RPPS group and although I live a long way from Gwen, we keep in touch regularly. Gwen says I'm a *'link in the chain'* because she'd already got the drawing of Steven before I ever knew her. It's all a long chain isn't it, for she has a lot of drawings in her cupboard. I wonder how many of them will find their way home ?

I hear from Steven often now. I know that he still plays his beloved guitar, so I know that his brilliant mind is not wasted. It also seems that in his new life in the Spirit World, his knowledge of physics and mathematics is not wasted either. Steven knows that I will always search for him and love him as only a mother can.

Now before I end my story, I thought I would share some of the evidence that Steven has brought me.

The Medium Val Williams, told me exactly how Steven had died. She also told me, that he'd had a dream about his own death, a few years before - which is true. About fifteen months before he died, Steven knew that his time on Earth had nearly come. He knew that he and his brother Richard, had been together in a previous life and that they had been Buddhist Monks. I also learned that he was very, very angry with his father.

Through Val, he said, *'I know when you get here you are not supposed to be bitter Mum, I'm not bitter, but I am so angry at the way it all happened, and the way my father handled it.'*

He then said, *'Gwen has helped my Mother more than anyone else and I thank her for that. Gwen's not going anywhere yet Mum, but when she does we'll all be together.'*

Steven also said, *'Mum, don't think that it wasn't right - my death. It was right for <u>me</u> ! I have grown and expanded so much. I know my death ended your life in a way, but it began it again in another. I know about Leah,* (his little niece, my granddaughter) *I love her so much and I'm like a guardian angel for her. I will always care for her Mum - don't worry.'*

Another Medium and friend of Gwen's, Rachael Hunt-High, gave me evidence of Steven with a good description of him and his passing.
She said, *'he has a great love for a Pink Rose for you, as his 'symbol.' He was very, very sensitive. He tells me he has two brothers whom he loves and misses so much, and he says how much they miss him.'*

She mentioned a special wreath in the shape of a guitar. His brothers, Richard and Andrew had it made for him. Steven so loved music *and* his guitar ! Rachael said, *'he says Richard used to play guitar with him and he's saying that you have just moved his photograph.'*

Both these statements were true. All our photographs were together, but then I put one photo of Steven on the table. Rachael went on to say, *'his eyes seem to follow you around. He is smiling, as your hair is different and he says he likes it.'*

This made sense, as a few weeks before I'd had a really curly perm, but hadn't worn it like that for years. Rachael then went on to say, *'Steven is asking why you're not wearing your chain Mum ? He was used to you wearing a cross and chain.'*

This was true. I hadn't put it on because the fastener was unsafe. Rachael told me that Steven had sat with me at night and that he'd held my hand when I'd cried myself to sleep.

'I'm with my grandfather' (my own Dad who passed 23 years earlier) Rachael told me. *'They enjoy each others company now and have long talks, and go for long walks.'* She said. *'they are very much alike and very loving, but neither of them knew how to show their feelings.*

I saw the Medium Mavis Pittilla, who also gave me a description of Steven and told me he was saying,
'I didn't really take my own life, I gave in to reality ! It was just a matter of

time Mum. I know you will never understand that fully, but you want to so much. It wasn't anything to do with my way of life, or the way I was brought up.'

In two separate sittings, one with Val Williams and one with Mavis Pittilla, they both confirmed that Steven had met up with his hero John Lennon. Mavis said,

'Steven would have loved to have been a composer.' That was true. 'Steven chats to people like John Lennon, to get quality of music. Eventually he will be a guide of someone, to help them.'

Mavis went on to say, 'he is saying that yesterday you talked to his photo and that his skin tone is a lot better now.'

This was true because I had done just that. I was talking to his photograph, telling him where I was going and hoped he would be with me. I found myself looking at his complexion and thinking how his skin wasn't too clear. Mavis went on to say, 'don't think that he's gone away. If you don't feel him around, he only goes away to learn how to do it better - he is going to learn how to try to pass thoughts to you.'

I realised that was what he was doing when I looked at his photograph. This made me realise that there wasn't only myself who knew about suffering - there was a lot of cruelty in the world ! He was saying that one of the good things about being over there is that he is away from it all. I feel that these remarks helped me in my decision to go over to Bosnia. I went with a group because I just wanted to help, that's all ! I saw so much pain and sadness, but I do feel that I helped in some way.

The Medium Darren Brittain also spoke of Steven. He said,
'he's a lovely lad. I know whatever charitable, humanitarian or Spiritual work you do, know that he will be there - whether you can feel him or not. He doesn't want you to dwell on the way he passed, accept it if you can because he is so happy.'

Darren also said that Steven said, 'I had to find out what it was like Mum !' To me this meant the amount of time that Steven would spend on his own. 'I know I seemed as if I didn't take any notice and I was stubborn, but at the time I thought it was the right thing to do.'

Darren told me that Steven said he loves me and his brothers and that part of him loves his Dad, but he still can't forgive him for the things he did.

I know that I will go on searching but this is my life now. I take one day at a time. Of course I have some happy times and that's something that just happens suddenly. For instance, I was recently packing to go on holiday and as it was so warm, I opened the living room window. I sat down to rest my leg, as it was swollen and aching at the time, then as I did, a big beautiful butterfly, a lovely reddish colour, came in through the window and went straight into the corner, where I keep all of Steven's photographs. Then with a swoop he vanished !

The very next day, Steven's brother Richard called to visit and I was telling him about the butterfly. We were in the kitchen when all of a sudden in came the very same butterfly ! It was as if he had heard me. I was astonished and excited. That was my first butterfly experience. I think my Steven must have learnt from Gwen's son Russell, how to make a butterfly 'net' to catch them, the way that Russell does. It was a lovely experience and I know it was Steven that brought him.

This search can be very challenging and exciting at times. It can also be very disappointing and hard, as I have learned. But when Steven *and* knowledge is at the end of it - then it's so worthwhile. I will tell any mother that. In everyday life I do seem to meet many mothers who have lost children and of course I urge them on. I often drop in a seed of thought, for it may help them to come to terms with their pain and I do know it will please their 'lost' child. This now is my life.

God Bless you, my dear son Steven.

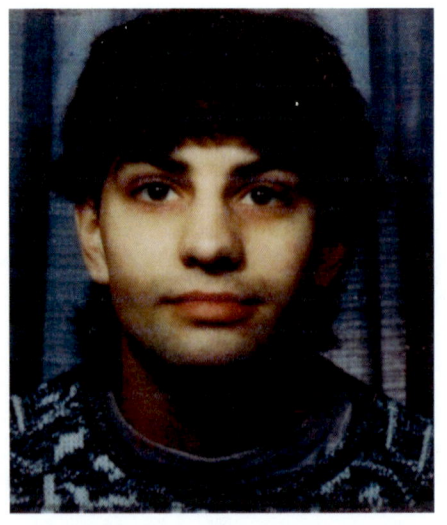

Gill's son, Steven Smith

Nine

America, I Love You !

July 1993

*'Just like a little baby, climbing his mother's knee,
America, I love you, and there's a hundred million others like me !'*

~ Edgar Leslie, 1915.

I think I should say, that if I had listened to the sitting by Shirley West where she told me, *'you are going to America'* I may not have had such a shock when it happened !
Serves me right, for I had been warned. Yet I was still puzzled by the songs that were coming at me, thick and fast. I awoke one morning to, *'Nothing could be finer than to be in Carolina, in the morning...'* by Al Jolson. I took no notice. Then I received, *'California here I come...'* another by Al Jolson.

I was really puzzled and hadn't got a clue what they were trying to tell me. So after more tries with, *'America, I love you'* then *'I like to be in America'* from West Side Story, I think they gave up ! Well who wouldn't ? I'm certain that Russell must have thought, *'oh Mother ! I'm trying to tell you that you're going to America !'*
If only we would listen !

Alfie and I had been away for a few days, minding some friends animals. On our arrival home the phone was ringing like mad - it was my daughter-in-law Chris. It turned out that my friend, Rachael Hunt-High had been trying to contact us. She said that I had to be ready by July the 24th, because it I'd been invited to the USA *and* I had to be ready in seven days ! I had been invited to go on a week long 'Life Spectrum Conference' which was being held in none other than, *North Carolina !* Suddenly all those songs came back to me.

During the next seven days, my life seemed like a dream. Alfie had to travel all the way to Peterborough to get my visa sorted out and a new passport photo. Then someone warned me by saying, *'it's hot out there, you know !'*

Well I don't know how I managed to pack. I hadn't a clue what to take or what I'd need - for the *heat,* for the Conference week or anything for that matter. I did know I had to take my music, for I'd been asked to sing during the week of the Conference. Then before I knew where I was, I was off to Gatwick Airport with a suitcase which was much too big and totally full of unsuitable clothes. Alfie took me to airport departures and saw me off. He waved saying, *'cheerio - see you in twenty days time.'*

All I knew, was that after an eight hour flight I'd be landing at Charlotte Douglas Airport and I needed to look out for a lady holding up a banner with 'Queen Guinevere' written on it !
Eight hours later and there she was waiting and didn't I get some very odd looks from other passengers ! However, I was quickly seen onto yet another plane, for a twenty minute hop to Harrisburg. By now I was totally in a whirl, but I thought the Americans were such fun people !

I waited at Harrisburg Airport for Rachael to meet me. She arrived with her long time friend named Roxan - who I actually knew ! Eighteen years earlier Roxan and I had met at Stansted Hall in Essex. Isn't life odd ? It's just like a circle, for after all these years we met again !
Anyway, I was whizzed around in a huge car - and boy, was it hot and humid ! We headed straight on to Sandy and Larry's - Roxan's sister and brother-in-law - and I discovered that I'd *also* met these two people before at Stansted.
Even as I am writing this, I really do think I've dreamt it all, because I think, *'crumbs ! Did I really do all these things ?'*

That very evening I found myself sitting in a hot tub, in a huge back garden. I'd never even seen a hot tub before - yet here I was sitting in one ! Oh it was so lovely and such fun. Lots of people were invited and drinks were served out on the deck in front of this gorgeous tub. I didn't feel one bit like a stranger in their midst, for these Americans were such lovely, kind and warm people. I remember sitting on the side of the tub watching fireflies dart enchantingly across the lawn. I'd never even seen a firefly before either, so my first evening was both enchanting and unforgettable !

We travelled on to Roxan's home, where Rachael and I were staying for a time, before we travelled on for the Conference. Rachael was off here and there with her work, so I spent time with Roxan and we really had some fun. Each day Roxan took me to the huge shops and I can't remember how many times I got lost ! Roxan is a hairdresser and has a salon at home, so I soon had a new 'hair-do' too. I also quickly learned how to wield the dustpan and broom, to sweep up all the different colours and clippings of hair. I know it might sound crazy, but I had such a lot of fun. Plus, when her ladies came for *their* hair-do's, I was not only sweeping up, but singing songs for them too. I had some wonderful backing tapes as accompaniment and between us, we entertained them.

I think if we played *'Phantom Of The Opera'* once, we must have played it a dozen times ! There we were, with Roxan giving the ladies wondrous hair-do's and me singing my head off ! The customers did seem to love it and of course we had some ladies who were weeping to the music. They were dabbing their eyes with their rollers in their hair ! Roxan and I had such a laugh though and I met some lovely people from all walks of life.

One of Roxan's pets was a small squirrel that lived in the house and he was named Albert ! It seems he had fallen out of a tree and had paralysed his back legs, so Roxan had hand reared him. Now fixed up, he would run around the kitchen in the evenings, joined by another pet - Roxan's gorgeous green parrot, named Baby. He could actually sing too. One of his was *'I left my Heart in San Francisco'* and if you sang to him, he would flutter his wings up and down !

This was really a nutty time for me, but wonderful. I don't think I will ever forget it. Though I do have my photo's to look at, in case I want to recall the memory.

Through Rachael's work I met some other mothers and fathers, who had all lost beloved children. One beautiful Summer evening we all met up in the backyard of one of the Mum's homes. We sat outdoors on the deck and we just talked and talked.

I was a bit amazed really, because in my ignorance I thought they would all have automatically heard of the wonders of Physical Phenomena. Especially since *'Modern Spiritualism'* had begun in America, but alas, they had not. So we talked on the subject for hours and they listened to me, intently. They were such sad, sad parents. We had to say our good-nights of course, but two of the dear mothers, Kimberley and Lauren, took me out to lunch the next day. We went to an amazing restaurant named *'TGI Friday'* where we talked throughout our meal about our respective sons in the Spirit World - my Russell and the mother's son's Bryan and Brian.

That first week had just been one whirl of activity and I'd really have to think hard to recall everything we did ! To cap it all though we three, Rachael, Roxan and me, went to visit a real Native North American Indian family. This was an experience that I keep very close to my heart, even now. For I have loved and admired their race - long before anyone had even seen the movie, *'Dances with Wolves'* ! We listened to the men drumming and were allowed to see their handicraft work in progress, so it was a *special* time for me. I remember meeting the mother of the family, to whom I instantly bonded with - the lovely Cherri Dancing Sun.

Only recently, I received a beautiful pair of hand-made earrings from her, with a note enclosed *'to my favourite English Auntie Gwennie'* ! My goodness, they are such special people. They have an air about them which I can't explain, but this was an experience of a lifetime for me and I feel so grateful and lucky.

We didn't have a minute to waste though, because next we were in a large van and off to *'Carolina in the morning'* ! As we set off, I realised that these girls really had much more organisation than me. I think Roxan drove all the way, though I didn't realise we were travelling through *'Gone With The Wind'* country - the soil was so red, and soft. We laughed and sang all the way. Then Rachael said, *'oh, Gwennie you must write all these songs down'* but I couldn't remember them now if I tried. I do recall the radio playing the Desmond Dekker song, *'The Israelites'* - whilst we were lost in this desert, temporarily ! Then when the heat was really on that day, we all sang, *'Hot time, Summer in the city...!'*
It was such a happy time, with such laughter !

En route we had a pit stop and I said I'd stay with the car, so that the boot - or the *trunk* - could be opened for a while. You see, we had Roxan's dear little squirrel friend Albert with us. He was in his cage in the back, on top of the suitcases. So I waited with the car at the side of the highway, just with Albert, or so I thought...

As I stood there in the sun, I knew that I had been joined by Russell, as an adult. I didn't see him or hear him, but I just *knew* he was beside me. It was such a beautiful feeling. I stood there with such a wonderful feeling, then as it gradually faded, I heard the ladies coming back to the car. So off we went once more and finally we came to the University where the week's Conference was to be held.

We got to our rooms, and oh dear ! The lifts, or should I say *elevators*, were so different to our English equivalent. Then the taps in the showers went the opposite way too - and the door knobs ! Well at least we were here and I had a nice little room-mate Jeanine and we immediately become friends. Not long after there was a banging on the door. It was Rachael, who said, *'come on Gwennie, over to the Auditorium.'*

'Where's that ?' I said.

'Just follow me,' says Rachael.

So I did just as I was told. Then lo and behold, before I knew what was happening, I was on a stage surrounded by microphones and warbling the Perry Como hit *'Because'* to a very appreciative audience. Well I was almost working on auto-pilot and in a complete daze. How can one sleep when you are on such a high ?

Next morning it was time to look at our programmes - what to go to and *where* the heck was it ? Which was *my* main problem ! We were given name badges, to pin on ourselves and I don't think I'd ever met such a lovely crowd of people. In the programme were a wonderful variety of workshops to go to. You name it and it was there. I thought, *'now it's time to take your pick, Gwen !'* My eyes spotted one workshop called *'Sufi Belly Dancing - Getting in Touch With Your Body.'* Well that was the one for me and boy, did I enjoy it ! The class had a lovely teacher called Sandy, who wore harem pants and wow, could she dance !

We were each given a veil and taught how to do the movements. It was tricky at first, but by the end of the week, the class had got the hang of it. We were all feeling it though - waving those veils about does make your arms ache ! Well you don't usually do that do you ? Oh, and our poor hips from all that wriggling - or as I learnt later *'undulating.'*

When we had first arrived at the Conference, we had all been given a slip of paper, which said that we had to be a 'Guardian Angel' to someone for the week. Thank goodness I got a man I knew ! John was someone else I'd met at Stansted years previously. The idea was, that we should find out where their room was and every day leave them a small gift. Well I had a problem with that, for if I'd have left the complex to find a gift - I would have *really* got lost. It was bad enough for me *inside* the complex ! Anyway, Rachael came to my aid with all sorts of ideas. I had to be a Guardian Angel to John, but I could leave the daftest things - even lumps of rock ! Really.

I never did find out who my 'Angel' was, but they left me the most delightful gifts outside my door. There were little frames with cherubs on and dear little hand-made angels. Each day was a joy.

I'd been asked to sing in the main Auditorium, on each evening before our lecture. I'd never got ready so quickly. There was no time to worry about what to wear or what to sing - I just did it ! On the last night we'd attended a healing ceremony, then our Belly Dancing class all got together

and got dressed up in the whole works. There were Harem pants, beaded bras, veils and bangles and beads everywhere - plus long dangley earrings. With such make-up too that no one would know you ! Of course, while all this was going on, guess *who* was singing to me ?
'If my friends could see me now...' by Cy Coleman. Yes Russell, if only they could - they'd never believe it !

So off went into our dance - which we could hardly do for laughing. No one had told us that we'd have to leap around and collect five dollar bills to put down the front of our costumes ! So we are all having the time of our lives, draping our veils over poor unsuspecting fellas - I could never have explained it at home if I hadn't had Rachael's photographs. Moreover, I don't ever expect to have a holiday like it ever again !

Before the week came to an end, I'd done my very first lecture to a very interested crowd. This led into what they called a 'Rap Session' – which is really just an informal discussion. They all wanted to know more about Physical Phenomena and my book 'Russell' - which was due out the following year.
Then all of a sudden I'd done it all, and in one week it was over ! We said our farewells on the Saturday morning and on leaving the college, I heard Russell with the line *'thanks for the memory'* - a song which Bob Hope made famous. So *'Cheerio and toodle-oo, thank you so much.'* I couldn't have said it better Russell !

We stayed two nights at my 'Guardian Angel' John's home, where he and his wife Barbara made us so welcome. Then we were off to the airport once again, for a night flight back to Harrisburg then on to Rachael's. Once there and settled, Rachael and I ended the evening watching the TV when, believe it or not, the Peter Sellers film *'The Pink Panther'* came on, *and* the biscuits I was eating were in the shape of a butterfly - when all the rest were square except mine - honestly !

Talk about pulling out all the stops, Russell ! We were two very weary gals, how on Earth were we going to get eight hours sleep ? Some hope !

I was back in England soon enough though, where Alfie was waiting for me at the airport and I was totally knocked out by the time we got there ! It all seemed just like an amazing dream to me, but I've got my lovely photographs and my hand-made angels and I still do some belly dancing ! So as the song goes, *'thank you very much.'*

Ten

Two Little Sisters

by Shirley Gifford

*'A dream that is not understood,
is like an unopened letter'*

~ Anonymous

My name is Shirley Gifford, and my story begins at 1.25 on the morning of October 6th, 1973 when my first baby was born. I named her Melanie. She was such a beautiful baby with the darkest brown hair and huge brown eyes. For my late husband Stuart and me, it was the proudest day of our lives ! Two and a half years later, on May 26th, 1976, our second baby was born, another beauty, who we called Kirstie May.
I was really over the moon. All my wildest dreams had come true. I had two darlings, my two little girls. My happiness was complete.

One day, a few weeks after Kirstie's birth, I noticed there was something wrong with Melanie. As I watched her, I saw that she was walking rather awkwardly. She was holding herself differently from other children. There was also something about her speech that to me, as her mother, just didn't sound right. But it was when she began to fall over for no apparent reason that I first took her to our doctor.
'You are over reacting !' I was told. He said, *'she is knock-kneed and pigeon toed'* and in his opinion, she was acting up just to gain my attention.

As you might imagine, I went home very, very anxious and deep down, I knew there was more to it. My heart told me there was something wrong with her, however, I tried to put it out of my mind - especially since my husband Stuart, was having severe medical problems himself at the time. The horror came in September 1977, when he was diagnosed as having a terminal illness named Huntingdon's disease. Stuart could not cope with it all and a few months later, he left us. He moved away up North and we divorced two years later.

Then one morning, it suddenly dawned on me whilst dressing Melanie. Her symptoms were so similar to her father's. Again, I went to the doctor, but this time saw a different one. He listened to me very intently, and instantly referred Melanie to the Bristol Children's Hospital, where she underwent a long series of tests. Then came the waiting for her results. *'Well,'* the doctor said, *'there's definitely something wrong with her. But, Mrs Gifford, not Huntingdon's disease, she is far too young. Huntingdon's disease only affects the middle aged'.*

Melanie had two years of tests. It was a long nightmare - during which time she gradually got worse. She was now at the stage where she could no longer attend a normal school. However, she was accepted at Courtland's School for the Disabled in Bristol and was so happy there, for it was a wonderful school.

When Melanie was five years old, she saw another consultant. He told me that he'd seen Huntingdon's disease in a child of thirteen. So finally, I had the answer that I had always really known and dreaded hearing. Melanie had Huntingdon's disease the same as her father. Even though this is so very, very rare in children. In fact, Melanie was case number 50 in the whole world, of those with the disease under the age of ten ! I was totally devastated.

My beautiful little girl - my Melanie - passed into Spirit on October 31st, 1982. To my utter horror, in the same month, her sister Kirstie was also diagnosed as having this same awful disease. Now the bottom had completely fallen out of my world. I cursed God over, and over again and asked *'why me ?'* What had I done to deserve such anguish and this terrible punishment ? The only thing that kept me sane at this time, was the fact that I had since remarried and had a beautiful baby boy. He was two and a half years old, plus I was expecting another baby in six months time !

About a year after Melanie's passing I had my first vivid dream. To be truthful, I know it was much more than a dream, so much so, that it changed my whole perception of life. I'd been very aware of a disturbance by the side of my bed. It was like a rustling sound. Then I felt a presence and someone patting the bed. The whole room seemed to become electrically charged. I sat up very slowly and there was my lovely Melanie, sitting on the bed by my feet.

I was filled with a wonderful feeling of love. I actually got out of bed and went to her. We just cuddled each other and it seemed like forever. I cannot recall talking to her, not with words anyway - just *love* ! Then I awoke, yet the sense of her presence was still with me. It filled the whole room. I could still smell her. Then I drifted back into a dreamless sleep.

A few weeks later, the same thing happened again. This time Melanie had a gift for me. It was a roll of drawing paper and as I unrolled it, I saw scene after scene of lovely little pictures. There were woodlands, lakes, flower filled gardens, and so on and the colours were indescribable.
'This is my life Mummy,' she said and she gave me a beaming smile.

When I awoke, I actually searched the bedroom for the drawing. I really did expect to find it too, for it was so real.

The next dream took a different turn. Once again I felt and heard the disturbance, but in addition I clearly heard a bell ring. I sat up and saw people coming up the stairs. By now, I was out of my bed when I saw a woman just walk into the bedroom. My Melanie was with her and there were two other little girls too. One of them had very long, blonde hair, which was plaited and tied with pink ribbons. Melanie ran towards me, but I noticed how different she looked from the last time I saw her. She had a new hairstyle ! Her hair had been cut into a pageboy bob style and around her neck she wore a pretty, delicate necklace. She proudly showed me her lovely new dress and I thought she looked so beautiful and well.
She seemed to glow with life and I remarked on how much she had filled out. Melanie replied, *'well Mum, I am ten now !'*

I asked the woman who was with her, whether she was also dead.
'Oh no, my love,' she replied. *'I am on your side, but I have chosen this as my life's work. I help to reunite children with their mothers in sleep state. Although not many are able to remember on waking up. Children in Spirit are never parted from their parents until all are ready.'*

As she said these words, the same bell rang again. *'We have to leave now,'* the lady said with a smile, *'but remember my dear, Melanie is a special child with a gift that will be used later.'*

As they left the room, I awoke still with Melanie's kiss on my lips.

I had many such lovely dreams over a period of 12 months. I once saw Melanie in a schoolroom with other children and they all looked so happy. By now I'd learned that I was only separated from them by a flimsy blue veil - like beautiful sticky cobwebs. I once put my arm through this veil and Melanie kissed my hand. As she did so, it was as though an electric charge had travelled up my arm and this stayed with me when I woke.

In 1986, just before Christmas, my other daughter Kirstie became very ill. I had a deep feeling that her time on Earth was also coming to a close, but I didn't feel strong enough to let her go. I prayed to God to let me keep her a little longer.

Well, my prayers were answered and she pulled through her illness - much to the amazement of the doctors. I noticed that Kirstie was fascinated by the Christmas lights on the tree. Even when the tree was taken down, she still seemed to be communicating with *something*, on the spot where the tree had been, long after it had been removed. I asked her what she was looking at and she managed to let me know that it was her sister Melanie. I asked her if Melanie had visited us over Christmas. Kirstie let me know in her own way that her sister Melanie is *always* there.

I felt a cold chill go down my spine, because I just knew that Kirstie was only waiting. She wanted to go 'home.' She was always more alive when silently talking with her big sister Melanie, than when she was with me. I asked her if she was ready to join her sister and her beautiful smile gave me the answer. I said, *'ok God. I'm ready now.'*

I was allowed Kirstie for Christmas, but I knew she wanted to be with her sister Melanie on her birthday. A few months later, Kirstie suddenly went into a kind of decline, then on the Sunday evening of May 24th Kirstie joined her big sister Melanie - just in time to have her birthday with her on the 26th. Kirstie left me with a precious gift - the gift of memory. The look of pure bliss on her face, as her Spirit left her body, stays with me to this very day. She had gone 'home' with all my love.

This isn't quite the end of my story. For six months later, my youngest son Scott, then aged four and a half, began pointing up to the ceiling and announced, *'Mum, Melanie and Kirstie are up there.'*

'Yes, I know Scott,' I said, *'they are in heaven.'*

'No, no Mum,' he insisted. *'They are UP THERE'.*

I said, *'Scott, what can you see?'*

He told me that Melanie and Kirstie were in a beam of light that came through the ceiling. I asked Scott, *'what colour eyes has Melanie got?'*

'Dark brown,' he said, *'can't you see them?'*

I was disappointed and I replied that no, I couldn't see them. However, I told him that I believed him and said that he was a very special boy to be able to see his sisters.

A week later, the same thing happened again. *'Mum'* he said, *'they are here again!'* He was so proud as he announced excitedly, *'Mum, Mum! This time a man has come with them.'*

I asked Scott to describe this man to me and tell me what he looked like.

At the time, all he could say was that the man had grey hair, a beard and nice eyes. He also told me that Melanie and Kirstie had come to say goodbye - and that they were very, very happy.

As I write, Scott is nearly twelve years old and still vividly recalls these two special events in his life. A few weeks ago he drew me a picture of the man he'd seen with his two sisters. A copy of Scott's drawing is reproduced here...

I know my two girls are always with me and I talk to them, as if they are there physically. I expect they even had a hand in helping me to write this, their story. And although I cannot always remember, I have my dream visits to look forward to.
Yes, perhaps I do live in both worlds, but then so do we all. We do not have to see to believe, but I did *see* them. I cannot physically prove any of this, but there again, I do not have to. *I know* !

* * *

Gwen: At this point, it seems right for me to comment on Shirley Gifford's lovely story. She had her own experiences of her two daughters survival. She never went near a Medium and yet she knows her children live. Most of the mothers contacting me have had similar experiences, but in a small way. Like waking in the morning, having known you've been with your child and either touched them, held them or felt their skin - *soft as a baby* ! I've had similar experiences myself and it proves just how much our children *want* to communicate with us.
To me this makes nonsense of the advice of so-called 'experts' who say that you are not supposed to communicate with Spirits. They say *'it is evil'* and other such rubbish. I wonder how they would explain Melanie and Kirstie's wonderful communications with their Mummy and brother.

For me, these are magical experiences, but then children are magical little people aren't they ? Some would say that these two little sisters *knew* they were only here for a short time - and perhaps they never felt 'at home' whilst on Earth. I know quite a few people, including myself and others, who all agree that we do not and have *never* felt at home on the Earth. We feel like strangers with a feeling of homesickness. As a child, these feelings can't always be as defined and if you dare to tell a soul, then its trouble with big T !
Who would listen to a child that says, *'I feel like a stranger here, Mum !'*

Childhood is meant to be a magical time, like in fairy stories - but it rarely is. Today's fairy stories seem to consist of 'Star Wars' or 'Captain America.' Yet there is always the wonderful Mr. Disney ! We might recall from our own distant childhood, the crystal coffin that Snow White lay in. Then there were books that gave us visions of crystal skies or Crystal Mountains - always *sacred* mountains. These were *only* supposed to be fairy tales, but I wonder...for when you look into them, they all seem to carry a message. Children can see that message, but rarely adults.

There certainly seems to me, to be an increasing awareness now taking place throughout the world. People from all walks of life and all professions seem to sense that we are heading towards great transformations. If this is true, I'm sure the people of the Earth will be led.

After Shirley Gifford's beautiful story, I know she won't mind if I ended this chapter with a poem. This is one that Russell sent through the Mediumship of another Mum, Frankie Brown, on January 8th 1991. It doesn't have a title, but I was told to think of the Irving Berlin song, *'I'll be loving you, always'* whilst reading it...

*'Chains are broken, bonds are set free,
I am now not bonded to one, but three.*

*In the year of ninety one,
There is so much that must be done,*

*The poem the brave sent down to you
Do heal his wounds for all are <u>true,</u>*

*I haven't been around you for a while,
To make you laugh or see you smile,*

*For we have been trying with all our worth,
To stop the global warming of your Earth,*

*And trying to prevent a war,
That would indeed make temperatures soar.*

*For how can souls be born again,
If the Earth's not here, do I make myself plain?*

*The help we can do is only to change the mind,
The prayers must come from all mankind,*

*We're very worried over here,
Looking at your Earth so full of fear,*

*If only each soul the truth did know,
There would be no war, and each would know,*

*I cannot laugh or joke any more,
Unless we all can prevent this war,*

*We do not know in our plane, so we sigh,
The answer to all of this is known only up high,*

*So I'll sign off now, there is work to be done,
I love you all, your loving son...*

~ *Russell*

This poem came before I met Shirley Gifford and even though her experiences are rare, to me they are nothing short of miraculous. Shirley and I have talked on various subjects; dream experiences, crop circles, parallel worlds and many of the mysteries of the Earth. Yet surely the Spirit World is trying so hard to help us, by showing us such wonders.

Physical Phenomena has been proven to me, but I feel that if we *struggle* to find a certain thing, then that struggle keeps the certain thing *away* from us. If we *stop* struggling with so much effort, *that* which we desire, comes to us by itself. For me, we are now in the *'Age of Miracles'* and all things are possible with God.

Many thanks to Shirley for her wondrous and beautiful story. If any of you were to meet her you would see with one look, that she seems to have an inner light switched on. For me, it is the light of *Truth and Love.*

Melanie and Kirstie Gifford

Eleven

Angel of Music

Summerland Tape 2
July 26th 1994

*'God make my life a little song, that comforteth the sad,
that helpeth others to be strong and makes the singer glad.'*

~ Matilda Betham-Edwards

Russell: *'This tape is dedicated to my mother Gwen Byrne. It includes 'Norman, Ray of Light', myself Russell Vernon Byrne and a finalé by an unknown friend.'*

Norman, Ray of Light: 'Hello dear Gwen. Hello dear Alf.
It is a long time since we have spoken. Remember I told you a long time ago, that out of the darkness and into the light came a boy, with bright shining eyes - Russell. Now that boy has grown up and become a man, who has chosen to work with those on the Earth plane.

I have composed a piece of prose for you. It is called, *'Angel of Music, Goddess of Love.'*

*Bring forth the music,
Lead the souls back to the light.
Music awakens love in us all,*

*Team it with light, laughter and dance,
And God speaks through music and love touches all,*

*Composer, conductor, musician join forces,
To link the channel and release God's forces,
Inspired by music from heavens Great Halls,
They transcribe the melody that nurtures the soul,*

*Team lyricists with music, to write down the words,
Then add a singer and each note they sing,
hears God speak to all,*

Each note the singer emits pure and true,
Heals and replenishes each soul <u>and</u>
the listener - and makes them brand new.

For each note contains a healing ray,
Intensified by the words that the singer relays,
Add musicians and singers and all goes bright,
God sends down his magical spiritual light,

Auras of rainbows shine forth from the stage,
To replenish the auras of the audience that wait,

So gentle reader, when a song makes you cry,
That's God's healing light healing your soul,

When you tap your feet and sing along,
That's God healing your soul, restoring your soul,

When you grow quiet and thoughtful as you hear a song,
That's God speaking to you of his peace and his calm,

When you tingle or jingle and know not what to do,
That's God showing his power lying dormant in you,

When the music makes you dance - be it waltz, jig or rock,
That's God introducing the rhythm of life to you,

For all of this Universe was formed on one chord,
Each piece of music ever written is a variation, that's all,
So it comes directly from God to touch us all,
Add to this laughter, without malice of thought,
And this casts a shaft of pure light through the soul,

For when we laugh at our foibles we grow closer to God,
God loves laughter, he loves to see you dance,
He loves to see you happy, healed and restored,
So God Bless the people with music in their souls,
Who use their talents to enrich us all,

For musical people shine with light upon this Earth,
To act as a channel for God's wondrous love,
God will not rest until we all sing our song,
A universal love song for all mankind.

Musical people, keep playing your part,
God gave you this talent to share with us all,
Angels watch over to inspire your souls,

To teach us one love song for all of mankind,

Angel of Music - Goddess of Light
Bring forth the music, lead souls back to the light,
Love is the power that lights up the soul,
Music awakens love in us all,
Team it with lyrics, laughter and dance,
And God speaks through music and love touches all.

In the past, I spoke to you as *'Norman, Ray of Light'* though you knew this was only a pseudonym. My name is Raymond Lodge and I am the son of Sir Oliver Lodge.
I will now hand over to the boy with the beautiful eyes, to complete this tape for you Gwen - you are his own *'Angel of Music.'*

Russell: *'Hello Mum and hello Dad ! Once long ago, when I first heard about the 'Angel of Music' I saw her as you Mum. So I think it's only right that this Summerland Tape should be dedicated to you ! For was it not you who sang to me, when my life on the Earth plane was nearly done ? You sang Brahms 'Cradle Song' to me - and music is one of the most powerful forces in the Universe ! Teamed with lyrics, it becomes a very powerful tool for all of mankind.*

Mother, I've heard you sing like an angel many times - both before I left the Earth and many times afterwards. How wonderful it is that your beautiful voice can be recorded for others to hear. It is our wish for it to be heard to heal and restore, all those who need that need restoration and healing.

So how does music work ? Well, Raymond has explained that this whole Universe was created on one note - and every piece of music that has ever been composed, is a variation from that note. Musical inspiration comes from the Great Halls of Music in the Spirit World. It is through composers that Spirit people work, sharing their inspiration from the Great Halls of Music. This is the same for every piece of music that has ever been written.

Because music is such a powerful thing, it can be used two ways. The Great Rhythm of Life is in every song and people can literally feel it, when a piece is correctly played. Then with the words of a lyricist you can have an extremely powerful channel for Love, Light and Truth. It is also true that music may be used in a negative way. If the Rhythm of Life is heard in reverse, it may have an negative effect on those who hear it - but the majority of people understand this and it is very rare.

Many songs have been written on many themes, but most have the same basic thread running through them and this is no accident. This thread is Love, for Love is the key and Love is the power that lights up the Universe. It is Love that enables those in Spirit to come and link, with those who love and grieve upon the Earth. So it is only right that Love itself should be reflected in most songs ever written. Of course, there are also songs to make you laugh and it is right that this is so. For laughter is also very positive. Laughter, without malice, is very powerful and enriching for the human soul.

So what happens, dear Mother, when you sing ? Well, around all living things is an aura. It is an aura of light and within each aura, all the colours of the spectrum can be found. If the body is disturbed so the aura is disturbed and if the mental state is disturbed, so again the aura is disturbed - but what does an aura look like ?

Well, to begin with an aura is seen as a bright white light, which extends between one and two feet from your body. Now when a musician starts to play or a singer begins to sing, then the real magic occurs in the aura...

Imagine Mother, that you are on a stage in great hall. You are about to sing and behind you is the London Philharmonic Orchestra. If you could see the aura as I can, around every musician you would see their own bright light, this is their own life force. Then all around you would be seen the bright light of your own life force too. As the musicians begin to tune their instruments in order to play, their auras then begin to show wondrous lights around each of them. These lights then begin to form a rainbow. Then as you begin to practice and warm up that wonderful voice of yours Mother, your aura becomes a rainbow too. Of course since a rainbow contains every colour in the spectrum, so does your aura - since while you sing it is operating on a higher vibratory pitch.

As you and the musicians begin to work, your bright auras now show all the colours of the rainbow. Then God sends down his Spirit lights. These Spirit lights are like little white balls, which reflect all the rainbow colours in your auras. These little lights are basically bright balls of energy which go out to link with the musician's auras and your own. This then intensifies the colours that are all around you, so you all look like little rainbows on the stage.

Now the audience who wait in front, also have their own auras of light around them. Perhaps their auras are imperfect, especially if they are tired or jaded by life. Or maybe they are grieving - for a loved one or a *broken relationship, or lost dream or cause - so their auras could be in various states of disorder or disrepair. So Mother, what do you think happens when you start to sing and the musicians begin to play ? Your auras grow brighter like rainbows and from them, little shining rays of light, which contain all the colours of the spectrum, go out into the audience. They go to replenish the auras of those individuals who need healing, for each rainbow colour in the aura contains a healing property of its own. Pink is for peace, blue is for healing and green is for clear-sightedness. While yellow and sometimes gold, is for wisdom, orange is for energy and purple is for power. So these coloured lights go out from you, as you perform on the stage and they reach the aura of each individual.*

Such is the wonder and the magic of all this, that each Spirit light going from singer and musician will always reach the right member of the audience. You will understand Mother when I say, that as you work and sing and your musicians play, a great atmosphere can build up in the hall. Especially since those in the audience are now absorbing the coloured rays of light from your auras - the audience become alive ! They become happy, emotional, even tearful ! They experience many, many things, but it is all healing. Then as their auras grow brighter, so little lights come away from their auras and go back to you. So now you can emit even more power, beauty and wondrous sound - to further replenish and restore.

So we have almost a two way love song, between the performers and the audience. This is true of every musician and every singer. It is true of all who entertain. For if you add to this the power of laughter, without malice, the soul is lifted even higher. Laughter produces shafts of white light which raises the soul to an even greater and more powerful feeling of well being.
So, my darling Mother music heals and love through music, heals on one of the greatest and best levels.

It is important to remember Mum, that the human instrument God uses to distribute music to the world, is by its very nature, sensitive. The better the singer or musician and the more talented and gifted the individual, most often the more sensitive they are.
It isn't good for such people to live in an atmosphere of negativity. Their 'batteries' always need replenishing with positivity after a performance - even though it is true that the audience themselves give off a great deal to the performer. It is very necessary and important for the performer, whatever entertainment they practice - that they live in an atmosphere of positivity. The reason so many musicians, singers and entertainers suffer a

great deal within their lives, is because they do *not* understand the importance of living in a positive energy.

Mum, you are very lucky to have Dad, for he provides a positive energy for you to operate within. Not all entertainers are so lucky. So many do not have that positive energy in their lives or even understand how to find it. Yet negativity will not sustain them !
So many artistic and musical people in general, do not fare well in their everyday world, basically because they are sensitives. They are Mediumistic, though they would never admit it ! I'm afraid some don't even understand it, but every one of them is Mediumistic. Also, the better musicians and singers are at interpreting their music, the more talent they have and the more ability they have to link with the 'higher Spiritual reality' - they can then become purer channels for God's Love and Truth.

Sadly, so many of them do not understand this. They do not realise the necessity, that they are gradually building up their heightened awareness. A lot of them take their work as a matter of fact. It is good for all artistic people to gradually build up their awareness, but also gradually come down to a lower awareness. Of course, they have to practice while living on the Earth, but you cannot go around on a permanent high because it would destroy you ! Some artists find it easy to go up to communicate with the Spiritual levels, but then they find it very hard or forget how, to come back to Earth in a positive and sensitive atmosphere. All sorts of things can happen to their bodies. They can develop all manner of ailments, from twitches in the eyes to headaches and throat problems ! So it is very important that once you get up to a Spiritual high, you have to come down to Earth to a positive energy level.

This is not just true of singers, but of dancers, comedians and actors, who often wrestle with a part, or the artist who tries to create an image of God's wonder and beauty upon the Earth, or great writers who search for Truth and then try to encompass these Truths in their themes or story lines. All creative people are sensitives and special Mediums. They need to come up the levels very gently, in an atmosphere of positivity. Positivity enriches and enhances the soul, but then all creative people are beloved of God. God understands them, for did he not give them their creative talent ?

Negativity has always destroyed the artistic soul. Unfortunately, a lot of creative people immerse themselves in too much negativity for their own good. That is why so many of them seem to lead such tragic lives. If only they understood the great Power that they are dealing with. Perhaps if *they realised that it is indeed, God's Healing Light and Love that they are channelling through themselves, they'd be able to cope better with everyday living. I hope they can, for it is the creative person that enhances this world and it is through the creative person that God speaks.*

I hope that all you creative people who may read this, remember that you are the instrument, you are the channel. You are the equivalent of the most exquisite piano or priceless guitar. You are the highest and the best ! Do not treat yourself with any less respect than you would treat a wondrous musical instrument, great painting or great book. Please love yourselves, for there is much to love !

I think it's very important that each and every one of us learns to love ourselves. It is the beginning of a compassion we can feel for another human soul. It's the beginning of a higher understanding of life and the beginning of learning to love others - for we cannot truly learn to love others, until we learn to love ourselves. Though it isn't easy to love one's self. So many people find it difficult, but if you truly wish God to teach you how to love - then you have to begin by learning to love yourself. Once you do, then you can begin to learn to love others.

Love is probably the most highly talked about thing upon the Earth and it is sought by so many. What we all seek is unconditional love, though there is a difference between unconditional and conditional love. Conditional love exists, only if a person will <u>do</u> a specific thing or <u>become</u> a special person. This may have no individual relevance to their own spirituality. So just love...

Now it is my wish to finish this part of the tape. I will speak again once my beloved channel has had time to rest. I think we should end this side with a song !'

At this point Russell suggests that B- plays her copy of '*Ave Maria.*' This was my duet with Russell, recorded previously at a Physical Phenomena séance during the mid-1980s.

* * *

Side two begins with a special recording of the song '*Memory*' from the musical '*Cats*' by Andrew Lloyd-Webber. This was another duet I sang at one of the séances of the 1980s - this time with my dear Spirit friend Laura. Now we continue, with B- and Russell speaking on the tape...

B-: 'I could not make this tape without including this duet Gwen. Russell had asked for it.'

Russell: *'How could I speak of music without remembering the time I sang with my beautiful Mother ! Although she is many miles away while I am here with B-, I thought the duet would enhance the tape.*

Mum, do you remember those days when I came to you in the Physical Phenomena Circle ? We used to sing together and I came through as a small boy.'

(Here, Russell makes imitations of his younger self, by shouting *'Oy'* and making his old boyish noises.)

'Now I come back as a man, for I have grown.
It had to be like that then, for this to happen now, for you Mother and for you too Dad. You have accompanied Mum on this quest and backed her completely throughout and during the publication of the first book. So here is a thank you from me, Dad !

Getting back to music - remember that all music is formed by playing just seven notes; C, D, E, F, G, A, B and it's through these seven notes that all music originates. Seven is a psychic number and the number of the Spirit - or the Spiritual number, so remember this as a sign that seven and music and God are all linked.
Now psychic is not the same as Spiritual. This comes from a far higher level than the psychic ever could. Most people are psychic and even some psychic people are Spiritual ! Although today, in the Spiritual movement, I'm afraid there are more who are psychic than Spiritual.

Now I want to mention those days of the Physical Circle, that we shared with you and Dad and the others. It was in this circle that I asked you to form 'Russell's Pink Panther Society.' This was to try and help other bereaved parents cope with their grief, in losing a beloved child and you, my darling Mother, went and did just that. You formed the RPPS which became almost like a sisterhood and brotherhood - populated by parents who have lost children.

In this second book that you are now compiling - in which I hope this tape will be included - some of those mothers of the RPPS, have been asked to tell the stories of their own Spirit children. They have some fascinating stories to tell and I hope this will help many others who read them. So I say to those Mum's of the RPPS,
'do write your wonderful stories. We need them and people on the Earth need them ! This is the next stage of the great story that is yet to unfold. So God bless each and every one of you !'

Some may say 'why write about the death of a child ?' Some may even *accuse you of capitalising on it. Well, I say to all of the Mums who are writing their stories - you are not capitalising on your grief. You are <u>sharing</u> the grief, the shock and the sense of loss that you felt when losing a child. You're sharing it with others out there, who still grieve. You're also sharing with these people, the wondrous realisation that you came to know for yourselves - that there is NO DEATH and your children SURVIVED the death experience. They are simply living in another realm of life.*

This is a wondrous knowledge and a wondrous Truth. But knowledge is no good by itself, unless it is shared with those who need it. By asking those mothers of the RPPS to share their stories, is not encouraging them to capitalise on their grief, but to share your sense of loss and then your JOY at discovering that there is no death.

So why is the RPPS so strong? Why does it contain the Truth? Because within it is contained the Divine Spark of unconditional love. This love is the strongest power in the Universe - and as it was written long ago, by the Master, 'by the hand, our children shall lead us.' Perhaps it is time.

So as your children led you to a greater awareness and understanding, your children can now take others by the hand and lead them to greater awareness and understanding. The RPPS is for to all who grieve, to all who have lost a child. It is open to fathers, to mothers, to grandparents, aunties, uncles - whoever grieves for a child.
In fact, it is your children who teach you how to love. For your children will love without condition, yet if we do not love them without condition, then that love will turn sour and grow cold and distant, instead of growing strong and true.

Now you may say to me 'you died on the Earth aged nine and three quarters - what do you know of children?' Well of course I had no time to marry or have children of my own, yet it has since been my privilege to adopt a child in the Spirit World. So I do have some understanding of parental love. Though some may say, that unless a child is truly your own, you cannot love that child <u>as</u> your own. Well I would say that is rubbish! There are many children who are adopted on your Earth very successfully, by parents who offer unconditional love and, since everything that happens on the Earth is a reflection of what happens in Spirit, then I too was allowed to adopt a child - and I love this child.
She has become the light of my life, and she truly is a joy. Well it's true!

We do have negativity in our world, just as you have it in yours, but here that negativity is banished to the lower levels of Spirit life. Yet there is nothing you can suffer on Earth, that we cannot understand or comprehend. Yes, we may live on a wondrous level of light and love, but we are encouraged to go and help those souls who are stuck in the lower levels - who are prisoners of their own negativity and conditional love.

We love without conditions, therefore we are not prisoners, we are free. Every one of you too, can love without conditions, so you are able to know the great freedom and the great joy of Spirit. You were born a free soul and a free Spirit and the most precious thing that God ever gave you, was your own free will.

Now it's not the purpose of these tapes or books to deny anyone the right to think for themselves. We would never tell anyone how to think or believe. People have to decide for themselves. All I can do is share what I have learned and all my Mother can do, and others like her, is share their experiences with you. It is up to you to decide for yourselves whether any of this is true !

Mother, I mentioned on the very first Summerland Tape that you and I knew each other in an Egyptian incarnation. At that time in history, you were a Priestess of Isis and you had me as your son. The High Priestesses were not supposed to have children, so I was adopted. During that lifetime someone tried to replace you in my heart and this experience was repeated in a way, in this lifetime - but that has passed and finished. We move on and walk through pastures new !

All creative talents are a gift from God and they are nurtured in past lives. So if you are a singer in this life, were you a singer in a past life ? Well, I would say that God doesn't give his talents lightly, for we usually earn them in one lifetime or another. Although it is possible for someone who plays piano extremely well, to come into another life and never play a note in their lives - but still feel an affinity to that instrument. This can be applied to any instrument or skill of course - because even though you may have been a pianist in one life, it doesn't mean that you will be again !

Those who misuse their gifts in a lifetime, may reincarnate without any creativity at all. All rights to that gift are lost because of their misuse. However, if the creative streak is strong and one chooses to incarnate within an atmosphere where the creativity can be nurtured, then this is where we may find the child prodigy. This is how they come into being on the Earth - there is no great mystery to it.
Sometimes, people do not understand how a creative gift can be misused, but any human soul can cause problems. If this is so, then in the next incarnation, the creative gift may be denied to you - or it may be given in

such abundance that you have to work even harder !

Some people wonder whether pre-recorded music has the same effect on the aura, as does live music. Well it doesn't, but it is a good substitute ! It's not the same as a live performance, but a recording does have good therapeutic value. As electronic equipment becomes more sophisticated, greater reproduction of sound is increasingly possible, in clearer and more precise reproductions. So in these recordings, the true power of the music can be released, giving a greater effect. Of course, nothing beats the atmosphere of a live performance !

It is a great shame that in this day and age, so many children forsake musical instruments, instead they channel their energies playing computer games and electronic gadgets for hours Anyone who plays a musical instrument well, has the ability to enrich those who hear it being played. So instead of buying your child a computer, why not buy them a musical instrument - or better still, buy them both !

We should never underestimate the power of music. It is very therapeutic, it helps plants to grow better, it helps people with nervous disorders and will restore the mental balance. Music calms those fellow beings that walk as animals upon the Earth plane - animals love music. The whole Universe is alive with music. Bird song is music. In fact, bird song is a vibration of the one note on which the whole Universe was created. The wind makes music as it rustles through the trees and bushes. Music is everywhere.

We often need silence and solitude to hear the music of nature. It is God's music and there is nothing more lyrical than listening to a stream running over stones, or the crash of waves on a beach. This is the 'Lyric of Life' and can never be devalued, because it is more precious and priceless than anything. It soothes the soul. Human beings live in a very noisy world of mostly unnatural sound, which does not feed the soul and Spirit - it actually coarsens and deadens the Spirit.

Although it is wonderful to have and enjoy pre-recorded music and all the advantages the technological age offers, but please do not forsake the old for the new. Change for the sake of change is rarely of any use - except for progression ! It is good to improve the quality of life, but much of the change in the world at this moment, doesn't improve life for anyone, not really ! There is too much noise, confusion, pollution and general pandemonium. Humankind seems to have lost the 'Rhythm of Life' and lost touch with nature and it's own inner self and this can be very dangerous.

When that begins, mankind sows the seeds of his own destruction - so it is wise to always think and question the way forward.

Is it right to always question ? We should not always agree with others because people tell you it is right. Only accept something if it rings bells in your soul and feels right for you. Each and every one of you knows deep down inside what is right. No one should have to tell you, you will know with your own inner awareness. There are so many people in this world who are very clever and always busy telling everyone what's right for everyone else, and many people believe what they are told by so called experts. Well there is no one more expert on what's right for you, than you ! Never lose sight of that.

Now I don't think it would be fitting to end this tape on music, without saying something about the Great Halls of Music - although it is very difficult to describe in Earthly terms, what they are like. Try and imagine a vast building of the purest, whitest marble, which has many corridors and many stages, which each have the most perfect acoustics - then you have and idea of what the Great Halls of Music are like.

Then we have the Libraries of Music, within these Great Halls. These are vast and they contain every piece of music ever created on the Earth. Then we have the place of music and melodies that we hope may one day be transmitted to the Earth - music of all diversities and character. It isn't all classical ! All music is incorporated, every piece which is ever created and all variations upon the theme is celebrated, enjoyed and sung and played.

There are also meeting houses where great composers sit to discuss what form of sound should next go down to the Earth plane - those sounds that can lead people on Earth, back to God. Sounds that give them a greater understanding and awareness of God. It isn't just hymns they create either, it's all types of music. There is no mistake about this and it may be very hard for some of you to accept, but God's presence can also be found within the music of a rock group !

Thinking about the generation divide within music, I can say that one variation of a rhythm speaks to one age group, whereas another variation will speak to another and so on. They are interlinked, since there is music all over the Universe and beyond it. There is, what you might call, intergalactic music also kept and recorded in the chronicles of the Great Halls and of course, all the great composers and musicians are there.

All those who arrive in our world are able to sing for anyone who cares to listen. They don't even need an audience. Some just sing for the joy of singing and they play for the joy of playing. Musical instruments in our world may be very different to the ones you are familiar with, but they can create the purest, most sweetest notes and our choirs have the sweetest voices too. The tone of my Mother's own voice resembles those I've heard in the Great Halls of Music. Which is why I feel it's important that her voice is captured by recordings. In fact she is recording one now and there is another still to follow...'

Gwen: (I was too - on the very day this tape arrived in the post !)

Russell: *'I feel it is very important that she does this, not for herself particularly, or for us - but for those who come after, to hear and be enriched and gain healing as they listen. I sing to my Mother myself and as she begins to unfold her awareness, she is starting to understand the meaning of the songs more. Also, we both enjoy music tremendously. It helps us strengthen our bond and we learn so much from that.*

Now I want to mention dancing. When you dance you are in fact observing the Rhythm of Life itself. Every dance that was ever created, is a variation on the Rhythm of Life. It doesn't matter whether you dance to a waltz, to rock or a jig, even the traditional dance of the Morris men. As you dance, you are tapping into the original life force. Dancing is very therapeutic too, it's good for everyone. The trouble is, people on the Earth can get very 'bogged down' with the negativity of life around them. They lose all contact with the Rhythm of Life, so they are unable to dance. You see, once again you should look to your children, they do not have any problems with this. Your children dance !

Many children are natural dancers, since they are in tune with the Rhythm of Life - for they have arrived new with the God force and dance naturally. It is only as they grow older and become involved in the rituals and taboos of life, that the negativity they find on Earth causes them to stop dancing. So many cultures find it easy to dance. Many traditional cultures have the most wonderful dances. This is because they feel and become 'in tune' with the Earth and the Rhythm of Life. They use their bodies to interpret that wonderful force, that wonderful rhythm. Yes, it is very good to dance.

Isn't it sad that in the history of orthodox religion, dancing was banned as being the 'devil's' work ? Well, I don't know the devil and neither do any of those I work with. We only know God and I know God loves to see his children dance - just as you love to see your own children dance. The children here in Spirit dance. They always dance. They never really walk - they skip, they hop and they dance. Just as children on the Earth should do. You know how little children find it impossible to simply walk beside you, because they jig along and play around ? Well all they are doing is expressing the Rhythm of Life itself. It's very therapeutic for them and often therapeutic for you to watch them ! It would also help many of you to absorb and express the Rhythm of Life if you danced yourself !

I often dance ! I dance the waltz and sometimes I dance with B- when she's a little down. We sometimes just have a little waltz round the kitchen ! I wish you would all dance, for it is good for the Spirit and the soul. The Spirit of music is so strong and powerful in your soul, it's God's greatest gift to his children. So never, ever turn a deaf ear to music and never, ever say that you can't dance, because you'd just look silly. You will not look silly, you are wondrous.

I've heard people ask if you can learn to play a musical instrument once you die and arrive in the next world. Oh yes, you can ! If through of your life you've wanted to play a musical instrument and never had the chance while on Earth, then you can come to the Great Halls of Music and learn to play an instrument. It's possible that you could become a great musician over here. You might become a beautiful singer over here or beautiful dancer. You see, there are none of the terrible inhibitions associated with the Earth plane.

Do you know what makes a wonderful singer or dancer - or a wonderful anything ? It is thought. You become wonderful by believing in the possibility of becoming wonderful. If you believe that you are good and capable of all things and that you <u>can</u> do it - you <u>will</u> do it. The power of thought is very, very strong. Never underestimate the power of thought, for it can take you into the depths or the heights. A positive thought can make you reach for the stars, because you are ready for them. Thought is very powerful, so if you think you can do something - then you will do it. This is not just true in my world, it's true in yours. If you want something to be, if you wish something to be - then it <u>will</u> be. Positive thoughts are so very, very important.

Finally, I want to just mention that the greatest riches upon the Earth, are not those purchased by money. Money has absolutely no value in the Spirit World - so it might be a good idea to not become too immersed in the material world. I know you have to use money and need to deal with money - but you do not have make it your God. Use money as a tool, only as a tool. There are a great many things money cannot buy. It cannot buy your health. Money cannot buy back the life of a beloved child, or beloved husband, mother, father or friend. In the real sense, money has little value at all. So, if you are going to collect treasure - collect Spiritual treasure. Invest in Heaven !

I will now conclude this tape, for my lovely channel is becoming tired now. I hope it has helped and enlightened those who read the words. I say to you all - just bring back the music in your life. Feel the music in your soul. Dance. Sing. Play musical instruments and stretch out and find God therein.

Goodbye Mum, Goodbye Dad. We'll all raise a glass on August 14th ! I'll be there, thank you for everything...and the work continues.'

An unknown Spirit helper: 'May the blessings of almighty God, nurture and heal all those who hear or read these words. God Bless all of you and may the Universal theme, sing in your souls.'

* * *

Modesty allows me say very little about this tape. I understand music and the strong emotions it can evoke, so I will allow the tape to speak for itself.

Whilst staying at B-'s, I had the privilege of Clairvoyantly seeing her beautiful Spirit daughter - who we know as 'Rainbow.' It was just a quick Clairvoyant picture, yet I was able to *hold* it in my mind. Once I'd returned home, I felt a great urge to *try* and draw her, in all her loveliness. I have done quite a lot of reasonable artwork, but I've never been trained.
I had been given a tiny photograph of Rainbow, as a baby of about six days old - taken just before her passing at the age of twelve days. I began to draw continuously for two or three days and actually turned out about nine or ten different drawings. They were all drawn from this one Clairvoyant 'flash' I'd had, but I didn't quite understand why the drawings were all at different ages. They were two months, two years, four years, five years, six through to eleven and one as a young teenager. I was puzzled, but I knew the face was hers, but the reason for the 'ages' - plus the clothes I had drawn her in, were bothering me. I truly didn't know why, but *she did.* I will explain...

After finishing them all, I looked at the one I'd drawn of her as a beautiful baby of around two months. I'd drawn her wrapped in a white shawl, with pink roses. Unknown to me, B- had wrapped her baby like this for her burial, in a shawl with the same flowers - just as I had drawn. The drawing of her at two years old, looked the image of her brother and I remember when I drew it, that it had just unfolded before my eyes. Then the one of her at four years old, could easily pass as the image of her sister.

One could argue that I know both children - but again, they just appeared as I drew. I puzzled over the older ones, because I had her in a ballet outfit and there was one of her in a red choir robe, singing, with all the colours of the spectrum and their corresponding notes surrounding her. In another she was wearing 'moon-shaped' earrings, and in the one as a young lady, she wore pearl button-type earrings.

Summerland Tape two arrived, incidentally crossing in the post with these drawings I'd sent to B-. I don't really think this was an accident. Listening to the tape, there is a part where Rainbow is speaking about while in Spirit she can be *any* age she wants to be. The tape also speaks of dancing and choirs, yet I had no idea these subjects were going to be discussed on the tape. As for the earrings, I later learned that B- had bought some moon-shaped earrings and had also got married wearing pearl button earrings ! So *something* was going on somewhere, plus the evidence of this little girls love of music. The large drawing of Rainbow, as I'd seen her in Spirit form at the age of six, ended up having pride of place on the wall in B-'s home.

Before I finish this chapter, I'd just like to relate an amusing little tale. This happened before I received Summerland Tape three, which was going to be called *'All Things Bright and Beautiful.'* It hadn't even been communicated yet and the dates all verify this.

Towards the end of July 1994, Alfie and I had returned home after being out all day. To get in or out of the house we have to go through two doors, with a porch in between. Once home, we were in the kitchen talking as the kettle boiled for a cuppa. Alfie was in the corner of the kitchen, near the conservatory door - which hadn't been opened for days. Without wearing his glasses, he bent down to pick up, what he thought was a used tea bag. But suddenly the 'teabag' just leaped out of his hand !

To our astonishment, he'd found a darling little green frog - a real live 'Kermit.' Well we laughed so much, then Alfie finally managed to catch him and put him into the garden. Having one of nature's creatures appear in our home, made me think, *'well if Russell can bring us butterflies, maybe he brought the frog ?'* Because many times during the séances, Russell had often promised to bring frogs. He likes them - but I admit, I'm not so keen !

Now Alfie and I both know Russell's humour and later on Summerland tape three, we heard him explain how he brings us live butterflies at special times. So I realise that he *could* have brought in 'Kermit' and I believe he did. Yet in spite of what some people may think, both Alfie and I are very logical people. We both know that the frog was very definitely *not* in the kitchen that morning before we left the house and he certainly hadn't come in through both doors of the locked porch. So how did he end up in our kitchen ? All I know is, it gave us such a laugh and that's good, isn't it ? However, I've since told young Mr Byrne *'no more frogs !'*

So mentally now, as I say thank you to all those concerned for this 'Angel of Music' tape, I half expect to hear Russell's familiar voice singing to me. This time I don't. So as it's rather late, I drag myself off to bed. Then at 2.30 in the morning, I'm awoken by a loud *knock* on the teasmaid clock. I sit bolt upright in bed, because very clearly I hear Russell with,

> *'Tonight the world is just an address,*
> *A place for you to live in,*
> *No matter wrong or right,*
> *For here we are,*
> *And what is like a dream,*
> *is a song tonight.'*
>
> ~ from West Side Story by Stephen Sondheim

This is meant a duet, but I just laid there and listened. I could only mentally join in anyway, for I couldn't *physically* start singing in the middle of the night or I'd have woken poor Alfie, who was oblivious and sleeping like a baby !

In the morning I awoke to hear Russell singing words from the wonderful Jimmy Webb song, *'MacArthur Park.'*

> *'Spring was never waiting for us girl,*
> *As it ran one step ahead as we followed in the dance,*
> *There will be another song for me for I will sing it,*
> *There will be another dream for me and I will bring it,*
> *And after all the loves of my life,*
> *You'll still be the one...*
> *...after all the loves in my life,*
> *I'll be thinking of you and wondering why...'*

Twelve

I'm a Music Man !

May 8th 1995

'With a song in my heart, I behold your adorable face,
...I always knew, I would live life through,
With a song in my heart - for you.'

~ Lorenz Hart

I've enjoyed years of entertaining people with my singing and the songs have always had meaningful lyrics. Now I realise just *how* important they are - for within lyrics lie some wonderful messages.

Just like today as I write, it's the 50th anniversary of the end of the second World War and on the TV, Dame Vera Lynn is singing *'We'll Meet Again.'* For years she sang this wonderful song so poignantly to the troops, but the *lyrics* have meant so much to so many homesick soldiers, sailors and pilots. That is the power of music.

Many people say they're confused when I say that I hear Russell sing to me. This is of course Clairaudient hearing - I just 'tune' in and it takes no effort at all - but why shouldn't he sing to me ? Now, I sometimes even hear songs outside of my head, but most often it's Clairaudience. Once I realised that I *could* hear in this way, I began to look even more closely at the meanings of the lyrics and what a great joy it gave me !

On reflection I guess I've had this ability or gift for years, yet I never really realised the very deep and powerful effect lyrics can have on people. I've always had songs whizzing around my head, but was truly unaware that a lot of it was coming from those in Spirit, including Russell himself ! It wasn't until I met one particular Mum during the 1980s, that I became aware that these songs - which still come at me 'fast and furious' - were indeed from Spirit.

I'd like to share some examples of this musical inspiration from the Spirit World, yet there are so many songs that come to me, where do I begin ? They always have a message - some are humorous, some arrive when I'm either angry, scared or depressed. They arrive when I'm happy too. I will try to share a few here that are varied, and even if you're not musically inclined, you should see how the message in the song always seems to suit the occasion ! It is said that *'music is a bridge between Heaven and Earth'* but then so are art and poetry. Music urges the Spirit onwards, although surely the greatest bridge there is, can only be 'Mother Love !'

    I will just use a few lines of each song, then end this chapter with the tale of how Alfie and I ended up with the two best seats in the house - by arrangement of Russell and I guess, a little help from his friends. I do think all this musical awareness is for a reason, at this precise time, although I'm not sure exactly just *why* it's happening, but I must say it is very enjoyable. I'll start with a few humorous songs, like the time I was once charging around the supermarket, with a wobbly trolley and I clearly heard the words, *'Bang, bang, bang went the trolley, clump, clump, clump went the wheels,'* (from Judy Garland's 'Trolley Song' in the musical 'Meet Me In St. Louis.')

Then one time my car suddenly stopped and I heard, *'If you're ever in a jam here I am, if you're ever in a mess S.O.S.'* (from the Cole Porter musical *'DuBarry Was A Lady*.')

    My favourite pastime is just lolling in the bath. I really could stay there all day, enjoying every minute. The face pack goes on, I have bubbles, oils, *the lot !* I was doing just this once while listening to Michael Crawford singing his wonderful songs, when Russell suddenly sings, *'Flash, bang wallop - what a picture, what a photograph ! Poor old Mum, there with nothing on, face all white and her rapier gone...what a picture...stick it in the family album !'* (From the Tommy Steele musical 'Half a Sixpence.')

Ok Russell, thanks - message received ! Although what's a *rapier* got to do with anything ?

    Once when Alfie was away from home at Loughborough University, one song had me puzzled. I'd heard it *outside* of my head and I think Russell was trying to impersonate Freddie Mercury, because I woke up with a start hearing *'Barcelona'* ! Freddie Mercury and Montserrat Caballé sang it together in 1988 as an operatic duet, to celebrate Barcelona hosting the 1992 Summer Olympics. Well, the Olympic Games are about winning medals and Russell was still singing this same song to me the next day, so what was it all about ? I was still wondering, when Alfie called me from Loughborough to let me know when he'd be home and then he said, *'oh by the way, I've won a medal for archery.'*

Ha, ha, well done Russell. Message received again !

Another time, I was in a clothes shop and trying on a dress. I'd just decided it was awful, when Russell pops in with a Deanna Durbin number, *'you're as pretty as a picture...you're the vision of an angel from above'* !

On my birthday one May, I was astonished while opening my birthday post, to find I'd won £50 in Premium Bonds. Sitting there thrilled to bits, I hear the Bing Crosby song, *'every time it rains, it rains pennies from heaven...you'll find your fortune falling all over town, be sure that your umbrella is upside down.'*

While I was waiting for the first book '*Russell*' to be published, one morning I awoke to hear these words from the musical 'The Sound of Music.' *'You wait little girl on bended knee, for fate to turn the light on,'* How true ! Then Russell quickly follows that with the Marty Robbins hit, *'some day I'm gonna write...the story of my life.'*

'Oh ! Are you Russell ?' I say out loud. *'Don't you mean I am !''* To which he immediately replies with Franks Sinatra's, *'if they asked me...I could write a book...'*

Isn't this what you might call a musical conversation !

I know Russell was aware of every single thing relating to his story, as I worked through the manuscript for the book. For even when I was posting it off, I heard the Irving Berlin song, *'now it can be told, told in all it's glory...every other tale of boy meets girl, is just another story !'*

Thank you Russell !

I'll move now from the humorous side, to speak of his more serious side - simply because the lyrics so fit the situations. I do wonder and am continually amazed, by how it all fits. Even when I'm sad and weary, he finds a song. My down times are met with words like these from Gerry and the Pacemakers, *'Don't let the 'son' catch you crying...'*

Life brings us lots of sad things to deal with and Russell knows this. The sad memories have to come out somewhere.

Waking on January 17th 1989 he gave me a song by Mel Tormé *'It's the most unusual day.'* He was right too. I had my friend Val Williams the Medium, staying with me and her son was away fighting in the Middle East. This was the day the Gulf War broke out and it was *my* job to wake her that morning, with the news. An unusual day ? It was indeed.

That night I heard, *'Each night I make a song for you, each night my Spirit longs for you'* - an Ivor Novello tune this time, thanks again Russell !

110

Russell certainly knows all the latest pop songs, yet he is clearly aware of sacred music too. I am glad that I also know them, otherwise he'd have a few problems, such as at Easter. For every Good Friday, *outside* of my head I always hear the same wonderful songs like, *'Were you there when they crucified my Lord ?'*

These kind of songs bring with them a great joy for me. If I'm feeling somewhat shell-shocked by life's traumas, and saying to myself *'God, I'm tired,'* back he comes with, *'Art thou troubled, music will calm thee, art thou weary, rest shall be thine'* (Handle's aria, from his opera 'Rodelinda.')

Whilst looking at a holiday brochure on Jerusalem, I heard words from the Dorothy Lamour song, *'Hide your heart from sight, lock your dreams at night, it could happen to you.'* Oh Russell, I hope so one day !

It's a nice feeling to wake to a song in the darkness some mornings. It helps to get the day going ! *'Just one voice, singing in the darkness...'* by Barry Manilow, is one I know Russell is fond of. That kind of, sums up his songs in the morning. Sometimes we have lyrics with his own touch, like this old time Music Hall song, *'The boy you love is up in the gallery, the boy you love is looking down at you.'*

Or this one by Anita Harris, *'I could spend my life just loving you...I'm not the laughing child I used to be.'*

Russell does seem very fond of Andrew Lloyd-Webber songs. One of his favourites is named *'Unexpected Song'* with the line, *'an unexpected song that only you are hearing.'* Clever, eh ?

What can I say ? These songs are always unexpected !

Sometimes he'll sing, *'I want to be the first man in your life'* Well Russell is just *one* of the men in my life - there are seven others and he knows all of them only too well !

I could fill a whole book with these if I went on, so I'll finish with just a couple more. This first one came so clearly, while I was reading about the legends of Glastonbury. As I read, I looked up to listen, as I hear my son singing so sweetly to me, the words, *'as if we never said goodbye,'* which is a gorgeous song from the Lloyd-Webber musical 'Sunset Boulevard.' I'd just completed my first professional singing tape at the time. It had no title, but this song was on it and I realised then, that this was just the title I'd been looking for ! Thanks again Russell.

It has been difficult choosing which songs to discuss here, as there have been many hundreds. The final one I will tell you about, came while Alfie and I spent with our grandson, young Russ. It was his tenth birthday and we'd taken him to London's Natural History Museum. He'd had a choice between two exhibitions - either Jurassic Park or the Egyptians. It was his birthday and his choice, so of course Jurassic Park won !

We travelled into London by train, which in itself was a novelty for him, but talk about a Byrne family day out ! The London Underground was new to him too, as up and down the escalators we went. He was having a great time and laughing all the while. Then we got on the wrong tube train, which was comical, then we repeatedly found ourselves at Russell Square. Young Russ thought it was great having a station named after him !

Then we were looking at monsters - real bones of dinosaurs ! Although it was Alfie and me doing the looking, for we were forever looking for Russ. He was busy playing with all the interactive museum gadgets. It seems he was more interested in pressing buttons than seeing dinosaur bones. In truth, he was a bit young to comprehend the reality of these great creatures. I mean, even me 'Nanny Byrne' was having the same problem !

We'd been watching a big screen video, when young Russ just vanished through a door marked *No Exit,* so off we went through the same door to find him. Relieved, we found him staring at an enormous *chrysalis* slowly changing into a butterfly. By now I had realised that we weren't just three, but *four* Byrne's, on a day out ! We felt that Russell senior was obviously with us too and he was clearly having a bit of late birthday fun himself, with young Russ. He was just 30 years and just a few weeks old, so was he missing this one ? No way !

Poor 'Nanny Byrne' was longing to get into the Egyptian exhibition. I almost managed a small peep, but no luck, I was too late ! At that point, Russell gave me a song Clairaudiently,
'Once I had a secret love, that lived within the heart of me. All too soon my secret love, became impatient to be free...'
Russell was being clever here, for I knew what he meant by these words. He was referring to a time we'd been together in a past incarnation, in Egypt. We were a mother and son then too, but we'd sadly had to part. There is more on the experiences in this lifetime, later on in the book.

* * *

In 1990, I was in Derbyshire attending a residential Lynwood Seminar. Although it had been a long while since I felt that I needed a Spirit message, it was nice to have the occasional sitting with a Medium. So while I was there, I arranged for a sitting with my friend Val Williams. As usual Val delivered the goods - the sitting was excellent. At the end, Val

asked me,
'Gwen, have you seen The Phantom of the Opera ?'
'Some hope Val !' I replied. For at that time, tickets were like gold dust.
'Well you're going to see it. Russell's fixing it and I don't know how !' said a puzzled Val, to an equally puzzled Gwen. She went on to say, *'you need to watch for a young man born, in the same year as Russell and under the same birth sign.'*

Now I felt like Cinderella, who was told *'you will go to the ball !'* Well I can dream, can't I ?

Later that day at the Seminar, we were all settling down to our evening meal. I was oblivious who was at my table, because none of us had ever met before. I got chatting to the man sitting next to me and he asked my name, so I told him, *'I'm Gwen,'*

Oh, that's my wife's name,' he said. *'So you must be the Gwen named on the programme. The singer ?'*

'Yes' I told him.

'So you sing ? Well I took my little niece to see Phantom of the Opera the other night.' he said.

'Oh, it's alright for some,' I replied, *'some people have all the luck.'*

Then he turned to me and said, *'Why, do you want to see it ?'*

I can't believe he even asks me *if* I want to see it ! Excuse me while I choke on my dinner, of course I'd love to see it !

Then just casually he says, *'I'll get you a couple of tickets for next week.'*

I was so amazed - and what had I been told that very day, by Val ? All I could mumble with a squeak, was *'what birth sign are you ?'*

Of course I knew the answer before he even replied.

'Virgo' he said with a flashing smile. Well what can I say ?

So the following week there we were...Alfie and me. We were sitting in the *front row* circle at Her Majesty's Theatre in London, watching *'The Phantom of the Opera'* in all its glory and wonder ! I felt like I was in a dream and I might wake up and find myself back in bed. But no, this was real ! Perhaps I'd somehow *'wished upon a star'* ? Because as this favourite Disney song of Russell's goes, *'it makes no difference who you are, anything your heart desires will come to you.'*

But then isn't Russell like our little friend Pinocchio ? I know that beautiful night in the theatre was engineered by him - Russell I mean not Pinocchio !

'If your heart is in your dreams, no request is too extreme' as the song goes.

What more can I say in this chapter on music ? Except it is truly wonderful for me to have this musical communication from my son in the Spirit World. For it's only that which comes from *his* heart, that reaches into mine...

Thirteen

Hello...? It's Time !

December 1994

*'there are more things in Heaven and Earth, Horatio
than are dreamt of in your philosophy...'*

~ Hamlet Act 1, Scene 5

Although it's now December 1994, I would first like readers to rewind with me to 1979. Alfie and I were getting ready to go to the Festival Hall for an Operatic Evening. I remember it well, for it was Easter time and although by now our son Kevin had married, we had not as yet been blessed with any 'little Byrne's.'

The time was dragging on that Sunday and we had time to kill. So switching on the TV to some now forgotten channel, we saw a film beginning. We wondered what it could be about, but as we watched a most wonderful film unfolded. *'The Blue Bird'* is a film that I can honestly say neither of us had even heard of, yet we sat enchanted. We were so engrossed that we were late for our Operatic Evening. I feel sure that the writer of this story must have had great knowledge of Spirit - and I mean great, for in this tale lies some very deep *Truths* !

However, this chance happening started me on a search for the original book of *'The Blue Bird'*, which was originally written in 1909 as a play, by the Belgian author Maurice Maeterlinck. In my first book *'Russell'* I tell how I eventually found a copy in Somerset - success ! I need to mention here, that this was some years before the wonderful Physical Phenomena séances that we attended, for these first came in August, 1982. I came to love *'The Blue Bird'* film and eventually the book, which now stands on our bookshelf, along with other 'specials'.

What follows is an extract adapted from the third scene of Maeterlinck's original Belgian *'Blue Bird'* play and I promise there's a good reason why I include it here...

'...in a huge hall called the 'Azure Palace' with shining sapphire columns and polished floors, there are two enormous doors in iridescent opal. There are many children here in sky blue robes and they are either playing, chatting or just day-dreaming while they wait. You see, all these boys and girls are here, waiting to be born...

Two Earthly children have just arrived in this dimension, brought here by an entity called 'Light.' The girl is named Mytyl and her younger brother is called Tyltyl. Their friend 'Light' tells them this is just one of thousands of similar halls, which are all full of children waiting to born.

'Light' leaves them to meet some of these children and they approach one boy who is curious about Tyltyl's hat ! Tyltyl explains to the boy that his hat keeps his head warm when it's cold. The boy looks puzzled and asks Mytyl 'what is cold ?' The brother and sister just look at each other, bemused. Then the boy tells them that he's invented something to take to Earth when he's born, which will bring happiness to many.

...Mytyl and Tyltyl are then joined by other children, who all begin to show off their own inventions they are taking to Earth - everything from cures for diseases to something that grows giant flowers ! 'Must you all invent something to take to the Earth ?' Asks Mytyl. Together, the children all respond at once with a resounding 'Yes' ! They say that Old Father Time insists on it.

Then Tyltyl notices one boy walking around with his eyes closed and asks another what he's doing. Tyltyl is told that he is practicing his blindness for when he is born...

Suddenly, a small girl in blue robes rushes up to Tyltyl's sister, saying 'Mytyl, it is so good to see you !' Mytyl's confusion is eased when the girl explains that she is soon to be born to their family - as their new sister ! Tyltyl asks if she'll be bringing anything to the Earth when she's born. The girl says she must bring three severe illnesses with her. So sadly, they will not have her for a sister for very long...

At that moment the giant opal doors begin to open, flooding the hall with a golden light. They see Father Time himself step down into the hall. Behind him they see a huge wooden sailing ship, and they learn he's here to collect those children who are going to be born today !

Many keen children rush up to Father Time, but he refuses passage to some, saying, 'you will need to wait a while longer, you know you are not yet expected on the Earth !'

One older boy refuses to be parted from his girlfriend, who is now crying and pleading for him to stay. Father Time explains that the boy must come, as he is due to be born. As he leads the boy aboard Father Time tells the girl, 'Do not cry. Your love is not going to die - he is going to live !'

...Eventually, the huge ship sets sail for the Earth, with hundreds of children on board. 'Light' returns to collect Mytyl and Tyltyl and together they all watch the ship of children leave.

Far off in the distance, Mytyl and her brother Tyltyl hear the most beautiful singing. Light explains to them gently, that this is the song of the Mothers who are waiting to meet their children...'

(End of Scene)

Now some of you might be wondering what this is all about, for it may seem a long way round to the subject I am coming to. Firstly, I thought it would be lovely to share the Spiritual wisdom and knowledge of such a writer as Maeterlinck. For me, *'The Blue Bird'* contains some beautiful *Truths.* Now, let's get around to why I include it here...

The year *'Russell'* was published many people wrote asking me, that in view of the experiences I'd had, had I ever received a Spirit telephone call from Russell ?

Thinking of that particular phenomena, I thought very deeply whether I should write of 'phone calls from Spirit' and decided to keep it for book two. I think this was the right decision, for only recently there have been others coming forward with their own experiences of this rare phenomena.

However, my answer to that question is yes ! I had many, many phone calls from Spirit. I intend here to only describe two I received from Russell - although I did have calls from other dear friends in the Spirit World, they contained no evidence of Russell himself.

On September 20th, 1983 I was dashing home from Yorkshire on the coach. My youngest son Gary and his wife Sharon were expecting their first child, although it was a 'wee bit' early. When I eventually arrived at Southend bus station, Alfie met me with the news that Sharon had gone into hospital. Today was also the anniversary of Russell's birthday and he would have been or should I say, was *going* to be 30 years old.

That evening was a real flurry of activity. I cannot recall exact times, but it was already getting quite dark, so would have been around 9 p.m. I was bustling around the kitchen getting ready to go to the hospital, when there was a knock at the back door. Answering it, I was greeted Sharon's mother, who was coming with us to the hospital, so in she came.

Now part of me was *so excited* that grandchild number three was coming soon and although it may seem silly of me after 20 years, but Sharon was in Dowsett Ward. This was the very same hospital ward from which my Russell had passed to Spirit - so part of me was *not* so happy to go at all.

Just then the phone rang and in a rush I ran to answer it, then I just *froze* !
This was my very first phone call from the Spirit World and of course, it was Russell. I was completely rooted to the spot and somewhat restricted in what I could say, for Sharon's mother was standing right nearby !
The call went like this...

Russell: *'Hello Mum it's Russell. I'm ringing to tell you it's Time. It's Time. Hurry up and get to the hospital.'*

Gwen: (Stammering) *'Oh...erm...hello dear. Yes, we're going very shortly.'*

Russell: *'Poor old Gary is throwing a wobbler. He can't believe what's happening Mum.'*

Gwen: *'Oh, he'll be ok. He'll be alright !'*

Russell: *'It's time...you know, Father Time ? Hurry. Goodnight Grandma !'*

Then the phone went dead.

To say I was thunderstruck would be very much an understatement. I felt like a robot, but we had to leave, so we jumped into the car and headed for Rochford Hospital. By the time we had parked up and walked the long familiar corridor to Dowsett Ward, it was roughly 10.30 p.m.
We walked into the ward and Gary handed me a beautiful blonde bundle.
'Here you are *Mum'*, he said, *'this is Russell.'*
'Oh, how lovely !' Then I just cried.

There were other happenings on that evening, but I have already written of them in the *'Russell'* book. As this chapter is dealing with Spirit phone calls, I'll just continue with call number two...

We must fast-forward to April 14th, 1988. By then, we hadn't been to a séance for at least a year and Gary and Sharon were expecting their second child. This time I remember the time - it was 8.30 in the evening and I was alone in the house when the phone rang...

Gwen: *'Hello, this is Gwen....who's that ?'*

Russell: *'It's Russell. It's bluebird time again Mum...in the morning. Don't panic. You've got Time. Remember Father Time ? Got to go now Mum ! We can only do this at certain times !'*

Then the phone went dead.

I know readers may find this unbelievable but it's *true*, it happened ! I've found that the most incredible incidents are *Truth*. I'd been wondering about 'Bluebird' and 'Time' and clearly Russell knew of my love for this great book. However, I think that both Gary and Sharon would have loved a baby girl, but it wasn't to be. Little Brett arrived the next morning, yet another beautiful blonde bundle, just as the phone call had said. Bluebird Time indeed !

At a séance some time later, I asked Spirit how they managed this wonder and strangely we were met with a some reticence. I had the feeling they didn't want to say too much about it, although Russell did tell us *'we have to wait until the Medium is either in Trance or asleep, Mum...'*
and that was that - subject finished !

Now I know many of you will have a thousand questions and perhaps as many explanations will spring to mind, which is fair enough. I understand that and I don't mind criticism either, but *both* calls came from Russell and *both* calls related to the birth of babies *before* they were born - and on both occasions *'Time'* and *'Bluebird'* were emphasised.

At another séance I recall speaking to Russell of these phone calls he'd made. Of course he joked in his familiar way, but then we heard the sounds of him promptly calling his brother in Yorkshire !

'I'll have a chat with Kev, but I don't think he's in !' Russell said.

That's was right, he wasn't !

'Oh well !' Russell said. *'I'll have a chat with the local vicar. I'm dialling a number...brr...brr...*
Hello, my name is Russell and I'm speaking from a house in Leicester. Can you help me please ?'

Well now we were laughing so much that we missed the rest of the conversation. But when we heard the sound of the phone going down, Russell said, *'there you are. Just to show you how easy it is for us.'*

I am not the first to write of phone calls from the so called 'dead' and I'm certain that I won't be the last. If one wishes to learn more about them, there are a few books available on this phenomena. So once again, I'll leave this to the scientific brains, although how I wish they would open their hearts and minds more. I can only hope that one day they will !

Other than in Maeterlinck's book, the nearest I've read about what I now call 'Bluebird Time', is in a book called *'The Children that Time Forgot'* by Peter and Mary Harrison.
According to the Harrison's, when little Daniel Jones of Preston was two and a half years old, he actually recalls waiting to be born ! Little Daniel

loved being in the water. Once, after his first ever visit to the seaside, Daniel had excitedly been splashing about in the sea. While his mother was towelling him dry, he said to her, *'I had to go into the water to get born Mummy. It wasn't the sea though, it was a river.'*

'That's nice dear, where was that ?' said his Mummy.

Daniel answered his mother by saying, *'it was in Heaven, of course. You know Heaven. Where all the little boys and girls live before they get to be born !'*

So Daniel remembers very well when it was his time to be born. He said he was told well in advance how he'd be leaving his little friends for a while, because he had to come to Earth - and his Mummy and Daddy would be there waiting for him. It really seems to me here, that we are on 'Bluebird Time' again !

* * *

We live in an age when Christian teachings are vanishing. Our world is hard to live in and children no longer live in a world of fairy tales. It seems that they become grown up far too quickly. I sometimes feel terrified by this age in which we live, for everything mysterious has to have an explanation, but I guess that's just how it is. Yet even scientists develop an instinct to realise when people are being truthful.

For those of us who are dealing with another dimension, contact with it often brings another state of consciousness. I have been aware of this myself throughout all the wonderful experiences I have had. However, some of these can be very personal matters and hard to describe.

Children are very close to the Spirit and no amount of television and horror stories will change that. There will always be children. I thank God for the animation work of Walt Disney, for at least through his wonderful work, we can all be children again. Of course I'm still waiting for the Disney version of Maurice Maeterlinck's 'The Blue Bird' !

I wonder sometimes if I'm still old fashioned, but as I have said before - today's fairy stories seem to be mostly 'Star Wars' or 'Jurassic Park'. At least Mr. Disney has kept to the fairy tales of Aladdin, Cinderella and Jungle Book ! It pleases me very much when I see our own young ones with whole collections of Disney films - although some still have pictures on their walls of huge dinosaurs. Ugh ! Jurassic Park and all that, but then boys will be boys !

The next chapter is by another mother and friend, Dorothy Wheatley. She has had many Bluebird times of her own, in her priceless story.

Fourteen

What I Think About My Daughter's Death...

by Dorothy Wheatley

It's January 1989 and my deepest inner thoughts tell me that my young daughter Anna Marie, *knew* she was going to die.

A month before her death, she just wrote and wrote - as if there was no time left. It was like watching a person rushing to catch a train. She even asked such things like, *'why were there all these killings and people dying in the Holy Lands'* which at the time there were lots of. In fact Anna Marie would even start to cry. She told me she really and truly believed in life after death. She even said to me, *'there's a lovely place called heaven'* and one day soon, *very soon*, she would go there. She just seemed to know it. She said she felt it deep, deep down inside of her. She also said, she would get a brand new body, but not at all like the one she had then. She told me that she would have no more nasty pain from when her joints locked, for her joints would never, ever lock again.

Anna Marie believed in all this very strongly and deeply, so who was I to doubt her ? I do believe all this as fact now and I even asked her how she knew it. My daughter told me that a nice, kind, gentle person had been to see her in her dreams many, many times and told her.

I asked her who this person was and right away she said,
'it was the Teacher !'
Of course I thought of her class teacher at school Mrs Christie. So I said,
'how nice of Mrs Christie to come and visit you in your dreams.'
Straight away Anna Marie said,
'oh really Mum ! I mean Jesus. He and only he comes to visit me in my dreams. He comes often.'

I must have looked a right idiot - a real fool ! I just sat there, staring at her. It was obvious and plain to see that she knew what she meant. She believed every word she was saying. Bless her! And I believed her too. She took my hand in hers and gave it a gentle squeeze as she said, *'please, please Mum, try to understand it's all for the best.'*

I do feel that these things have true meaning, even at times like this. We may not really understand it all, but perhaps somewhere deep down, we do. Then we wonder why we never ever understood, but at the time we may have been so upset. I am so sure Anna Marie knew what was happening to her. My wonderful, sweet darling daughter.

She and I were *and still are* very, very close. The things she told me then, I hold very close to my heart. At the time, Anna Marie only had a few days left to live - we did not know that then. I am sure she was getting herself ready to leave us. More than once, she told us that if she died before she was twenty-one, she would like to be cremated and not buried. She said she believed it to be a lot cleaner and far more healthier. She wanted no fuss and said that her family and friends should remember her just how she used to be.

When Anna Marie died on December 4th 1988, I was so deeply unhappy and felt so lost without her - as did the rest of the family. Though we all agreed that we did not want her to live, if she was to suffer any more nasty pain. She had gone through such a lot in her short life, yet she had many happy times with us and left us with many wonderful and lovely memories for us to treasure.

'God bless you our darling sweetheart Anna Marie. May God keep you safe in his loving arms until we all meet again and we are united as one whole family once more.'

It was because of her free speech about life here on Earth and life *after* death, that made Anna Marie so popular. She would often talk about heaven and how she would get a brand new body, as soon as she died. I will always remember the determined way she lived her short, but happy life. Her Dad, two brothers John and Simon and me, miss her so very much and always will and for all the memories we are so grateful. I just wish we could have done more for her. She always said that it didn't matter how you came into the world or how you went out of it - but only how you live your life while you're here on Earth. She believed in this so strongly and had a wonderful awareness of the Spiritual life. She once wrote,

'we are all the same to Jesus. We are all very special to Him - our King, Lord, Master, Teacher, Shepherd and Friend. My life has been good to me, so I thank God for this and as the water ripples over the stones, they

remind me of my memories. My life is just like those stepping stones !'

Anna Marie was born on a cold windy day, on December the 29th, 1973. She was born prematurely and was very long and thin, measuring 21 inches long. She had been born with a rare muscle and bone disease called Arthrogryposis, which affected mainly girls. We were told that children with this condition usually died at around two years of age.

Well how wrong they were ! Anna Marie lived into her fifteenth year and was, or is an amazing child. Our daughter passed away in December, 1988.

In her final year on Earth, she cared for a beautiful horse during a holiday in Bridlington. How she enjoyed that week ! She did manage to ride this horse and with a lovely smile she promised, *'Mum and Dad, I'll try my best to win a rosette for you.'*

In fact, Anna Marie won *eight* rosettes and we were so proud of her. We have them at home now in a frame and it's no wonder we look on them with such pride and love.

Anna Marie had been a happy baby, toddler, child and blossoming teenager, yet she was in such pain most days. Her doctors couldn't give her medication, since they felt the drugs could cause her more harm than good. So she just had to grin and bear it. She truly was a brave girl and always full of fun and jokes. Any tears she shed were only ever because of her pain. Most of all she gave us happiness - to us she was LOVE and still is, to all of us. We are so proud of Anna Marie and we miss her so much, but even though we cannot see her, we are fully aware of her presence. She does this by bringing a beautiful floral scent, which cannot be mistaken once it's recognised. This scent always comes with her when she visits.

For six years Anna Marie would dream the same dream. Now I know that this dream was showing her the way of things yet to be. Our daughter also wrote poetry and about her life. We feel that she was wise beyond her years and I realise that all she had learned on Earth, made her so thoughtful.

Anna Marie was not ill on the day of her passing, but she had said how very tired she was. She had taken our dogs, Tina and Gemma, out for their walks and on her return had asked for her favourite pyjamas. She put them on, laid down and simply fell asleep. She was so at peace and with such a lovely smile on her face. She had even chosen her own hymns for her funeral - *'All Things Bright and Beautiful'* and *'Morning Has Broken.'*

I realise now that she knew her body was getting weaker. She'd also told me how she'd be able to help us all *more* after she passed - even more than she could on Earth.

My husband Laurie and I had lost three stillborn babies, had four miscarriages and lost three sets of twins. One set were a boy and a girl who lived one week. We named them Kevin and Lucy. We had also lost a little girl of four years old, named Tracy Jayne. She had died through cancer in her voice box. There was no wonder cure, nothing could be done. The cancer had gone too far.

My husband will still not talk of Tracy Jayne and for me, that's hard. It's as though she never existed, which is a great pity, for I have lovely memories of her. I do believe that one day I'll see all my lovely children again - when I finally go *home* to the Spirit World. Of course, I get very sad at times, but I never give up hope ! I've made lots of friends, including other Mums who have lost children and I tell them that there *are* people out there who understand.

One of these ladies is Gill Smith from Sheffield. She's a member of Gwen Byrne's RPPS club. Gill told me about her son Steven who passed away. *(See Chapter 8)* She'd been to see a a psychic artist named Frankie Brown, who also became an RPPS member. *(See Chapter 23)*
Frankie draws pictures of people that come into her mind. Gwen Byrne had a pile of Frankie's drawings and Gill told me that one of them was a portrait of her son Steven - which was made before she'd even met Gwen.

Gill wrote to me and said that Frankie had drawn a picture of a young girl, who looked very much like my Anna Marie. Frankie gave permission for Gill to send the drawing on to me, because they both agreed there was quite a resemblance to my daughter. Now that I have received it, I *know* the picture is of my Anna Marie. I must state here, that I didn't know anything about Frankie Brown until Gill wrote to me, but this has certainly helped me to understand the loss more. I even received a wonderful evidential poem from Anna Marie, through Frankie, which was given to her via her own son in Spirit, Alan. Perhaps it was all planned !
Frankie also sent us a beautiful sketch of a nun, who's a Spirit helper for my husband Laurie.

Frankie introduced me to Gwen and Alfie Byrne, who have since been really good friends to me. They'd experienced their own sad loss of their son Russell, at the age of only nine and three quarter years.
Then something really wonderful happened to Gwen and Alfie. At a séance with a Medium, their son came into physical view to them - and he did not come empty handed. He brought with him a Pink Panther bendy

toy, then asked his Mother if she would form the RPPS.

I feel very proud belonging to this special friendship club and I call both Gwen and Alfie my very special friends. I'm quite sure that along life's lanes, after our loved ones have passed away, certain friends we meet are meant for us. To me they are special and I give them many thanks for their kindness and for the chance to share Anna Marie's story, to show other parents that they are not alone. I also thank Gill Smith and Frankie Brown from the bottom of my heart, for without them none of this would have been possible.

I know my daughter's life was not in vain, for she lived life to the fullness of her ability and with it, she taught us *Love*.

She'd written this poem for Mothers Day in 1989, although she had passed away before then, so couldn't give it to me herself. I will explain later how we found it...

For Mothers Day and Fathers Day

For all those first years that you both cared for me,
For all the tears that you both shed for me,
For all the hopes that you both had for me,
Most of all, for all the prayers that you both prayed for me,

For all the help that you both gave to me,
For the sacrifices made for me,
For all the examples shown to me,
For all these things and many, many more,
and the debts I cannot ever repay - I send my thanks.

With all my love just for you, my Mum and Dad,
I love you both forever more.

Happy Mother and Fathers Day 1989,
Your Daughter Anna Marie
Lots of Love xx xx xx

* * *

Like a lot of children, when my own Grandmother died, I felt I'd lost my best friend. She was and still is, a wonderful lady.

My parents were unmarried when I was born in 1944 and to be an unmarried mother in those days, was the greatest sin of all. How times have changed ! Years later in 1976, when I gave birth to my last born son Simon, I was very ill. When I arrived home from hospital, I felt so very sick, but kept it quiet. Four days later I was rushed back into hospital. Later, I was told by friends that I'd actually *nearly died* - although over the next six weeks, I began to recover very slowly.

Simon was a lovely baby and a joy to have. This weekend in November I had been at home about four days, when I just fell asleep in my arm chair. I remember clearly, as I was nodding off, that I felt myself floating - as though I was the air itself. Such a wonderful feeling came over me. I remember looking down at my family and I could even see myself, fast asleep in the chair. I saw Anna Marie in her pushchair. I could see my older son John, helping his Dad to knock nails into wood and really enjoying themselves. I could see Simon, my new baby, who was now two months old and fast asleep in his carrycot. I recall feeling really proud of them all - especially since my last three children had been premature. To me, this was such a lovely sight !

For some reason I started to float down a very long tunnel and could see a very lovely, shining bright light. It was very far away at the end, although the tunnel itself was dark. I could also smell lovely flowers, but did not see them. I remember being near to the light, perhaps four feet away from the end of the tunnel, when all of a sudden my Grandmother, my wonderful Nanna, just stepped out in front of me !

I couldn't believe my eyes and just flung my arms around her, then we just clung to each other. I told her how I'd missed her and we both cried together. She looked and sounded just as I remember her. She told me how proud she was to be a great-grandmother and how she loved all the names we had chosen for the children. Then she said something to me that made me stop and stare at her. She told me to go back !

I just couldn't believe my ears and just stared. Looking back now, I realise that what I said next was very silly. I said, *'you don't love me any more Nanna !'*
She gave me a stern look and waved her finger at me as she said,
'Love ? Now you listen here, my girl. I've loved you since the day you were born and I always will - but just now is not the time for you to join me here, not yet anyway.'
She turned me around and pointed a finger at each of my family saying,
'they all need you very much; your boys Simon, John and Anna Marie and husband Laurie. There are things yet to come and you must be there for them.'
By now time I was sobbing my heart out.

I could see my great-grandparents standing behind her and also there was

my beloved Grandfather, who I called '*Poppsie*'. All around there were lots of lovely colours, each one in seven shades of each and nothing like the ones here on Earth. Beyond, I could see lovely gardens and houses and green, green grass everywhere. Even the trees seemed to have a soul of their own. I gave my Nanna a kiss and she felt so warm and safe.
Then she whispered in my ear, *'remember lass, I'll love you always and I am always very near you.'*

Suddenly I was no longer in the tunnel. I was standing at home, looking over at my sleeping body. Looking up I saw Nanna and she blew me a kiss and believe it or not I *felt* it. It was warm and seemed to flow right through to my soul. How she'd missed me all those years. Then I felt I was being drawn back into my body and I felt a pull, like a sudden jerk. Just then, Laurie rushed over to me saying, *'are you ok ? You look very grey.'*
He hugged me and kept asking, *'are you alright ?'*

Once I'd calmed down, I told him everything that had happened. He could see I was not making up a tale and told me that I'd had an O.B.E ! Now I've never forgotten my 'out of body' experience. What I call my *floating* has meant so much to me. It has shown me the nice things that are in store for when I pass over. Although I never spoke about it, I realised it was silly to keep it to myself, when I found there were others who'd had similar experiences.

Later we moved to a three bedroomed council house, since all the children were growing up fast and Anna Marie now needed a bedroom of her own. After a couple of years, my husband Laurie became ill. He began coughing and sneezing so much that he blew three holes in his right lung. He was rushed into York hospital and put onto a life support machine. He was there for two months and when he was well again he needed to learn to speak and write all over again - just like a child. It was so hard for him. Apparently he had also torn his oesophagus, so spent another twelve weeks in another hospital. The nurses all spoilt him. Laurie's throat was so badly damaged he couldn't eat and it took him nine out of the twelve weeks, just to be able to talk again. All the things my Nanna had told me came flooding back, but now every day is a bonus to us.

Laurie and I had met as children at a children's home. As we grew up I discovered that, when they were young girls, both Laurie's mother Alice and my mother Rose, were best friends. My Mum told me that when I was just two days old, her pal Alice came to visit and she brought her little three year old boy with her - Laurie. They came to see *me* the new baby

Dorothy Hannah !
I was really surprised when I learned all this. It seems our marriage was blessed from the day I was born. Laurie had wanted to take me out when I was just fourteen, but because he was seventeen, he needed permission from the 'Mother' of the children's home. Laurie had fallen in love with me at the tender age of fourteen and he still tells me how much he loves me.

We were married on May 11th 1963, over 40 years ago now, yet we are still as in love as we were in the beginning. We have wonderful memories of our lovely white wedding, so many years ago and if ever a couple were meant to meet, we were ! I guess it was all planned.

Anna Marie loved both her brothers, John and Simon, but my youngest child Simon was always there to help her. He kept her smiling and happy and she'd given him the nickname 'Smiley' !
Simon was very close to his sister Anna Marie and I would say they had a very special bond and friendship, so when she passed away, Simon felt it so much. In March 1989, just three months after Anna Marie had passed away, Simon saw his sister. She spoke to him and told him not to be afraid. She said that she is so happy and without pain. She said he should, *'not to be sad. He must be happy,'* because she was near to him. She told him jokes, as she did when she was on Earth and she gave him a kiss on the cheek - which he could feel. Simon believes that the warm air that came with the kiss, was the love that she brought with her.

Laurie and I also know when she is near, because she always brings with her the scent of flowers - and her own special 'flavour' ! Yet Simon *has* seen her and he wasn't dreaming. Anna Marie is still part of our family and we all speak of her daily, although I haven't seen her in the way Simon has, I do live in hope !

Our friend Trisha saw and communicated with Anna Marie too. Trisha told me things that only my daughter and I know about - very personal things. So now I never say, *'how do you know all this ?'* because I know it's Anna Marie.

My Grandfather *'Poppsie'* was given his particular nickname, because he brewed home beer, cider, wines, Dandelion and Burdock and lots of fizzy drinks for the children. All these drinks were home made and the corks would go 'pop' when opened. That's how we christened him Poppsie.
My friend Frankie Brown never knew my Grandad, but she did give me his name. She also gave me a word - the word 'ace.' Now dear Frankie didn't know that 'ace' was a word that my Anna Marie used a lot, but we knew. It

was a word she used to replace the word 'brilliant.' It's the little things that *we* know, that mean such a lot. I do believe in all that the wonderful Frankie Brown tells me, for I know she speaks with our beautiful daughter.

I feel sad for people who *don't* believe and say it's rubbish. Our loved ones *don't* die, they go on living and are *never* far from us. It only takes a thought or two in their direction. I know they help us with our worries and woes, and all the things that those left behind have to endure and face.

After Anna's passing, we asked Simon if he would like her room. Of course his eyes lit up and soon he was moving in. One day, he called me into the room because he'd found something. He had seen a piece of paper between the floorboards which was blowing in the wind, after the front door had been left open. He asked me if it was okay to take it out, because it was annoying him, but as he promptly did so - what a surprise the two of us had ! For even though the paper was blank, it led to us finding what seemed like an Aladdin's Cave under the floorboards - and I know Anna Marie meant us to find it.

We found two lots of monies in a purse. Anna Marie hadn't saved it for herself, but for her brother. There was £95 wrapped in a piece of paper and it was for *his* holiday. This was a special holiday he'd been looking forward to and Anna Marie knew how badly he wanted to go. She also knew that her Dad and I didn't have that sort of money. In a second paper we found £25 towards Simon's spending money. In plain words she clearly *wanted* him to go !

At first we couldn't understand why she hadn't saved up for herself, but I am sure now that she knew she wouldn't be around. There was money left for her Dad too, so that he could take Anna Marie's little Yorkshire Terrier Jemma, for a haircut. This too was wrapped up separately. Each piece of paper was marked - who it was for, and why.

We discovered all of Anna Marie's poems, writings and pictures too, all written and drawn while she was ill. One picture was of the Earth, like a map and she'd drawn a dove flying over it, with a piece of grass in its beak. She had called it 'Peace to the World' and in each corner Anna Marie had drawn lovely blue, yellow and purple Primulas. Anna Marie had always been upset by news on the TV of wars and fighting, so this drawing did not surprise us.

Even as close as she was to her brother Simon, he was not aware that Anna Marie had this special hiding place under the floor. Yet everything was so well wrapped, for she had intended it all to be kept well, so we could all read her lovely writings. In fact, it was a surprise to see how much she *had* written, even though she did spend a lot of time in her room. I believe her writings show just how advanced she was. She had continued to write up to a few days before she passed away, using an old typewriter we'd got for her. This helped her with the pain in her fingers and the type she did in her own fashion.

Anna Marie was a happy child, who was just blooming into a teenager. Though she never had the chance to have a boyfriend, the boys certainly liked her. One time she asked me, *'why do they pinch my bottom ?'* We laughed about this of course, but she *did* have a nice behind and such lovely blue eyes too ! When she was very tired with the pain they would go an even deeper blue, yet on a good day, they would be as bright and blue as the Summer skies.

When Anna Marie died, she was only three weeks off her fifteenth birthday, yet she was so grown up and wise for her age. Oh, I do miss her terribly ! Thankfully, my life here on Earth makes it possible for me to know that I *will* see her again. This is why I do my best to listen to other Mums who have lost a child or dear ones. We all need someone to care and just knowing there are other people out there, can lessen the pain.

My dear friend Gwen has suggested that I include some of Anna Marie's writings in this chapter. There are so many, so I will leave it to Gwen to choose which to include, so I will sign off for now.

A Very Special Person...

I have a very special person,
I know this very special person, who means a lot to me.
His name is Doctor Heggerty.

I write to him as often as I can,
As he is a good and wonderful man,
I agree with Mum, he is worth his weight in gold,
A hundred fold.

He works at York District Hospital,
He comes to see me at my school.
I am so proud he is not just a doctor to me,
But a good and trusted, special friend
to me and my family.

My friend's at school think he is just great,
Of course I agree with them.
I am glad he is there if I need him to help me.

I have a very special person, who means the world to me,
His name is 'Pal' and 'Friend' to me,

But we all know him as my - Doctor Heggerty...
God Bless and keep you safe in His loving care,
Now and always and forever.

~ By Me, Miss Anna Louise Wheatley Age 14
December 3rd 1988.

<u>Very Dear Friend Caroline</u>

As you may know, if you know me, I have lots of really 'ace' friends. I have one who is very, very special to me - it is my Caroline Dale. (My Mum knows I have always wanted a baby sister, but my Mum had her tubes done soon after my baby brother, young Simon, was born - so no way can I have my deepest dream come true, or be fulfilled.)

But in my heart, and deep in my mind, I have a secret, only Jesus knows all about it, as he knows all things.
My secret is that my Caroline is my adopted sister. I love her so very much. Caroline is a very poorly girl and at times can be so ill, that my auntie Val (that's Caroline's Mum) thinks, 'is this it?'
But like me, Jesus knows there is a strong family bond with Caroline and her Mum and Dad. It is this that keeps my sweet Caroline going.

I know I have not got long to live, and I have been told from Jesus I can keep my eye on Caroline. Jesus has told me that my love and my friendship I have for Caroline is so unique.

Jesus says I can help my family and Caroline more after I die, than I could ever mean to, if I was alive. I wish I could explain it all to my dear sweet Caroline, just how I feel without hurting her. (I would not hurt her for the world).
Jesus has told me to write all my feelings down on paper, so in time if my written work is found under my loose bedroom floorboards, (I hope they are found by someone who knows me and my friend Caroline, so they can explain all this to her very gently and kindly, as I did not mean to leave Caroline so soon, but I am now so very, very tired.) I know she will need my help and I will always be there, just for her. I am so very proud that my Caroline is my bestest and really 'ace' friend of mine.

Oh Caroline, I do love you so very much. It does hurt me so to have to leave you. But one day, in the far distance of the future, you will really realise how poorly and so tired I am.
I love you now and always and forever, my dear sweet Caroline.
From your pal, Anna Marie.

~ By Me. Miss Anna Marie Louise Wheatley. Age 14.
***PS:** With Jesus' help I will take care of you.*

Burnholme School

I am now going to an ordinary school, (I go one half day a week) it's to see if I can do the same work that the other children do. (Their lessons, I mean.)
The school where I go is called Burnholme School. Now, I live at Acomb, which is at one end of York, and Burnholme School is at the other far side of York - near to Tang Hall Council Housing Estate. I like the staff (Teachers) here, and the children are not too bad really, but the school itself is far from my family and friends.

I have only one great fear. It is, if I get very poorly, I may not get home in time. I know I have not long to live, so Please, Please, don't ask me why, but I feel it deep...deep down inside of me.

I just know I will never get to my twenty-first birthday. So it means a lot to me to die at home with my family near and round me. So apart from me liking my new lessons at this new school, I feel this ever so much. I am now getting more and more tired every day as I am getting older.

I will be fifteen soon, on December 29th 1988. I am sure my time here on Earth is much nearer to its end than I think. I am so sure my Mum has noticed me getting more and more tired now every day. But she tries her best, her hardest to hide it. But I can see it in her eyes.
I wish I could die without hurting my loving, caring family. My family mean the world to me. I hope I can leave Burnholme School and I can stay fully at my own beloved 'Northfield School.'

I love my own school so very much. All my friends are at my school. I have told my Mum why I want to leave Burnholme School, and she knows my deepest, deep inner fears on how I feel about it. Also, my Mum is coming to my own school - Northfield School, to see my head master Mr Bill Ford, about it all.
My Mum says I needn't stay at Burnholme School if I don't want to. I know my schoolwork is good, but I cannot settle at Burnholme School - my fears are still there at the back of my mind.

~ By Me. Miss Anna Marie Louise Wheatley. Aged 14
November 6th 1988

Teach College on Tadcaster Road, York

I have been going to Teach College on Tadcaster Road York. I am studying office work, and how to answer the phone properly, as there is a right and wrong way to do it. And I am also learning how to keep office files neat and tidy. I am also studying beauty care, on how to look after *myself. I love going there.*

There are girls who go there who really do remember me, when I used to go to Westfield Infants School with them, to their nursery school on Askham Lane.

I am really proud to be able to say I can go to Teach College. I know my Mum and Dad are very happy for me. Their love has made it all possible. I think to be able to go to Teach college makes me feel normal, as I am a handicapped girl.

It makes a lot of difference to me when I get my reports, on my work I have done. I will send a copy to my hospital friend my 'Doctor Heggerty' and he can see how well I have done.

I know I have done my hardest, my best. My Mum and Dad are always pleased with my schoolwork. Mum has always said, 'just do try your best and that's all you can do.' So my best I do.

I am now feeling my tiredness more, I am so sure that my time on Earth is much nearer its end than I think. I will never ever be far from my family when I die, as my family's love is so strong, and that is the real bond.

~ By Me. Miss Anna Marie Louise Wheatley
November 8th 1988

My London Visit

1988 has been a really full year for me. If I could live it again, I would. Nothing would I change, it has all meant so much to me.

There is one place in the whole of England I would love to visit - mainly because of its history (I love history) - and that is London.
So when the York Borough 'Round Table' people, asked my Mum if Simon and I could go with them on a mini weekend visit to London, I was overjoyed when she said yes, we could go.

I saw lots of lovely and different places. London is such a big town, much bigger than my own hometown of little York. We stayed at a posh hotel. The food there was just great, lots to eat. We saw Andy Crane from the London BBC children's TV. He came over to me and had a few words with me. I also saw Anneka Rice, she let me put my hand on her tummy to feel her baby kick out at me. It was a lovely feeling knowing there was a little person growing inside her tummy.

I still think that a baby is the most wonderful and best thing that a man and woman can make. Even if, like me, the baby is not perfect, it is still wonderful and lovely - also a very special little person in the eyes of Jesus.

I also saw Spike Milligan. He told me a joke and made me laugh. He also told me, back in the 1960s he was known as one of the Goons. It was a show on the radio, called The Goon Show.

We saw lots of very interesting buildings - and what history! I saw Buckingham Palace and The Houses of Parliament. Yes indeed, London is such a wonderful City. It has such a lot of History. History is like a large book - on opening it we find a family tree of History (or so it seems to me.)

In London there are lots of cars and many, many people rushing everywhere. Even my young brother Simon really enjoyed himself. We went down Carnaby Street, and Petticoat Lane, and Portabello Road. We even saw the house where Sherlock Holmes used to live and the road and street where the TV series came from in Upstairs and Downstairs, called Eaton Place.

I asked Andy Crane to write to me, and he did. He even sent me a photo of himself signed to me, Anna Marie. When I got back I asked my Mum, I said 'I'd love Andy Crane to send a photo of himself to each of my school friends (about 10 of them) signed to each of them, in their own names.' So my Mum said, 'why not write back and ask him?' (as my Mum knows I like writing).

I will be glad to but just now I feel ever so tired, I also feel I must rest a while first. As soon as I've rested I'll write to Andy Crane.

I really did enjoy my visit to London - it was great, really Ace. God Bless You Doctor Heggerty, my Dear Friend.

~ *By Me. Miss Anna Marie Louise Wheatley.*
November 28th 1988

Anna Marie's last wish, was that Andy Crane should send all of her school friends a signed photo. This wish was carried out after her Mum, Dorothy, wrote to him and told him of Anna Marie's wish.

The Rainbow
(and what I think, as it means a lot to me.)

What the Rainbow means to me,
as I see all the colours smiling down on little old me.
Oh, what lovely colours they mean a lot to me.
It is as if our dear Lord is saying,
'Look dear souls, on Earth down there'
This lovely Rainbow is what you'll all always see

when you all come home to me.
I know in my heart, and deep in my mind,
I believe when I die and My Lord I see,
He'll be so proud of me.

This is what the Rainbow colours mean to me.
These are the lovely colours Pink, Blue, Mauve,
Purple, Yellow, Orange and Green.

Pink is the colour of LOVE,
as it has always been since time began.

Blue is the colour of life,
as it surrounds and keeps the baby safe
in it's mother's womb.

Orange is the colour of deep happiness
within the family circle, or so it means to me.

Mauve is the colour of sleep,
and many, many dreams, that is what it means to me.

Yellow is the colour of peace
for all the children everywhere.
(It is the light of the yellow of deep dew,
that we children choose to follow
when we come home to you, our Heavenly King,
which we follow at our passing over.)

Green means to me, fresh veg, growing flowers,
trees, grass, it means life in all it's living glory
that is what it means to me.

Purple is the royal of all the colours,
it is fit for Kings and Queens.
(Who but our dear Lord should wear this colour,
the colour of many, many Kings?)

This is what the Rainbow colours mean to me,
as it is sent from The Heavenly Father,
for all of us to see.

I like to think when I see the Rainbow,
it is smiling down on me.

This is what the Rainbow means to little old ME.

~ By Me. Miss Anna Marie Louise Wheatley. Age 14
November 3rd 1988

November 1988

My feelings run deep and true for my Mum and Dad. As I am writing all this down, November 1988 is drawing to an end. This year has really been a full and wonderful year for me. Things I have done, seen, and places I have visited. I can honestly say I have got to my goal. All this I have done with the help of my loving caring family.

My Mum and Dad have let me do these things. They have never, ever tried to stop me and to them, I'll always be forever grateful for the deep love and understanding.

Even my own family doctor has always supported me, in everything I have done. And not forgetting the most important person my dear and loyal friend, wonderful, faithful friend Doctor Heggarty. (Anna Marie's Specialist)

In just a few words I love you all deeply. God bless you all, always and keep you safe in His loving care.

The Dream - December 1st 1988

I keep having the same dream now, over and over again. It's about a nice kind and gentle person. I say 'person' as I am not sure if it is a lady or a man. This nice, kind, gently person, comes to me as soon as I am fast asleep. I am asked 'do I feel tired?' 'How do I really feel?'
I never, ever feel tired when this person is near me - in fact all my tiredness goes away when this person is near me. Then I was asked, 'would I take this person's hand, and go with them?'

For some reason, I don't know what, but I said I could not leave my Mum and Dad just yet. The next time I had this dream, I asked,
'Who are you, and what is your name?' The person did answer me, 'Well, Anna Marie, my pet lamb, I am the Teacher.'

He said his name was Jesus, and I believe it was. I was pleased and felt very proud that Jesus had come to visit little old me.

I must say it again...I just felt ever so proud that Jesus had visited me. I told Him I did not think I was that special. He said 'all people are very special' to Him. Jesus has told me, He knows I love my family very much and that is why he has let me stay with them. He also knows I am much more tired than I have ever been before. He knows about the joints locking and the nasty pain. He said I have been brave and he was very proud of me. I felt ever so warm and wonderful, deep, deep down inside of me.

He knew all about my one, great fear in the back of my mind - what if I die in some strange place ? What then ? He told me that would never ever happen.

He would make sure I would die with my Mum and Dad right beside me. He also told me that my Mum and Dad were very special people and that is why he chose them for me to be my parents. I asked him 'why do I feel ever so wonderful' when He is near me ? He said, 'that is how it should be' as He takes all known fears away. I asked Jesus 'is it silly of me to keep asking of Him WHY all the time ?

Why this and why that ? I asked why I know I am going to die ? Why is it that I know deep down, inside my heart I will be happy to die...yet, I don't want to hurt my loving, caring family ? Jesus said it was because my Mum has always told me never to be afraid of the 'time.'

Anna Marie told her mother all these things, who said to her, *'why do you have to go ?'*

She said, *'because now I am feeling ever so tired and I know deep down inside I want to go.'*

Her Mum said, *'then you must go with mine and your Dad's blessing.'*

Anna Marie said, *I could see the hurt in my Mum's eyes.*

I know now what Jesus meant when he said, my Mum and Dad are special people. Indeed they truly are. I am so proud of them. I love my family very, very much. I know that Jesus knows this, and family love is a deep thing. Yes, indeed I love you all my loving caring family... Thanks for being there.

This is the last written work I have done, as I am much more tired now.

Earlier in Anna Marie's writings, she had written, *'it is not how you come into this world, or how you go out of this world, it does matter how you live your life on Earth. That was what Jesus was interested in.'*

However, Anna Marie who had written very perceptibly about her school friends, wrote about her *'very close'* friend Caroline - who she described *'more like a sister'* and *'who meant the world to her.'*
Here again, is part of what she said on December 3rd 1988.

'I wish I could explain to my dear friend Caroline, how I really feel without hurting her. Jesus told me to write my feelings down. So in time, if my written work is found, I hope it is found by someone who knows me and Caroline - so that they can really explain to her. I did not mean to leave Caroline so soon, but I was so very, very tired.

I know I won't be far from Caroline. I know she will need my help even more and I will always be there. I am so proud that Caroline is and always will be, my 'bestest' and 'Ace' friend.
Oh, Caroline, I do love you so very much. It really hurts me to leave you so soon, but one day in the far distant future, you will really realise how poorly and deeply tired I am.
Love you always...
P.S. With Jesus' help, I will take great care of you.

The very last words Anna Marie wrote were,
'... Jesus has told me, my love and friendship for Caroline is unique. He says, I can help my family and Caroline more after I die, than I could ever mean to do if I was alive.'

Anna Marie Louise Wheatley died the next day, on December 4th 1988 in her own bed, with her family around her as she had wished...

Anna Marie Wheatley
with her rosettes - July 1988

My Memorial

    I would like to dedicate my story and these poems of Anna Marie's, to my beautiful son of 27 years, John Matthew Wheatley. John was born on January 15th 1972 and died on September 23rd 1999, when he joined his beloved sister and all my other children in Spirit.

    John was killed under the wheels of his own lorry. At the time it seems it was a tragic accident. He was a courier. Often he would take his best pal Ian, for company. He was crushed by his own beloved lorry. He was known to other truckers by the nickname 'Azwad' on his C.B. Radio - both here in York, as well as on other runs. He has left behind two beautiful children - Danielle who is six years old, and her elder brother Liam. He adored his children, they were his life.

Now he has gone. I so strongly know that there is a 'Life After Death.' I have one son left now on Earth - Simon. All my other children are together in Spirit. I do thank God for that knowledge, but I miss them all so much. John was the last to go. So goodbye for now, sweet son !

    I finish here with two poems by John's ex-partner, Dawn Lamb, mother of John's children Danielle and Liam...

Life's Not That Bad

When I'm really down and feeling very sad,
I look at what I've got and say,
life's not that bad.

I've got a son Liam - our lovely little lad,
He helps me see that life's not that bad.

Danielle is our daughter and looks just like her Dad,
And she's another reason my life's not that bad.

I've got my friends and family,
Sometimes they drive me mad,
But look at what I've got compared to some,
My life's not that bad.

So when you're really down and feeling
Oh so sad,
Just look at what you've got.

Just thank God and say,
Life's not that bad.

~ Dawn Lamb

From the Heart

*Oh John, I just don't know where to start,
The hole you've left, is deep in my heart.*

*I don't know what to say
or even what to do.
All I know is -
in my heart you will always stay.*

*Now as a father you were the best,
And you John, outshine all the rest,*

*I know I never said before,
that I really do love you.
I only hope that this, you always knew.*

*Stubborn pride, stopped me from telling you,
But you know me, that's nothing new.*

*Now all that's left for me to say,
is that I'll really miss you every day.*

*Most of this I never knew,
Until the day I lost you.*

~ Dawn Lamb

Russell Vernon Byrne

Gwen Byrne

Gwen & Alfie Byrne
Taken for Woman's Own Magazine

The 'son' has got his hat on !

The mysterious Egyptian named Raymar

Stuart Borley & Tony Stockwell
In Egypt with their *Russell* book

Toy Pink Panther
as was apported by Russell

Raymond Lodge
WWI Soldier & Russell's friend

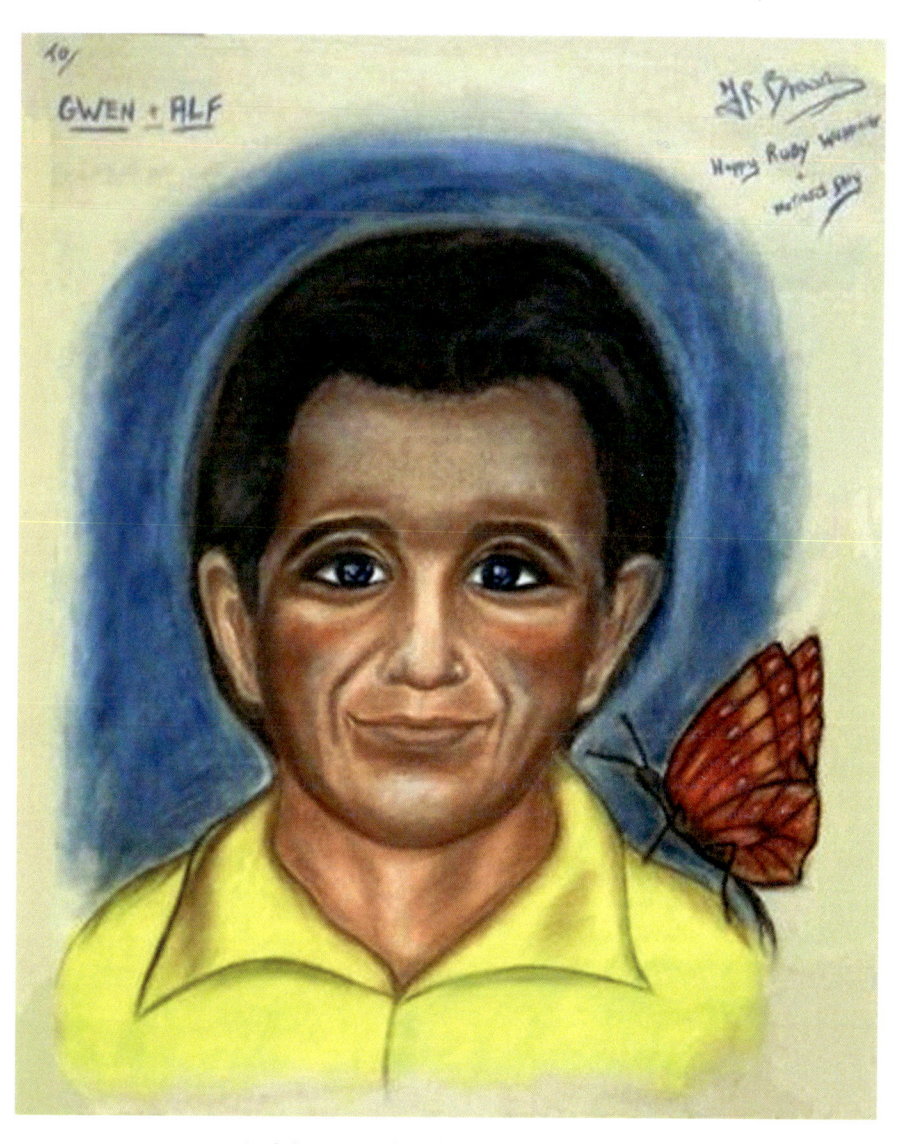

Spirit Portrait of an older Russell
painted by Frankie Brown

Farewell To A Little Boy...

"Darling...there'll be a hoop with hills to roll it down,
God wouldn't give a little boy, the burden of a crown,

He'll show you lots of trees to climb
and where he keeps the swings.

~ God, let him have a bat & ball, instead of shining wings ~

And will he let you fly a kite up where the sky is clear,
'without tall buildings stooping down?'
Of course he will my dear!

Now close your eyes and I'll kiss them shut,
The way I always do,
I must...I must not cry dear God,
Until he's safe with you..."

~ Anonymous

Fifteen

I'm Nine & Three Quarters, So There !

February 1993

'When did he grow to be so tall ?
Wasn't it yesterday when love was all ?'

~ variation of lyrics by Sheldon Harnick
from 'Fiddler on the Roof'

Now we are reading of Russell the *man* and I have to say that I'm totally amazed by his wisdom ! I can reminisce on the hundreds of times we used to talk with him so intimately, at the Physical Phenomena séances.

I came across a cassette recording of one of these séances from February 1983. A young reporter named Alan Cleaver had come from the Psychic News newspaper to 'interview' Russell, after he managed to get himself featured in the newspaper. The circumstances at the time decreed that the interview must never be used - I don't know why, but on listening to it once more, I thought it would be nice to share with readers - especially as we are now hearing from Russell the man.
'From Boy to Man' - so to speak !

At the time the recording took place, I must have been to roughly sixty-five séances and had seen them develop from trumpet phenomena to Direct Voice and later on to Independent Voice - to say nothing of the wonders of materialisation that came later ! At the time Russell was the clown of the communicators. During the evening séance that this particular recording was made, the sitter's laughter almost drowned out the voices of Spirit - which made it a bit of a problem for me to transcribe. However, not only was he very, very funny back then - but it was clear that he was learning a lot or *had* learned a lot.
Of course, he was acting the age of nine and three quarters, but in reality

he was roughly thirty years old. Listening to it now I find it very amusing and interesting, but we do hear him channelling real knowledge and wisdom. Somehow I can listen to him being nine again, without a trace of sadness. Well, *sometimes* - depending on my mood - but when I listen to my recordings of the 'man' Russell Byrne, at times he says things that 'ring a bell' even now.

It can be so difficult to write out humour, especially because readers can't hear the silly noises Russell makes or appreciate the other Spirit communicators who are laughing too. It's more tricky to write, but here goes anyway...

It's early February 1983 and a freezing Saturday evening. I'd been staying for a week at the home of Rita Goold the Medium and witnessed many wonderful happenings. I'd travelled by car to the séance venue together with Rita and Alan, the Psychic News reporter.

The séance began and within a short time Rita was in Trance and with the music quietly playing in the background - instantly he's there !

Russell: *'Hello Alan. I've got my best suit on Alan, you'd like it !'*

Alan: *'Hello Russell, I've got here at last !'*

Russell: *'As long as I'm here there's nothing to worry about, is there ?'*

Here we hear loud thudding noises in the middle of the room.

Alan: *'What are you doing there Russell ?'*

Russell: *'I'm riding a bicycle ! Just let me get off this bike ! Oops ! Right I'm here, sitting on my little chair. I'm here to answer any questions that the world wants to speak to me about...'*

Alan: *'How old are you ?'*

Russell: *'I'm nine and three quarters I think tonight. I might be, and I might not be !'*

Alan: *'What decides whether you are, or you are not ?'*

Russell: *'I decide how old I want to be !'*

Alan: *'You're really older than that, aren't you ?'*

Russell: *'Yes, I can be any age I want to be.'*

Alan: *'What do you do all day ?'*

Russell: *'I've got three occupations; I'm a time and motion studier !'*

Alan: *'How can you be a time and motion studier, when you are over there ?'*

Russell: *'Well I have to set things in motion and I've got plenty of time - but sometimes I'm a trumpet player !'*

Alan: *'Ha ha, I see. Can you see in the dark ?'*

Russell: *'It's not dark to us - that's why I'm a lighthouse keeper too. I can see you Alan. I've got a very important occ-u-pation...I'm master of all and Jack of none !*

Alan: *'Ah, I see. But you've got another title haven't you ? You're the chairman of the RPPS.'*

Russell: *'Right ! I'm the Top One. If you can see us and talk to us, you get the title bestowed upon you, the 'RPPS' - Russell's Pink Panther Society !'*

Alan: *'Where do you live Russell ?'*

Russell: *'Sometimes I live here - sometimes I live there. Sometimes I'm everywhere ! I can go anywhere I want. For me it's easy !'*

Alan: *'When you're not there, where do you go ?'*

Russell: *'Well I must be somewhere ? Well, I'm in my life and I can carry on like you do. What do you do when you're not here ? You go and see your brother and your dog, and you go and see my Mum and Dad. Then you go back to work - all kinds of things. Well I do all kinds of things too - see ? My world's as real as yours. I don't have to worry about clothes and things, but I've got a body.'*

Alan: *'Well people might find that hard to understand. I mean to use the expression 'your dead' and...how can you have a body ?'*

Russell: *'My other body's dead - like the chrysalis and the butterfly, you see Alan ? In your world there's things...two things inside one. You've got butterflies inside a shell, like a grub - a nasty little thing, it crawls about - it's alive - and one day it stops and probably has a little sit down and it has a think...and all of a sudden it drops down and it goes POP - and out comes a bea-u-tiful butterfly - and it hasn't got it's old body. The other one's gone to dust - the grub, I mean. That's two lives in one, but its brain is still the same. Its mind is still the same, that's a butterfly.*

Alan: *'Well, I rather like the analogy that you were a grubby little thing crawling about and now you're a beautiful butterfly !'*

Russell: *'Yes, well ! That's right, but I'm not a butterfly. But we've got perfect minds and we've got perfect bodies ! Nothing can harm us. That's right, nothing can harm us. Somebody could harm my mind, but not much. Do you understand ?'*

Alan: *'Can you explain a bit more...?'*

Russell: *'Yes ! You've got a body and a mind that could get harmed in some way, yes ? But we can't get harmed, because we know what we are doing. We are quicker, we think quicker.'*

Alan: *'Right Russell. You've got a body. Do you breathe, like we do in air ?'*

Russell: *'Yes we can walk about and we breathe - sort of. We're not a 'see through' until we come back here. It doesn't hurt and we can change a little bit.'*

Alan: *'What do you mean Russell ?'*

Russell: *'Well you can reflect back and reflect on memories of when you were a little boy.'*

Alan: *'Mmm...yes.'*

Russell: *'Yes and you become that little boy in your thoughts and your body. Well we can do it here - what we used to do, but you can only do it in your mind. Well we can do it and be it ! It's the power of the mind. We can do things...wonderful. We can't change into a frog, but we've got to be what we was. You have a lot of bodies really. You can see a lot of old photo's of yourself and say 'Cor, that's not me' - but it was you. If you saw yourself on TV you'd say 'is that me ?' But it is you ! Three people in one. People don't know the cap-a-bilities (oh, I can't say that word) of their own minds ! Right ?*
Next question Alan !

Alan: *'Mmm...can you be an old man, Russell ?'*

Russell: *'No I can't do that. I can only be what I've been. Sometimes, if you've not been very good, do you understand ? If I'd been about twenty-five, then I'd have to stay about twenty-five, so that everybody would recognise me and everyone would know that I was the person that did the bad thing, until I said I'm sorry. But it's complicated really for you, do you understand ? I have to come back as me, to help people, as me. Right ?*
Next question...

Alan: *'About your world - are there buildings ?'*

Russell: *'It's a very large world, I've not been everywhere, I don't know it all. It's got lots of beautiful places, beautiful water and beautiful flowers. Flowers don't die. Every flower that's died in your world, is in our world and every tree that's been in your world, is in our world. Every living thing that's been alive, that has the Life Force, doesn't die. Mmm...Oh, now you are going to ask me about prehistoric monsters !'*

Alan: *'Well I don't know.'*

Russell: *'Everything that's got a love of beauty, is reborn.'*

Alan: *'Good question ! In our world I see prehistoric monsters of a former life, are not prehistoric monsters in this life. I see.'*

Russell: *'No you don't....I can't explain that. I don't mean we've got prehistoric monsters running around here. People evolve - right ?'*

Alan: *'Where is your world ? People here tend to think of it as 'up there' to us, the Earth - around the stars, galaxies...'*

Russell: *'If you look down from an aeroplane and you see the size of things, right...yourself - you're nothing ! I'll explain to you...*
The Universe is a bit like you, only in our plane. What I'm saying is, you look at Time and Space and the depths - everything's a different world. You <u>see</u> space - anything that you can see, you can reach, sometimes. Right ? You can't put your arm up and reach the moon, but you <u>could</u> reach it, man is doing it ! So everything you can see, doesn't reach heaven - our world. If you went into a space ship, you wouldn't reach us. No. But if you put your hand out one day, you would put it through our world'.

Alan: *'Mmm...you sure ?'*

Russell: *'I don't know ! I don't know ! It's difficult for me, 'cause I woke up here. You can't come back...come and visit us, unless you're asleep, right ? Some people never do. Sometimes they dream and they don't remember. But <u>we</u> can come to you in your dreams, rather than you come to us. You visit us - meeting for a while. Right ?*
Next question !'

Alan: *'Yes ! On the train on the way here, I got talking to someone about death - people are scared of death.'*

Russell: *'Yes, but some people are scared to go to Australia !*
My advice is don't be frightened. But 'cause they don't know, they have to take my word for it. I could say, 'don't be scared, I'll catch you, trust me.' Take my word for it. Otherwise you wouldn't jump. You won't die, you carry on and someone else meets you. Yes ! It's not knowing where you are going that's difficult, 'cause it's one thing you can't practice. There's nothing to be afraid about. I'm still Russell and I'm here ! I've got brothers and sisters - shall I tell you about my family ?'

Alan: *'Yes, that would be nice !'*

Russell: *'There's Kev, my brother and Gary, my brother. Gary's got a married lady named Sharon. Oh, they <u>are</u> married - just a while. And*

Kev's got a wife called Chris and they've got two little boys named Graeme and Jon.

Alan: *'Oh, then you're an Uncle, Russell?'*

Russell: *'Yes and you can laugh all of you! Do you know what Graeme says to Jon?'*

Alan: *'Yes, tell me?'*

Russell: *'Graeme says Jon's a pain in the bum!*
Oh, you all look so serious! My Mum's here tonight and she's sitting there biting her lip and saying, 'Oh dear!''

Gwen: *'I'm listening Russell, I'm taking it all in...'*

Russell: *'Right, I'll sing my Mum a song now,*
'she loves me, yeah, yeah,yeah, I love her, yeah, yeah, yeah...'
That's why she's here!'

Then we heard some whispering between Alan and Russell about a particular black box. I will explain at the end of this chapter about that, at least the knowledge I have of it.

Russell: *'Any more questions? I'm the one and only Russell Vernon Byrne as Raymond says 'Touché!'*
Mum, I know the Pink Panther's sitting at home with a big sock on his head! I'll never forget that night when I brought him, shall I take him back?'

Gwen: *'No, no, Russell. He's mine!'*

Russell: *'Well all right then. Mum, I'll never forget when Dad put the cats out! Well I should say threw them out, but that's not nice! It don't sound right. My Dad wouldn't hurt them, but the kitchen was such a mess! I've got a confession to make to the world. It was me!*
I stood in the middle of the kitchen and Dillon, the cat, saw me and leapt into the air and the telephone went flying! They both, Snowy __and__ Dillon, saw me!
Right, time for a break everybody...

* * *

As the séance begins again, we hear the very beautiful Spirit voice of Laura, soaring up so beautifully with *'On the Street Where You Live.'* As this wondrous voice finishes singing, another Spirit communicator, the Medium Helen Duncan, begins to speak before Russell comes in...

Helen: *'Hello it's Helen Duncan speaking...it's not 'Hands Across the Sea' Gwen, it's 'hands across time' and we've made it ! Charlie* [one of the sitters] *once said, they're more intelligent than me...well he's an intelligent fellow for making a statement like that !'*

Russell: *'I'm back. I'm at the ready ! Hello Alan Cleaver. I've got another friend Alan Crossley as well. I've got lots of friends. Any more questions ?*

Alan: *'Well,* [my friend] *Lesley has given me about a million questions to ask you.'*

Russell: *'Well she's intelligent, isn't she ? Even if she has got a funny face, big ears, big feet and a funny little turned up nose ! Oh, I've not to say that...but she's nice, ever so nice. That's for the tape - to make her laugh !*

Alan: *'Well, she wants me to ask you whether, in the Spirit World if you might meet up with a young lady and get married ?'*

Russell: *'Well we don't get married, because a marriage is something you make in your world.'*

Alan: *'I was...'*

Russell: [Interrupting] *'Yes, I know you are going to say 'marriages are made in heaven.' He's more intelligent than me ! But it's something you've got to work it, through everything, 'cause marriages aren't made in heaven. You find what you want by looking for it and sometimes you find them, but you can't have them ! Well anyway, that's the question you asked ! But in my world we don't go around saying, 'Oh well, I must get married, I must find someone.' People get pressurised into getting married, but some people find someone they like. For us, when we find people we like, we can be together all the time if we want. We don't have to sign a piece of paper - but we can still find someone and love them.'*

Alan: *'If someone gets married twice, and then one goes to Spirit - is the first and second one waiting for them, when they go to the Spirit World ?'*

Russell: *'Not always. Depends on who you love the most. Sometimes you find the people that marry again, don't love the person quite as much as they thought they did. Some never bother with any one else 'cause if you really, really love someone - then you don't want anyone else...'*

Alan: *'When people are born in our world, are they born in your world first ?'*

Russell: *'I can't answer that, it's beyond our control. It's nothing to do with us. I can't give you a baby - do you know what I mean ? That's something else. We're just a bit ahead of you - that comes...I don't know, I can't answer that !'*

Alan: *'Lesley wants to know - are babies born in the Spirit World ?'*

Russell: *'No ! We don't have babies born in the Spirit World. We <u>can</u> get younger. Oh, tut, tut - babies are not born here ! I don't have babies. If Rita [our Medium] was with us and she'd never had any babies, she couldn't just lie down and have a baby ! But if she really, really loves babies, she could look after them over here. But I think she might have had enough with two ! Perhaps I shouldn't have said that ?*
Barry [another sitter] have you got a question ?

Barry: *'Well Russell, I wondered if there was anything that you didn't like, anything that upsets you ?*

Russell: *'Well we don't get upset like you do. We don't worry the way you do. When you're sad or upset we stay at the side of you and say 'oh don't be like that'...and try to help. We try and change your minds by loving you.'*

Barry: *'You mean you try to impress our minds ?'*

Russell: *'Yes ! We try to keep you loving...I do worry about people who are cruel to people and hurt them and make them sad. We don't like anyone being unhappy. Though if you cry 'cause you laugh - we love it ! But if we could wipe away the tears for you, we would. We know that sometimes you have to be sad or happy, but we like to be part of your life and help in every way. But some people never get out of their sadness. We don't like that, and we can't always help them then.'*

Barry: *'It's nice to know that children who pass when they're very, very tiny are looked after.'*

Russell: *'Course they are ! We don't have them rolling about the streets Barry ! When babies are tiny, you should know that someones looking after them. One minute your bending over their cot and saying cooee...then the next minute they come to us and then <u>we're</u> bending over the cot. They don't know any different. They are so boo-tiful !'*

Alan: *'Are you allowed to go where you like ?'*

Russell: *'Up to a point.'*

Alan: *'Which point ? Where can't you go ? Can you go to the bottom of the sea ?'*

Russell: *'No ! No ! There are divers. There's no point in going to the bottom of the sea is there ? No I don't want to go down there. It's dark and murky. I don't have to go to dark places. Some people do. They've got a problem. They have to go to places that are not nice. I don't go to houses* that I don't like. I don't say bad things. Some people do. It's not my job.'

Alan: 'Do you eat over there?'

Russell: 'I did at first when I came, I wanted to. I don't want to now. Now I've seen my Mum and Dad and my brothers, I feel all full and nice and I don't want to eat!'

Alan: 'You don't have to eat? I expect Rita would want a cigarette! But only for a time, after a while she wouldn't.'

Russell: 'Well, say if you were crippled and someone says, 'get up and walk' - you'd say, 'no I can't.' But you can suddenly, say, take a step - that's all. Gently does it. Then they know they can!'

Alan: 'Do you realise you're dead?'

Russell: 'Everybody doesn't - it's quite a nice feeling. A nice lady told me I was dead and I was able to walk and not be ill.'

Alan: 'Do you feel frustrated when you can't make us see you?'

Russell: 'No - a bit sad, but it's quite natural really Alan...'

Now Laura's Spirit voice is heard once again singing, *'On The Street Where You Live'* from the musical *'My Fair Lady'* - with original lyrics by Alan Jay Lerner, although once more, the words are changed to suit the occasion:

'...just to be in the room where you are.
And, oh, that towering feeling,
just to know, somehow you are here,
the overpowering feeling,
that any second we might suddenly appear!

People came and stared,
they don't bother us.
For there's nowhere else on Earth
that we would rather be.
Let the time go by
we don't care if I,
can be here in this room where you are.
Just to be in this room where you are.'

Russell: 'Don't forget the best reporter in the world is listening folks! Well we've got to get on with the proceedings, alright? Just a minute, our [Spirit] *friend Walter is going to play his music on the xylophone!'*

On the cassette we hear, *'Younger than Springtime'* by Rogers & Hammerstein, then our lovely Spirit musician Walter is playing a toy xylophone along to the music ! We're sitting and listening, enjoying every note. It's all so lovely, we are struck dumb when Helen Duncan comes in asking, *'do you have any questions ?'*

Helen: *'Well it's going to be a chatty evening then ! So I better sing then, but I haven't got such a golden voice as somebody else I know. So you'll have to put up with me !'*

Barry: *'I've got a question for you Helen. Is it true that Clairvoyance and Clairaudience go together ? I mean, can you comment ?'*

Helen: *'Yes, well people get so confused. They call everybody a Clairvoyant, which is just to 'see.' I think somebody like Doris Stokes is not Clairvoyant at all. She hears down her ears, but she doesn't 'see' - do you understand ? It doesn't matter, because if you've got a contact with us it's wonderful. So if your radio's tuned in, you can carry on the good work and can improve with practice !'*

Barry: *'Are these Mediumistic gifts hereditary ?'*

Helen: *'No not really, but if you've got a Mother or a Grandmother that's a Medium, then you're more aware and you can give more time to it. You work at it and sit in circle...*

Now, we're going try something special. Don't get worried...turn up the music a wee bit...'

Then we hear Russell go to Rita, our Medium who is in deep Trance...

Russell: *'I'm just going over to Rita. Don't get worried.'*
'Hello Reet, wake up. Wakey, wakey. One of your best friends is here waking you up ! It's Russell Vernon Byrne, your bestest ever friend. I'm here Reet. Wakey, wakey..!'

Rita is coming out of Trance now and speaks...

Rita: *'Oh ! He's touching me ! Oh, I don't believe this, it's amazing !'*

Then along with Mario Lanza on the tape, Russell sings, *'Do you wonder why I love you so, do you wonder why I'm here at all. It's because I love you so...it's because it has to be...'*

Rita: *'Oh my God it's Russell !'*

Russell: *'Silly thing. It's me, it's good isn't it ?'*

I think 'good' was a bit of an understatement ! Rita, our Medium was now wide awake and actually having a chat with Russell !

Earlier I spoke of a particular black box, well Alan our young newspaper reporter had made a special box for an experiment. It was made of glass and plastic, then super-glued together. We stood it on a table in the corner of the séance room, placing a seven inch toy Pink Panther on top of it. Alan told us that inside the sealed box he'd placed a toy mouse. I guess he was hoping that Russell would wave his magic wand - and with a bit of the old 'abracadabra' - just take the mouse out ! Well, during the séance this black box vanished and with it, the toy Pink Panther too ! All Russell could say was, *'it's in my big fridge in the sky, Mum'*.

Of course someone asked him where the Pink Panther toy had gone and he said, *'oh I've got him, don't worry !'* I never saw the box again, but there is more to the story...

Later in 1983 our Medium Rita, came to visit my son Kevin and his wife Chris for a couple of days. When a séance was suggested we were all delighted of course.

Kevin's house has high ceilings, which we knew would be great for our lovely Spirit friends, the singer Laura and our friend Walter - who played the xylophone. Walter could also make a pair of drumsticks do such wonderful things and he could whistle in such a superb manner, to any song that was played. He was a true musical magician if ever I heard one !

So that evening we prepared for the séance. Now Kevin had a friend staying that night, who I will call A-. We asked him if he wanted to stay for the séance and he said a very firm *'Yes'* which really surprised me, since he was a very orthodox man in the ways of religion. Anyway, I felt a little apprehensive to say the least.

During the séance A- was sitting next to me on the sofa, then as the music played, Rita went into a deep Trance. The drumsticks, which were tipped with luminous paint, were quite a sight as they began to dance way up - almost *on* the high ceiling. To our newcomer it was much more than that ! Then we heard Russell speak, in Direct Voice,

'Hello A- I've got a present for you !'

and onto the table dropped the missing seven inch, toy Pink Panther !

By now I could literally feel A-'s heart beating. I knew he was petrified as he stared up at the drumsticks, probably with his mouth wide open. His arm hung on to me in apparent distress. Yet it wasn't only to me that this was apparent. One of the Spirit communicators suddenly said,

'Stop the séance ! Wait now and we'll bring the Medium out of Trance.'

And they did ! When the light was switched back on, A-'s face was ashen. He just went straight into the kitchen to eat something, so I suspect his pride was hurt, though nothing was said by any of us.

That night we all prepared for bed, somewhat disappointed and subdued - but here's the rub, I had picked up the Pink Panther toy and put it in my pocket. A- was still looking somewhat 'mind-blown' but was not going to admit it, naturally. Was it pride - or fear ? Since he was staying the night, he had a sleeping bag to sleep on the sofa - in the very room we'd tried to hold the séance. Now I knew he would never sleep in that room, so I said, *'I'll sleep down here. You go and sleep in my bed upstairs.'*

To which he gratefully did and the subject was never mentioned again.

But as I snuggled down for the night in the sleeping bag, guess what I found as my bed mate ? It was the little Pink Panther toy that I'd placed in my pocket ! I have him still and he now hangs in my car.

As for the black box, well years later we were visiting Rita in her new home, when she told us that it had reappeared there - in her garage of all places ! Lord knows why it had landed there, but we never had a further explanation and that was that !

Whilst visiting Rita that time we sat for a séance. There were only three of us and Rita. She had moved into a new home which had a large and beautiful garden and after wandering around admiring it, we enjoyed a superb meal Rita had made for us - then sat for the séance.

This particular evening wasn't recorded unfortunately, but a very interesting happening occurred. Roughly half way through the proceedings there seemed to be a lot of chat coming through. We could hear at least four different Spirit voices and they were all talking at once. It seemed that one of the voices, a man, was being quite difficult and the other Spirit communicators were trying to pacify him. We heard him shout out,
'It's my house. Who are these people ? Who does this b--- child belong to ?'

We sat quietly and realised that something was 'up' so to speak. Then we heard Helen, who was one of the other communicators say,
'Now ! The people in this room, are here for a séance.'

The man's voice replied,
'what's that ?'

By now the man was quieter and said,
'but it's my house, my room.'

'It was !' said Helen. *'But you are now in Spirit. In other words, you are what they call 'dead' !'*

Now the man seemed aghast. Then Helen said,
'Russell, go and explain to your Mum and Dad.'

Which of course he did, although we'd already got the gist of what was happening. Russell was whispering to us when Helen said to the man, *'Now if you will be quiet, you can speak to these nice people.'*

We spoke to the man very gently and explained his situation to him and that fact that he didn't *live* here any more. He told us that his name was Mr Snow, then for the next half hour or so he talked to us about his beautiful garden. *'There's a crack in the pond...'* he said,

'...and in the Spring the garden will be alive with tulips and daffodils. You won't forget my geraniums in my greenhouse will you?'

Once he got chatting naturally about his beloved garden, he seemed to calm down and quite enjoy talking. We sat quietly and listened. At one point he did speak to Alfie and me, asking, *'is this child yours?'* To which we both replied a definite *'yes!'* To be honest, this was pretty apparent since Russell was calling us Mum and Dad !

Clearly Mr Snow loved his garden and this was a very fascinating evening for us all to experience. Of course, Russell couldn't help himself from singing a song from the Rogers and Hammerstein musical *Carousel - 'When I Marry Mr Snow.'* Plus he was making up all sorts of his own daft words and acting the goat !

Needless to say when Spring came, Rita's or what had been Mr Snow's garden, *was* a wonderful sight, with daffodils and tulips and his beloved geraniums were in full bloom. Oh, and the pond did have a huge crack in it, just as he had told us. I imagine he just loved his garden and still wanted it looked after. Well what's wrong with that ? I think it's rather lovely of Mr Snow, but I hope by now he is nicely settled in the Spirit World with his loved ones. I'm sure he now has a far more beautiful garden and a pond without a crack in it ! So I guess this séance had been a sort of 'Spirit rescue' by our Spirit friends, with us lending a hand !

Whilst describing these wonderful séances from the 1980s, I want to just mention some talks I did. One lecture was in the USA, during my visit there in 1993 and the audience seemed spellbound. We went way over time, yet I could have carried on all night ! A similar public talk I did in Rayleigh went on and on, with many questions fired at me.

Once, a radio chat show I took part in brought in some amazing phone calls. Ninety-eight percent of callers wanted to know more about the subject of Physical Phenomena, although one very nasty man called and suggested I was making money from a 'dead child.' I soon conveyed to him that my son *LIVES* and as for making money...ha ha...forget it ! So he shut up. After that, I made up my mind to do *no more* public speaking.

One séance I recall had a more serious nature about it. There were just four of us present, Rita and her husband Stephen and Alfie and me. The first half had been wonderful and was full of laughter and music, but then our Spirit communicator Helen Duncan said,
'We want to carry out an experiment, so after a break we will start again...'

In the second half, we sat quietly as Rita went back into Trance. Her deep breathing was the only sound we could hear. Now I have to be very careful here, for I don't have any direct notes and I wasn't recording at the time, but Helen's voice began to speak.

'Now Gwen and Alfie...shh ! We're doing an experiment. I told you before, so that you wouldn't be anxious. Please stay as quiet as mice...and we do not want you to tell the Medium what happens here tonight.'

She made us smile by making amusing little threats to Rita's husband Stephen, if he did tell ! But we did as we were asked and remained as quiet as three little mice. Needless to say, we were very puzzled and wondered what was going to happen next.

We began to hear the familiar tones of Russell as a child, but *not* as a clown this time. A more serious Russell seemed to be taking instructions. We could hear him being encouraging and urgent towards someone unseen, yet he seemed so kind and even a little sad. We were transfixed and hardly dared to breathe. We strained to hear, for it seemed as though Russell's voice was so far away. Then it became gradually clearer and we heard him saying, *'come on, come on. My name is Russell.'*

There were other voices which we couldn't identify and we heard sounds and murmurs - we had no idea what was happening. Then we heard Russell again, *'it's alright, I promise you. Don't be upset, hold my hand. Shh, shh, shh ! I'm taking you to the light. Look ! The light...there it is.'*

Then we heard a kind of sob, then Russell again,
'Look at the light, it's so beautiful.'

Then, *'Yes, yes, come on, where's your hand ?'*

There was a shuffling sound, then suddenly a woman's voice broke through in a clear English accent. Breathlessly she said,
'I want my blouse ironed.'

Then Russell's voice, *'It's alright, it's ironed.'*

The woman's voice raised louder, *'my hair, my hair. My makeup ! I want my peroxide for my hair, please.'*

As we sat listening to this, we found the whole experiment achingly wonderful. Then out of the silence came Helen's lovely Scottish accent saying, *'come on lassie, go with the laddie. He will take you to the light, you don't have to worry. Go on. Go on Ruth.'*

Helen's voice sounded cracked with emotion - so yes, Spirits feel emotion too and this was very apparent to us all that evening. This was clearly a 'rescue job' - as Russell would call it. By now we had learned that the lady being helped was Ruth Ellis. In July 1955, Ruth was the last woman in Britain to be executed for murder.

I had thought for a long time about whether I should include this séance in the book. Only a week ago I had read somewhere that Ruth Ellis's family were hoping to have her name cleared. I don't think it was simply a coincidence that I'd read this at the time, for I don't believe in coincidences. Here was a woman who was in a highly charged emotional state. She was suffering the after effects of a miscarriage, brought on by her abusive partner David - who was confused by drugs and drink *and* pathologically jealous.

Ruth Ellis never had a lot of luck in her life, but using a revolver, Ruth shot her partner in a crime of passion. It wasn't a crime that deserved execution - but how easy it is to judge. Any relationship is a learning experience.

During the séance that evening, I know we took part in something beautiful. I know *I* felt very emotional. There was a sudden *'goodnight'* that came from Helen, then quietness. Then I remembered that Spirit had asked that Rita was *not* to know what had happened. Thank goodness the lights were dimmed as we three - Alfie, Stephen and me just looked at each other, as Rita came out of Trance saying, *'*
Oh, there's something round my neck.'

We kept quiet as the Medium came round and began enjoying her coffee and biscuits. We never knew whether Stephen ever told - maybe he did ?

My thoughts were with this lady going towards the light, hand in hand with a small child, yet didn't Jesus say, *'...and a little child shall lead them ?'*

* * *

Time and time again I've been asked, whether there was ever a public séance with Rita the Medium ? Well, yes there was and it was held in the Autumn of 1982 at the 'Arthur Findlay College of Psychic Science' in Essex - otherwise known as Stansted Hall.

I had been booked into the College for a week when I was asked if Rita could come to Stansted Hall to give a séance demonstration. Rita later agreed and we all talked it over with the regular 'outer circle' of Spirit friends. Of course, they knew exactly what would happen and soon, this 'secret séance' was splashed all over the Psychic News !

It was decided that Alfie and I would attend, but not the others in the group. Our Spirit friend, the singer Laura, would be able to duet with me during the séance and Alfie could help out with any problems, him being a business man. I remember being quite nervous, since physical phenomena was quite new to me at the time. It was arranged to be held in Stansted Hall's Library. First there was a talk about how it all began, then the plan was to hold a short séance that first evening, again in the Library. Our group consisted of Rita as the Medium, with her husband Stephen, then Alfie and me and four others acting as sitters.

We used the trumpet, which whizzed round and round, but we also had apports - mostly of small toys and flowers. I can recall that it was quite a shorter séance than usual, but those who spoke briefly were Helen Duncan and Russell, followed by Arthur Findlay himself - who chatted to all. After all, Stansted Hall had once been his home !
When the séance ended and the lights went on, there on the small table were six beautiful pink roses, which had been apported and they were still covered with moisture !

The next séance followed on the Sunday evening and I was already feeling traumatised - simply because of my own personal involvement ! We had all wondered what would happen in front of an audience and what their reaction would be.

However, I was amused during the preparations for the coming evening, for all and sundry were in the library that afternoon, trying to black out the windows. I don't think I will ever forget the look on the face of Stansted Hall's Manager, Charles Sherratt, when he saw Rita's husband Stephen putting large safety pins through the Library's thick velvet curtains. You would have thought poor old Stephen had committed a murder. There was so much fuss and commotion caused. Oh dear, dear ! I mean, there we were in the *'College of Psychic Science'* and those who were supposed to be *in charge* of the proceedings, seemed to fail to understand at all, so I stayed well out of the way.

Many skeptics fail to accept that séances of this kind *have* to be held in the dark, so proceedings are heavily criticised. They fail to realise that there are good reasons for this. All Spiritual manifestations are governed by Spiritual laws.

However, the College was full to the brim that week and those who were there, knew they were in for a treat. The evening soon arrived and the Library was packed to overflowing. Alfie and me sat up on the platform with Rita, Stephen and two others sitters this time.

The audience were packed in so tightly and I noticed there were some new faces present. Obviously some had arrived just for the evening séance, but some of these were researchers, who'd been specially invited. Along the way, I had met many of them before. I made eye contact with one lady who seemed to realise that I recognised her face. She was the author and researcher Anita Gregory. A year or two later I learned that she had passed to Spirit, but at least she'll know the truth herself now.

As the séance began, I felt light headed and a strong pull on my solar plexus. Helen Duncan spoke full and loud through the trumpet, which was painted with luminous paint and whizzed about from one end of the library to the other. Helen answered numerous audience questions in her own inimitable way, then we heard one lady in the audience, who had been good friends with Helen Duncan during her lifetime, chatting with her quite naturally.

I later learned that my young reporter friend Alan Cleaver, went out of his way to find this lady. He was successful and reported back that she had indeed spoken with her old friend Helen Duncan, of that she had been one hundred percent sure.

However, I was still in a bit of daze myself, when Helen said to me, *'sing Gwen...'* Now that did start me off ! The trumpet was still whizzing about, but I could hear the wonderful singing voice of our Spirit friend Laura. She had begun to sing the Richard Tauber song, *'Vienna, City Of My Dreams'* - so I did as Helen had asked and sang along ! It was quite an experience I can tell you.

Then Russell spoke and did his *'little boy act.'* He kept talking about the lake at Stansted Hall and how it was full of *'great big frogs'* and spiders. I just sat there thinking, *'oh Russell, you're scaring all the ladies !'*
Of course he was, but they were loving it and we could hear laughter coming from them all. Amongst the laughter, we heard Russell threatening to put frogs and *'great big spiders'* in their beds. It was obvious he was just trying to lighten the mood, for there were clearly people there who just wanted to shout *'Fraud !'*

Speaking to one of the audience, Russell politely addressed one lady using her name. Nobody else knew who she was, except for me and two or three more. Yet amongst all the laughter, there was a lot of serious scrutiny going on, but I do not want to speak of that - that's a problem for the researchers, not me !

This second séance was over soon enough though. It had blown my mind, but I was absolutely shattered and glad to go straight to bed.

Next morning there were ladies coming down stairs carrying flowers which had just appeared in their beds. A few were quite stunned who had even found Physalis flowers (Japanese lanterns) had appeared. I said, *'don't look so worried, they'll just be a gift from Russell.'*

One lady had hopped out of bed in the night to visit the bathroom and on her return discovered a dew covered rose lying on the bed ! She came to me with it, all smiles and I just said, *'good job it's not a spider or frog !'*

After breakfast, I went for a long walk to get away from the hubbub of the Hall. I walked and walked round the grounds, but could find no Japanese Lanterns growing anywhere. I didn't have them in my garden at Rayleigh, although I know Rita's garden did have them in abundance.

The rest of the week just dragged for me and I wanted to go home. I was naive about people back then, but I stuck to my guns during the week, for there *were* people there ready to tear the whole experience to shreds. It made me feel sad, that people who are supposed to know better can be so treacherous. In part, the atmosphere had been very unpleasant and I learned some really *big* lessons that week - but *no one* could budge me from the wonder of it all !

Those in the audience who had booked in for the week, had loved every minute of it. I still hear from some of them and they talk of it to this day and wish they could experience even more. One small group of young people went to further séances on Rita's invitation, to her home. One of them said to me, *'Gwen, it has changed my whole life !'*

Surely, this is what Truth is all about ? Thinking back, I can smile now but in a way it changed *my* life too ! However, some audience members did make me laugh when I was asked questions like, *'can Russell tell you the winner of the Grand National ?'*

I often tell of one incident when asked this sort of question. I wrote of it in the first book...

In the middle of a séance, Russell decided he would make me a cup of tea - right in the middle of the circle ! We could hear cups and spoons and water running - the whole lot ! He did this quite a few times, but one night I recall him saying, *'oh dear, I'm spilling the water everywhere...can I have a dishcloth ?'*

He kept on and on about this dishcloth and we were highly amused by his antics. I remember thinking, *'why doesn't someone just give him a dishcloth ?'* But oh me, if only I'd have known...it turned out that *'Dishcloth'* was the name of the winning horse in a race which ran the very next day ! I could have been rich by now if I'd have listened - but Russell was just having some fun with his Mum, that's all.

I hope that one day Rita's own story will be published. Yet how could she tell it ? For we have to remember that the Medium is in a Trance state, so sees and remembers absolutely *nothing* !

As for me, after our thought provoking séance week at Stansted Hall, I ceased to call myself a Spiritualist. I found the negative aspects all so very sad, so I will say no more about them.

The so called 'scientific tests' of researchers, seem very unscientific to me. Then they say that we invent our own 'Spiritual laws' to suit ourselves and say it is fraud if the phenomena doesn't conform to theirs. If they want séances to be held under test conditions, so be it - but they shouldn't let the conditions be so nonsensical that they are not possible.
Too often researchers demand that séance phenomena should be produced in conditions which may violate fundamental laws of the psychic world.

Negativity is yet another undesirable condition for phenomena and boy, was there negativity that week ! Test demonstrations always tend to work much better for the sympathetic enquirer...

However, the paragraph that follows is taken from many notes that I've kept over the years. I love these particular words by Sir Oliver Lodge, Raymond's father and I think lot of people would do well to study them...

'Bigoted hostility is a complete bar to the production of any phenomena at all. An open mind is desirable and certainly no hindrance. The out and out scoffers need not wonder that their investigations are so successful and if they will condescend to read their New Testament - where they will find it recorded even of Jesus, that
'He could there do no mighty work...and he marvelled at their unbelief.'
'Could' not - please observe, not 'would' not. Again a natural law of Universal application, if Jesus could not break that law for the purpose of healing, we may be sure that the lesser Mediums of today, cannot break it for less essential purpose of convincing the scoffers, that there are more things in Heaven and Earth than are dreamt of, in their somewhat limited philosophy.'

During my many thought provoking times, I have pondered on the great mysteries of life. I once read something that appealed to me, which I will now repeat here. In 1897, some ancient papyrus documents were discovered in Egypt - they are believed to be part of the Gospel of Thomas, which contains new sayings of Jesus. I want to share with you, one of these sayings here. I think these words say it all !

'Let not him who seeks, cease,
until he finds.

And when he finds,
he shall be astonished.

Astonished, he shall reach the Kingdom,

and having reached the Kingdom,
he shall [not] rest.'

Sixteen

Bridging Two Worlds

December 1999

'My child is a phenomenon...
really the most natural production I ever beheld'

~ Lady Elizabeth Holland

When I wrote *'Russell'* I wrote mostly of my son. It seemed like the right thing to do at the time. However, almost ten years have passed since then and now I can say more. I've been asked so many questions over the years, about the Physical Phenomena séances, so I want to take every opportunity I can, to talk about them in this book.

First I must satisfy the curious regarding our first ever séance, which we attended on Saturday, August 14th, 1982 - Russell's anniversary. For me, it was the most heart stopping moment that I have ever experienced. There were such an array of wonders ! There were also other wonderful Spirit communicators - and I will speak of them all a little later in this chapter.

We drove to Leicester and neither of us had been to such a séance before. We *had* been to what were 'supposed' to be séances, but it would be wise not to speak of them here. I feel that time either erases a memory or clarifies it, but this particular night is imprinted in my mind with indelible ink ! It also stays in my heart as a 'hallowed' event. When I think of it now I could weep *still* !

Once we had arrived, we were ushered into a room where we exchanged greetings with people who were strangers, but who were so kind. I was aware of Alan Cleaver, the Psychic News journalist, he sat to my right - but in no time at all, the séance began. I really thought that my heart would stop there and then, as the luminous séance trumpet advanced towards us.

There are no words that can convey the depth of feeling I felt that evening. I seemed to be glued to my seat. Yet out of this trumpet came this lovely boy's voice and he was singing *'Where is Love'*- from the Lionel Bart musical, *'Oliver!'*

I gasped in amazement, for here was my own beautiful boy and he was singing to us about Love. My head started swimming. I truly felt I was dreaming ! But the song was so beautifully delivered and the diction was so, so clear. It was as though it wasn't Russell - my own 'Artful Dodger' that I remember so fondly and so sweetly - but Oliver himself singing.

As the last refrain of *'Where is Love'* came, the materialised Spirit body of my boy, calmly handed me a piece of willow tree. Now I'd heard all about apports, but I would never have expected to receive a piece of *tree* ! Then Russell spoke to us for the first time. His first words to us were,
'Hello Mummy and Daddy'

I recall replying *'Hello Russell'* but my heart was spilling over with such love for him, and his achievement, that I sat there completely stunned and speechless ! I couldn't think of a thing to say to him. I was tongue-tied and totally blown away. I do recall that Russell seemed shy - to me, his Mother, which was unusual for Russell. Yet when I think of how happy he must have felt that evening, I was so proud of him and he must have been as nervous as I was - until we got more used to it.

Suddenly things swung into action and Laura's glorious Spirit voice could be heard, as she began to sing us. Well you'd have to hear it to understand the wonder of it ! I don't recall how long the evening lasted, but next, dear Helen Duncan introduced herself. At first I had a problem with her strong Scottish accent, but soon got used to it. I had heard somewhere that Raymond Lodge was a communicator at this circle, but he didn't speak that night.

I think our Spirit friends were aware that this had been a very special and emotional evening. My mind and emotions were on hold that night, although I didn't realise, until it was all over. I know that nothing happens by accident and every event has a reason, but a curtain was lifted that night - and it was to be seven years before it came back down again !

That night I found sleep hard to come by, for my mind was so busy doing mental gymnastics. Then I woke up the next morning to find a beautiful, lilac coloured, sweet pea flower on my pillow ! I soon began to realise that we were on the verge of a wonderful adventure !

However, I stayed on in Leicester that first week, but Alfie had to leave for work. That first night had been such an emotional roller coaster for me and I never thought I would return to write of it here. For me, being a part of those first séances felt as if I was almost 'walking on Holy Ground.'

I have five precious tape recordings of these séances. Yes, only five in all the seven years we sat ! Apart from one I call the 'Birthday Tape' which I have copied and given out to other bereaved mothers, our Spirit friends didn't want too much taping and copying done. They had their reasons and after all these years, I think I know why !

Now I didn't play these tapes for sixteen or seventeen years. I had put them on the back burner. I knew they were *Truth*, but I needed time. I knew I was going through a great learning experience...

During that first week I *got to know my son again* and what a joy it was. Yet I found myself sadly lacking in questions. I was so spellbound by it all.

By now his humour was really rolling and we spent a lot of time laughing, which of course relaxed us all. But when you can't find anything to say and need time to take things in and sort it all out, repetition is very useful. Now it was me who was shy ! This did gradually vanish of course and I tried writing notes during the séances, but in the dark this was definitely not easy ! All I ever had was writing on top of writing, so I eventually gave up on that idea. It was hopeless !

One thing that struck me that first week was, that Rita had been in deep Trance for up to four hours or more. Yet when it was all over she was absolutely full of energy. This puzzled me, but at that time I had no understanding of the energies involved. After the séances, when all the sitters were having tea or coffee, I would find Rita down at the bottom of her garden watching the stars. Once I joined her and asked,
'where do you go when you're in a Trance ?'
Rita would just answer, *'oh it's like a sleep or a dream.'*

One time we were told there was an outer circle of Spirits, a team who apparently organised every séance, so that everything was well in order :

No.1 was Raymond Lodge, the son of Sir Oliver Lodge the great scientist and pioneer of Spiritualism. Sir Oliver already knew the truth of survival, before the death of his son. His classic book entitled *'Raymond'* is one of the finest books ever written on the subject. Raymond was killed in battle, during World War One on September 14th 1915. He was 26.

No.2 was Helen Duncan, the great Physical Medium who died as the direct result of a police raid during a Nottingham séance in 1956.

No's 3 & 4 were two of the sitters Spirit guides.

No.5 was a Spirit called Galma, which is all I know.

No.6 was Walter, a musical director in life and the Medium's father.

No.7 was Michael, the son of sitters Pat and Barry Jeffries, who died on his motorbike, aged sixteen.

No.8 was Dr Albert Schweitzer, the medical missionary, philosopher and musician.

No.9 was John Campbell Sloan, the superb Direct Voice Medium written of by Arthur Findlay in his book *'On the Edge of the Etheric.'*

No.10 was Florence Marryat, the Victorian actress and Spiritualist author of *'There Is No Death.'*

No.11 was a Native North American Indian guide.

No.12 was Arthur Findlay the great researcher, author and historian.

No.13 was Russell Vernon Byrne, my son and the joker in the pack !

This list was made for me by Rita herself, so I know it is accurate. Our dear Spirit friend, the glorious singer Laura, didn't seem to have a number placing in this group, perhaps because she didn't speak very much at the seances - but oh could she sing !

It may be generally known by now, that Rita Goold later withdrew from her Spiritual work and Mediumship, because she had become a victim of frightening threats. Vicious lies were spread about her and she received threatening phone calls and worse - anything to discredit her wonderful work. She was deeply upset by this since she had dedicated herself and her gift, hoping to bring some enlightenment to this crazy world.

She never received one penny for her work. In fact she was well out of pocket, because of her good nature and hospitality. She readily fed and accommodated those who came to the séances - she is that kind of lady. But little thanks was what she received in return, by people who were supposed to know better.

I don't know all of what happened, but what I do know - and knew of at the time - made us all very, very, angry. I later realised the reason why Alfie and I were never there when the psychic researchers came. I dread to think what would have happened. Yet as always, our Spirit friends knew exactly what they were doing. Mind you, I am very glad we were not there at these times, for I would have felt it almost an invasion of privacy.

When I held Russell's materialised hands in the séances, my own hands trembled. It was an achingly beautiful experience for me, but it was all so wonderfully natural - just as when he was in the body.
When Raymond Lodge introduced himself to us one evening, I could only answer, *'hello Raymond, so nice to meet you.'*

'How are you dear lady ?' he asked me.

Even though I could only just mumble a quiet *'very well thank you'*, I had a very definite feeling of *knowing* him somehow.
I think it's well known that women relate with their hearts, but at that first *'hello'*, I felt I knew him ! Yet from where or when, I don't have the slightest idea - but my soul level of consciousness said *'yes you do !'* So I just accepted it.

One evening, a visitor came to the séances. A researcher and writer named Michael Roll. He was a very kind and pleasant man who clearly knew his stuff, because he asked very intelligent questions. To Helen Duncan, he said,
'Helen, I am very worried that what happened to you, will happen to Rita.'

Helen replied, *'Ever since I was killed in 1956, scientists on our side have worked very hard to refine the ectoplasm that killed me. Now - if our defences are breached and we are grabbed by people on Earth - there is a good chance that our Medium will not be harmed.'*

Note: We knew that this was Helen Duncan the Medium, since on a previous occasion, Helen's own daughter Gena had attended one of Rita's séances and conversed with her for over an hour. Gena later verified, that without doubt, this was indeed her mother Helen Duncan.

Michael Roll also spoke with Raymond Lodge about different Spiritual energies. He was referring to the new energies that were, at that time of the 1980s, on the verge of being discovered. This was what Raymond's father Sir Oliver had referred to as etheric energies. Sir Oliver knew that Spirits have substantial bodies, but that they are made up of sub-atomic particles - a much finer substance than the ones that make up our own physical bodies. This is the sole reason why our 'dead' loved ones, are normally out of range of our own five physical senses. Rather like all the TV and Radio waves, which are operating in the *same space* - but at different frequencies.

Recent discoveries into human survival by the scientist Ronald Pearson, now show this to be a perfectly true. His scientific paper, called *'Quantum Gravitation and the Structured Ether'* was published by the Russian Academy of Science in 1993 and peer reviewed in 1997. His discoveries apparently begun in the late 1980s. To quote Dr Pearson,
'When matter is repeatedly divided, the atom is eventually reached. Then further division shows this to constitute sub-atomic particles...our Universe now appears...built from real energies but these are intelligently organised.'

I must admit that I have to make notes on this scientific stuff - for I have said before that I do not understand it all. I only know that energy cannot be destroyed or created.

Now I will completely change the subject to one which seems to interest many people. I have been asked so many times by readers of *'Russell'* - why did entertainers and movie stars appear at the séances ?

Well, I guess they will communicate where they can. After all they are only people, the same as us. Yet I do really believe that as we meet and interact with people in the body, there is an interaction of energy that comes into being. So it is with Spirit. It's really quite simple. You could call it the 'Law of Attraction' or even an 'Affinity of Vibration.'
In my case, most of those lovely show-biz and film star people who visited during séances, were singers. I spoke to Mario Lanza, Judy Garland, Maria Callas, and Marie Lloyd. Even the lovely Marilyn Monroe was also a singer. She spoke to me once asking, *'are you an actress ?'* I replied, *'no dear.'* Her only plea was, *'I did not kill myself !'*

To this I could only say, *'I know dear. God bless you.'*

Maurice Chevalier popped in once and sang his famous song, *'Thank Heaven for Little Girls'* - very cheekily too, but he was so charming. I remember trying to imitate him when I was six or seven years old !

Friends have asked me 'but what about Alfie ?' Well he had a super chat once with Joe Louis the American boxer. Mr Louis has been a life long hero of Alfie's and why shouldn't he pop in ? They had a chat about how many fights Joe had and all sorts of secrets were discussed. I know Russell had bought him along for his Dad, as he had brought along others for me. I smile to myself to this day, when I think of Russell telling Maria Callas how to sing down the séance trumpet. We heard her say,
'this damned infernal instrument !'
I still have mental pictures of that scene, believe me !

Another evening, Russell brought along Harry Houdini, another hero of Alfie's. I remember having trouble understanding his Bronx accent and what with Russell's antics too, that was some night ! 'The Great Houdini' was chatting away to Alfie, quite naturally. He talked about his life and how he wished he had *'helped, instead of hindering'* this communication *stuff* ! Russell clearly wanted magic that night - like he did in 1962. For that year, his last ever Christmas present on Earth was a children's magic set, complete with wooden magic wand ! In the séance I'm afraid I missed a lot of what was said. Houdini was teaching Russell a card trick, I think it was called the Russian Shuffle, but all we could hear was the laughter of both of them. First Houdini the expert shuffled the cards, then said, *'you try Russell.'* Then Russell laughs saying, *' whoops ! I've dropped 'em all.'*

Lord knows what the trick was, but we laughed until we ached. I think personally it was all part of an act, just to give us a laugh. The circle also had visits from Mr Presley, Mr Lennon and Laurel and Hardy, although I wasn't there those times, so can't speak of them. I imagine there were probably others too. I cannot forget Winston Churchill, however. When he came in for a chat, he said to me,
'you're the lady that paints Bluebell Woods...hello !'
'Yes I have painted Bluebell Woods' I said. *'Can I ask you a question ?'*
'Of course you can,' he replied.

I asked him about a little daughter that he and his wife had lost at a very early age. I said, *'I love her name - Marigold. Who chose it ?'*
'No my dear' Churchill said, *'that was only our pet name for our little girl. Clemmie and I both knew of life after death. She is with us now and we are very happy, but I am still very interested in the politics of the Earth plane.'*

Then someone interrupted, but before he moved on he said, *'keep up the good work and your painting !'*

To me it was all so natural. It would have been so easy to slip into a pool of complacency, but to me it was so enthralling and awe inspiring. Though if you approach 'Mr or Mrs Average' with such tales, they're not interested. They'd rather just watch the TV ! It's only when something in life disturbs or bewilders them, that they really take the time or trouble to even think on such things.

Now I must stress that in the very early days of Rita's séances a trumpet was used, but this was dispensed with as things progressed. As time went on we were able to see this *'new energy'* at times. It usually came when the evenings were - as Helen put it, *'Special Evenings.'* With these evenings the vibrations were so powerful and this energy, when seen, was like a vapour. Perhaps the best way I could describe it would be a bit like the vapour from an inhalant. I understand that many new Physical Mediumship circles now use this *'new energy'* so for me that has to be good news !

I once asked Russell how long he had worked with Rita, as the Medium to do this work. He said, *'seventeen years of your time, Mum !'*
So working that out, means that he had started his work with Rita at about 13 years of age - which was about the time I'd 'settled in' to the certain

knowledge that he lived on *forever...*

'Look in the mirror Mum,' he once said. *'You'll see a likeness of me now I am older. Though I can be like Peter Pan and stay 'frozen in time' as a little boy, but I won't 'cause I've got a lot of work to do !'*

It's this book which tells of Russell's work - his mission in the Spirit World.

   I do recall noticing that whenever he was being serious, which wasn't often, his intonation sounded just like mine. Now the researchers *would* have a field day with that. The mind boggles, it really does ! The politics of the psychical researchers and the Spirit World is much more interesting than the every day politics of Earth, believe me.

However, before I get on to that subject I would just like to say something of the really special times in the séance room. Those overwhelming - even *hallowed* times - like Christmas and the simple and beautiful apports. There was my Pink Panther, which is now rapidly falling apart and Melvin the toy monkey or the toy frog. Sometimes pounds of liquorice allsorts would come landing onto the séance room table.

   Once I was given a beautiful feathered headband and Russell said it was, *'cause Mum wants to be like an Indian !'*

He even brought us little, fluffy mice for our cats to play with ! There were all sorts of daft things. Yet they all became our treasures and some still are to this day. Some of those evenings were so beautiful and intimate that you could have heard a petal drop in the quieter moments. Then suddenly a huge bunch of grapes would arrive, brought by Spirit - which became a nice feast for later in the evening !

   Talking of petals, I'm reminded of one séance when Barry Jeffries, the father of sixteen year old Michael in Spirit, asked Russell a question...
'The front of the house is a bit bare Russell, can you give me a bit of advice as to what would grow quickly ?'

Well it seems that now my son's a gardening expert, because he suggested Barry planted a Russian vine. One was apparently acquired and need I say more ? They don't half grow fast !

   There are no words to convey the humour of these séances. I would have expected our squeals of laughter *must* have been heard outside - yet, to my knowledge no one every complained !

* * *

   Now it's 1999, and I have just received the final Mum's story to add to this book. Then finally, after many long and late hours, it all seemed finished ! Yet something was nagging at me, somehow I just *knew* that I'd left something out. I took note of these feelings, but told myself that I'd dotted all the I's and crossed all the T's - yet still the feeling persisted...

Then during early October I felt strangely detached. I was alone in the house and still thinking. Mentally I heard Russell call me the scarecrow from 'The Wizard of Oz.'

'Well thanks very much !' I said.

'But Mum, you ponder about things that you already know the answer to.'

The next morning I lay awake listening Clairaudiently to two beautiful voices. One I knew was the singing voice of our Spirit friend Laura - the other I think was Russell. They were singing a version of the Tim Rice duet *'I Know Him So Well'* and they had changed the lyrics !

> *'Nothing in this world will last eternally,*
> *perfect situations can go wrong...*
> *It took time to understand the man*
> *Now I think it's true.*
> *I know him so well...'*

I lay there and just pondered on these words. What in heaven's name were they about ? Later, whilst still feeling detached and miles away, I wandered into my music room and began looking through an old box of audio tapes, which had laid unopened for many years. In a sort of daze, I took the box to the kitchen, yet after a closer look I discovered that inside were my séance tapes from the 1980s - all five of them ! I hadn't listened to them for almost sixteen years, because I just couldn't. Now idly I put one on for a listen and to my amazement heard the voice of Raymond Lodge, speaking in his beautiful Oxford accent,

'Hello Gwen, how are you dear lady ?'

Well at that moment it hit me like a ton of bricks,

'that's it ! 'I know him so well', the song !'

I knew then that I *had* to listen to these tapes, no matter what. So I armed myself with a box of tissues and listened. After all our Spirit friends had worked so hard on these 'Special Evenings' and now I felt it was my duty to write about them. This became another huge task and soon I was surrounded by papers and new notes. Now I intended to write all about Raymond, Helen, Russell and all the gang - I owed them that at least.

'So no more thinking about it Gwen. Just get on with it !' I told myself.

Listening once again to the voice of Raymond in these recordings was quite a surprise for me. The individual way he spoke and the personality of the man was there and I realised that if I didn't write about these tapes, no one else would. So, rigorously and meticulously I forced myself to listen to these voices of Truth, over and over again !

I began transcribing the tapes around October 6th 1999 and writing it all down was quite a task, oh boy ! I did have help however from two lovely ladies. My friend Margaret Prentice did her stuff and Linda, another RPPS Mum, helped too. Thank goodness for them !

* * *

In 1917, through the Mediumship of Gladys Osborne Leonard, Raymond Lodge told his father Sir Oliver, that he would always work to prove 'Life After Death.' Well after listening to these tapes, all I can say is that he really kept his word !

When listening to the recorded voice of sixteen year old Michael, you can tell that he and Russell are close pals. Although Michael's personality and accent are so different to Russell's, he certainly makes himself heard, although in a quieter way...

'Hello, this is Michael. We're all ever-so pleased to see you, it's really exciting.'

'That's because you're here Michael.' I said.

'Well I am here' said Michael, *'and Russell's my friend. We've been friends for a long time. Friendship's very precious, real precious. We make friends in our world as you do in your world. We don't have enemies here. We have preferences.'*

He went on to explain that he'd made a Spirit phone call ! He spoke of his brother and how he'd been amazed to receive this special call from Michael in the Spirit World. Then Michael talked some more...

'Russell and me, we are good mates. Nothing will change that. We don't get up to mischief. When people come and talk to us Gwen, sometimes they are frightened and they try to cover it up. It's nerves ! We put up a front to cover up for them and then they are not afraid to talk to us.

Life is beautiful, so be happy and laugh with us, don't cry. If you cry, they are tears of emotion, not tears of sadness. We don't cry. Our bodies are not quite the same as yours - we don't need tear ducts like you've got...

Well I've said my piece haven't I ? There's so many people who want to come and talk to you ! It's so wonderful, all this.

Don't thank me - I'm really happy that you come and talk. Ain't it lovely ?

Talk to you another time !'
Then he was gone.

The night before the Psychic News journalist Alan Cleaver was due at the séance, Russell addresses him on tape...
'I'm here. It's Russell Vernon Byrne - so there ! I'm on tape, so you'd better get a coffee and sit down and listen to us, 'cause we're all here. We're very sorry <u>you</u> can't be here, so <u>we'll</u> come to you. So the mountain comes to Mohamed ! You know what I mean, don't you. They are all going to talk on this tape for you in a minute, so you've got to listen to every word, right ? I've got to go for a minute, got to carry on with the proceedings, alright ?'
Then the singer Laura comes in singing *'On The Street Where You Live'* but with the words changed !

> *'...just to be in this room where you are.*
> *There is nowhere else on Earth*
> *that we would rather be.*
> *Let the time go by, I don't care if I,*
> *can be here in the room where you are...'*

Then we hear Russell once more,
'oh, I'm here again. You got to remember that the best reporter in the world is listening on the other end, so there ! My friends, we all love him. I'm going to sing 'Edelweiss' to him when he comes. He'll like that.'
...and apparently he did like that !

Russell continues his speech to Alan,
'it's no good if Walter's banging his drum sticks on the ceiling, 'cause you're not gonna see them [on the tape.] *Put them little things in your ears* [headphones] *and listen to every word. Oh, Laura wants to sing 'I don't talk to strangers' to you. You'll know what she means won't you ? You should have been a detective !'*
'Right,' said Russell, *'now I'm going to wake up Rita.* [the Medium] *She's lovely. She's got a funny little face and a nose like a chisel - you know, what you use to soften putty. Her nose is just like that. But all gone wrong. She's got great big ears...*
None at all of this is true by the way, in fact it's all just the reverse !
'She looks like Laura don't she Mum ?' said Russell.
'Yes she does !' I replied. *'Well she is Laura's granddaughter, Russell !'*

As I listened to this tape, I recalled that it seemed that Russell and his friends had their own secrets and codes, so unless you were in on it, you could only listen and wonder. Though as time went on, Russell and I had our *own* secrets - things that will never, ever pass my lips !

Back to the tape and every now and again Russell is actually waving a torch in the darkened séance room. Then he uses it to show me his legs ! *'They are like yours Mum. Skinny ! Now look at my hands Mum. Hold them !'*

So one minute I'm looking at the skinny legs of a little boy and the next, I'm holding his hands - but they are the size of *man's* hands. Now *I know* my son's hands and they haven't altered in shape, only in size - they have just grown !

'Mum, look at my cowslip.' He meant what we call the 'cowlick' in his hairline. Russell always did have an unusual fringe, it would never stay down - because of this 'cowlick' !

Looking back, it amazes me how Alfie and I were able to just sit there - but we were *trusted* that much ! Russell knew that we wouldn't try and reach out and grab him. Of course we would have loved to, but we knew better. We knew the rules. Sometimes it really felt as though we were in another dimension ourselves, but then anything was possible with this outer circle of Spirits !

In that group we also had Helen Duncan and what a character. Talk about calling a spade a spade ! If anyone asked a daft question - and you'd be surprised at the questions some visitors put to Spirit - she would tell them so, in no uncertain terms ! She would also say something to Russell, if he got a bit out of hand, which at times he could. He'd get in trouble with Helen for shouting '*Oy*' or humming with his 'dum-de-dum' sound.
'I'm not being daft' he'd say, *'I just like 'dum-de-dum'-ing'*
Of course, this was all part of his act.

Helen was always with us when the Spirit team were practising with the energies. Now I can only repeat what I heard, but once she did say, *'bloody hell, I feel like I'm in a suit of armour, it's so heavy.'*
I imagine this was a reference to the materialisation energy Helen was using, although Russell whispered, *'she's like the Tin Man from the 'Wizard of Oz' Mum,'* - until Helen told him to hush !

Helen Duncan has a heart of gold and a great sense of humour. If ever we were laughing at the boyish antics of 'his nibs' during the séance, Helen would join in with the laughter too. We would even hear her collapse on the séance room sofa, which would literally rock and roll with her laughter.

I do find it difficult to convey humour into words, but how could we not laugh at Russell, when he was there running around the séance room in a pair of size 13 shoes ! Someone in the group had supplied him with these and prepared them with luminous paint, so we could see where he was. Then he would stand on his head on the sofa, banging these shoes on the wall - at the same time singing,
'Right said Fred, have to knock the wall down...'
If Helen hadn't stepped in to stop him, I think we all would have just burst from laughing !

It was all so informal, but Russell still had his work to do. All of a sudden, amid the laughter he would say something like, *'right, now Helen wants to talk to you'* or *'now Laura's going to sing for you'*

Now this was *always* a joy, for I often got to sing with Laura. Music from two worlds, sung together. What could be more magical ?
Although I mustn't forget Rita's father in Spirit, Walter. In life he had been a musician and musical director, yet unless you hear it you can't describe his brilliance. If he came through in the séance room, his whistling was as magical as any singing bird and even though the xylophone he was playing was only a toy, every note was perfection. I used to sit there enthralled and almost cross-eyed by it !

If he used the luminous tipped drum sticks, they would go up in the air, touch the ceiling and fly all around the room, such is his brilliance ! Then of course, if these toys ever needed fixing, we could rely on Russell to bring in his hammer and we'd hear him, *'bang, bang, bang !'*

Singing was always such a feature in the séances. I've already mentioned the evening that the Music Hall entertainer Marie Lloyd popped in. We all had a 'sing-a-long' together, even though we didn't know all the words !
Another evening Helen said, *'well, we've got a treat for you tonight.'*
One of the sitters had acquired an old tape, which had the voices of Violet Lorraine and George Robey singing their old wartime hit from 1916, *'If you were the only girl in the world.'* As the tape was played we heard the Earthly voice of Violet singing on tape with Mr. Robey, but then the Spirit voice of Laura came in and sang along with it. Oh it was wonderful !

One evening Helen surprised us all by saying, *'well I can't sing, but I'm going to talk my way through a song.'* Then she began with her own version of '*My Way*' by Paul Anka...

*'And now the end is near,
this is not the final curtain,
There will be times,
the hard and slow,
we'll win it through - of that we're certain
There were times,
'they' tried to stop this, lassie
But I know you know,
I'll do it my way.
They tried in vain to stop us all,
Oh yes, we'll show them all - the final curtain.
There will be times, though hard and slow,
We'll win it through,
We'll get them all along the way,
I know you know,
I'll do it my way !'*

Now isn't this the song of the individual, doing things their own way ? Straight afterwards Russell came in singing, *'I'll do it the Russell Vernon Byrne way.'* Typical !

I have to say that I wasn't present on that particular evening, but this recording was given to me on tape. In trying to decipher Helen's meaning, it seemed that *'they'* and *'them all'* were references to certain people, who had done all they could to try and stop this wonderful phenomena ! I'll speak a little of this a little later. However, I understand that most of the sitters were in tears that evening and is it any wonder ?

I can see what Helen means when she says 'get them all' - she doesn't mean violently, although there are many ways 'bad' people can be tripped up. Those that lie and cheat get caught in the end, somehow. Perhaps she means that the Truth of Spirit will catch up with 'them all' in the end ?

Many scientific researchers were invited to the séances over the years and some actually mocked these wonderful experiences. I won't bother to give them much space here, I mean they're supposed to be experts, right ? During one séance, the well known researcher Maurice Grosse called out to Russell saying,
'cut out the big act ! Why are you talking in such a silly voice ?'
'Because I'm Russell' replied Russell.
Later, Russell said to me, *'Mum, if only he hadn't been so sarcastic !'*
If I had known *how* this man had spoken to Russell at the time, I would

have said *'No !'* when he asked to come and visit us at home. He was so nasty and sarcastic with us too and he talked to us as though we were idiots. He even suggested that as a singer, I was the voice of Laura during the séances. I said to him,

'how can I be at home - here in Rayleigh, Essex - watching TV and knitting <u>and</u> singing at the séances at the same time ?'

'Well' he replied, *'you could be projecting your voice.'*

I mean really ! How daft can you get ? I needn't go on, because out of my door he went.

After his voice had been ridiculed, Russell made a suggestion. He said that we should try to compare these séance recordings with an old recording of Russell that Alfie had at home. Russell said,

'Dad's got an idea in the back of his mind, that he's got my Earthly voice on an old reel to reel tape. I know Dad and Mum will try to find it. I know the Rolling Stones are on it too. If they do find my voice on this tape, don't let old Maurice Grosse have it !'

I'm pleased to say that we didn't let him. I didn't think I could trust myself to speak to researchers after this anyway. I think our Spirit friends knew what they were doing, during the times we weren't present and the researchers were. It's amazing how they protect us.

Another time, two other researchers had been invited to sit in on a séance. They said they were both writers - but to me, they were unworthy of their titles. One arrived armed with a case of booze. I guess, he was hoping to get the Medium drunk - some hope he had ! Thankfully, the séance didn't last long, since the researcher was nasty to everyone, so it was stopped. He went rushing out the door, still clutching his booze. The other man lied to Rita before he arrived, with all sorts of tales about why he was late in arriving. He hadn't reckoned on our wonderful Spirit friends. They told him he was a liar.

'We know where you were and who you were with...' they said. I don't think he stayed long either. How can a dedicated Medium work with such people ? Although Alfie and I were not present at these type of events, we were told about them by Helen during the following week's séance. Spirit do not lie !

I have one recording of a special evening arranged by our Spirit friends. Helen says, *'oh, we've got a house full tonight ! We always do, but tonight's special. I know it's cold outside, but we'll warm you with our love.'*

Then Russell pops in saying, *'hello Mum and Dad. I'm coming over to sit next to you in a minute - I love you, yeah, yeah, yeah'*
Then someone says, *'shut up Russell !'*
'Oh I'm in trouble again' Russell replies.
'Just like with old so and so...' [the researcher]
'Ooh, now Raymond's wagging his finger at me, that means shut up ! Got to get on now - tonight comes first ! I'm in charge. We've got something very exciting for you tonight. You've got to listen to every word - all my instructions. Mum's sitting there and Dad's banging about in the collapsible chair - watch out Dad ! I've got so many jobs to do, I'm the organiser...oops ! It's a bit like [the TV comedy] *'Some Mother's Do 'Ave 'Em' tonight Mum - but I'm doing it...ooh !"* [imitating Michael Crawford's TV character]*'...shh, shh. Here's Raymond...'*

The music quietly playing in the background is a Mario Lanza song called *'Beloved.'* As we wait, we hear a soft voice speaking the words,

*'Tonight is just a
masquerade,
tomorrow's just another day
but come whatever,
tonight or never,
I'll throw the mask away'*

Then Raymond says,
'I can't sing but, I do enjoy music so. It's very nice speaking to music...'
Now we hear lots of thumping and scraping sounds. Apparently it's Russell dragging a box, to gasps of amazement from me ! We hear someone say, *'what on Earth are you doing Russell ?'*
Russell replies, *'I'm waving my torch and I'm getting the clothes ready. Hang on - hang on. Oh...!'*

Then Raymond says, *'feast your eyes on me in the corner.'*
As we do, we can see all six feet two inches of him, standing in the light of the Spirit energy. His hands show up clearly and his arms. Then together we all chorus, *'oh Raymond, how wonderful.'*
'Yes, this is very exciting.' Raymond replies

I say, *'oh Raymond, what a knock out you are.'* Well I'm just agog by now ! *'I can see the toecaps of your boots !'*
Then Raymond says to my husband, *'Alfie, I like your cap. May I put it on ? It's very interesting.'*

'Well, it's in the car Raymond.' Alfie replies.
'No it isn't,' says Raymond. *'It's behind your chair. I'll get it.'*

So the Spirit of Raymond Lodge promptly retrieves my husband Alfie's chequered cap from the back of his chair and puts it on his head !

Raymond: *'You know, we had caps similar to this Alfie, except the crown was much bigger.'*

Alfie: *'Well you can take it back with you. They'd never believe me when I say, I gave my cap to you Raymond.'*

Raymond: *'Alf it doesn't matter. <u>You</u> know that I'm wearing your cap, so let them say what they will...'*

Pat Jeffries: 'Raymond, you know how we look forward to certain events in the future, do you have things to look forward to, as we do ? Because you tell us it's such a marvellous world.'

Raymond: *'Why of course. If one does the same thing all the time, one gets bored. We do not get bored, for all the wonders of our world are never ending. Every day there's something new for us to absorb, but you find it difficult to absorb new things everyday with your busy material lives.'*

Alfie: 'Can I ask you about your recent sessions with the experts ? We discussed it today and it centred around whether or not they actually believed, that when they came here they *would* see some phenomena. I said most of the researchers had never seen anything over the years - that could really be called phenomena.'

Raymond: *'Absolutely true Alf, they wouldn't know it. So when you see a piece of furniture hurtling towards you and there is no one at the other end, then it stops full short of your brain and doesn't hit you - then that's phenomena of sorts. What I mean is, oh yes, they have seen something which they call 'supernatural' which is uncontrolled, then what are they calling this ? You understand me ?'*

Alfie: 'I think they are completely unprepared for it.'

Raymond: *'Oh yes exactly. They know I am here.'*

Alfie: 'But will they clearly define what they have seen ?'

Raymond: *'Well they can say we have spoken and there's no other way another body can be in the room, that is all. I am not worried. They <u>ask</u> to come, we didn't ask them ! Understand Alf ?'*

We all murmur, *'yes Raymond.'*

Raymond: *'They were invited to witness what is going on, you know. We are here...but we only give them a taste of that. The minds who want to play around with the scientific are very welcome to come along and witness it. Whatever they want to make of it or not...though I cannot give them a formula if I do not know it myself!*
One thing I would like to stress to you, is the link of the Higher Beings. I'm sure that those scientists who do come, cannot be scientific <u>and</u> believe in God - and <u>there is</u> a God Almighty. What would they do then? That is the main point that I want to make.'

Alfie: 'It means a complete change of approach by them.'

Raymond: *Well doesn't it? They suddenly say 'my God, I've seen Raymond Lodge' and then go out to the outside world. Can you imagine what would be changed in history? Not a lot really...*
People who have believed have made a few waves. Then those who didn't want to know come along and try to stop it - you understand?
So they don't go ahead too far. But <u>we</u> all do and we know how much to give them and how much <u>not</u> to give them.

Alfie: 'I don't believe they will go away and use what they have seen. I think they'll break it down into small bits, but I don't think they will conclude anything, because I'm not sure they know or expect to see what they see. You see they can't explain it anymore than before they come here.'

Raymond: *'Yes, they can't say this is what I've witnessed. They can't explain it and say <u>this is what I have seen.</u>'*

Alfie: 'It's against their standard. They can't explain it, so they sidestep it.'

Raymond: *'I don't think so, because every time they come they can't explain it. Archie Roy comes all the way from Glasgow you know and stops overnight at a hotel. He wouldn't do that if he didn't need to come. He would sidestep it too and quite frankly I hope he wouldn't for that reason - if he didn't need to come. Now Alan Gould has sat in quite a few séances, many hundreds in fact and he behaved like a gentleman, a very thinking man. So these people wouldn't be phoning on a weekend saying that they think they've got a 'scoop' - and they haven't got it at all.*
I'm just a part of a whole. We advocate peace at that point.
Would you believe that men get assassinated in the name of peace? Martin Luther King did and Mahatma Gandhi. Where there's peace there is no wealth. A war always makes riches. It's black market and many people making arms and ammunition. All those people would lose money where peace is concerned...'

Alfie: 'How do you cope with the difficult researchers ?'

Raymond: *'Well it's a matter of warning people off. Yes if you want to go on an ego trip, I suppose we could all be in America or somewhere or other. Rita's afraid of flying, isn't she ? You see it's her who has told people 'NO WAY' will she be in the Psychic News. You must remember this !*

They have published articles that are untrue about me - and that has turned Rita away from the Psychic News forever. It's not that important to get things in the PN, but it's the only defence I've got on Earth, as you people have. Mind you, many people could believe it was me in there. Understand ? So it's a fascinating subject of ours. Now I think we ought to take a break...

...No Russell, you can't sing 'Valencia' !'

But Russell comes in singing it anyway - while we all have a breather.

Then after a few moments Russell is back and shouts,
'all back to your places now.'

Then he goes over to Rita the Medium, who is in Trance. Gently tapping her chin he says, *'hello...it's Russell. It's me. X X Kiss-Kiss...'*

Rita: 'Oh where is he ? He touched my face but he's not there.'

Russell: *'I'm up in the air...Boo ! Now I'm in the box...oh dear...whoops !'*

Just then, Raymond begins lifting Rita out of her chair as he says,
'I'll give her ghost stories. She does love to read them !'

Then together, Russell and I sing *'Ave Maria'* while Raymond gently puts Rita back into her chair.

I know this all sounds fantastic, but it's all there on the tape !

You may have been wondering what was in the box that Russell mentions. Well Pat and Barry, the parents of Russell's friend Michael Jeffries, had tall sons, so they were able to bring a pair of large leather boots, a jacket and a hat to the séance room. These had previously been covered with luminous paint...and now Raymond had the lot on !

So suddenly there he was, this very tall man (over six feet) standing there and walking around the room. When you looked at him you could see his army uniform, underneath the luminous jacket. I saw two little badges on his collar and he wore a leather strap across his body. On other occasions we were told he'd been seen wearing his Lieutenants cap - and people *had* seen and touched his leather boots. He could be heard with the cane he carried, tapping on his boots. You could even smell the boot leather.

This had been an amazing evening and we *'oohed'* and *'aahed'* and laughed so much. Someone had asked Raymond how tall he was. Raymond replied by saying, *'I'll lay down and you can measure me...'*
We heard someone say *'six foot two and a half!'*
Then Raymond quipped, *'I think I had better get up now, otherwise you'll all think I'm dead!'*
Raymond's humour was great, so he'd have said that in fun. Honestly, sometimes we'd laugh so much during these séances, that we'd literally be rocking in our seats!

Russell told us, *'when we're laughing Mum, like you are, we lift off the ground like Mary Poppins. You'd all need a helium balloon and then you can hang on the end of it - that'd be fun wouldn't it?'*
Next we heard a crash and a wallop, which sounded just like Russell landing on the floor, like a parachutist!
Then he asks, *'oh can I sing a song - can I?'*
And off he goes with his own version of a Perry Como tune...

*'You can tell when you open the door,
you can tell when there's <u>love in the home</u>,
Every table and chair seems to smile.
Come on in, come and stay for a while.*

*You always know that you've been there before,
by the shine and the glow in the room,
and the clock seems to chime 'come again any time!'
You can tell when there's love in the home.'*

Crumbs! I think we needed our tissues after that one...

This particular evening, Raymond Lodge had even bought his dog Larry with him, from the Spirit World. Larry went round and round the room, jumping about as any dog would, with his tail wagging all the time. Yet he did respond when Raymond said, *'sit Larry.'* He seemed to be enjoying proceedings as much as we were!
Whilst animals are on my mind, I did asked Helen Duncan once about my own little white cat, Snowy. She was so frail and old then, yet I hadn't the heart to have her put to sleep. Helen told me,
'I'm not able to answer that Gwen, but just use your own judgement.'
Snowy was so well loved and we managed to hang on to her for another three weeks. Then so tragically, Snowy actually died after running under the wheels of my son Gary's car. He was totally devastated and so was I.

Before I share another cat story, I want to include something here which many readers of my book *'Russell'* have asked about. During a séance in 1983, one sitter asked Raymond Lodge, *'exactly what are UFO's ?'*

Raymond: *'...well they are not from our etheric wavelength. I am adamant that Spirit do not need a vehicle to travel about in. UFOs come from other solar systems where, on their planets, physical people programme their vehicles to dematerialise and then materialise in another Solar System. This is also the method by which etheric scientists move apports about. These are physical objects that are transferred from one part of your world to another.*

There was once a very interesting experiment, carried out in this very house in the early days of the circle. The etheric scientists teleported a large easy chair - together with the family cat, who was sound asleep - from one room to another and the cat came to no harm !'

Raymond also said to this sitter,
'it is surprising how much light can come, into an open mind.'

I know this story of the teleportation of the armchair and cat, will always be hearsay until the experiment can be repeated. The only problem is 'where do we find a Physical Medium to help repeat such an experiment ?' I'm certain there are some out there, but the way Medium's are treated, is it any wonder they don't dare come forward ?

Now I would like to finish this chapter on a lighter note !

We mustn't forget that there is such a lot of good in this world. The human capacity to love expands as we get older. The so called 'death' of a child shows me that there are no rules to life. Yet if there *are* rules, that loss has such a life changing effect, you break the rules. In my case, I was filled with such determination to 'find' my child again - no matter what !

At the moment, the TV and the media are full of horrendous crimes. There seems to be such evil about. We are inclined to forget about the goodness all around us - which seems to speak to us in whispers. Yet it escapes the headlines because it *isn't news.* Looking around us, we find so many acts of kindness and generosity from so many people, every day. Imagine if these acts of kindness, goodness and love were recorded somehow, let's say on a computer in the Spirit World. It would show that in the balance of goodness against evil, the scales would crash down on the side of goodness - of ordinary folk everywhere.

We hear enough about the baddies in authority, but we rarely hear about the goodies - those who give out kindness to people who are lost, confused, sad or bewildered. We are learning now to jeer at our politicians. Some are clearly crooks and liars, yet a lot of them have a passion for justice and a desire to do good - we just never hear about them. It almost seems that trying to do good is almost a dangerous thing to do. Yet there is good everywhere and those who are, just carry on without ever being noticed. Being noticed is not important to them. Simple words exchanged in bereavement or illness, can do more good than all the newspapers and politicians put together.

So now I'll get off my soapbox, for I have said enough...
When all people *know* there is no death, things *must* change. I have written about Truth in this chapter and for those who look for it, may I say '*more power*' to your elbow ! But please don't just keep it to yourself, share the news with people everywhere. It will bring it's own rewards, of that I am certain.

As I write it is almost Christmas 1999, so let me end on an amusing discussion involving Christmas. Before we finished the last séance, Russell came to his father and said, *'give me your hand, for a special reason Dad.'*
Helen Duncan said, *'well it's got to be a new little trick. I'll tell you the truth - don't get too excited over it !'*
Russell was going around to people in the séance room and grabbing their hands. Then he would dematerialise his own hands whilst still holding theirs ! He did this once with a gentleman who'd been invited. He'd got his two hands around Russell's, which then just disappeared as he held them. For those invited, this was the type of experience that really got them. They would just gasp for breath and not want to leave !

I asked my husband, *'did Russell say anything to you Alf? Some special words ?'* Alfie just replied, *'he never does anything without a reason Gwen - but I think you know that already !'*

However, during the séance everyone began chatting about Christmas. Michael told us something he remembered from his life on Earth. One Christmas his father Barry had fallen asleep after eating his Christmas dinner. Michael told us.
'...and he'd still got his glasses on. Well you know those bows that you stick on parcels, the ones that stick on automatically ? We stuck one on each lens of his glasses and when he woke up he thought he'd gone blind !'

Then Alfie and Russell began discussing their memories of Christmas 1960 - when Alfie had fallen down the stairs with a pushbike !

He'd been trying to put it at the top of the stairs late on Christmas Eve - for one of the boys to find on Christmas morning. *'I was playing at being Father Christmas'* Alfie said. *'and yes, I'd had a fair bit to drink !'*

'Then he slipped down the stairs' Russell tells everyone, *'and we all had Christmas at two in the morning because we'd all woken up ! My Mum wasn't very pleased about it. I can remember Dad was sitting on the stairs holding his head !'*

We really had such fun at these séances. I remember one time Helen jokingly suggested they should try and materialise Father Christmas ! This did make us laugh, yet I could go on and on with similar stories in this chapter. However, I'll finish here with this short poem, which came for this purpose, through my friend Frankie Brown...

*When you see white doves,
you think all doves are white.
If you see a black dove,
then you know all doves can't be white.*

*When you see nobody appear from the other side,
Then you think there's nobody there.
But when you see one child materialise,
Then you know there must be somebody there.*

*So the parable here, is seeing is believing !
That's why the boy's story has been told,
and the Age of Aquarius is starting...
to bring forth multitudes of materialisation.*

~ Signed 'The Light Bearer'
Through the Mediumship of Frankie Brown

Seventeen

A Magical Mystery Tour ?

'I'll get by with a little help from my friends...'
~ John Lennon & Paul McCartney

It's June 1996 and like most of us when searching for something we've lost, we often find something else ! In my case I'd found a piece of paper, which brought back memories of a very wonderful surprise that our Spirit friends sprang upon me.

On the day of the magical 80s séance, when we received the apport of the Pink Panther, I was invited once again to join Rita for a weekend. I can't recall where Alfie was at this point, but I travelled up to Leicester by train and Rita was there to meet me. I don't recall the date, but the weather was foggy, wet and murky, so it was perhaps around February time.

We had a beautiful séance the first evening, where we chatted about family matters and such things as the mysteries of planet Earth ! If my memory serves me right, there was a man there who was very much interested in such things. He spent time talking to Raymond Lodge on space travel, time travel and the moon landing. It was very interesting to listen to such a conversation and of course we had our lovely Laura, who sang to us at regular intervals. Now and again Russell did his usual clowning around and it proved to be an altogether very enlightening evening. It was very, very relaxed and so, so natural.

Now everyone has their own pet subject, so to speak, and this evening ended with Raymond saying, *'...these are the mysteries of the Earth, they are there for man to solve if his free will want to do it, it's up to you friends...'*

Although most of this went straight over the top of my head, I did notice that Russell's friend Michael kept calling him 'Rusty.' So I asked him, *'what's with all this 'Rusty' business Michael ?'*

Michael replied, *'you'll see tomorrow !'*

Well this nickname, 'Rusty' was only ever used for Russell by his father and since Alfie wasn't there that evening, I just said, *'oh, okay.'*

Finally, Raymond said to us, *'early to bed tonight my friends'* then he promptly apported a handwritten note, in his own handwriting. By now I became very puzzled, but since note was for Rita, naturally I never read it. I recall that we did all turn in somewhat earlier than usual that night, but next morning we were up early.

We were going out in the car that day, but I was still dying to know what was in Raymond's note to Rita, although I never said anything. I just got in the car, settled down in the back seat and we were off !

Rita had very kindly packed the boot with a super picnic for us - with all sorts of wonderful goodies. There were flasks full of soup and tea and coffee and I as I watched all this food going into the boot, I was aware of a kind of excitement. I said to Rita, *'where are we going ?'*

Rita just said, *'here Gwen, read this'* and to my astonishment, she passed me Raymond's note. I'd thought it was a private message and Rita's own property, but no. It seemed some instructions had been given and I was the one who was to try and solve the clues in the note.

Being extremely right brained, I'm not even capable of doing a crossword puzzle and as for cryptic puzzles, I have to admit I'm useless ! Our Spirit friends must have been very amused by the puzzled look on my face, when I tried to work it all out ! Raymond's apported note was written thus:

> *Well, well, well, you're here at last,*
> *To join as one among the past,*
> *These stones stand proud as we do too,*
> *A memory circle through and through,*
> *Now here is what you have to do...*
>
> *Norman's house with weight on so -*
> *From there to ground where we don't grow !*
> *Where we are and what we do,*
> *When last of breath has gone from you.*
>
> *Then add to this a coinage <u>true,</u>*
> *And bull will shine - that is the clue.*
> *The keys to stars in heaven's blue.*
>
> *~ Norman (Raymond Lodge)*

After driving for a couple of hours through the misty morning, I studied the note, but still hadn't got a clue. The clues were all there yes, but silly me had got them all wrong ! We stopped at a dear little village and we strolled along, chatting. I remember staring through the window of a bric-a-brac shop and spied a row of books. Knowing my obsession for old books, we went into the shop, where I immediately found a book called *'Rusty'* ! Soon enough however, we were off again and I had this lovely book tucked under my arm.

I have to say, that at this point I had no idea that Raymond Lodge was the son of the scientist Sir Oliver Lodge. In his father's book *'Raymond'*, Sir Oliver explains that a favourite pastime of theirs was to write to each other - and *both* were fond of puzzles and cryptic clues. Some time later, I read a copy of Sir Oliver's great book that I'd received as a gift and I could see their games for myself.

However, I was still pondering Raymond's note while sitting on the back seat of the car. *'Perhaps there's a pub called The Bull'* I thought, but Gwen was wrong again ! I remember searching through the mist for standing stones and didn't see a single one. I must have seemed like a right nut ! We did make a big joke of it though and we laughed a lot. I guess our unseen friends were laughing with us too.

We had arrived in the county of Wiltshire and at the time, I'd never been to this part of the country before. To be honest I was totally lost, but I happily chatted away to my friends, since I knew they were well in control of our logistics. I really thought we were driving through the back of beyond, when suddenly we pulled into a car park and stopped. We had actually arrived at Stonehenge - and the mist outside made it all seem even more mysterious ! I clutched Raymond's note and looked at the poem,
'these stones stand proud, as we do too,'

'a memory circle through and through...'

Indeed ! At least a piece of his puzzle was solved. Our visit to Stonehenge was really memorable, for I had never experienced the wonder of it before. Our walk around it felt truly mystical to me, for it is an amazing place !

After we'd tucked into some lovely hot soup and crusty rolls, we sat feeding the pigeons for a while. I'd helped to solve some of Raymond's note at least - with a little help from my seen and unseen friends, then we were back on the road again.

We had another stop soon after, where we pulled over to the side of a pretty road. Looking through the car window, I found myself staring down a long tree-lined drive towards the most beautiful house. I discovered that this house was where Raymond's father, Sir Oliver Lodge, had retired to

with his wife Mary and spent the rest of his life. My travel companions had already got it all worked out from Raymond's note,
'Norman's house, with <u>weight on</u>.'

At the time this bit really puzzled me, what did he mean *'with weight on'* ? Well, it turns out the house was called 'Norman*ton* House' !

We continued along many country roads on our expedition, yet we still had half of Raymond's note to make sense of. We arrived at yet another mystery location and got out of the car. Walking through a very tiny alleyway, we could see a very small church and the smallest cemetary I think I had ever seen !
'From there to ground where we don't grow...
...when last of breath has gone from you.'

I just stood in amazement, because we were actually standing in the Lodge family cemetery ! I was totally lost for words but found it all so interesting. We looked at the names on all the stones and found, Sir Oliver Lodge, his wife Mary and all of Raymond's brothers and sisters who had passed on to the Spirit World. Rita did tell me that at the time, she thought there might be some of Raymond's sisters still alive.

'Then add to this a coinage <u>true</u>'

To my knowledge we never solved this bit, although I vaguely recall a coin being found, but I couldn't swear to it.

The grass in the cemetary was long and very wet and by now my feet were soaked, for as usual I was wearing completely inappropriate shoes ! But I didn't care too much, for we were having such a great time. We looked around at all of the Lodge family gravestones, when suddenly we saw one tiny stone which seemed very sunken.
Oh, it was so small ! Engraved in the stone was a memorial to a baby named *'Lily Lodge'* who had apparently passed shortly after birth. As we stood there, the sun came through the mist briefly and seemed to shine on this tiny baby's grave. As it did, we saw something glistened in the long grass. One of us bent to pick up this mystery object and we found that it was a 'Taurus the Bull' keyring - which is my birth sign !
'And bull will shine - that is the clue.
The keys to stars in heaven's blue,'

So said Raymond's note. I held this lovely keyring in my hand, which was red and depicted a white bull and blue stars.

What more can I write about this lovely trip ? We'd had such a glorious day and it was a long journey back. Though just to bring me back down to Earth, we stopped off so I could buy some sensible shoes - for now I was soaked through and up to my ankles in mud. But who cares - I have memories of a magical day that will stay with me forever.

At a later séance Russell told us that the keyring was a gift to me from the two R's - Russell and Raymond. I still treasure it now and it hangs on the arm of my apported Pink Panther toy.

On the following evening we enjoyed another séance. Although I didn't make notes at the time, I do recall Raymond said he was delighted that his 'Mystery Tour' and 'note' had been so appreciated.
'There will be other notes Gwen' Raymond told us *'and other 'Tours' as you call them, in the future. You will see.'*

Raymond was right, there *were* more notes - *and* tours, but they came years later. How clever our Spirit friends are though, for a constant interaction is going on. Yet we can only fully understand this when our Spiritual awareness is switched on.

I made up my mind that I'd revisit that tiny cemetery one day, for I wanted to know more of the Lodge family. I now truly felt that Raymond was one of my dearest friends in Spirit. His gentle voice with his 'cut glass' accent always has me captivated. If someone would have told me years ago, that some of my most wonderful friendships would be with 'invisible' people, I'd have thought they were crackers ! Now I know that these Spirit friends are all around us, unseen and unsensed by most and existing at a much higher frequency. This doesn't cause me any problems, because to me they are *more real* than we are.

I wish I could have tape recorded *all* of our wonderful chats - especially one about Raymond's Bible ! He told us that it was still in existence somewhere and he spoke of his favourite passages, which he'd underlined within it's pages. In fact, we agreed that we enjoyed the same pieces, for I'd underlined them in my own Bible. We also talked of coincidences and of course Raymond replied, *'Gwen, you know there are no such things. We make them happen !'*

These chats with Spirit now remain as precious memories for me. I'm reminded here that years later, my friend Val Williams felt she had to send me a tiny butterfly as a gift. Beneath it were these words from Acts 1-8, *'You shall be my witness'*

Well I hope that I *have* done this, for I know my Spirit loved ones can see that I've done my best. One can do no more than that.

Eighteen

Summerland Tape Three

February/March 1992

'All Things Bright and Beautiful'
$\sim$ C.F. Alexander

Russell: *'Hello Mum ! Hello Dad !*

I promised that I would tell you how I bring inanimate objects to the séance room and how I put them on your lap. How do I do it ? Well it's basic for us, but hard for people to understand. Yet whether they are animate or inanimate objects - they are all made up of molecules. All we have to do is to alter their structure. This allows us to transport the object through time and space - your time and space - then rebuild it in the séance room and that is exactly what happens !

This may seem extremely unusual for you, but it is possible. I was very young then and had much to learn, but then there is nothing new to discover in this Universe. Anything that scientists discover today, you can be sure was known long ago. It may have been lost in the abyss of time and ignorance, but these things just lay dormant to be rediscovered again.

Great civilisations have come and gone and they have amassed much knowledge in their time. Catastrophes may have befallen them and in the chaos and confusion that reigned, their knowledge was lost. Yet it exists to be rediscovered again ! It is not so much discovering the knowledge, it is the timing that's essential for it's rediscovery. That's just how it is !

Timing is so important for everything. For if a concept or ideal is discovered too soon for people to grasp it, then that concept or ideal will be of no use to whoever discovers it. The discovery has to be at the right moment and time. It is the right time for this tape to be channelled. I'm not telling you anything that's not already been said or that you do not already know, deep down in the core of your soul !

What is sad, is that these Spiritual wonders, instead of being quested in true and rational ways, are steeped in mystery, intrigue and general silliness. They are not studied in the true light of knowledge and understanding. It is time that superstition was lifted - <u>and</u> all the mystique and silly preconceived ideas that go along with it. These happenings are not weird. They operate within the natural laws of nature. It has always been possible to move inanimate objects from one place to another through time and space. Civilisations have been able to do it in the past and they have achieved it in two ways - using machines and the power of their own minds.

It was once possible for machines to do this and it soon will be again. Yet there is one machine that is little understood and little known. It is far more powerful and complicated and intricate than the most advanced computer - and that is the human brain. It is possible for the brain to work on a certain thought or vibratory pattern to be able to move inanimate objects through time and space !'

* * *

Russell: 'Now my friend Raymond Lodge wishes to share some of his own words..'

Raymond: 'Once long ago, a boy with eyes so bright,
walked out of the darkness and into the light,

we had many adventures, this young lad and me,
Lighting the darkness for others to see.

But this beautiful boy grew into a man,
and now walks with a child on his hand.

A beautiful child with eyes so bright,
who works with us now to bring others to the light.

There's Rainbow and Russell,
Richard, Ronald, Steven and Ray,
and they've all come to say,
"God Bless you our Mothers."

My own Mother and Father are here with me in Spirit and you may recall that my Father told his own story for others to read. My Father still works, but from our side of life - to heal and help the knowledge to grow.

Now all the dear children written of in this book,
send their blessing upon the words you have put...

For your love it is wondrous, your love it is true,

It is through that love, that we come back to you.
Love is the answer, love is the key,
Through love we will show ourselves - to those ready to see.

But first let our words take root in your hearts, to feed you, to guide you, and bring you back to God...

God is love, Love is God,
to know God is easy,
Just make Love your God.

Material things have no place with us, so use them but don't worship them, for they will not feed your soul...

Don't break laws, there for the common good,
But never lose sight of the <u>True Laws</u> of God.
Divine in their making and absolute in power,
The Divine laws of God rule from one world to another.

For they alone have the ultimate power, the Divine Laws as given on slabs of stone - but since altered and re-written...

So the Divine Laws are lost in confusion and doubt.
Now we return to help you sort them out !

We always come in humility and we come in love - for you and the planet you damage, because you have forgotten *how* to love. We work with the Torch Bearers on Earth, to lead you out of the darkness of your own souls.

Your children will lead you, your children will show,
the wonder and glory of Love - as it grows...

Through your children's love you find truth. Through truth wisdom shines, but wisdom - the only true gold - is the hardest to find. To find wisdom look to a child - just watch their face as they discover the perfection of a flower ! Only when you can look on a flower with those same eyes, can you begin to understand the wonder in that child's eyes.

Look within to know what is right.
Don't look for others to lead you into the light.

The light is within you, but we can only point the way. You should keep your mind open to God and his ways. Do not let fear condition you or doubt blanket you in darkness. This keeps the love light out ! Don't let envy, ego and greed set up barriers. Trust God's way instead.

Trust God as a child trusts you.
Trust in God's Love - it will see you through.
Changes are coming - changes big and small,
the chance will come to get in touch with your soul once more.
Let go of your fears, neuroses and doubt.
Let in Love, Trust and Faith and the noblest of thought.

Keep thoughts for the whole, not just of the one - thoughts for *all* living things and your planet as a whole...

Give, do not take.
Love, do not hate

and the darkness of your planet *will* lift to become a bright light.

Love, truth and wisdom, walk hand in hand,
Feel love in your heart,
Find truth in your mind.

You can feel Love, you can find it - and
wisdom will follow very closely behind.

The power of God's Love is alive in you all.
So accept only the words that ring bells in your soul!

But never forget the first Divine Law, that you were born with free will. It is your right to choose, but responsibility for your actions is also your own. So be careful my friends...at-one-ment exists. For that which you give out, will come back to you.

Love is the answer,
Love is the key,
Love has the power to set the soul free.

Free to discover the greatest of truths
and free to discover your true Spirit home!

I made a promise long ago that I would not rest until the Truth was given to mankind, for them to truly see and understand. I have not forgotten my promise. I still hold dear to my vow and I will work to see the Truth presented to you all. So each may choose their own road...

There is nothing that can cure the soul
but the senses...
Likewise, there is nothing that can cure the senses
but the soul...'

Russell: *'I would like to begin this next piece by asking a question. What is time, space and distance?*

You know it from within the confines of your own dimensions, but outside of them that concept is different. This may seem a very odd thing to say, but it is truth, so it must be said.

Imagine for a moment that the entire Universe is just the size of an apple. It is there floating in the vastness of infinity when a Great Traveller - or Time Lord if you'd like to put it into the realms of Television - comes travelling through this vastness and sees this small round object, no bigger than an apple.

Our Traveller moves closer then enters the first layer. He discovers it's vastness and many galaxies within. He is now <u>within</u> the dimension of our apple-sized Universe and not simply viewing it from the outside. Once there, he finds galaxies upon galaxies.

He then he travels through the next layer and discovers your galaxy. That too is vast, yet he is small and tiny within it. Then he finds your solar system and the planets around your Sun. All the time, the vastness to him is increasing. Then he finds the Earth and once there, he lands upon its surface.

The Earth is also vast and wondrous, but he forgets what he has been through and how long he has been travelling. He forgets the many layers and he forgets the dimensions through which he has travelled. He settles to live upon the Earth, without recollection of his journey.

But this Traveller I describe is not really some great Time Lord created from a writer's imagination. This great traveller is you!
Because every one of you has viewed the dimension in which you now live, from the outside! All of you have some understanding of that which I speak, for it lies dormant within the very core of your being. You all know!

Yet you have become tied up in the vastness of the Earth and the vastness of the dimensions which you have grown to love. By doing that, you have lost the true reality of dimensions, space and time. This is what we all did, when we grew to love the planet called Earth!

We all grew to love it, so when the time came for us to return to being on the outside - we did not wish to go...
Then the whole concept of reincarnation began. So now we have souls trapped in these vast dimensions within our Universe.

Not only do souls like you exist within this dimension, but also those who have passed on to a greater understanding - and they choose to return to this dimension time and time again. They simply want to continue their voyage and quest within this dimension.

Now we are all free Spirits and just as you have the knowledge within you, of that first journey into this dimension, you also retain the ability to travel outside of this dimension !

You may say, 'how do we do this ? How do we make this great journey ?' Well, you begin from within, then you stretch out your mind to comprehend the vastness of your world, then of the galaxies and of the Universe. You must go on a Spiritual journey from within, to discover your true being - which is of God's creation.

Within your physical body you live in one dimension - this is reflected in your life on Earth, but from within your soul and your mind, you have the ability to soar. You do not need to stay rooted upon the Earth, you can travel up into the Universe and through the galaxies. You can try to grasp the true oneness that you possess, with the creative power which you call God. There is only one power in this Universe, in this galaxy and beyond. That power is the ultimate, supreme power we call God. Others might call it the White Master - there are many, many names, but there is only <u>one</u> power.

Each and every one of you have the spark of Divinity within you. You can link with that ultimate creative force and be alone with that power - so that the inner journey reflects your original outer journey. It is how you came here in the first place - and it is through your outer journey that you will one day return. It is within the realms of possibility, that if you choose to link with that ultimate creative power, you will find that time, distance, space and physical being are all an illusion ! Each of us only believe what we see and hear within the dimension that we live. Take that experience outside of that dimension and it becomes nothing.

So how do we see something that we perceive to be physical ? We see it with our eyes and it registers within our brain. Our brain recognises the reflections of the image from our eyes - and we give it a name. So if we look at a beautiful view and see a mountain in the distance, our brain registers a mountain, likewise a valley, tree, river or house. But how do we get that vision of wholeness that on the Earth we call 'reality' ?

Remember that all things are composed of atoms and atoms join together to create molecules. The things we see, gain their substance and their density by the vibratory pattern of these molecules - created when they vibrate with the living God Force within them ! This vibration creates a light, which all living things have. Some call it the Aura, but it is simply a physical reflection of the life force.

Every blade of grass has an aura and every tree. Stones have auras as does the Earth itself. If you could view the Earth from the moon you would see a rainbow aura of light around it. It does look wondrous !
This is the life force of the Earth - the aura. For the Earth is a living thing.

If you create a piece of furniture from of a piece of wood, it is no longer a tree. You have cut off the living life force from the wood and turned it into a cabinet or chair or desk. Although it will still contain a faint aura of its original life force. Plastic toys, such as my Mother's Pink Panther and little Dinky cars are inanimate objects and contain no aura. Living things do contain an aura. Every animal and every human being that walks upon the Earth has their own aura.

The aura is a bright light which shines around six inches to a foot, all around a person. A healthy aura shows white, with bright rainbow colours indicating a healthy soul and mind - this usually means a healthy body ! A dark aura shows disease within the body, the soul or the mind. When combined these three produce physical ailments in the physical body.

All human beings are three in one, Soul, Mind and Body. These three conspire and exist together to produce the aura around each and every living soul. So you have a Physical Aura produced by the vibration of the molecules within your own body. You also have your Spiritual Aura which joins forces with it. This combination is what those who are blessed to see auras can use, to perceive certain illnesses or diseases within the body.

For many years gifted seers have spoken of auras. These are seen depicted in the holy paintings and stained glass windows of your churches. They are there for you all to see. That bright light around Holy figures is simply the aura of those that lived in the past. Of course, it is not a light reserved only for Holy figures, it is the light of all living things and you all have it.

Despite these historical paintings in your galleries and churches, many people deny the existence of auras. Many laugh at those who speak of auras, but auras have been photographed. People can now have photographs of their own auras. The scientific establishment were initially very distressed when they saw this. It was not within their preconceived ideas and this is the tragedy !

You have an establishment on the Earth, which cannot come to terms with ideas that go against their existing patterns and beliefs. This is indeed a great sadness for us. When these people block the truth, it is very sad - for nothing can be gained by that. It is only when human beings truly grasp the power and might of themselves, that this wonderful planet can be rescued from the ravages that have been inflicted upon it.

You may wonder what all of this has to do with a book about the continuation of life after physical death ! Well it is exactly these things which makes the continuation of life after death a reality. In order to explain, I would like to bring you to the first law of physics, which proves that energy cannot be destroyed. Energy can be transformed and it can change form - but it cannot be destroyed.

So what is a human soul ? Well if you could see a human soul outside of it's body, it appears as a ball of white light in the form of a circle - and this is significant. The circle is the key to all life, as all time is circular. The circle is also the shape of the Divine Spark from the God Force. This was given to make you and that white ball of light - which is your soul. It is pure energy. Energy without the interference of matter, therefore that energy, that white bright light, cannot be destroyed. It may take other forms, but it cannot be destroyed.

Shapes are very important, for example even to this day the mysteries of the Great Pyramid of Giza have still not been fully uncovered. The key to the Pyramid is its shape. It is no accident that the Pyramids or series of Pyramids in Egypt, were laid out to reflect the stars up in the sky. The ancient Egyptians had knowledge contained within the Great Pyramids and in the Sphinx. If this were to be fully revealed, people would not be ready to grasp the implications of all it contains.

There are Spiritual 'Torch Bearers' now working on the Earth to light the road to that knowledge. This is why that now is the correct time for these words to be channelled. The reason for this will become apparent in a few years from now, but it <u>will</u> become apparent.

The first book entitled 'Russell' will probably make some people think 'why is it that Russell's Mother has seen Physical Phenomena ? Why can't I ? Why should she have the right to see it ? Why should his Father ? Why should any of the circle see it ?'

Well I tell you truly, that all those who sat in that Physical Phenomena circle had earned the right to be there. Each and every one of them had the opportunity to use that knowledge for the benefit of all. Not all those present in the circle have chosen to use that knowledge for the benefit of all however. One of the reasons that my parents witnessed the Physical Phenomena, was because my Mother was destined to write the first book. My Father had to witness it alongside her, to be our witness - and to back up that which my Mother saw. There are other reasons which I will not go into now, but I can say that they both earned the right - in this lifetime and others. Even so, you may then say, 'but I've lost a child ! Why can't I see Physical Phenomena ? Why haven't I been given this blessing ?'

Well I will ask you this, if a person who you know to be 'dead' materialised in front of you, what would you do ? What would be your true reaction ? And why would you want to see it ? If you did see it, would you believe the evidence of your own eyes ? What is more, what would you do in order to share that knowledge for the benefit of all ?
So before people begin to shout about not being able to witness Physical Phenomena, first of all look to yourselves. Are you really ready to witness the laws of your dimension suspended for a brief moment in time - to witness that which is beyond many people's conception of belief.
Are you ? Look into yourself ! For if you <u>were</u> able to witness it and share it with mankind, then you would see it !

So how do we produce the Physical Phenomena ? Well to begin with, it is not a thing that is done willy-nilly. It has to have the blessing and the direction of the ultimate power, the ultimate creative force, which I have always called God. For this phenomena to occur you also have to be in the presence of a Physical Phenomena Medium. This would be a human being who has the ability to produce a substance known as Ectoplasm in order for the soul or souls, that live in another dimension, to be seen in yours.

The molecules of those souls vibrate at a higher frequency than your own, this renders them invisible and impossible for the physical eye to see. Of course, there are those on the Earth who can heighten their own vibrations, just as there are people on our side, who can lower theirs. This allows the blessed communion to take place, this is the moment when our two worlds join. In order for us to physically manifest, we have to have a Medium in our circle who can produce Ectoplasm, which is a mix of chemicals and fluids released from the Medium's body. This is used to allow those who live in our dimension, to materialise.

This is not based on witchcraft or any form of untoward action, thought or deed. It is based on science. It is science that makes it possible. It is based on a scientific principle that is not currently understood by the scientific world. This is mainly because they do not <u>wish</u> to understand it, for they have closed their minds to any work on this form of discovery.

Physical Phenomena is not a game or trick or any other form of weird conjuring. It is a thing based on very real scientific laws, rules and regulations - as well as Spiritual and philosophical laws, rules and *regulations. It is only when the Spiritual and scientific are joined and people come together in love, harmony and fellowship, will this sort of thing occur - and only on the understanding that a Physical Medium is required to produce the right combination of fluids and chemicals known as Ectoplasm. This has occurred throughout the ages and will continue to occur. We are saddened by how Physical Mediums have been treated in the past. It is not the will of God that anyone should be persecuted for doing this kind of work.*

Of course, not all Mediums who claim to work with Physical Phenomena are true Physical Phenomena Mediums at all. This is true of the last 50 years and it is true today. I'm afraid there are frauds and there are tricksters and they should all be exposed. For they are taking something Divine and beautiful and misusing it with the intent to defraud many. This will not aid the understanding of life and life beyond life - so it is right that the charlatans be exposed !

On the other hand, it is not right to oppose, humiliate and in any way abuse or misuse genuine Physical Phenomena Mediums. Also, we will not work with those who abuse their own abilities. We choose who we work with, just as Mediums should choose who they work with. Any legitimate Medium should always choose to work with the highest and the best, and it is our wish to always work with those on the Earth, who have only the highest and the best motives for doing what they do.

So how does Ectoplasm make Spirit people, who exist at a higher frequency, materialise ? Remember that Mediumistic people communicate with us by heightening their own vibrations, as we lower ours. Then between us we blend and communicate, so the two worlds are temporarily joined. In order for us to manifest in the séance room, we need to clothe ourselves in Ectoplasm from the Physical Medium - which lowers our vibratory level even further, so we appear as solid mass on your Earth. It is the Physical Medium that we need, in order to produce this phenomena.

Some people do not realise they are Physical Mediums, while others develop the gift over years. In the first 50 years of the twentieth century, Physical Mediums produced Ectoplasm which took the form of a white gauze looking substance. It is now the wish of my mentors and guides to do away with that particular form of Physical Mediumship. It is our wish that the Physical Medium should no longer have the very selfless role of needing to go into a semi-coma type Trance state, to produce Ectoplasm for us to materialise. This is what normally used to happen.

We now want to encourage our Physical Mediums to simply go to sleep, then we can bring the Medium back awakened into their normal state - so they may enjoy the wonder of the phenomena themselves. We are now working on the production of Ectoplasm in such a way, so that there isn't masses of the white substance physically appearing - but that it is rarefied into an almost invisible coating. So perhaps the most you might see is a vague white mist or at the very most a white glow. My guides and mentors are working on this principle of Physical Phenomena for the future.

We hope the day will come, when the world will be free enough that we can show the wonders of Physical Phenomena to many, not just a few. We would like to bring it into the realms of your reality even more and show it to the entire world. Perhaps then, some miraculous things could be seen and brought about, with the full knowledge and involvement from the Physical Medium. But then again, it's all a question of timing. If we were to try this before the world was ready to receive it, what would happen?

Sadly, I suspect that the Physical Mediums would be misused or abused and at worst their lives ruined. It is not our will that this should happen, so we have to be extremely careful, for the safety of our Mediums is absolutely paramount.

We will not risk the life of any Medium we work with - they are too precious to us. We must be one hundred percent sure that they will not suffer through our use and we never betray the great trust they place in us. We have to be sure that the world will not misuse or abuse them, for it is our wish that many will see Physical Phenomena for themselves - but this is all in the timing! It has to be done at the right moment for people to understand and perceive it. On its own, Physical Phenomena is no good whatsoever, unless it is studied and understood within the knowledge and context of the philosophy of life itself. Just as Spiritual fact is part of the philosophy of life, so the philosophers and the scientists will have to come together and work together, to understand the wondrous philosophy of life.

Religion always looks on the scientists as its enemy and scientists always look on religion its enemy. This is not meant to be so - if only they would understand. If the two could join together and become one, then truly they could set about discovering the philosophy of life itself, for it can be proved in many ways. There are many pathways to God and there are many pathways to the truth - this doesn't always have to be a religious pathway.

As far as orthodox religions are concerned, none of them contain all of the truth, but then all of them do contain a portion of the truth. Once again, only when all religions can come together and become one, will we truly get some idea of the philosophy of life. Together, they can become more enriching and enlightened than they are today. While ever they are apart, they are but fragments and seen as complete and utter nonsense.

The scientific world has already discovered that man and all living things are not just matter - and the scientific world has already discovered the reality of life after death. They reached their conclusions a very long time ago, but I'm afraid this information is suppressed by various interested or self-interested bodies. They feel that this knowledge would be a threat to them - yet it is time that this information was opened up. There is a generation at the moment who are coming along now - children who are growing up. Those children will be the adults of the future. They have been born with an inner knowledge and an inner knowing - that there is more to life than the material. It is our hope that they will quest for the knowledge of truth and bring it to the attention of many. It is so sad that science has already crossed the barrier of understanding life after death and yet still suppresses it.

One other Physical Phenomena that people often wonder about, is how we can produce living things - at just the right moment and the right time. My own Mother has shared with you how the 'Red Admiral' butterfly is my special sign to her. Rainbow's is a white butterfly.
(Well it was a white butterfly when she was a baby, now it is turning into a yellow butterfly, because she has gained some knowledge.)

It's very different for us to produce a living thing in Physical Phenomena. It's easy enough to alter the molecular structure of an inanimate object, because it has no vibratory level of being. But with a living thing, it has a vibratory level of being and it is very important that we do not interfere with that vibratory level.
There is no way that we would damage a living thing, purely to bring it to you as proof of our existence or nearness. We would not do that for it would not be right. So how do we do it ?

Well, we use our minds to weave a kind of 'net' which we use to carry the little creatures to you. By the power of our world we weave these nets with love, in a kind of gossamer material very similar to Ectoplasm. It is of a much finer design and the same fine material that we are currently experimenting with in Physical Phenomena. If we capture these little creatures in our gossamer nets, we bring them and release them beside you, for you to be entranced by them. They are our signal to you that you know we are near and the creatures are never, ever harmed. For if we did, *purely to prove our nearness to you, it would be unacceptable to God. This is something not of our egos, but of our love. These gossamer nets are materialised on a higher vibratory level than your dimension can visibly produce - so you cannot see them, but they are there !*

If we bring something like a pearl, which may seem like an inanimate object, the pearl was once part of an oyster - a living thing - so it still contains a real life force. So again we gently wrap them in our gossamer nets to bring them to you, to show our love.

In a similar way, if we choose to bring you a flower, then through the power of our thoughts we can transport it to wherever we wish. Now you might argue that we have damaged the flower by picking it, for it is a living thing, but we would never damage a flower. We always beg its pardon before picking it - we ask its forgiveness first. Then if it is willing to give up its transitory life for our use, we can bring it to you. Even the humble snowdrop is never picked, without us first asking its permission !

To those of you who eat the flesh of living animals I have a question: how often do you thank the creatures that give up their lives, for you to feed yourselves and you families ? That animal has sacrificed its own life for you, but perhaps you should ask yourselves whether any animal should make that sacrifice for you ? This is something you need to consider within your own hearts. It's a decision you have to come to, by yourselves. Once again, there is always free will.

We think it's so sad in many ways, that although God has given the human race dominion over the animals - still many humans choose to dominate them. They abuse that gift of God. Our animal friends put up with so much from human beings, yet they still choose to return to the Earth in animal form. Animals that live close to human beings, return to give unconditional love to their chosen people. Other animals come back to work out their own Spirituality, their own voyage, their own soul growth and their own understanding. They choose to come back.

All animals have much more to teach us, than we have to teach them. It is no accident that human beings share the Earth with so many of them. They were given by God to teach us, even though so many sadly claim dominance over them. Those who do claim that dominance, approach it from an angle of ego. If we had no ego, we would not dominate our animal friends. It is our ego that makes us try and dominate one another. Dominance has nothing to do with dominion. God gave us dominion over the animal world, not dominance. It is a shame that human beings often get lost in their own ego.

Animals are able to manifest their Spiritual selves to Mediumistic people, because they have the Divine Spark of God within them. They have a soul - not the same as human beings - but it is a soul ! So when an animal dies, or 'ceases to exist' in your dimension, it goes on to exist in another dimension. It's very important to remember that there is no such thing as death ! All living things continue with their own spiritual journey, long after their own physical body has fallen away. Our animal friends are no different, they are as Divine as we are.

There is also nothing wrong in mourning the passing of a friend that walked on four legs. Nothing wrong whatsoever. However, it is very wrong to substitute an animal for a human being. One cannot use an animal purely to shower love and affection upon, as one would with a human being. Animals have their own right to be. They are wondrous and Divine creations, but they should not be used as any substitute for children, for husbands, for partners or for human friends. They can be friends that walk on four legs, but give them the dignity of their own being. Give them the importance of themselves and the right to be - do not abuse them.

To humanise an animal is almost as bad as threatening them in a cruel manner. They are not human, they are different, but this does not make them any less of a being. I often think that if we treat our animals as human beings, we are debasing them and not able to learn that which they came here to teach us. The most important thing they come to teach, is unconditional love.
An animal friend will give you unconditional love in the most glorious and wondrous abundance. They will give you loyalty and they will give you understanding - they will give you a great deal. They will give and ask very little in return. This is what animals have come to teach human beings. They become friends - personalised animals - that you can share your lives with, on an intimate level. Remember a cat or a dog is a great teacher in many ways, they can teach you and show you how to love !

It is very important that you respect the animal for what it is, in its own being. In its wholeness, its wonder and its dignity, we learn the lesson it comes to teach us. Your dog is probably your greatest teacher.
Since your animals have come to teach you something, get to know them as the wondrous and Divine creatures that they are, but don't use them as substitutes. Human beings they are not. Their role in your life is far greater than that ! They have come to walk with you and to teach you how to love - this is very important...

I will now conclude this third 'Summerland Tape' and say goodnight. Goodnight Mum and goodnight Dad ! God Bless and 'thank you very much, so very, very much' for all that you have already done. Thanks also to my wonderful channel for allowing me to work through her and I will leave the last word to her daughter, Rainbow...'

Rainbow: *'Hello Mummy, I love you. Night ! Goodnight and God Bless.'*

Gwen: Then we hear a short prayer on the tape, by an unknown voice of such beauty...

'May the Divine Laws that have been spoken of here, stretch forth into the world of darkness and lighten the world in understanding. God Bless all who listen and all who participate in this work.'

* * *

Gwen: After receiving this tape in the post, I first used headphones to listen to it - whilst at the same time writing out what I heard. Not being able to do shorthand, I had to take it down a few words at a time. It then had to be deciphered in my own fashion. Then I wrote it out in longhand and listened to the tape once again, whilst reading through my transcript. I found that one simple mistake, could make some of it read incorrectly. This third Summerland Tape took me about 19 hours in all to transcribe - but I really don't mind, for it makes for fascinating reading.

As I was finishing this work, I again heard Russell's now familiar tones singing to me...

'Thank you very much, thank you very much, it's the nicest thing that anyone's ever done for me...'

This song is from such an amusing scene from the 1970 film 'Scrooge' - and I'm amused at Russell's antics. Years later, I learned that his name is even seen displayed on a shop sign, in this part of the movie !

However, as I eventually wend my way to bed, my is mind boggling on everything I'd written out for him - molecular structures, inanimate objects, pyramids, and so on. I wonder how it is all done ? The wisdom of my own son, now grown into a man and the terms he uses in this script - I mean, I have practically no knowledge of any such things. Physics may as well be a foreign language to me !

So with these thoughts, a very preoccupied Gwen finally goes off to bed and I hear yet another beautiful song...

*'You give your hand to me,
and then we say hello,
and I can hardly speak,
my heart is beating so,
and any one can tell,
you think you know me well
but you don't know me...'*

~ *words by Eddy Arnold & Cindy Walker*

I think here I'd have to answer, *'no Russell, I don't know you - the man !'* This man with so much wisdom and knowledge and so much love. Now tears well up within me, for to me, he is still a laughing child and I guess he always will be. Yet I'm continually amazed by the way he expresses himself as an adult. Although if I get too pensive in my thoughts, I always receive another full rendering of the song, *'Thank you very much....!'*

I'm only able to comment on the things within this tape which I understand and have experienced. I've already said that I know very little on the subjects Russell speaks of - and the same can be said for his Medium. I *can* comment on the 'gossamer nets', because we do have a lot of wonderful experiences with these apports - but I'll put these in a chapter of their own, for I think them worthy of that. The 'scientific' part of the tape I cannot comment on at all. I'll just say, that it's really not my thing !

Many of the Mothers in the RPPS have had their own experiences with butterflies, brought to them in the way Russell describes. So much so, that each of their children in Spirit bring their very own species of butterfly. That is if they can find them, as some are so scarce these days. These Mothers relate their own stories as we go through the book.

Russell also spoke of a new form of Mediumship that they in the Spirit World are working on - the form where the Medium will be able to witness the wonders whilst *out* of Trance. From my own experience I can speak of two or three similar happenings that we witnessed in the séances.

At the end of one four hour séance, Russell said,
'we want to do an experiment Mum and Dad. Can you all be very quiet ? We are going to bring the Medium out of Trance and I am going to say 'hello' to her !'

So as usual, we all did as we were told by our 'boss' and we sat there, almost holding our breath. Now normally at this point, we would hear the Medium gradually coming out of Trance and asking us, *'are you there ?'* Our usual response would be, *'okay, we're here. We'll just switch the light on.'*

However on this occasion, as we sat in the quiet, hardly daring to move, we heard, *'hello, it's me ! It's Russell !'* Followed by Rita the Medium, who was now wide awake saying, *'oh my God, it's Russell !'* And it was. He was talking to the Medium ! This happened a few times and we were totally amazed.

After another four hour séance once, our friend Raymond Lodge took over and said, *'please be very quiet and I will show you what we can do. Watch and listen !'*
Again we sat perfectly still - waiting...

This time we heard Raymond speak to Rita saying, *'hello, it's Raymond !'* Then he lifted her out of her armchair and briefly held her, as we watched in amazement. Rita was then gently placed back in her chair and a moment later Raymond, together with Russell and all our other Spirit friends, simply joined in with their usual goodnight wishes.

There are few words to describe our feelings at these wonders. I wrote in my first book of this 'new energy' seen and felt at the séances. Perhaps wondrous *is* the best word to use ? I don't know.

As I was writing out the lovely piece from the tape about our animal friends, the morning post landed on my doormat. Sitting at my table to open it, I found that my publisher had sent me the chapter entitled *'What about our animal friends ?'* from the first book *'Russell.'* Somehow, this chapter later found it's way into *'Cat World'* magazine ! But here it was now, lying amongst my paperwork, as I was writing out the very lines about our beloved, four-legged creatures. Oh the timing...which is the very thing that Russell seems to excel at !

There is one final 'happening' that I feel I need to share with readers. Alfie and I have two young friends, who we've known for the last four years. One is Tony Stockwell, a jolly good Medium who works around the Spiritualist churches - and now the world ! He is so devoted to his work. The other is his partner Stuart Borley, a young man who also has a great love for the Spirit World.

A few days after Summerland Tape three had been recorded, they had both travelled to Egypt for a friends wedding. Naturally they were full of excitement and off they went, armed with all sorts of sun screen and vaccinated up to the max ! I would have loved to have sneaked into their suitcase to go with them ! However whilst they were away, I'd received Summerland Tape three in the post and had finished transcribing it by the time they arrived home, at the end of the month.

On November 3rd they came to visit us, bringing lovely gifts for me and such photographs - which I am sure they'll treasure forever. They gave me a few pictures to keep, of themselves posing alongside the Pyramids and Sphinx. They'd even climbed the Great Pyramid itself!

Now Tony and Stuart had taken their own copy of '*Russell*' with them on holiday and they told me how they'd sat and read it by the Pyramids - the very Pyramids that Russell had spoken of in this tape!

I was astonished to hear where the lads had been, but I was doubly astonished of what they told Alfie and me next. They said that after they'd been for a swim one day, they went for a walk - whilst carrying 'his nibs' book around with them. They were meandering down a little Egyptian street, when to their own amazement, they saw a Red Admiral butterfly flying around them both as they walked - in Egypt!

Tony and Stuart already knew of Russell and his butterflies, so they loved this experience. They told us that they'd literally jumped up and down with excitement - and who can blame them?

Yet here I was, now with the information of *how* Russell brings his butterflies, with the explanation of how he makes the gossamer nets to do so and all in his own words.

Now I don't believe in coincidences, but I do know that Russell must have had joined the lads in Egypt and made himself known to them in his own special way!

Whatever next I ask myself?

'I'd love to go to Egypt' I remember saying to Tony and Stuart. But I did eventually and you can read more of that later!

After this tape was completed, Russell had said to his Medium, *'well B-, I thought I'd better explain it all, because I don't want the whole world to think that you and my Mum are a couple of daffy old ducks do I?'*

Well thank you Russell...

Though I really *do* thank you Russell - for your love, your knowledge and obvious wisdom. Thank you for the songs you sing to me, with such meaningful lyrics and thank you for your humour.

Daffy Old Ducks indeed!

Nineteen

Gossamer Nets

September 1996

*'In dreams, through nets of wonder,
I chase the bright elusive butterfly of love'*

~ Bob Lind

Here I'd like to share some amazing butterfly stories. First, I include this tale from the book *'Phantoms of Soap Operas'* by Jenny Randles. I found it so interesting because it blended so well with my own experiences.

'Pantomimes are a very British tradition around Christmas time. These involve performances of a number of fairy tales, across the country. Well known actors star in these ritual comedy performances and they covet the lead roles in the best theatres.

Around seventy years ago actors in the Theatre Royal in Bath were rehearsing for their Christmas pantomime. Part of the scenery for the show included a hand-painted butterfly, but during rehearsals a dead butterfly was found on stage. Shortly afterwards the shows producer Reg Maddox, collapsed and died of a heart attack.

Despite the tragedy the show went on and during opening night a live butterfly was seen fluttering around the stage - the show was a success and a theatrical legend was born. Many years later, the actor and comedian Leslie Crowther had a role in another Christmas pantomime at Bath's Theatre Royal. On opening night, a butterfly which was attracted by the spotlight, fluttered onto the stage, flew around the entertainer and promptly landed on him!

The audience saw it, but weren't to know the legend - that should a live butterfly appear on opening night, it guaranteed a successful production. Whereas the appearance of a dead one heralded certain doom! As the audience looked on, Leslie paused in his performance and carefully picked up the butterfly, he then gently passed it to a stagehand. Knowing the legend as he did, there was no way he was going to let the creature come to any grief!

Butterflies are extremely rare at Christmas time in the UK, when Leslie's pantomime had opened. Yet the legend lived up to its reputation and the show went on to break box-office records! Theatre staff do take the legend very seriously - and so do the actors. Afterwards, Leslie Crowther was booked for the next pantomime and staff were hoping that another butterfly would turn up this time, to ensure the show's success!'

I'm very pleased to say, that this delightful story links in very nicely with one of my own. In my case we did not have a dead butterfly on stage, we had a Red Admiral back stage, on stage *and* in the audience. It was even captured on video for the show's recording.

Two friends of mine - local musicians, Colin Chaston and Tony Lloyd - had written their first ever musical entitled '*Tarot*' and somehow I'd found myself a part in the show, where I could be seen leaping around the stage and generally having fun! On opening night some of the ladies were getting made up and into costume. While some were glued to their scripts, some were practising their musical scales, *'ah, ah, ah, aah!'* and *some* were smoking cigarettes like mad. All the usual things one does on an opening night!

I was all ready to go on and waiting with a nice cup of tea, when someone called out, *'look, there's a huge butterfly in the dressing room. It's a Red Admiral.'* The butterfly was swooping and fluttering around the dressing room as if to greet everyone. One young lady said,
'he won't like all this smoke. I'll take him upstairs and release him.'

Later we were all on stage while a couple were singing a duet entitled '*Soulmates.*' Suddenly back came the butterfly and he was hopping right across their faces! The lady singer was highly amused, for she was a friend of mine and knew all about 'Gwen and her butterflies.'
Next, our butterfly visitor decided that he would join the audience and to their amusement, could be seen flying around them all. Alfie was there to watch the show too and he was sitting with some friends who were also 'in the know.'
Our Red Admiral returned for all three of our nightly performances and each evening he did his 'stuff' so I think there must have been lots of 'gossamer nets' around, during these three evenings!

Another incident was when Alfie had gone to away to Loughborough University for a weeks training course and I was at home alone. It was Russell's anniversary, August 14th 1990 and I was wondering around the house, singing away like mad - as I do when I'm alone, when suddenly I spotted a Red Admiral butterfly. He was sitting in my lounge, looking at me and of course I was delighted. I'm sure I even said something like, *'hi there'* to him ! He was busy opening and closing his wings for me to see his beauty and I was enchanted. Then the phone rang and it was Alfie calling from Loughborough. He was in his room at this point and said to me, *'guess what I've got in my room ?'*

I said, *'but guess what I've got in our lounge ?'*

Yes ! We both had a Red Admiral butterfly at the *same* time - me in Rayleigh in the South, and Alfie up North in Loughborough ! We took photographs of our butterflies and both said, *'Happy Anniversary Russell.'*

To finish this short chapter, I want to share another very special event. Although we have so many of these, I could almost fill a book with them alone, but this last one occurred in Dallas, Texas and was focussed around another boy named Russell. I will leave it to Mary, his mother and my friend, to tell her story. We will call it *'The Ice Butterfly'* by Mary Jones.

* * *

'We have all had experiences where we meet someone and find there is an instant communication, on a soul level. You feel yourself being flooded with Divine Love from a higher dimension - and you 'know' that you have walked with that soul on this Earth before. There is an instant connection. Some would call it 'coincidence' or good Karma, but by whatever name, it is a most wonderful experience. That's what happened to me, the day I met Gwen Byrne.

As it often does, Fate has a way of guiding our footsteps to places more wondrous than *we* could ever direct them. One Autumn day in 1987, I was busying myself around my home in Dallas, when the phone rang. It was Don Galloway from England, he was an old friend from Lincolnshire, who organises Spiritually orientated, metaphysical seminars under the name *'The Lynwood Fellowship.'* He told me, *'we have just had a space come up and I think you should come.'*

Much to my surprise, I agreed without even thinking about it and three weeks later, I found myself in England in the middle of the beautiful Derbyshire countryside. I felt as if I had been lifted up from my home in America and transported to a magic kingdom. Little did I know that things had only just begun ! The people at the seminar were more warm and loving than any I had ever encountered in a group in my own country. I was especially drawn to one lady, yet at first we seemed an unlikely pair. Because my friend Don had told us we should dress casually, I did. Now we Americans are known for being more casual than the rest of the world, but this lady was beautiful, inside and out and she dressed with a flair that was not only becoming - it was her.

After dinner the evening programme began and when I looked up, I saw her standing by the piano as she prepared to sing a song. When the music began and she started to sing, the sound of her voice began to strum on the very chords of my soul. She had the voice of an angel and it lifted my consciousness to great heights. It was a truly magical moment.

Over coffee, after the programme was over, we began talking and our words just came tumbling out, almost non-stop from us both. This lady was of course Gwen Byrne and we found that one coincidence after another revealed itself. Her son Russell in the Spirit World, was born on September 20th, which is the date of my birthday. I too have a son named Russell.

I had been told by one of the Mediums during that week that one of my new friends would present me with a red rose. She had said,
'it would be an indication that Spirit was indeed looking after your son Russell...who had been through some very trying times.'

This message came early in the week and it was such a wonderful week, that I actually forgot about it. On the last day, Gwen came up to me saying, *'I've just been into the village and when I saw this I just had to buy it for you.'*
Gwen held out her hand and I saw she holding was the most beautiful red, porcelain rose. Then she said, *'I guess this means that my Russell will be looking in on your Russell.'* And indeed he did.

I'd put my son's name on just about everyone's healing list before coming home. He was twenty three years old then and living the life of a lost soul. I knew there was no prayer more powerful than a Mother's prayer. After my visit to England ended, just before my birthday in September, things continued as usual once I'd returned home - until one freezing cold December night.

At about three in the morning, something woke me and I abruptly stood up beside my bed. I was wide awake when saw a bright flash of light across my bedroom wall. It was the light of my son's motorcycle and I thanked God for bringing him home safely once more.

Now Russell usually turned off his light as soon as he arrived in the driveway, but this time it stayed on. I went to my window and looked out

and I saw him aiming his motorcycle light onto the boot of his car. I put on a robe and quickly went outside to see what was happening.
'Mom, look at this' he said to me, in awe.

I looked in the direction he was pointing and saw a perfect and very large butterfly in flight. It was framed in frost which covered the entire boot of his car. It was absolutely beautiful. I ran inside to get a camera to take some photos. I'd taken two, then handed the camera to Russell who also took a few. He asked me what I thought it meant, but as I started to answer him I asked what *he* thought it meant.
He simply said, *'I've been freed.'*

And that was exactly what had happened. His soul had been freed from the bondage of drugs, alcohol and fast living. God and those in Spirit, who had been watching over him, chose this way to show him, in an indisputable way, that he was free. The rest was up to him and he knew it. Within a week he had repaired his car, sold his motorcycle and left his pot-smoking friends. He also had his straggly hair cut and then returned to University.

Russell was now restored to the son I knew, after hiding deep within the chrysalis of the butterfly which had manifested so dramatically to him. Every morning, he'd gone out to look at the boot of his car to see if it was still there. Miraculously, it lasted for five weeks and then finally faded away. His message had been received and today, we are all very proud of the man he became.

When Gwen and I had first met, she told me story after story involving her Spirit son Russell, his butterflies, herself and her family and friends. Since that time, I have been much more aware of these beautiful creatures - especially in light of what happened to my son Russell and me.

* * *

I think *'The Ice Butterfly'* is a wonderful story with amazing links, names and dates. It's all there !
Of course I guess the sceptics will find another explanation. Although...

'Sceptics do pad their intellect by the intrusions of the inexplicable, because nothing happens to rationalists that cannot be explained naturally - that is the most miraculous marvel of all.'

~ Words by Eckhart Tolle

It is said that *'Silence is the Wise'* and who am I to disagree ? All I am writing is *Truth* - not only of things that have happened to me but to others. Truth has many witnesses and to me, to have real intelligence means being open-minded. Perhaps one's mind needs to be opened to these wonders. I'm very grateful that mine is, for what empty lives those with closed minds must have !

I think it's no coincidence that as I complete this chapter today, on television I've just seem a tribute to the actor and comedian Leslie Crowther, who passed to Spirit just one week ago.

Russell Jones's Ice Butterfly

Twenty

The Great Master

'This natural life is a piece of the life everlasting'
~ Martin Luther (1483-1546)

It is not my way to copy from other writers. Yet in places, I've shared some of the work of others, simply because I felt it was important. Since forming the RPPS I have also learned a lot and I am not ashamed to say, that it has been the children who have been my greatest teachers.

In my first book, Russell had spoken of Jesus and in view of the phone calls and letters I have received, I now feel that I can write of my limited knowledge in that area. Many of the RPPS Mothers have a 'Jesus' story to tell, in connection with the passing of their beloved children and it does strike me as odd, that it is the little ones that speak of *The Master*. Perhaps the older we are when we pass to Spirit, somehow makes that particular man less of a Spiritual reality, I don't know !

I have in front of me a scrap of paper given to me some thirty years ago. At the time I hadn't a clue what it was all about. Perhaps now with my own experiences and this scrap of paper, I might weave them into a chapter. I sincerely hope so. One man who telephoned me after reading *'Russell'* told me he was extremely puzzled. In his own words he said,
'Gwen, how can you write about Jesus and use texts from the Bible, in a book about Spiritualism ?'
Now I know that after the death of his son, this gentleman was on his own particular search for the Truth, so I tried my best to explain.

The scrap of paper I mention is in pieces now. It's all that remains of a pamphlet called *'Spiritualism and Jesus'* by Geoffrey Griffiths. It was written in the 1970s and distributed by the Spiritualists National Union. Mr Griffiths has kindly given his permission for me to share the following amended excerpts from it...

'It is often said that the founders of the great world religions all taught the same religion. Yet these separate religions are so different today, that some of their followers are even prepared to kill each other to prove superiority.

It is only when we realise that Jesus was not a Christian, Buddhist, or Mohammedan, that we begin to grasp the fallacy...these individuals did not come to lead vast religious empires, they came to teach some very simple ideas.

1 - That there exists a central creative force
2 - That all men are brothers
3 - That all life has a Spiritual foundation.

These Universal teachings are common to all major religions. We find the same pattern of teachings in the life of many of the Great Masters.

Following the stories of Jesus of Nazareth, we can clearly identify these Universal teachings. He taught his followers to look to God - not to himself. He pointed out the 'God' within each of us and whenever a miracle occurred, he told his followers it was because God was working through him.

The account from the New Testament of the Transfiguration, where the Spirits of Moses and Elias materialised, was simply a Spiritual séance. Jesus also performed Spiritual healing many times, yet he always resisted personal glory - so his messages did not take second place.

It is said that the big things unite us and the little things divide us. In Spiritualism, our philosophy is based on these Universal teachings, but if our philosophy focussed on the personality of Jesus we would soon be worshipping the messenger and not the message. Our movement would then resemble the established church, which teaches about Jesus rather than his Spiritual truths.

Today Spiritualism promotes these Universal teachings in much the same way that Jesus did...

Our demonstrations of Clairvoyance often contain the kind of message that Jesus shared with the woman at Jacob's Well - to be understood on the level needed, by the person receiving it.

Spiritualist séances provide the 'touchable' reality of Spirit life and a unique experience for those attending, which can remove the fear of death forever.

Less than ten percent of orthodox churches today, carry out healing as Jesus practiced it, whereas Spiritualist Churches doing the same, are closer to a hundred percent.

Spiritualism is itself a Universal religion, but is often presumed to be against the teachings of Jesus. The paradox here is, that through Universal teachings, it may be closer to the original ideals of Jesus than orthodoxy is today.

Spiritualism is unique in two particular ways...
It is the only Spiritual movement that emphasises our Spiritual heritage and destiny - in the same way as Jesus did, and Spiritualism presents Spiritual realities as facts which are not purely based on faith.'

* * *

Now I can only share my own thoughts here. It is clear to me that Jesus the man was *not* supernatural. He even told us this. But as a boy, Jesus *was* a special child. Once, after he had been missing for a time, he said,
'did ye not know that I must be in my Father's house.'

He said this beautiful phrase to his parents, who I think must often have been baffled by their own son !

He longed to go to Jerusalem to gain knowledge. One can only wonder at the books he read, maybe the Old Testament ? When he finally did go to Jerusalem, the great teachers were amazed at his Spiritual knowledge. Although I think they may have failed to understand this wondrous, Spiritual boy. It seems too that Jesus' parents also possessed psychic gifts.

One can read of Clairvoyance in the Bible and we can easily find examples of Clairaudience, it is there for all to read. For without these gifts of the man Jesus, I don't think there would be any New Testament !

One can also find examples of automatic writing in the gospels. So what did Jesus write ? Well, from one story I remember learning from my school days, the scribes had brought a woman to Jesus. She had been caught committing adultery and they told Jesus that she should be stoned for her offence. Ignoring them, Jesus asked for guidance from the Spirit World. Next, he placed his finger on the ground and wrote out,
'he that is without sin, cast the first stone.'

This was automatic writing - words given by *'the hand of the Lord.'*
So Jesus wrote these now famous words, under true Psychic conditions.

Now let's look at the psychic phenomenon of apports. From the Gospels, we have the well-known story of the 'miracle of the fishes.' In school we were all taught that this *was* a miracle. But then what we called a 'miracle' yesterday, becomes today's natural law.

The story goes, that Jesus asked Peter to row him out from the shore into deeper waters to fish. Peter explained that they had fished all night long and caught nothing. Although, since it was Jesus himself asking, he agreed to try once more. Later, as they began to pull in their nets, amazement set in for the huge amount of fish they'd caught !

This it seemed, was a very remarkable happening. To me, this is clearly an example of Spiritual apports ! One has to read the whole story to discover the full wonder of it. If in these days we have Eastern wise men like Sai Baba, who can materialise objects out of thin air - why should this Biblical miracle seem so different ?

Now, let's look at the materialisation of Spirits - which was a wonderful phenomena that *we* were privileged to witness so many times.

In the Bible, the story of the Transfiguration saw Jesus take Peter, James and John up a high mountain. The air was rarefied and very, very still as they sat in the darkness - of course these conditions were needed for the experience that was to come. As Jesus prayed, his companions saw that his appearance began changing to a dazzling white. He had dematerialised his physical body and now stood before them in his Spirit form. These conditions and the dazzling whiteness is well understood by students of Physical Phenomena. Not only that, but the forms of Moses and Elijah materialised and spoke to Jesus too.

Whilst I will not suggest that our own psychic experiences were of a Biblical nature, I do see a great similarity. After the crucifixion, Jesus appeared to his disciples. Clearly they were afraid, but Jesus asked them not to be so disturbed saying,
'Look at my hands, look at my feet. It is me. Touch me and see.'

I humbly suggest that this is similar to our own experiences. During one séance, Russell said to us, *'Mum, I will show you my feet'* - and he did. We also held his hands. Sometimes they were the hands of a ten year old, sometimes the hands of a man. Touch me and see ? This was a miracle to my mind.

Jesus never used the word *'miracle'* for he worked in strict accordance with natural and psychical laws. It makes sense when you understand these laws. I do not understand 'educated' people, who believe in the happenings in the Bible, yet when faced with explanations of Physical Phenomena as seen in the Bible, they are full of disbelief ! No one of intelligence today believes in miracles, but again I say, *'that which we called a miracle yesterday, becomes today's natural law.'*

It is 1994 as I write and for me, it's orthodoxy that's being rejected by society today, not Jesus the man. Those who are 'educated', like the scientists, fear facing facts that are known to us through their own prejudice. These scientists must be bigots !

Whilst on the subject of psychic gifts of the Spirit, I must write a little of Frank Leah. This man was the gifted psychic artist who drew Russell's wonderful portrait, which can be seen on the cover of *'Russell.'* The story of Frank Leah's wonderful gift is told in the book *'Faces of the Living Dead'* by Paul Miller and for me, a drawing of a loved one in Spirit, is proof on paper that your loved one has survived death. Unfortunately it is quite a rare gift and as with any gift, it should be trained - although it can occur with Spirit guidance in the untrained.

Through the accomplished psychic artist, Spirit operators can create artwork that would rival anything displayed in gallery. There are many books about this. Spirit painters draw close to the artist and work through them, often from a distance. I have noticed that this 'inspired creativity' also occurs with singers, poets and musicians - all of which I have been privileged to witness.

Whilst I understand that Frank Leah was already a trained artist in his Earth life, I was so very lucky to have been guided to him for Russell's drawing. Yet I was not looking for an expert drawing, although I received one of the greatest technical ability. Having drawn and painted myself, I am aware that being trained in this particular gift can be a great advantage to the psychic artist, as in Frank Leah's case.

* * *

During the early 1990s I wanted to find evidence in the Bible of another subject - 'the biggie' of reincarnation ! Yet I couldn't find anything of satisfaction, although I know there are people who say references to it *can* be found there. However, it was around this time that began to feel happy again after the séances had ended. I was enjoying my music and my friends and my family, so I forgot about reincarnation for a time.

Then in 1991 whilst staying at Grail Haven, I attended an utterly amazing lecture at Bath Church. It was given by Keith High, who was married at the time to my friend Rachael. Listening to Keith, I literally had my ears pinned back ! I had recorded this talk, but like a fool I had loaned it out before I could listen to it. Then when only one of the two tapes came back I was furious. So again I waited and in 1992 a book came into my hands which also covered Keith's ideas - this was *it* !

The book was called *'Journey to Infinity'* by Peter Nichols and published by Finbarr books. I was glued to it then, as I still am today - especially with all the exciting discoveries in physics and energy that have been made since. In his book, Peter Nichols talks of the *purpose* of reincarnation - and how it is necessary to try and contact our 'Higher Selves.'
Here is an fascinating extract from Peter's book.

'This distinction is what set Jesus apart from the multitudes. He was continually in touch with his Higher Self. He came with a message for those who have ears to hear. As Jesus progressed along, focussing his consciousness upon the Higher Planes, his physical desires became more and more remote. He did not chose to cloister himself away like some recluse...he faced these challenges head on...through his contact with Higher Powers emanating from the Super Celestial dimensions...Jesus brought a message instructing us how to realise our full potential but as usual...certain men didn't approve. Their selfish desires included ruling...over the masses...by keeping the common man in ignorance...so they obscured...these vital truths...in their place they set up a watered down...legend which included worshipping his person - a concept which was totally alien to Jesus.

He wants...each of us [to] start making progress along the pathway of evolution, which he trod over two thousand years ago. When this incarnation is complete...we gladly move on to the next dimension. It is an eternal glorious undertaking.'

All this is in a small book on reincarnation ! For those who wish to study this controversial subject further, Peter's book is a must.

I have spoken in this chapter of automatic writing, so I will seize the chance to go back to it now and describe a short, but very remarkable happening from July 1994.

My friend Rachael was over from America and with us in Rayleigh for a few days. As today was a Friday I was also expecting my other friend Marion, for our regular Friday evening sessions of automatic writing. For weeks we had received nothing - the pen just *refused* to move, although we decided to press on regardless. However, that evening the pen *did* begin to move and a name was spelt out. It meant nothing to Marion and me, but Rachael's ears pricked up because she knew exactly who it was.

We sat around my table, with Marion holding the pen. Now unfortunately I have to rely on memory for this, since Rachael took the original notes back with her to America and somehow they were lost. But the pen began to move...

Pen: *'Hello Ladies - and Good evening Judith.'*

Us: *'Good evening, but we don't have a Judith with us.'*

Pen: *'Yes Rachael is Judith - but in another lifetime in France. Your mother passed when you were very young, but you travelled extensively with your father. He was a business man.'*

Us: *'Can you tell us more ?'*

Pen: *'Judith you had four sons.*
I would like to say, that before the end of this year you will be a married lady. Goodnight Ladies...'

And it was as short as that !

Later that year Rachael met a man named Robert and before the year ended, they *were* married. We learned later that it was Robert who had played the part of Rachael's father, in the earlier lifetime in France.

So what can I add here ? Often our Spirit friends can be way off in their timing, but they were right this time. Rachael and Robert married in America on December 11th, 1994. So the automatic writing was a hundred percent correct ! Alfie and I were so happy for them, but sorry that we couldn't have made it to the wedding. Within hours of their happy union in America, I was at home transcribing Summerland Tape four from Russell. It has the subtitle of *'The Cycle of Souls'* and is on the subject of reincarnation - even Rachael is mentioned on the tape !

I spoke to Rachael after her wedding and told her of the part she plays in the fourth tape. Rachael said, *'how wonderful Gwennie, but I'm not a bit surprised. Nothing surprises me !'*

To me, Rachael is a very learned lady and a *true* worker for Spirit - I've already written of our adventures together and our very deep and powerful friendship. The whole story fits together like a great big jigsaw puzzle, but isn't that *exactly* how we can describe this life ?

Twenty One

Margaret Prentice's Story

Simon

From a really young age I'd always made the wish that, when I was grown-up and married, I wanted to have a baby boy.

As a child, I'd been injured after fall, which caused a slight deformity at the base of my spine, then from the age of eighteen I began suffering backache. By the time I was married at twenty, lifting shopping and doing housework only added to my pain. I thought this might have been why my husband Roy and I hadn't yet been able to start a family. So we decided to try and adopt a child and I'm glad to say, we had no trouble being accepted as parents *and* we didn't mind whether it was a boy or a girl.

In July 1964, we returned from our annual holiday to learn we'd had a call from the adoption agency about a baby boy. He was so lovely and fitted our looks and family so well, that the agency had already put him down as ours !

We were thrilled beyond words, so arranged to see our new baby. The excitement was almost unbearable, but I was so afraid that I'd do or say something wrong. However, when we saw the baby, he was more than all our expectations. He was absolutely perfect in every way and I wanted to take him home there and then !

At the time I was working as a receptionist in a computer company and my contract stated I must give a month's notice. On my first day back after our holiday I was so excited. Roy was too - to think that we were having a son *at last !* We'd been married for six years and thought we would never be parents.

When I saw my manager about leaving, he asked about our baby boy then wished me luck for the future. Then he said, *'we'll get your papers in order then you can leave at the end of the week - will that suit you ?'*

I was overjoyed ! Now I could be a real mother at last. Roy was *so* pleased.

We named our son Simon. He was a good looking boy and very clever. He was reading before he even started school. Even in Junior School, Simon would help other children with their spelling. Roy and I really had high hopes for him. He was a most loving and affectionate child and Roy and I took him everywhere with us.

As a baby, Simon had been heavy to carry, so by the time he was two, I'd developed agonising pain in my back. After two months of rest I was admitted to hospital in London, for surgery on a slipped disc. I spent so much time in and out of hospital back then, that my parents looked after Simon a lot. By the time I was well and came home, Simon was unsure of me. Now he wanted to be with his Grandparents, so we let him stay with them for occasional weeks now and then. They spoiled him all the time and he was always the centre of attention, but everyone really loved and fussed over him, because he was such a lovely child.

When Simon was three and a half, Roy and I adopted a second baby boy who we named Matthew and just like Simon, he was perfect in every way. Life was now wonderful for us and the boys got on well together. Whilst Matthew was still little, Simon would visit the neighbours or find things of his own to do. Yet as Simon grew up, it quickly became apparent to us that he seemed easily led and was a wanderer.

Once, when he was just four years old he'd disappeared with the neighbours dog. He'd taken it for a walk after putting a piece of string around it's neck. Three hours after the police, traffic wardens and most of the schools in Letchworth had searched for him, he told us that he'd only gone to see his Grandmother ! However, this little incident should have warned us of the great heartache that lay ahead.

Simon's teacher wrote to us once, to ask if we could visit the school. He wanted to discuss why Simon hadn't attended for the last six weeks. It turned out that Simon had been producing false notes from me, saying he was excused from school for any number of reasons. He had even forged my signature. So now Simon had become a master at telling lies.

In his final year of school, Simon spent more time away from it than he actually attended. He began spending most of his time drinking in the local pubs and soon became an alcoholic. Then once he'd found alcohol wasn't enough for him, he went on to begin taking drugs.

Simon also seemed to have an inferiority complex, because when he was sober he was so shy and embarrassed. It was really painful for him to be in company, because he felt so awkward. After he had left school, we only ever saw him either drunk or drugged up. He was sixteen years old.

When Simon was nine, my father died after a long year suffering with cancer. Simon grieved very much because they were very close. Afterwards, Simon spent more time with my Mum. We could see they needed each other and at least my Mum would have some company. This did become a happy time for both of them and they grew very fond of each other. While Simon stayed with his Grandmother, I found I could cope better with just Roy and our son Matthew at home. Matthew was six at the time and a very quiet natured boy. He was so different to Simon and would play for hours on his own.

When Simon was fourteen and Matthew was ten, I gave birth to our third son, who we named Richard. After nineteen years, Roy and I had finally had a baby - in spite of my bad back. Simon and Matthew were both excited to be having a baby brother and I'm glad to say, that they accepted Richard at once and really loved him. There was no jealousy whatsoever and over the next ten years we were a happy family.

It was at this time that Simon began to nag us to let him stay with my Mum. In the end we agreed, but it's easy to see your mistakes years later. We should have been more strict with him and kept him at home, where we could keep an eye on him. At fourteen, Simon was already playing truant from school and drinking - but we never suspected a thing. He had also been taking his Grandmother's sleeping tablets.

When he was old enough to leave school, Simon got a job after being picked from eighteen other applicants. For a time he was happy with his new job, but was still drinking, although now he couldn't sleep, so he asked our doctor for something to help. So at fifteen years old, my son was prescribed strong sleeping pills and he soon became absolutely addicted.

Eventually Simon was unable to work at all without being either drunk or drugged up - so of course, he lost his job. We began sending him to various clinics then, to dry out *and* psychiatric hospitals. He was often in jail too, for theft to feed his drug habit. This always seemed to be at Christmas time, on my birthday and on Mother's day too.

However, during Christmas of 1993 Simon was at home with us. That year we also had Matthew and his girlfriend and my Mother with us too. This was the first time we'd all been together for years. Simon was with us to try and control his drug habit for a few weeks, before going to London to yet another clinic. So we agreed he could stay, until he was due to leave on March 8th...

Richard

When you lose somebody really close, you never, ever get over it. That person is always on your mind. Sometimes it seems quite easy to cope, but that's because you've deliberately detached yourself from the agony of reality. Then suddenly, you think of that precious, familiar face that you knew so well and loved so much - then the terrible shock returns and you realise what happened. It all comes rushing back and you wonder how you've managed to live without them since.

If that person is a child, it seems so much worse because they are young. It seems so unfair to be robbed of life. We do not expect our children to die before us, but on February 5th 1988, our third son Richard died at the young age of only ten years. He'd been ill with leukaemia for eighteen months before that.

About six months before Richard died, a friend of my husband invited us to a party, we took Richard with us and that's where we met Graham. It was clear that Graham loved children and soon he and Richard became great friends. Graham seemed so knowledgable about *life*, but he couldn't believe Richard had been given only a few weeks to live. He thought he looked so alive and happy.

A few weeks later Graham asked if we would let him take Richard to the local Spiritualist church for some healing. He said it might not do any good, but it wouldn't do any harm either - and we had nothing to lose. So we agreed and on the following Tuesday evening as we got Richard ready to go, he said to his father,
'oh Dad I'm not too sure I want to go to this spooky place !'
However, I went along too and Richard had great fun in Graham's car winding the windows up and down and playing with the seats and gadgets. It was quite clear that Richard didn't mind going with Graham at all !

When we first walked into the church, it felt a little awesome. It was so quiet. People were sitting in two rows around the room, with a central circle of about six chairs all facing inwards. Either a man or woman was standing behind each chair and one lady, named Daphne looked up at us as we entered. She left her chair to come to greet us and Richard.

Graham had already told Daphne that he was bringing Richard along, so when she approached us, she walked towards Richard with both arms outstretched in welcome. Richard was a naturally loving boy and he went to her, smiling all over his face. Daphne said to him,
'would you like to come and sit in my chair Richard and you can tell me if

you have any aches or pains we can get rid of?'

Richard was happy to sit in the chair with Daphne standing at the back of him. Then there was a nice young man named David, who stood at the front of him who Richard seemed to like - perhaps because he had a beard and was so softly spoken and kind.

During the healing, I looked at Richard's face. His eyes were closed and he was resting back in the chair and seemed so relaxed. At one point, I almost thought he was asleep ! Richard later told me that he thought Daphne's hands on him felt so warm and he could imagine all the pain floating away. He said, he looked up at the big cross on the rostrum and imagined he was breathing in God's healing light.

When we left the church Richard seemed a different boy to the one we took in. He ran and skipped and jumped to the car and seemed so happy. *'Mum'* he said, *'this is all we need to cure me. All the pains in my legs have gone and I'm starving !'*

Graham looked at me and said, *'there can't be anything really wrong with him, can there ?'*

Then Graham took us to a burger bar in Letchworth, where Richard ate a big burger and had a large strawberry milkshake ! Apart from the times when Richard was having treatment in Barts Hospital, London, we never missed one Tuesday night healing session with Graham and they were always followed by a visit to the burger bar afterwards !

This had all begun in November 1987, but around the middle of January, 1988 it ended, because Richard was becoming very weak and needed to have blood transfusions. Then on February 5th, after a few days in bed, Richard passed away peacefully. The time was 4.20 p.m.

Earlier that same afternoon, Richard had woken and was looking towards where his drink was sitting. As he pointed to it his father Roy, offered it to him, but Richard shook his head. He was pointing *past* the drink and into the corner of the room. His eyes were wide open, as though he'd seen something, but because he couldn't make us understand what he was trying to say, he fell back on his pillow, exasperated. Now I can't tell if Richard really saw something or not, but personally I think he did. I have since been told that he *was* seeing something. He was looking at a boy named Russell, who came to meet him, with Jesus and my father.

Before Richard was buried, Roy and I went to say our last goodbyes to him, as he lay in his coffin at the funeral parlour. I had him dressed in his judo suit and I'd put a little white and blue flower by his neck. I put his teddy bear, who he'd named 'Vodka Pat' in with him and I tucked a photo of my husband and me under his jacket, over his heart. I said, *'there Richard, the three of us together, forever.'*

The next day we went to see Richard again, this time we took our neighbour Freddie. Richard loved her and used to call out her name twice and just run into her arms. After Freddie and my husband had said goodbye to Richard, I stayed behind to be alone with him for the last time. I touched the flower and 'Vodka Pat' and then bent forward to kiss him. In my mind I whispered to him, *'Richard I won't say goodbye, because I want you to come back and let me know where you are and if you know what's going on still.'*

Then I said, *'don't come back to any silly Medium. Make sure it's someone special, who is honest and can tell me what's happened here. Show her Vodka Pat, the Judo suit and the flower and the photo.'*

Then I went out into the street where my husband and Freddie were waiting for me.

I remember my thoughts clearly as I bent down to kiss Richard goodbye. I just couldn't believe he had gone anywhere without me. In my mind, I had no doubt at all that I'd be in touch with him again, sometime in the future. I'd been with him day and night for the last eighteen months and had the feeling that I only needed him to find the right Medium. I really felt that his death was the beginning of a new adventure.

Of course, the first few weeks were very miserable for us. I couldn't believe he wasn't coming home anymore. It was as though he was just around the corner at his friend's house. I'd taken photographs of Richard in his coffin and some more later, of all the flowers on his grave. I remember seeing Richard's judo instructor at the funeral. He was leaning against a tree with his forehead touching it, trying to hide his tears. Graham's sister told me that he had also broken down in grief one Sunday, during his meal.

The most memorable thing for me, was on the day I said goodbye to Richard in his coffin. I noticed the smell of pine and white wood and the musty smell of earthly embalming fluid. It wasn't unpleasant, yet it was very, very strong, although Roy doesn't seem to remember it at all. At the time, I remember thinking that I would easily recognise it again.

About three days after the funeral we'd decided to go away for a short break. I nipped into the photographers to collect my photos, whilst Roy waited for me in the car. Back in the car, I took out the photos to show Roy and the overpowering smell nearly knocked me back. It was the exact same smell I'd noticed at the funeral parlour. Of course I realise that the smell of the developing fluid that photographers use, is very similar to that of embalming fluid, but it was so very strong.

After we returned home, I knew Richard was trying to let me know he was still around. If I ran down the stairs, the smell would meet me half way or I would open a door and the smell would hit me full in the face. It was so powerful that I knew it was no coincidence. I'd never smelt it before Richard had died.

Not long after this, I was doing some ironing in Richard's room, while at the same time watching TV. There was a film on that Richard had liked, so I talked to him as though he was sitting on the bed watching it with me. Then I said *'oh listen to me Rich. If anyone heard me they'd think I was really mad, talking to thin air - but I wonder if you can hear me?'*

Then I went out of Richard's room into our bedroom and the smell hit me with such force that I stepped back before entering.
'Oh Richard, you are here,' I said, *'I know you are.'*

I followed the smell round the bed to my husband's side, which was where Richard had died. His other teddy bear was laying there covered up and as I lifted the cover the smell wafted up from the teddy bear, all warm. I could hardly contain myself, so ran downstairs to tell Roy.
'Oh Roy, Richard is in our room,' I said. *'I can smell him so strong.'*

Roy just looked at me and said, *'oh Marg, you really are gone aren't you!'*
He wouldn't even come upstairs to see for himself. It was as though Roy had buried Richard and as far as he was concerned, that was where he was.

About three weeks after the funeral, I began visiting the Spiritualist church where Richard had gone for his healing. I felt I wanted to learn as much as I could about Mediums and the Spirit World - if it really existed. I've always had a secret feeling that there *is* a world somewhere, that we all go to meet our loved ones. How can there be nothing after death? It's only the thought of meeting our family and friends that keeps us striving on.

Each week at the church I bought the Spiritualist Gazette newspaper. In one issue, there was an article by Michael Roll about Spirit people making contact with their loved ones on Earth. He also invited readers to send for his thesis. I thought about it for a long time then decided I had nothing to lose - providing I kept an open mind and didn't let anyone fool me. I was well prepared to let anyone know how I felt, especially if I thought they were trying to take advantage of grieving parents.

I wrote to Michael Roll telling him how my world had collapsed since our son had gone and if what he said was true, I wanted to know more. I posted my letter on the Tuesday evening and thought I wouldn't hear any more about it.

The next day I wasn't working, so I was pleased to just lie in bed. In fact I was so depressed and longing for my darling boy, that all I wanted to do was sleep. I was thinking of the letter I'd written the day before, when suddenly out of nowhere I had the strongest smell of oranges, but there were no oranges in the house. A few days before a Clairvoyant had told me that if I ever smelled oranges, it meant my father was around. So sitting in bed so unhappy, I said aloud, *'Dad is that you ? I don't want to face anyone or anything today, I'm just going to stay here.'*

Just then the phone rang and because of the orange smell, I presumed it was my Mother. Reluctantly I went downstairs to answer it and was taken aback when a man's voice said, *'is this Margaret ? This is Michael Roll.'*

Well I was amazed, as it seemed I'd only just had the letter in my hand to post to him, and I said so. He said, *'don't be surprised Margaret, your son will have arranged all this. Nothing is coincidence.'*

Since then, I've come to understand what he said is true. We think some things are just coincidence, when it's really our loved ones in Spirit making things happen their way.

Michael gave me Gwen Byrne's contact details, but at first poor Gwen must have thought I was mad, because I remember saying something like, *'what's your game, you and Michael Roll ? Is this a publicity gimmick to promote his article and thesis ? Maybe you two have got a good thing going here.'*

I know I shouldn't have said that to Gwen, because I knew in my heart that they were genuine, but I felt it would be terrible if someone was trying to fool grieving parents. However, Gwen was so understanding and said she would send me an article from the Psychic News, about her son Russell.

In fact, Gwen was really good to me in those early days and I know now, that Russell and my Richard were together all the time. They both found ways to bring proof to Gwen, as well as to me and they both made little 'coincidences' happen.

Now I want to share a few stories, which are absolutely true, of how Russell and Richard proved to me that they are both still very much alive *and* vital - but living in a Spirit World which is overlapping this Earth world of ours.

The Start of My Proof

After the Spiritualist church service one Sunday, an old friend who'd lost her own son, stopped me and said, *'Margaret, here's my phone number. Ring me if you need to talk or need any help at all.'*

A few weeks later, I was having a crisis at home over Simon. I was in such a state and wanted to call the police. But instead of phoning the police station, I mistakenly rang the number on a little card which was propped up in front of the phone. My friend from church had given me this card and it was her number I rang, although I don't remember putting the card there at all. When she answered, I blurted out my troubles to her without even thinking and she said, *'Margaret, I know what you need. Can you come somewhere this afternoon, if I can get a meeting fixed up for you?'*

I had no idea what she had in mind, but I felt very relieved that someone cared enough to try and help.

That afternoon my friend's daughter arrived and I discovered that she was taking me to see a Medium named Shirley West. Once there, Shirley said that her Spirit guide had already told her she would be seeing a lady that afternoon, who had a great need and was grieving. Showing us inside, Shirley explained that my friend, who'd arranged the sitting, had said only that I'd lost a little boy, but that was all she knew about me.

The sitting began and I was astonished at what Shirley told me. She began to describe what my son was showing her and said that she could see an image of Richard in a coffin. She told me there was a little white flower by his neck and that he was wearing a judo suit. She even mentioned a teddy bear. Then Shirley said,

'your son is saying you've forgotten the other thing you put in with him.'

I tried hard to remember what it was, then Shirley said, *'it's under his jacket. It's a photo.'*

Well that was exactly right, but I had to think whether I'd told anyone about this, yet it was all so accurate.

Then she said, *'he was standing beside you as you were looking at him in the coffin. You had private words with him that nobody else knows about. You told him to remember all this. Then you said that you were not saying goodbye yet, because you wanted him to come back through someone good, to let you know he still existed.'*

Then Shirley asked me, *'why is he is calling Freddie...Freddie?'*

At first I wondered why she'd said that name. I'd completely forgotten that at the time, Roy and I had taken our neighbour Freddie with us to the funeral parlour.

Later at home, once I'd recalled everything from the sitting, I realised just how evidential everything was that Shirley had said. As I thought it through, it slowly dawned on me - that my little boy did *still* exist somewhere and he could come and see me whenever he liked. After this, life was much more bearable and it was marvellous for me to know that Richard had taken notice of what I'd said to him !

The following week I thanked Shirley and said how wonderful it all was, then arranged to visit her again. This was a way I could feel near to my darling boy once more. It was just as though he was in Australia and was only waiting for me to phone him. When I arrived at Shirley's door this time, she said she was glad I could come, because Richard had a friend with him who wanted to speak to me urgently. I had no idea who this friend could be.

Sitting in the Shirley's little reading room she asked me,
'do you know who Russell is ?'

'The only Russell I know, is a friend's son in Australia.' I said, *'but we don't see each other.'*

I was such a dope at the time ! Shirley said, *'no, this Russell is in the Spirit World with Richard.'*

'Oh. Well I wonder if it is Gwen's Russell ?' I said. It was silly of me to even wonder, because of course it was him ! At the time I didn't know how the Spirit World worked and I thought Russell wouldn't come to me because I hadn't known him in life.

Then Shirley said, *'Russell is pushing past Richard to get to you. He is saying, 'hold out your hand. I'm giving you something and you have got to remember this, it's very important." It's a stone or a pearl.'* Shirley said. *'Yes it's a pearl - remember this.'*

Shirley went on to say, *'there's a man here with Richard now. His name is Peter. He's tall and slim with a beard and he's Richard's teacher. Peter is saying, he's doing what he promised you he'd do.'*

I was absolutely amazed at this, because Peter Barratt had been Richard's headmaster at school. He was going to take over Richard's class as his new form teacher in the next term, but had died suddenly during the Summer. How could Shirley possibly know about Peter ? At the time, the enormity of this message didn't sink in.

Peter had been so good to us before he died. He'd offered to help with Richard if ever I needed a break, by taking him to Barts Hospital in London or in any way he could. He'd said I could ring him day or night, because he would be there if we needed him. Knowing now, that Richard still had his teacher and friend with him in the Spirit World, was a great comfort. Peter had died the week after telling me he would help. He was still quite young, but he'd had a fatal heart attack. Richard died six months afterwards.

In November, I needed to go to hospital in London for a check up and Roy came with me. Whenever Richard had made this journey for his hospital visits, he always remarked on the time as it was shown on the big clock in Arsenal Football ground. This time, when Roy saw the same clock through the train window, he said, *'the time is now five to ten by the clock.'* Instinctively I looked at my watch, which had a digital readout. It was working perfectly, but in place of the usual digits, the screen now showed the letter R ! To me, it was as though Richard was with us and he wanted me to know that he'd altered my watch !

On Richard's second anniversary, Roy came with me to see Shirley West. The sitting was a success and towards the end Shirley said,
'Richard saw you put the roses on his grave. Now he's saying 'Butch' and also 'Bonsai.'
Well, we were was amazed at this, since Butch is the name of a little dog that Richard had wanted before he died. Also, earlier that day we'd visited a garden centre and bought some Bonsai tree seeds to grow in Richard's memory. I'd also bought red roses at the time and put them on his grave.

Gwen called me once, to ask if our friend Lotte had been in touch. She said, *'I think she'll ring you soon, because she wants to tell you about a mysterious phone call she had on Sunday.'*
I was intrigued, but didn't have to wait long because Lotte rang me that evening and it was very exciting indeed. This is what Lotte had to say...

Lotte: Margaret had given me a small bonsai plant in memory of Richard. About eighteen months later the plant seemed to be dying, so I moved it to top of my microwave in the kitchen, so I could watch and nurse it along.

One Sunday, I was putting the dinner together when I heard a faint clicking sound coming from the microwave behind me. As I turned, I saw the Bonsai plant move. I couldn't believe what I'd seen, but continued with my cooking - only for the whole process to be repeated. I thought that perhaps there was a vibration from the floor or something was shaking, so I did some experimenting. I walked heavily across the kitchen and even jumped, but nothing moved. My kitchen floor is solid concrete !

Perplexed, I went to leave the kitchen, but as I did - from the corner of my eye - I saw the Bonsai move again. This time I went and spoke to it. I implored it not to die and asked Richard to do something to keep it alive. I finally left the kitchen but suddenly felt very sleepy, so went to lie on my bed as the phone rang. My husband Ernie answered it, then came into the bedroom saying, *'well that was a funny phone call. A voice just said 'Ih-Oi Bonsai' and then the phone went dead.'*

Here are some other recollections of Lotte's, concerning Richard and the Spirit World and they fit my evidence like a jigsaw puzzle !

Lotte: In June 1988, I had a dream of being on a vast grassy slope and in the distance a group of children were gathered. I walked towards them and two small boys separated from the group and came towards me. One was reluctant to approach me, so the second boy was pulling him by the arm. As they came nearer, the second boy pushed the reluctant boy towards me shouting, *'remember him, he is Richard,'*
and as 'Richard' stood in front of me, he said,
'yeah, Richard, you remember Richard.'
Then they turned to run back to the group and I woke up.

I tried to remember my dream, but was irritated because I couldn't remember the boy's name. The name Russell kept coming to mind, but I knew that wasn't the name I wanted to remember. Anyway, at the time I didn't know anyone called either Richard or Russell. The pieces finally fell into place when I went to my first ever Spiritual seminar. At dinner, I sat opposite a lady called Margaret and later in the week she told me that her little boy Richard had died the previous February. She then introduced me to a lady called Gwen, who'd lost her own son some 24 years earlier - and his name was Russell !

Another incident occurred while I was in my greenhouse. I'd cut down a rather overgrown lavender bush and was taking cuttings, when I noticed my compost bag had split, so I squatted down to empty the bag into a bucket. Suddenly I was aware of someone behind me, when I was knocked into from the back, which caused me to fall forward. I got up to admonish two boys that I didn't recognise, who were wrestling with each other. I began to tell them off, but they pushed past me and ran from the greenhouse laughing and chanting, *'na-na, na na-na, we got you'*

They ran around the corner of the house and as they passed our outside water tap it started to run all by itself. My husband Ernie was at the bottom of the garden and called out *'who turned on the water tap?'* He hadn't seen the children at all.

Another incident was during an evening that my son, husband and I were sitting quietly in the living room, each occupied with our own interests. The room was silent, until we suddenly heard a music box begin to play. We were all puzzled and just looked at each other. No one had moved. We began looking for the source of the music and inside our display cabinet, we found that a figurine of a little dancing girl had begun twirling and playing music. I'd had this figurine for six years and until then, didn't even realise that it was a music box. It had lain there untouched for years.

One Winter's evening, I'd gone out to collect my son from the bus stop. I had my car headlights on and arrived at the same time as the bus. My son got in the car and we drove off. Approximately 200 metres down the road, two separate oncoming cars both flashed their headlights at us. Puzzled at first, I tried my headlights and found to my surprise that they were switched off. I quickly put them back on and thought no more about it.

That evening, Margaret Prentice called and asked what was wrong with my car headlights. I'd forgotten about the incident at this point, so said nothing was wrong. Margaret insisted, telling me a friend had called her, who had done some inspired writing that evening. She said, she'd had a message from Richard to say that he'd been playing with the car headlights. It was only then that I recalled what had happened in the car that evening.

Margaret: When I first started to write to Gwen Byrne, I learned that she was a singer! When a letter arrived from Gwen one day, I told Roy that it was from my friend *'Gwen, who sings.'* So Roy said,
'oh, so it's from 'Pearl the Singer!"

Thereafter, Gwen became known to us as 'Pearl the Singer' and once Gwen learned of this, she started sending me little things with pearls in - and I would send her butterflies. Little did we know then, that Spirit would begin to use pearls as evidence and whenever they could, they would even bring a pearl. They would also regularly make me aware of the time of 4.20 p.m. which was the time Richard had died. It seemed they were always looking for new ways of proving to me that they were there.

Shirley West and I had become good friends, though I was always careful not to give away any information about Richard, because I knew he'd want to give me more proof through Shirley's Mediumship. In the early days of my grief for Richard, he would appear to Shirley many times *and* when she least expected it. She could be in the kitchen or the bedroom, he would even show up on the stairs or while she was in bed ! She told me she could feel children pulling at her feet or lifting the covers. She would even hear their voices and laughter.

Russell Byrne was around all the time too in those days. I seemed he wanted to teach Richard how to communicate for himself, because Russell had other work to do. He was often busy in other countries, helping other children who were passing into Spirit.
After one cryptic message from Russell I contacted Gwen who said, *'oh he loves giving us riddles to solve. He might continue this now for ages - to give us something to do. For when we are busy, we're not longing for them so much, are we ?'*

About a month later, Gwen and Alfie travelled up North where Gwen went to see her friend Val Williams for a Mediumship sitting. Of course Russell came through and gave lots of personal evidence for the family, then he said, *'Mum, hold out your hand and you must remember this, as it is very important.'* Val said, *'he is giving you a stone or a pearl. It is a pearl and he says you know who to give it to.'*

I'd booked a weeks seminar in Clacton and during my first night there I had a terrible dream about Richard. It involved a certain unfeeling teacher of his from school, who Richard was afraid of.
The next morning a lovely lady came up to me and asked if I'd slept well. As she spoke to me, on her right side just above her ear, I saw coloured lights begin to build up around her hair. It started with a deep pink, which blended into a lovely green, then orange blending into yellow, which went around the back of her neck. I said, *'oh, you've got lovely colours around your head.'*
She was so pleased and asked, *'tell me what colours they are, because you're seeing my aura.'*
I was so excited, but I'd always thought it was impossible to see the aura - yet this was so natural. The colours faded as we talked, but we concluded that they hadn't come from anything around us that was reflecting light. Then I told the lady about my bad dream so she said she would introduce me to a Medium named Ivy Scott, who might be able to help me.

Ivy was so kind and considerate and she soon worked out my dream's meaning. She gave me a wonderful message from Richard too. She said, *'Richard gave you that dream to get it out of your mind. He wants you to know that he doesn't think about those times now, because he is so very happy where he is. His only regret is, that you and his father are grieving so much over him, when he hasn't really gone anywhere - he still comes home and sits with you. He is learning to communicate and one day, he will get through and you'll have no doubts ever again.'*

This seminar was becoming a real education for me and every day it seemed that Richard and Russell were doing their very best to get through to me. Before the week ended I booked a sitting with a Medium who nothing about me. She said that my little boy didn't quite know how to communicate yet, as it was still very early days - but he was saying thank you for putting his teddy bear in with him.

Then the Medium asked me, *'why would someone be handing you a pair of pearl earrings ? It's either the hand of a small lady or a child. To me, that means two things or two people, have come together.'*

Then she described a matching necklace, in which every pearl was *exactly* the same. She said, *'it's as though a lot of people who are all the same, have come together.'*

Well for me, his was excellent ! It was as though she'd described all the Mums in Russell and Gwen's RPPS. Eventually there were lots of RPPS members all over England and abroad and we keep in touch with each other and give comfort where we can. It's also wonderful to hear Spiritual evidence from other parents too. One thing is certain - we only want the truth when it concerns our beloved children.

A few of the times I saw Shirley West, she would say I had someone with me from Spirit named Daisy, but I've never known anyone of that name. Then for my birthday, Gwen sent me a pair of real pearl earrings which had belonged to Alfie's stepmother. I called Gwen to thank her and asked,
'what was Alfie's step-mum's name ?'
'Daisy' Gwen told me !

Once, I'd bought myself a pair of beautiful black tights decorated with butterflies. Gwen said that she liked them so much that I promised her, if I couldn't find another pair, she could have them.

Then one evening Roy and I were getting ready to go out and as I put on these butterfly tights I thought,
'oh Russell, if only you could let me know that all this is true and you are here with Richard.'

Just then Roy shouted to me that Shirley was on the phone and wanted a quick word with me. I put on a dressing gown and quickly ran downstairs. Shirley said, *'Margaret, Russell is here and he's saying, for goodness sake tell Richard's Mum I'm here and that she's wearing something that belongs to my Mum.'*

The next chance I got, I sent a pair of these tights to Gwen !

During the 80s Richard had always liked the 'Rambo' movies and he was longing to see the third installment. So when it was advertised on TV he said, *'Mum, we must get the video of that as soon as it's out.'*

I promised him that we would, but in my heart I knew he wouldn't be here to see it. After Richard had died, I was with Shirley when she said, *'Margaret, if the lights suddenly flickered at home, would you be scared ?'*

'No, I'd love it.' I said. *'Why ?'*

'Because Richard is going to try something,' she said, *'if he can...'*

Of course, I watched every day for the lights to do something unusual - but the weeks and months went by and nothing happened. Then, as soon as I'd given up being so alert, it happened !

After an evening out, Roy and I returned home at about eleven thirty. Our other son Matthew was in front of the television watching a film and the only light switched on in the room, was a single wall light. I asked Matthew, *'what's this old video you're watching Matt ?'*

Just then the wall light flickered once and I said to Roy,
'oh Roy it's happened, did you see that ?'

Roy said nothing at first, but Matt said, *'oh Mum, you know why it's happened now don't you. The film is Rambo 3.'*

I was thrilled. Clearly Richard had been waiting to do this light trick when it would give the biggest impact ! Of course Roy simply said, *'there must be something wrong with the lights tonight. The power must be low to make them flick like that.'*

I'd already told Roy that Richard might flick the lights at some point, but I think even *he* was a little surprised. Matt just looked at him and grinned. Roy does love to give the impression he's not interested, although I think he must wonder sometimes, whether it is evidence or just a coincidence.

Once Christmas, Roy and I were due to attend his company's annual dinner and dance party, so I went shopping for a new blouse. In a small dress shop I was the only customer, which I though was unusual for the time of year.

As I browsed through the blouses on display I remembered the time of the last party. I had to leave Richard in hospital to go, but felt terrible for leaving him like that. However, Roy had insisted, since his work friends had raised so much money to help us travel and stay in London, while Richard was in hospital there. So although I didn't feel like going, their help had made life so much easier for us, during a very dark period and I'll be eternally grateful for that.

All this was going through my mind now, as I browsed in the dress shop. Going dancing was the last thing I wanted to do, because life would never be the same again. I thought about my son Simon, who loved it when I got dressed up to go out. He'd sing *'Pretty Woman'* to me and Richard would say *'Pretty Mummy.'*

I remember thinking to myself, *'I wish you were here now Rich. You'd tell me which blouse to buy.'*

I picked one or two and held them up to light for a better look and thought, *'which one would you like Richard ? Do you like this one or this one ? I know ! You'd like this red one - it's your favourite colour.'*

Just then, all the burglar alarms went off by the shop door, yet there wasn't a soul was about. The assistant behind the counter looked over to me and said, *'strange ! That's never happened before - perhaps we've got a ghost !'*

I just smiled and thought, *'yes and I know who the ghost is !'*

Such a lot of 'coincidences' seem to happen to me now that I don't always tell people. I don't think they'd believe me anyway - but it's all *true*.

Lately though, I've noticed that whenever the subject of 'life after death' comes up, people seem much more interested than they used to be. Very often they even have their own little experiences to relate. People seem afraid to reveal anything, until they're sure you feel the same way on the subject. It's a shame we can't all be more open-minded about discussing the Afterlife and our fear of death.

One evening I visited Simon, who was being held at our local police station overnight. We sat at a small table with a chair either side and were talking about Richard and the way Simon used to make him laugh. Suddenly felt a pressure on the top of my head. I thought someone had got their hand on my head, so I raised my eyes and laughed, thinking it was one of the local officers I knew. I said, *'oh no it's not P.C. 49 again is it ?'*

I fully expected to see him, as I turned around and put my hand up to grab

his. A slight shudder went through me, when I realised there was no one there at all. Simon asked, *'what did you think was there Mum ?'*
I told him and we both looked up to the ceiling, as we thought something may have dropped on my head. It was obvious to me that it was the pressure of someone's hand and as Simon and I talked, it came back. I said to Simon, *'it's here again'* and quickly turned round to catch the culprit, but we couldn't see anyone there at all.
Was Richard there with us ? Or did I imagine it ?

In our family we have two cats - Bonnie and Minnie. Richard loved Bonnie the most, because when he was ill, she would jump up on his bed to play. After Richard died, Bonnie would still jump up on his bed and sniff around, while purring like a machine.

One morning Bonnie was pestering me so much. She followed me wherever I went and after almost falling over her a few times, I opened the door and said, *'go out Bonnie. Richard's not here anymore for you to play with, go out and find him.'*

So out she went - but she didn't come back. I was so upset, she'd never gone away before. I thought the worst, then began asking everyone to look out for her. I was becoming desperate with worry. Then out loud I said, *'oh Rich, please find your little Bonnie and show her the way home. I'll never make her go out again, if she doesn't want to. I promise.'*

I'd been asking Richard to send her home throughout the day, then at about 4.20 p.m. the doorbell rang. I was hoping someone had come with news of the cat, but when I opened the door I saw Richard's old home tutor.

I couldn't conceal my disappointment and my smile just fell away. I explained to the lady that Richard's cat had been missing for weeks, but the she looked surprised. She turned around and looked up the garden path saying, *'no - there she is, just coming over the gate.'*

When I looked, there was Bonnie just strolling towards me with her tail up as high as she could get it. She came and sat on the doorstep as though she'd never been away ! Well, who better to send his favourite cat home with, than his own tutor ? I thanked Richard saying, *'how clever of you to send Bonnie home with your old teacher.'* I could almost hear Richard reply *'of course'* which was his usual, familiar saying !

My feelings about this experience were confirmed later, when my friend Lotte sent me a tape where a Medium talked about the work Spirit children can do. She said that one of their jobs is to look after animals and if they are lost, the children help by safely showing them the way home !

One day I'd needed to buy myself a new purse. I'd given mine to my mother to replace hers, but I searched for weeks to find one I liked.

After about three weeks had passed, I came home from shopping one day to find a small parcel on the doormat. When I opened it, I found a purse exactly like the kind I'd been looking for ! I would have easily chosen it myself if I'd seen it in a shop. I was amazed, but couldn't remember mentioning it to anyone. There was a letter inside the parcel from Frankie Brown, another RPPS Mum and friend of mine and Gwen's.

In the letter, Frankie explained how three weeks ago, she had bought the purse for me. She wrote that Richard had apparently been pestering her to *'buy a purse for my Mum'* and he'd kept on about it until she did !

I thanked Richard saying, *'now all I need is a nice new bag to go with it !'*

Then I laughed to myself thinking, *'oh I've got a nerve. As though Richard would bother about something so trivial.'*

Yet I've learned never to underestimate how those in Spirit look for ways to give us evidence of their power and existence - so we should never be surprised at anything they do. In fact, I truly believe they are delighted, when they can really prove to us that they are so close.

Soon after this, I went to visit Gwen for a couple of days. Gwen said that Frankie needed cheering up and as she only lived a short journey away, that we ought go and see her. I agreed, as Frankie had been ill at the time, but I could also thank her in person for the lovely purse she'd sent me.

Once there and we'd chatted for a while and had tea, Frankie said to me, *'Margaret, your son sure knows how to spend my money. Look what I've got for you now !'*

Then she picked up a plastic bag and dropped it on my lap. Inside were two lovely shoulder bags, a large one and a smaller one. Gwen and I were amazed. Frankie said she thought Richard wanted me to have the smaller one and Gwen the larger one. Well thank you again Richard !

I could never believe that this had been just a coincidence. For me, it was very carefully worked out by my son Richard.

While at Frankie's, we decided to use the glass and board, because Frankie had a feeling that Richard wanted to talk to me - bless him, he really tries very hard to ease my grief. Now Richard did come through and seemed concerned about my elderly mother. He spelt out,
'she should eat more.'

Then another communicator spelt out the message,
'Margaret, you are so special. I will give you a nice bit of haddock !'
Well at the time, all I could get my mother to eat was haddock, I'd tried everything. Then Spirit spelt out, *'try a nice bit of plaice then.'*
Well I thought this was hilarious, because recently I'd asked Mum what she *did* want to eat and she'd replied, *'well, I could try a nice bit of plaice then.'*

Our friends in Spirit do try to help us in so many ways, but they must be really frustrated at times, when we don't even notice them ! Yet even the smallest things can be very evidential.

One small thing that stands out in my mind, relates to my friend Shirley. When we first met, she'd been worried about her worsening eyesight. She told me that she'd asked Spirit to protect her sight and not let her go blind. I thought to myself, how terrible it would be to go blind and it worried me a lot after that - but I never ever said anything to anyone. Then out of the blue in a letter from Frankie, she said that Richard had asked her to tell me, not to worry about my eyes, I wouldn't go blind !

To me, this was excellent proof that Spirit had heard my thoughts.

Another time I'd been really worried about how I would pay the electricity bill. So I said to Spirit, *'I wish you could magic me some money. Even just fifty pounds to help with this bill would be very nice.'*

Then a few days later, a premium bond dropped through the letter box, to the value of fifty-pounds ! This really tickled Roy, who thought it was all just a wonderful coincidence. So one time when he complained that he needed some money to fix the car, I said, *'why don't you ask our friends up there if they can help. They helped me didn't they ?'*

'Don't be daft Marg.' Roy replied. *'It wouldn't work a second time - last time was just coincidence.'*

But then he surprised me by saying out loud, *'can you hear us Rich ? Send your poor old Dad some money eh ? Then I can fix the car.'*

Then, when the morning post landed on the doormat a few days later, we found yet another fifty pound premium bond - which solved Roy's little problem nicely ! So was this another coincidence ?

About two weeks after Richard had passed into Spirit, my husband Roy told me of a dream he'd had. Richard had woken him in the night and said, *'hello Dad. I'm alright, I've just come to see if you're alright too ? I've been to see Christopher at his house. He's alright too.'*

Christopher was Richard's best friend, who lived just around the corner. The next day, his mother stopped me in the street and told me that Richard had been in her dream on same night. She said she'd woken up feeling that Richard had given her a cuddle.

She told me that she got out of bed thinking the dream was so real, when she heard her son Christopher coming up the stairs. She went to him and asked what he was doing. His reply really surprised her. Christopher said, *'I've just been down to let Richard in.'*

I was with my friend Shirley once when suddenly she said, *'Richard's here and he's saying he's got Butch.'*

Now I couldn't work this out at all, but before he passed away, Roy had taken Richard to see a friend who bred Yorkshire Terriers. He had several pups at the time and the tiniest one of all was a bossy little thing, which yapped all around Richard and kept dashing about - much to Richard's delight ! The pup was called Butch and Richard really took to him. He said how he wished we could have him and how much he would love him. We *had* promised Richard he could have a dog - but not until he was better.

Back home, I told Roy about Shirley's message and he said, *'well that must be wrong, because my friend would have told me if anything had happened to little Butch.'*

Two days later, Roy came home from work and said to me, *'you were right. I saw my friend today and he told me that Butch had died unexpectedly a few days ago.'*

We just looked at each other and instantly realised that Shirley had been right, so Richard now had little Butch with him at last !

Richard with his Dad, Roy

All these stories of mine are written just as they happened, although some people may think I just try and make things fit. Yet I know that our loved ones do watch over us. They try and comfort us by showing us signs that they are still alive and waiting for the wonderful time we can meet again.

I was once very sceptical myself, but when things began to happen that were so obviously meant to shake me up and make me search for an explanation, I learned there is more to this world than meets the eye. As time goes by, I know I'll get even more evidence and Richard will keep on showing me he's around, as often as he can.

My other son Simon was always interested in everything I told him about Richard in the Spirit World. Simon had been with us since Christmas and now it was March 1994 and he was attending a treatment centre in London called 'Turning Point.' Simon was full of hope that his addictions would finally be conquered and he said to me,
'Mum, I'm really going to try this time and I feel that I'm going to do it.'

I thought he would succeed this time too, but Roy disagreed saying, *'he'll never change now Marg.'* Yet I kept on hoping that one day Simon would come home, cured. I began looking forward to the future for the first time since Richard had passed away and I thought of having happy times at home again, with Simon sober and drug free.

Simon had been in London for two weeks, when one day he phoned to ask if I'd send him some money for toiletries. The next time he rang, it was to my mother who sensed that he was drunk. Now I became very worried, because he'd already been everywhere else for counselling and treatment and 'Turning Point' was his last chance.

At around 11.30 p.m. on April 14th, my mother's phone rang while she was asleep. The next day she told me that by the time she reached the phone, whoever it was had hung up. We decided that it must have been Simon, because this was the type of thing he would do. He would never consider the inconvenience to others or even seem to think of other people's feelings. So when he rang me the following evening, I told him what I thought. I said how selfish I thought he was, but he denied it. Then after arguing, Simon hung up without even saying goodbye.

The following Sunday, Simon phoned me back to apologise, but I said, *'I don't believe you are sorry Simon. It must have been you who called your Nan late at night - who else would it be?'*

We didn't hear from Simon throughout the following week and although I was worried about him, I also had a very uneasy feeling that something was about to happen. I seemed to just be waiting for the doorbell to ring, then find him standing on the doorstep saying, *'I'm sorry, I'm sorry'* - like he always did.

On the following Friday evening at 10.30 the doorbell *did* ring. We guessed it would be Simon, but when I opened the door I recognised our familiar policemen standing there. He asked to come in for a minute, so I said, *'oh no. What's Simon been up to now?'*

When the policeman spoke, his next words shook me to the core. He said, *'he's died this time Margaret.'*

It was such a shock.

After all our hopes and prayers, it was finally over for Simon and for me. Then I felt so guilty and blamed myself for not keeping him at home and helping him. Although Simon had pushed me to the limit of my endurance and there *were* times when I'd wished he would just go away altogether. He was so exasperating, but deep inside I loved him just the same, for he was still my longed for baby boy.

Nobody really knows what happened to Simon, but I think he'd just taken too many pills in his loneliness. Yet he'd always told us he would never live to be thirty. Now it was April and Simon had been just a few months away from his birthday - he was twenty-nine years old.

Simon knew of my understanding of Spirit, so I knew he would bring me his own proof that he was around, just as soon as he possibly could. My friend Shirley had told me to be aware too, saying, *'Simon will come soon, you'll see !'*

After Simon's Passing

I was sure Simon would do all he could to let me know he still exists - once he became accustomed to his new life in the Spirit World, with his brother Richard, their Grandfather and others.

A few weeks after Simon had passed away, my Mother said to me, *'Margaret, remember when my phone rang late at night and we blamed Simon ? Well my phone rang late again last night, but I got up to answer it this time and there was a whispering, hissing noise, which sounded far away. Then it went dead.'*
Now I don't know if this was anything to do with Simon, but we both felt it was something strange. Nothing like it had ever happened before.

Now Simon did make an effort to show himself *and* it was to his father ! One Summer afternoon, Roy had gone for a motorbike ride in the country. He'd come to a stream and stopped to look in the water. Roy was watching little fish swimming around in a circle, as they popped up to catch flies on the surface. He picked up a little pebble and dropped it in the water, then watched all the fish scatter about then form a circle again. Roy repeated this several times becoming totally engrossed in what he was doing. He was thinking of this and nothing else, when suddenly he became aware of a presence beside him. He turned around and for a brief second, saw our son Simon standing watching him. Roy said,
'cor blimey Simon, what are you doing here ?'
Then he was gone. Roy did tell me it was a bit of a shock, but very real to him at the time.

A few weeks later, on a gloriously warm and sunny day, I was walking back from my mothers house when I saw my neighbour Doris. She was sitting in her front doorway, so I walked over to her. As she saw me, she called me over.

'Marg we had a break-in last night,' she said. 'Now we'll have to change all the locks.'

'Was anything taken ?' I asked.

'Well that's the funny thing' said Doris. 'The back door was open and things were knocked off shelves and newspapers were strewn about the floor.'

As she said this I remembered something about Simon. The last time he was home, we watched the movie *'Ghost'* together. In one scene, a Spirit on a train knocks newspapers out of passenger's hands and onto the floor. Simon liked this bit and we laughed about it together, but he said, 'Mum, that's great isn't it ? I'd like to do that !'

I could just imagine Simon throwing these newspapers around in Doris's house - just to make us aware of him. Then I thought,
'at least this time, he can't be blamed for breaking into Doris's house - or ever again for that matter !'

I wanted to tell Doris that Roy had seen Simon, but as I opened my mouth to speak, I stopped - because as Doris stepped out of her doorway and into the sunshine, something happened...

Suddenly, I saw Doris's hands begin to glow ! They looked to me like green fluorescent light bulbs. As I watched in stunned silence, I saw these green lights grow larger and begin spreading up her arms, just like green flames. I tried really hard to keep talking, but I was so astonished at this phenomenon that I just stared.

These lights crept up my friend's arms and were now surrounding her whole body. Doris was wearing a pink dress at the time, but this bright green glow had completely covered it, until all I could see were Doris's features. Then I briefly turned to look away, but everything else around us looked normal. When I looked back, Doris was still totally covered in this green glowing light. It surrounded and glowed all around her, to about a distance of one foot.

Doris seemed unaware of anything happening at all, then she looked over to a lady across the road, who was coming to speak to her. The lady didn't see or react to anything either and we all talked together for a minute or so. They were both unaware of what I was seeing. Now I had to make an excuse, 'well, I have to go. I must start Roy's dinner.'

I started to leave, but don't even remember finishing what I was saying. Then as I turned away, I saw two big green balls of light which were bouncing on the pavement in front of me. As I walked along they came all the way around the corner with me and right up to my front doorstep. Then as soon as I got inside, they were gone. I quickly opened the door again and looked out, but they just weren't there any more. Before I'd walked out of sight of Doris, I'd looked back towards her and she was still there at her doorstep, talking - and she was still glowing green all over!

Now this was a first hand experience which I saw with my own eyes, but I can't explain it. I think it was perhaps Simon trying hard somehow to give me something - some proof.

Later on I saw Doris, though never mentioned the green light, but I did ask her more about the break-in. She told me how she'd actually been mistaken. She'd discovered that her son Christopher had come home a bit tipsy and he'd left the back door open. Although Doris couldn't understand why he would have strewn newspaper all over the place, Christopher had said that he couldn't even remember doing it.

A Message from Simon

I sat with Gwen, in the congregation of my local Spiritualist church once, where our friend Tony Stockwell was demonstrating his Mediumship. At the time, Tony knew only that I'd lost Richard, but not Simon.

During his demonstration, Tony addressed some people sitting in the middle row. He asked if any of them knew the Spirit of a tall, young man in his twenties, with dark hair and blue eyes. None of them knew who this was but Tony continued, saying,

'He is saying he is so sorry. He is confused. He has two other young men with him. One is very ginger-haired and died through fumes and the other died through drug abuse. The young man is talking about his own boy on the Earth and saying, 'love to my baby."

Still no one in the middle row could place this young man, so Tony asked if anyone else in the room knew him. Now I'd waited until I was absolutely certain that this wasn't for someone else, though I felt sure this was my Simon. I spoke up and told Tony that I could place all that information, except the man with the red hair. Tony said, *'I know this young man wants to speak to someone very close to him, someone as close as a Mum. Now I know you are in touch with other Mums but I know this is not for them - it's definitely for you.'*

Tony knew my Richard was a boy of only ten, but I don't think he could understand why a man in his twenties, wanting to speak to his Mum, would come to me. I said that I knew exactly who this was. So Tony continued, *'well, he's telling me you are the right one. He's going on about bean bags*

in a room he had and that he is so sorry for the pain he caused. He sends his love to you and to his baby. He says he made a mistake with the amount of tablets he took and he didn't mean to take too many. He was confused and says he wouldn't have got better, had he lived and that he would have had an awful life.
He says that the people you have been to for messages, have given you a load of cr*p - but there are good times ahead.
He says, you are not allowed to see the boy and he knows you want to. He says he's going to try and do something about that, if he can.'

What Tony had said about the bean bags made sense to me. Simon had some bean bags in flat he once had and when Roy and I paid him a visit, he was sitting in one and saying how much he loved them - and I'd told him that I did too !

All of what Tony said about 'the boy' was also correct. This was Simon's son. The baby was adopted straight from the hospital - around the time that Richard was dying - but because of the adoption, I was not allowed to see or know anything about him. If things had been different back then, I could have looked after Simon's baby.

That evening, both Gwen and Tony stayed over at my house for the night. Whilst we chatted, Tony said he felt that Richard wanted to tell him something, so I showed him into Richard's old room. When Tony looked at the patterned wallpaper, he pointed to a scene of rabbits in grass which had a little brown butterfly flying over it. Pointing to the butterfly Tony said, *'I can see a little boys face in there and he is saying, 'that's me."*

Then Tony said, *'Simon is saying that his Dad has his Marks & Spencer's t-shirt.'*

This didn't mean anything to me at first, but then I remembered. A few weeks before, I'd found a t-shirt in Roy's wardrobe and suggested Roy tried it for size. Roy said, *'Marg, the arms are much too tight for me. This must have been one of Simon's shirts.'*

I said, *'well I'd have given it to Simon when he next came home - if he was still here Roy ! Anyway, Marks and Spencer's shirts are usually nice and big, so you should have been able to get into it okay...'*

I think Simon must have been with us when Roy and I were talking about his shirt that time - and this was what Tony was referring to.

Times of Awareness

Several Mediums have told me that I have the Spirit guide of a Japanese lady, but I'd never really thought much about it until one night, when I couldn't sleep.

I'd been suffering from insomnia for a while and was in bed wondering if I'd ever get to sleep and I began thinking of Richard. I pictured him in the American Wild West and he was walking behind an old-fashioned, covered wagon. Everything was so very hot and dry and there were mountains off in the distance. I could see Richard holding onto the back of this wagon, which was part of an entire train of similar wagons.

Then suddenly, the scene changed and I was looking down a long and narrow, reddish coloured room. I could see someone slowly coming towards me and it was a young Japanese lady.

I think I must have been to sleep, although I knew my husband Roy was beside me. I tried to bring the wagon train back into mind again, but before I could open my eyes, the face of the Japanese lady rushed towards me. She came so close, right up to my face and I literally pushed my head back into my pillow - in case she collided with me !

I remember she was looking at me very intently. She was very pretty and a little plumpish. She had lovely almond eyes and two soft rolls of hair each side of her head. She wore a round necked, t-shirt style top which seemed quite modern to me and in both hands, she held a round, flat basket to one side. I couldn't see what was in the basket, but it was small and looked like it had little square tickets or papers inside.

The moment I realised I was seeing this Japanese lady guide, Roy's arm flopped over me and everything vanished. She had looked nothing like I'd imagined her to be and I was disappointed because I couldn't bring her back.

A few months later, I began sleeping in our spare room, because I was becoming very restless at night. I was always up and down the stairs making tea, writing to other Mums or just watching the television.

One night I'd been sitting up in bed writing and felt tired, so I lay down to try and sleep. I turned off the light and began saying a mantra. I started to feel really drowsy, when suddenly I could hear the sound of wind chimes, a little way off to my right. Great - now I was alert and awake again !

'But what was making that noise ?' I thought, as it came nearer and nearer. At first it was very lovely and delicate, then it seemed to come right over my face and was quite loud. I couldn't make it out, so I put my hand up and switched on the light. I could still hear the tinkling wind chime sound, as it slowly passed to my left and gradually trailed off into the distance. I was quite disappointed when it had gone.

As usual, when something like this happens, you wish you'd made the most of it at the time, because these things always happens when you're relaxed and least expect it !

Orange Blossom

One hot day, I was with Gwen in her garden. We'd been out visiting and had been looking forward to getting back to relax. Gwen went inside to make some tea and when she brought it out I could smell orange blossom. It was very strong, so I said, *'Gwen, what's that lovely perfume ?'*

We both looked round to see where it might be coming from and sat there sniffing the air. I even went up and down the garden looking for an orange blossom tree. *'It can't be orange blossom'* Gwen said. *'We haven't got an orange tree and neither have any of our neighbours.'*

Then Gwen could smell it too. It was so strong and every now and then it kept wafting past us, all the time we were sitting outside. We couldn't place it or explain it.

When I got home I went to see my mother and as I opened the front door to step inside, the smell of orange blossom just hit me. It was as though there was a big bunch of it in the room. My Mum couldn't smell it at all, but she was very interested when I told her about it. There were no flowers in the room at the time and nothing to make such a strong perfume, but it was so beautiful. By the time I went home, the scent had completely gone and I still had no explanation.

After the orange blossom incident, Gwen and I were talking on the phone and she told me she'd had a song going round in her mind. It was the *'Flower Duet'* from Puccini's opera *Madame Butterfly*. I'd never heard of this music before, until Gwen told me about it. She said that Russell loves that particular opera and that he often sings parts of it to her - especially when he wants to make a point ! Well on that day, she told me that she just kept singing it and the song just wouldn't go away. Now Gwen and I both have Japanese ladies as Spirit guides and Gwen has always thought of this duet as being about her and me.

However, that afternoon I went for a wander around the shops in town. I just had to go into, what I call my *'magic'* charity shop, because I knew there'd be something there for me to find. Sure enough, right at the front of a rail of shirts was one in white, with *two* Japanese ladies on it ! They were in a garden, like two friends together.

I've sent Gwen all sorts of things over the years and I know it's either

Russell or Richard who lead me to find them. I didn't think there could be anything more I *could* send, but after carefully washing and pressing this lovely shirt, it was like new - so I sent it Gwen straight away. It did look great and it showed just how I imagined the two ladies from the Flower Duet would look.

A couple of days later, Gwen called me and she was so excited. She told me she'd been humming the Flower Duet when the postman bought her my 'surprise' parcel. Gwen really loved the shirt and had put it on straight away. She really was bubbling over with excitement, because once again that 'little thing' that could have been a coincidence, we agreed was so obviously *not* a coincidence at all. We talked about the wonder of finding something, yet when I bought it, I was not aware what good evidence it really was.

More Proof

I'd read somewhere that God never gives us too much to bear, so that we cannot cope with the pain of it. Several times, I found that when I'm really desperate with longing for my two boys, I somehow come over very tired and need to sleep. I usually feel this intense longing early in the morning. I suppose it's the realisation once again, that it isn't all a dream. My sons *did* die and leave me all alone with my terrible grief. They left me to struggle without them, thinking and longing for them day after day.

Both a mother and father's grief are different. Each one is locked up inside with their own personal pain. Each one's suffering is as bad as the other's - but different, because of the different memories shared. The beloved child who was so very vibrant and alive, is now so very absent and gone from our lives.

It's said that 'no man is an island' - but it feels so very isolating when you are continuously longing for a child, who you know has gone from your life forever or at least for the rest of your life.

One morning recently I'd woken at six yet again, after a very restless night. I had been longing so for my two boys and I asked God to help me cope with the awful emptiness I felt. I pleaded for Jesus to ease the pain of my grief and to give me some sort of comfort and relief. I felt I really couldn't endure much more and my heart felt as if it was on the point of breaking.

Now, I don't normally fall asleep again once I've woken up in the morning - but that morning I did. Suddenly I felt that my son Richard was behind me in bed. I knew I was asleep, yet I could still feel his body so

solidly. His leg was over my hip and my hand was on his thigh. I could feel his arm around my shoulder and his face was pressed into my neck. He was laughing and cuddling me. I said, *'oh Richard how can you feel so solid when I know it's only a dream ?'*
He giggled and said, *'no it's not Mum.'*

I briefly opened my eyes, but didn't want this lovely feeling of Richard's presence to go, so I closed them again. He was still there as I patted his leg and he felt so solid. Next in this 'dream' I was looking up at Richard, who was standing in the room. I was cuddling my little Spaniel dog, which had been laying on a nearby chair and Richard was watching us and laughing. I really felt that God had answered my prayer and just when I needed it the most.

The day I spent with Gwen when we smelled the orange blossom, was the same day we gained some really good evidence of another kind. Sitting in Gwen's kitchen, we decided to make contact with Richard via the glass and letters. Once we'd established that Richard was speaking to us, we asked him to give us some proof that he could see what was going on around us.

We asked him where he was the room and he told us that he was standing between Gwen and I - but in a flash he could be with Alfie, who was upstairs and then back again just as quick. So Gwen asked him,
'can you prove that Richard, by telling us what Alfie is doing ?'
Richard then spelt out the name of a daily newspaper, which we really didn't understand, so Gwen said,
'do you mean Alfie is reading the paper ?'
All Richard said next was,
'King Richard was not so bad after all.'
Well this really foxed us. At first I thought he might mean himself as 'King Richard' and that *he* was not so bad. I asked him what he meant and he simply said, *'ask Alfie.'*

Just as he'd said that, Alfie came into the kitchen with his newspaper under his arm. It was the same edition that Richard had named, so Gwen asked Alfie if there was anything in the paper about King Richard. Alfie said not, but Gwen took the paper and we searched ourselves. When neither of us could find anything, Alfie had another look. He searched through every page and then said, *'oh look, here it is. The headline says, 'King Richard was not as bad as people said''*

Richard was right ! There was a long piece down one side of the centre page with that very same heading. We all thought this was wonderful proof that Richard knew what was going on, so we asked him how he knew ? Richard came back and told us that he'd looked at the newspaper, over Alfie's shoulder ! Now wasn't that clever ?

Spirit Knocking

The evening that Simon first came through a Medium at the Spiritualist church, made me so happy to know he was trying to prove his existence. So when I went to bed that night, my mind was full of Simon.

I lay thinking about him for a long time and recalled the times he and I had talked about his brother in Spirit, Richard. Simon had been amazed at the things I'd told him, about how his brother had tried to bring me proof. It seemed that Richard often tried very hard to give me evidence at specific times. Simon said, *'Richard will always give you something when he can - especially at 4.20 p.m.'*

I was deep in thought as I lay there and remembered that a few days before, I'd been thinking that now Simon was in the Spirit World, could he bring me his own proof in a similar way ? Just then I heard a loud knock which came from my bedside table. I looked up and noticed that the time was 11 p.m. Over the next few nights, I waited for another knock at the same time, but nothing happened.

A few nights later I was wide awake yet again and I said aloud, *'Simon - or anyone who wants to - can you try and knock again for me ? I know Gwen gets them every day from Russell - even though Russell has told her that, 'it may be your Mummy or Daddy."*

I hoped that these type of knocks might be from someone in Spirit, though I did realise that any faint little knocks or taps could just as easily be the wood moving or pipes banging, as they often do. So I said out loud, *'when you do knock, make sure I have no doubt that it is Spirit. Make it loud if you can !'*

It was quite late by now, so I soon settled down to sleep. In the silence, I was suddenly awoken by a series of loud knocks coming from my computer printer, which was over in the corner of the room.
'Bang, bang, bang, bang.'

They were so loud that I jumped up to see who was there, saying *'what ?'* My heart was racing, because at first I thought there was someone knocking from outside. Then when I looked at the clock, it was 4.20 a.m. and I remembered. At that moment I felt so excited. It seemed as though

Spirit were just standing there looking at me, saying,
'well that woke her up, didn't it ?'

Smiling to myself, I turned over in bed then thought, *'Simon, you nearly gave me a heart attack. Is that what you wanted - for me to join you ?'*

Many may feel that this was simply my printer making a noise, but I hadn't used it for days and it wasn't even plugged into the electricity. I'd heard four very definite knocks, which were loud enough to wake me. They made the same kind of sound as when you knock loudly on a door - and they came at 4.20 a.m. Was it another coincidence ?

Our Space Age Tunnel

In 1986 Richard had to go to London for treatment. His teacher, Peter Barratt, had kindly offered to take Richard and myself to or from Barts Hospital, anytime. We agreed that after a few days, I would call him at the school when we were ready to come home again.

At that time, as part of the A-1 road improvements into London, the Hatfield Tunnel was being built and Richard was very interested in this. In fact, we all looked forward to the time when we could actually drive through it.

After Richard's treatment I called Peter. He was true to his word and he collected us both from Barts Hospital in London. On the way home Richard was exciting at being a passenger in his teacher's car *and* he tried to get him to speed up - cheeky boy ! There was clearly a great rapport between them and I know they admired each other very much. Peter told me that he'd be happy to take Richard to his next treatment, when it was due. So when the time came, he collected us from home once more.

When Peter arrived, he told Richard that the time we'd been waiting for had finally come - the Hatfield Tunnel was open at last ! Now this time, the journey to London was quite exciting. Travelling through the new motorway tunnel was awe-inspiring - we all felt it, including Richard, who said to us, *'it's just like a space age tunnel !'*

We all agreed that it was very impressive and from then on we called it our 'space age tunnel.'

Several years later, after Richard had passed away, we received another good piece of evidence - and quite unexpectedly. For me, it was one of those times when something suddenly clicks into place and you realise everything is clear and you understand all at once.

On a day Gwen was visiting, we decided to use the glass and letters to see whether anyone from Spirit wanted to communicate. It went very well and as usual Richard was giving us riddles to think about. He never, ever wanted things to be easy for us ! He always seemed happy as long as we were somewhat baffled, so we always had to think things out.
On this occasion he spelt out the words,
'space age is here.' I thought he meant that we were now in the space age.

So I asked him if he'd been into space. Richard replied by spelling out, *'Peter has.'*

Gwen and I were puzzled, so we discussed what he was trying to say. I just didn't know what he could possibly mean. Then Richard spelt out, *'Pete B Tun'* - which I thought was perhaps someone's name.

Now Roy, who had been quietly reading the paper, but was secretly listening to everything that was going on, suddenly jumped in and said, *'he's saying Peter Barratt's space age tunnel !'*

After a few seconds it dawned on me.
'Yes of course, that's it ! How clever,' I said.

Richard was reminding us of the Hatfield Tunnel, yet it had been almost seven years since we'd regularly driven through it. I'd almost forgotten Richard's nickname for it, so I'd been on completely the wrong track - but Richard hadn't forgotten ! What a fool I was. Now I could easily imagine hearing Richard saying, *'oh Mum, at last !'*

A Set Number of Years to be Here on Earth ?

It's so very hard to understand why some children have to die so young and it's so very hard to understand why some people live to a ripe old age. What is it in their makeup that stops some people getting diseases ? Some people never seem to get ill at all, while others seem to get everything nasty that's going round.

When Simon was a baby, I protected him like a mother tiger. I kept him with me all the time and didn't expose him to anything I considered dangerous. I never even liked to give him medication, for fear it would upset his health. I always gave him the best food we could afford and in fact, he had the best of everything. I kept him away from smokers, drinkers, bad language and also violence and sex on the TV. Yet Simon grew up knowing all these things so well and in the end, it killed him.

I tried to protect all my sons in the same way and thought I was giving them all the best start in life that a child could possibly have.

When Richard became ill, I didn't believe he could die. I thought his body was immune to everything and mistakenly, I even thought that while I was there, nothing could get to him. I'm sure even Richard thought, *'Mum will protect me, whatever.'*

Yet who would have thought that out of three sons, two would die within seven years of each other ? I think there must be a reason. Maybe there's a 'code' of life and death, so that when our allocated time is up, we have to go. No matter how we've lived - good or bad, healthy or unhealthy, neglected or pampered - whether we're old or young, I do believe that when we've served our time, there's nothing that can keep us living on in our physical body.

I also believe that if a person's life is due to end, they *will* be taken in whatever way is necessary. So someone who we may expect to die as a result of illness, who is then helped along with medication, can get better. Yet I think, if it is their *time to go*, they might probably have a fatal accident or a heart attack anyway.

I will share a true story that explains what I am trying to say...

Living near to us was a young man named Steve. He was about twenty-three when he first became ill. We hadn't seen him around for quite some months, so I presumed that he must have gone away to study or something similar. He had a younger sister, but both their parents had died tragically, so they were alone in the house together.

Eventually, Steve's sister moved away to be with her boyfriend, so Steve got some young friends to stay, to help pay the mortgage. This worked fine until he got very ill.

As I had missed seeing Steve for a very long time, I asked Roy if he knew anything. Roy said that he'd been wondering where Steve was too, but told me, *'I've seen him in his garden and he looks as if he's had chemotherapy treatment, because he has no hair at all.'*

This news really upset me, because I knew of the horrors of chemotherapy all too well. Roy and I had both watched our dear son Richard go through the same thing.

Later, I learned that Roy had spoken to Steve, who'd told him that he did have cancer, but hoped he was on the mend.

Sure enough, Steve did improve and for two years he was doing really well, but then after his final diagnosis, he was told the cancer had returned. So once again, Steve began another course of 'chemo' and had to travel backwards and forwards for regular treatment.

However, Steve said he felt much better after all this and so he got on with his life. He passed some exams and got a better job and life seemed good for him for some time. Unfortunately the old signs of illness returned once more, so it all started again. He had to visit the hospital for treatment and his hair-loss returned.

After a few months I began to get worried as we hadn't seen Steve in such a long time. Then a few days later, I saw him through my window. He was in the street talking to Roy and they were discussing Steve's motorbike. Roy was concerned about the bike's brakes and he told Steve that if they were sticking, it could be very dangerous. Steve told Roy that he would get them fixed the next week. I joined them outside and told Steve how pleased I was to see him. I said I'd been worried because we hadn't seen him for so long.

Steve said, *'I bet you thought the worst? But I'm pleased to say, I've just had the all clear, at last. After my check-up yesterday they've told me I'm absolutely clear of cancer!'*

I was really happy for him and said, *'oh how marvellous for you Steve. Now you can put it all behind you and have a new start in life.'*

'I intend to' Steve replied. *'I'm going to live it up now!'*

The next Saturday night, just three days later, Steve went out to meet his friends. He went out on his motorbike, which was unusual for him, as he always went in his little car. At around 11.30 that night, Steve was travelling home, but missed a bend in the road and ended up in a nearby field. He was found at around three in the morning by a man on his way to work. Steve was dead.

Only a few days earlier Steve had said he was going to live his life to the full - but just like a little flame, his light was snuffed out in seconds. Steve was gone but the cancer couldn't kill him, yet it seemed he was to die anyway, so had the motorbike accident. I feel very sad when I think of all the suffering he went through, only to be killed after all. Three times Steve had cheated death, but still he had to go. It makes you wonder, doesn't it?

A friend told a me of a young girl who died one Christmas. She was just fifteen and had been fit and well, until only two months earlier. She had been complaining of pain and after a medical examination, was found to be very ill with cancer.

Towards the end she just kept drifting away and back again. Suddenly, she came back into full consciousness and said clearly to her mother,

'Mum stop pulling me back. They are pulling me and you are pulling me -

and I'm in the middle, not going anywhere. I want to go with them now.'
The girl's mother said,
'I'm not pulling you love. You can go now if you want to.'
The girl said, *'well cut the wire Mum. It's holding me down.'*
Her mother replied, *'you will have to cut it yourself, I can't do it.'*
'Alright' the girl said to her Mum. *'I'll do it now.'*
And at that moment, after those few words, the girl just quietly died.

I think she must have been describing to her Mother, the silver cord that many people say connects the physical body to the Spirit. It was obviously holding her back and when she agreed to let go she became free of her physical body.
For me, I think this gives great proof. Everyone who describes the life that's to come, can't be wrong can they ?

Before I lost Richard and Simon, I was always afraid to think of what might or might not come after death. Although after they'd died, I was forced to face all the questions that every parent has, when their child is no longer physically around them. *'Were they in oblivion ? Do they know where they are ? Do they still think about me ? Do they really still exist ?'*

If our loved ones are dead and that's it - if they no longer 'are' and there's nothing left of them, then why does our love for them still exist ? Why doesn't it just evaporate, as they did ? How can we still have such strong feelings for our loved ones, if there's nothing left to feel strongly about ?

I believe in an inner knowledge. A knowledge which tells us that we *are* all going to meet again and love again - and *be* again. That's what keeps us striving towards our heaven, with them in mind. If this is so, then nothing ever dies. That great power of love keeps everything alive. Wouldn't it all just be a waste, to spend our lives longing for our dead loved ones - if this life was all there was. I think it's the power of our love that keeps them alive, so they *must* exist. *Love* is the strongest and greatest power of any that exists.

One More Knock

I was sitting up in bed reading one night and thinking of Richard, Simon, my Mum and Dad, and Gwen's son Russell. Now they were all together in the Spirit World.
Mostly, I'd been thinking of Simon. Then I looked around my bedroom and said out loud, *'oh Simon it's been such a long time since I heard you knock*

on the printer. I wish you could do it again for me. I miss the times when I felt you around. Are you still near?'

I turned off the light and lay down, facing the wall. I was almost asleep when I heard a loud *'crack'* on the bedside cabinet. Instantly I was wide awake and I sprung round to turn on the light. I was smiling as I said, *'oh thank you Simon! Thank you, thank you!'*

But then I thought, *'was it Simon?*
Could it be Richard or Mum or Dad - or even Russell?'

Either way, I was so happy to have heard that knock as I lay back down again and turned off the light. Settling down I wondered which of them had made that sound. But then, in the silence and just as loud, I heard four more knocks on the cabinet in quick succession, all sounding exactly the same. Now I'd heard *five* knocks altogether - one for each of those I'd been thinking about. Weren't they clever?

I lay there thinking and was so pleased that they'd been able to show me that they *are* still around and *can* hear what we say to them.

'Ask and you shall receive' as it is often said. Now I know that's true and if they possibly can, *they will* oblige.

Twenty Two

Poetry By Another Bridge

November 25th 1994

*'There is no death,
only a change in worlds'*

~ Black Elk

Earlier in the book, I explained how I'd received poems from Russell during my 'dark times' - especially after the wonders of the physical séances had ended. He knew how difficult it was for his Mum !

Now I'd like to introduce you to another Mum, Frankie Brown. A lady who, in spite of health problems, received a succession of inspired poems. Some were from Russell the child and are full of humour - some were from Russell the man. I feel they're worth sharing with readers, before Frankie tells her own story in the next chapter.

I'll begin with the humorous ones first - Russell the boy's humour !

Here I am - shouting from the beyond !

*Have you tried your luck with the Premium bond ?
Or how about the lottery, at a quid a go ?*

Come on Mum don't be slow,

*'Cos I'm trying to tell you, honey,
From up here we can't materialise money !*

*See if you can win something - go and have a look,
This way I could help you, to publish my book !*

~ Russell
May 1992

Thank you Russell ! I *have* recently won a couple of bonds, but the National Lottery wasn't started for another two years. We've had no luck yet, but we can hope !

The following poem through my friend Frankie, illustrates a regular happening experienced in my own garden.

> *When you sit under the willow tree,*
> *Direct your thoughts right up to me,*
>
> *Then I'll say, 'God, my Mum is calling me,'*
> *And I'll come and sit right down by the tree,*
>
> *Then I'll catch a butterfly for you, my dear,*
> *And you'll say, 'oh crumbs, my Russell's here !'*
>
> *Oh what a happy day that will be,*
> *Just you and me, beneath the tree,*
>
> *You don't believe it ? Well, you'll see,*
> *Just sit under the willow tree.*

~ Russell
July 10th, 1991

To My Mum

> *When I was small you hugged me tight,*
> *And told me stories in bed each night,*
>
> *We laughed and loved and lived here together,*
> *And you moaned about the Rayleigh weather,*
>
> *I used to ruin my shoes and they had to go to the cobblers*
> *And I thought 'Oh my Gawd, she'll throw a wobbler !'*
>
> *Then I had to go to the Other Side,*
> *And I was sad to see how you cried,*
>
> *But I thought my Mum won't let anything beat her,*
> *So then I materialised through Rita,*
>
> *Then we laughed and loved and met again,*
> *And we joked about the Rayleigh rain,*
>
> *And how I really scared the cat,*
> *And you said, 'Alfie, did you see that ?'*
>
> *You've done well Mum ! We've done it together,*
> *We've helped all the Mums, just like birds of a feather !*

I <u>know</u> it's been hard, but I'm here now to say,
That I've always been with you, every step of the way,

Because you see Mum, the <u>great love</u> we have for each other,
Has enabled us to help many sad mothers,

So don't get down Mum, must look up to the light,
I'll always be there to help you in your plight,

Now I've grown up, no more sadness and tears,
I love you, you love me and though we've lost all those years,

I'll always love you and be by your side,
For you are my Mum and my heart fills with pride,

So when you can't bear Earth's old hustle and bustle,
Just know I am beside you, your loving son Russell.

~ Russell
September 1991

Happy Birthday Mum,

Happy Birthday dear Mother mine,
My word you're getting old !

But I wouldn't change you,
For a great big pot of gold.

Another birthday, another year,
My heart beats like a child, when a birthday is near,

From the loving realms above,
All the RPPS send their love,

I will not desert you, no not I,
Aren't I your great big red butterfly ?

Have a great birthday, enjoy it with all your worth,
For I'll be right beside you, here on Earth,

So make this birthday a happy one,
'Cos I really don't half love you Mum !

~ Russell
May 1990

Happy Birthday Dad

Happy Birthday dear old Dad,
You're getting old, but you don't look bad !

Just the greying of the locks,
I hope you don't get too many socks...

Your secretary will be going away,
So you'll have to finish your job some day,

So do the things that you like best,
And we'll take care of all the rest.

~ Russell
June 1990

This poem from Russell for his Dad's birthday, references Alfie's upcoming retirement. We knew the company would fold soon enough - and it looks like Russell knew too ! Thanks Russell, from both of us.

Rustle's & Knocks

Dear Mum, listen closely now and pull up your socks,
The ones with the bobbles on and listen to my knocks,

When the knocks come, listen and surely you'll see,
When the mind is quiet, the messages will come from me,

You know I've come down to Earth, when I give you the knocks,
So I am closer to you then, to help you through life's shocks,

For the cover of the 2nd book, dress up in your bustle,
Listen carefully now and I will rustle !

I'm glad to see you lighter of heart,
I can't say much, but it's just the start,

Sing sweetly Mum, with all your heart,
You know that you and I won't part.

~ Russell
May 10th 1990

Russell often did come through at home, with Spirit knocks or raps. We've been hearing them in our own bedroom regularly since 1983. I once

asked Russell about them at a séance and he replied,
'...Mum it's not always me. Sometimes it's <u>your</u> Mummy or Daddy !'

This next poem refers to an evening show, during Lynwood Fellowship Week. We were all able to let our hair down, including my friend Val Williams. She's a real comedian on stage and I think she might have missed her vocation !

Oh, would I love to see your face,
But I just can't set the pace,

So I'm flitting there and here,
Arranging things to give you cheer,

(I loved your warbling, when you helped to run the show)

What about Val's funny face,
Causing uproar at that place ?

I'll always let you know I'm here,
So don't be down - be of good cheer,

If only we could have our way,
If only we could have our say,

To help the world to know the Truth of life,
But how can we know the Truth of life ?

Never mind Mum, I'll change the knock,
So you won't wake up with such a shock,

So look around, be of good cheer,
Those little things show I'm near !

~ Russell
August 9th 1990

The first book *'Russell'* was supposed to be released on June 6th 1994 and the next poem references the book's actual release date of May 20th 1994 - my Birthday !

A trillionaire you may well be,
But spare a little thought for me,

For where the sun sets in the West,
That's where you'll see my face best,

Now when a child so good and true,
Is born to a Mother so caring as you,

Then is so quickly taken away,
Some 'Karmic Plan' must come into play,

There's only one thing I can say,
What a present, hey ? For your birthday !

Thank you for your patience, I mean about the long wait,
It won't be so long next time, when we name the date,

Maybe about 3 years, not 30 - I'm allowed to say,
Remember my promise, I'm there every step of the way,

I'll tell you what...behind closed doors,
There's lots of shuffling of people's jaws !

But fear them not - let all the tongues rustle,
For your son is here, still with hair stuck up like a bristle !

Oh ! Just one thing before I go,
Happy birthday Mum, I do love you so.

~ Russell
May 20th 1994

To Mum and Dad

Well blow me down, don't you two look grand ?
Like butterflies in shells of sand,

Two 'land lubbers' looking hale and hearty,
Will be at my birthday party.

I'm not gonna get any older, for I am in my prime,
No aching bones for me, 'cos we don't count the time,

When you both come over - old and grey,
I'll have to look at you and say,

'Cor ! Stone the crows, don't you look old ?
It must be the worry of the house not sold !'

Although loads of money will come your way,
It will be quite a while 'til you get full pay,

Then trillionaires you both will be,

And all because of little old me,

And stop chopping down the willow tree !
They'll be no apports left for me,

Well what a laugh you two had today,
Like two big kids, let out to play,

I said, 'Look at our two Mums, Al,'
He smiled and said, 'I love to see it, pal.'

She'll soon be on her feet again,
Smiling 'cos she's free from pain,

She doesn't believe me while she's writing this,
But soon her life will be pain free and bliss,

Anyway I have to soon go,
So watch for footprints in the snow,

And with my best top on and hair up like a Brussel,
You'll both exclaim, 'Cor blimey - it's Russell'

~ Russell
July 8th 1993

My word, all these promises about being trillionaires ! Good job we can take a joke Russ, but we're still waiting ! Here Russell refers to his friend *'Al.'* This is Frankie's son Alan who helps to bring the poems through.

As I'm transcribing these poems, it seems as though they are getting a little bit more serious as we go along. Although before we get to the serious ones, here's one of Russell's - to himself !

<u>Happy Birthday To Me !</u>

When I was much younger, about thirty-six,
I had the place in uproar with my little tricks,

It's great to change ages from ninety to one,
Though I decided to be nine and three quarters, for my Mum,

But now I've got older, and grown out of my coat,
I have to be responsible and stop acting the goat,

When I was around, it was easy you see,
To say 'Hello Mum, Hello Dad' - Happy Birthday to me !

But anyway don't worry, I'll do what I can,
I might even break through another man...?

But until then it's quite easy you see,
to say through this poem - Happy Birthday to me,

(and Happy Birthday to 'little Russell'
You're growing up fine,
When Mum looks at your beauty,
It makes her eyes shine...)

So no shedding tears, Happy Birthday to me,
Look out for the Robin, I'll make dance round our tree !

So put away that old hankie,
When she feels better - you can keep laughing with Frankie.

~ Russell
September 20th 1992

Chains are broken, bonds are set free,
I am now not bonded to one, but three,

In this year of ninety-one,
There is so much that must be done,

The poem the 'brave' sent down to you,
Do heed his words - for all is true,

I've been around you for a while,
To make you laugh or see you smile,

For we've been trying with all our worth,
To stop the global warming of your Earth,

And try to prevent a war,
That would in fact make temperatures soar,

For how can souls be born again ?
If the Earth's not here - do I make myself plain ?

But the help we can give, is to change the mind,
And prayers must come from all mankind,

We're very worried over here,
Looking at your Earth - so full of fear,

If only each soul, the truth did know,

There would be no war and each would know,

I cannot laugh or joke anymore,
Unless we all can prevent a war,

We do not know in our plane, so we sigh,
The answer to all this, is known only up High,

So I'll sign off now - there is work to be done,
I love you all. Your loving son.

~ Russell
1991

It's been difficult choosing the right poems to include here. Yet I <u>cannot</u> leave out the next one because it's so very lovely. *'The Crystal Castle'* came for me in connection with Russell taking care of B-'s baby daughter in Spirit. She is known as *'Rainbow.'*

<u>The Crystal Castle</u>

There is a baby castle, upon a cloud of blue,
Where colours so translucent, emanate a magical hue,

Through the coloured crystal, sweet music wafts & rainbows sway,
One gazes at this wonder, for it takes your breath away,

Now the pathway to this castle, twinkles and glistens with purest gold,
And in the sky above the turrets, rainbow colours sweetly unfold,

The keepers of this castle, enfold in their loving care,
All the babies that are grieved for, also the unwanted ones are there,

I came upon this castle when I walked the purple hills one day,
And I thought I'd adopt a baby, to be mine and take away,

So I took the path of glistening gold and knocked upon the door,
'Do come in Russell' a sweet voice said, 'I know who you've come for'

(Then into my arms she placed a child so sweet, with golden hair)

Now as I looked upon this lovely child, my heart was filled with joy,
This child untouched by cruel Earth, I knew nothing could destroy,

This purest soul lay in my arms, for me alone to care,
To cherish and to nurture, but I knew I had to share...

...this child's love with her dear Mother,
'til she came to this pleasant sphere,

So I took her to the Earth and told her Mum,
'Look quietly B - we're here !'

The 'Rainbow Baby' I call this little girl, as I gaze at her so proud,
'Hey Russell ! Watch me play' she says, as she dances with the crowd,

Of rainbow children, chasing butterflies and bluebirds in flight,
'My' little girl is growing up, she is such an enchanting sight !

No more will I feel alone, with someone so sweet to love,
We'll walk the purple hills together, 'til our Mums come up above,

So I'll cherish dear little 'Rainbow' - she'll have no need to cry,
Not for her to shed a tear or have a plaintive sigh,

I thank the 'Dear One' up above, for sending her to me,
For I know this Love that fills my heart, is the LOVE that's meant to be !

~ Russell Vernon Byrne

For me, the description in *'The Crystal Castle'* brings a clear picture of a little girl of about six years old - as she would be at this point. This poem reminds me so much of Maeterlinck's beautiful play, *'The Blue Bird'* and I make no apologies for mentioning it again here !

It also reminds me of the touching scene from Disney's Snow White. Who cannot fail to be moved, when seeing her asleep in the crystal coffin, surrounded by the seven dwarves - it's so sad, yet so lovely !

The meeting or reuniting that all bereaved mothers yearn for, is told very beautifully in another poem called 'The Meeting.' It was received by my friend Frankie shortly before she passed to Spirit herself. It is a beautiful poem for any parent grieving over their beloved child and can be found at the very beginning of this book.

Next I'm including a poem, which I think was the last one to arrive. It came on February 22nd 1994 - just three months before the *'Russell'* book was published. Here he is, still older and although his subject is serious, he still manages to be humorous.

The Butterfly & The Humble Bee

One day, out in the garden sitting on my dear father's knee,
We both sat idly gazing at the brown bumblebee,

Well I smiled and I chuckled, and began to contemplate,
The state of the world without the bees, to pollinate,

I thought, all the plants & flowers would have to get up and walk,
And I laughed as I pictured them - walking with legs on a stalk,

Then the gardeners would rage and shake their heads,
As they watched with anger, at their disappearing flowerbeds,

The farmer would find all their vegetable fields missing,
As the plants would need to go and find their own mates, for kissing.

For without the bee to pollinate,
There'd be no other way for them to find their mate,

Then I thought what would happen to the human race ?
As they searched for food all over the place,

We should all be so grateful you see...

for God in his wisdom sent out of the sky,
came fluttering into the garden, the sweet butterfly,

Of all God's creatures, seeing the world as a whole,
The butterfly's the supreme example, to show proof of the soul,

How like these two creatures is the whole human race,
One to multiply, one so full of grace,

Except they would not hurt each other,
Like man - who would destroy his brother,

But like man, nature will escape and change,
<u>Both</u> of these is within man's range,

...if you don't believe all this, just take a look,
For the Truth is in the pages of my Mum's book !

~ Russell
February 1994

I had so many letters from so many people after my first book was published. Many with lots of different questions - which I did my very best to answer. The only one I couldn't answer was the 'biggie' - that never ending question of reincarnation.

Was it true, or was it not true ?

Well I'm afraid I really don't know. I'll have to leave that to Russell for the next litany to come ! I truly want to know more myself, but the things he's told me keep me 'on the edge of my seat' so to speak.

In the past, I've been told I've experienced a previous lifetime in Egypt and another in a Jewish community. I heard more on this from B-'s Spirit helper John, but at the time I was so dumbstruck by the beauty and delivery of his oration, that I didn't dare ask any 'daft' questions. Who knows the truth ? I just await the chance to learn more.

Yet one day, I was simply drinking tea and chatting with my friend Frankie Brown - my 'Poet Mum' - when she felt inspired to write. Now Frankie is a very cheerful and humorous lady and she is creatively gifted with Clairvoyance, Clairaudience, art and poetry, although she still has her feet firmly on the ground.

At the time, Frankie was laying on her bed because her physical problems were so bad. But she began describing to me the image of a *'lady holding a light'* who was dressed completely in crystal. As usual I saw nothing, but it must have been a wondrous sight. I don't know how she does it ! After the image of the 'lady' was gone, Frankie said,

'Gwen, could you get a pen and take this poem down ?'

So, acting as Frankie's 'secretary' I wrote down the words, as she was being inspired. Now I know very little of these things, but this was a very exciting and educational experience for me. Oh boy, did the words ring true for me ! They were so deep, but made so much sense of my life, my character, my gifts and indeed the real Gwen !

Here is a transcript of Frankie's words, exactly as they came to her. It was only signed with the initial 'O' - but note the date, for it is of great importance to the story.

<u>The Golden Bird of Isis</u>

In the beginning,
we were the most ancient civilisation,
and our passageway to the stars and eternity,
was to sail through the Golden Lake.

As your Earth progressed, so did ours.

For instance, when you travel through the tunnel of light...

*Our only progress was to sail
with the boatman of the Golden Lake,*

*Your boy was the boatman, coming for you,
The Golden Mask was the Death Mask of Osiris,
Which you wore, when you were laid in the sarcophagus,
- that was taken off your head before burial,*

You notice you weren't wearing it in the portrait ?

*And as your son REN-EAY, (RAY-Nor) said,
'The bird was to show you the way to Paradise'*

*As with this Earth incarnation,
In past times your son preceded before you,
once again into the Spirit World, through malnutrition,*

So as we say, history repeats itself once more.

*He is in that position to meet you again,
He always has to go before you, because he is an older soul,
You are an old soul also,
but he is older and has to be there to show you the way,*

*If you cast your mind back, you will remember,
that the Golden Lake led to the Crystal Palace,
Where you were reprimanded
for choosing one life and living another,
So therefore, not learning what you were put on Earth for,*

*There are higher things to learn on the Earth plane,
than physical love,*

Which you are now understanding in this lifetime...

*People talk of us worshipping false Gods,
but they <u>were</u> our Gods,
They were our Spiritual Gods,
they existed and they were not idols made of stone,
they were separate, Spiritual Gods that ruled the Earth, the Wind
and the drawing of the day,*

Now all this merged, with progress, to the Supreme Consciousness,

*My name is Osiris - though names are not important,
I am the bearer of the Golden Light.*

More of your passing into the Spiritual Life will be given...

*You always had your voice,
so you went straight through to the teaching cloisters,
To learn more of music and to sing from the light of your soul,
to help your voice to vibrate into the atmosphere,
to enable you to reach deep down, into the souls of others,*

*You ask of psychic gifts ?
<u>This</u> is your psychic gift and what's more,
You have been told this many times,*

*Have you not seen the light and compassion
that shines out of others when you sing ?
Does this not enlighten the soul more than a message ?*

*Be grateful for this gift and use it wisely,
and be more grateful than you are,
of what a great gift you have been given,*

For many can sing - but few can touch the soul with the voice.

Good day.

~ O ~
February 14th 1994

Mentally, I said *'thank you'* to this lovely Spirit visitor and as I left Frankie's, I drove home to Rayleigh clutching tightly onto my piece of paper. I was so deep in thought, but who wouldn't be ?

Frankie Brown has a large part to play in this book and whenever we get together we really do have some laughs - and music too. But we do have our serious times, though I'll leave that for Frankie and the next chapter.

There is more to come on the mystery of Isis and more on the portrait. Personally, I think it makes for a truly fascinating tale !

Twenty Three

Alan Brown's Story

by Frankie Brown

*'I feel like I'm fighting a battle,
when I didn't start a war.'*

~ Dolly Parton

This story is how I met my very, dear friend Gwen Byrne and became a member of the RPPS.

My dear, sweet son Alan was murdered ten years ago. A psychopath had set out to kill six people and unfortunately, my son was in the wrong place at the wrong time. Alan wasn't one of the people he had intended to kill. He shot my son because he just happened to be in the way.

As you can imagine I was beside myself with grief and despair. I visited several churches and was told that I must have faith. This didn't help, in fact I felt even more in despair than ever. So I decided to search for the truth myself. For as every mother knows, after losing a child, you just can't survive on faith alone. You must search for the truth and question : Does your child survive or not ? And if so what are they doing ? *Is* there another life ? And most important of all - will I *ever* see them again ?

For eight years I searched and read all the books on survival that I could get my hands on - and I visited an untold number of Spirit Mediums. I simply couldn't rest until I was pacified in my mind - did my dear son still live, or was he gone from me forever ? Because I'm such a down to Earth person and one that calls 'a spade, a spade' - I must say, that I took a lot of convincing.

I received a lot of evidence through mental Mediumship, some that was so staggering, that it could only have come from my own son. Along the way I also developed the gift of psychic art and I began to draw people from Spirit, for others who had lost their own, dear loved ones. Yet I still had this niggling doubt - that is, until I met Gwen Byrne...

Through the awful trauma of the death of my darling son, I developed terrible spinal trouble. I had arthritis all over my back, which was bad enough that I needed to have surgery. One day, while I was lying in my bed in so much pain, a thought came out of the blue. I said to my partner Frank,

'do you think you could go down to the Spiritualist Church for me and pick up a copy of the Psychic Gazette ? There might be some scientific proof in there about life after death - something I can believe and understand.'

At the time I just presumed this 'thought' had been my own, but a few years later I know better. Sometimes, these thoughts are sent to help us.

Anyway, off Frank went and came back with my newspaper. Inside it was an article on the *'scientific proof'* of the Afterlife, written by Michael Roll. There was an address included, so readers could request free copies of his thesis. I duly wrote to Michael and his thesis arrived in the post, but to my great delight, he'd also sent me the account of a lady called Gwen Byrne. It told of how she had helped countless bereaved mothers, by relating how she and her husband Alfie had been reunited with their dear son, at a materialisation séance, nineteen years after his death.

Well, with great excitement I noticed that Gwen lived in Rayleigh, which is only a few miles from my home. So I looked up dear Gwen's phone number and with mounting excitement, I called her.

'Hello ?' Said a very friendly voice. I asked if this was Mrs Byrne, but then just blurted out what had happened to my dear son Alan. I had so many questions for Gwen, *'did you really speak to your son ? And did you really have material contact from another world ?'*

Gwen simply replied *'yes I really did, dear !'*

Then she said, *'would you like to come to lunch ? We can have a nice little chat and I can tell you all about it ?'*

Wow, I thought ! Would I ? *'Oh, yes please'* I said. So we arranged for me to visit Gwen at her home.

I didn't know much at all about Physical Phenomena and wasn't sure what to expect. When I arrived at Gwen's, I was met by the most lovely, kind and sensible lady and made most welcome. We had some tea and then Gwen proceeded to tell me, in great detail, how she had come to meet her dear son at last. Gwen talked of her experiences at the many séances she and her husband had attended. She showed me some apports - gifts from the Spirit World. Then she played me some tapes, recorded at the séances. I heard her son Russell speaking to her and he was talking as naturally as though he was there 'in the flesh', so to speak.

After more tea, Gwen answered all my searching questions, with the utmost truth and sincerity. She even kindly loaned me some of the tapes from the séances and after a very pleasant afternoon, I went home utterly gob-smacked ! My mind was going round and round in circles. I'd at last found my proof and this was no silly, misguided person. This was a very intelligent truthful and compassionate lady - who, let's face it, had nothing to gain.

I went home on cloud nine and played all of Gwen's tapes. When Frank came home, I played them all over again for him to hear, then I talked to him about the most incredible day of my life. I said, *'oh Frank, at last I've found out the truth. Alan still lives and we will meet him again !'*
Was it a coincidence that I met dear Gwen ? No, I don't think so !

I must just mention a little more about the séance tapes. You can clearly hear dear Russell laughing and joking, but that's not all. There are at least five other Spirit people heard talking, there's a beautiful operatic voice heard singing, there's even somebody from Spirit heard playing tunes on a toy xylophone - and there's lots and lots of laughter.
This only goes to prove to me, that we don't change when we pass over to the other side of life.

Anyway, since that day my life completely changed - it really did. Gwen and I have known each other for many years now, so from this point, at times some of our stories will intertwine. Gwen and I and our boys in Spirit, Alan and Russell, have all been working together, so where I might falter, Gwen will come in to help me out.

After I'd been doing my psychic art for a while, Gwen asked if I might like to try and draw some Spirit children, for other grieving parents in the RPPS. I don't mind saying, that with great trepidation I said,
'Yes, I'd have a go.'
They lived all over the country; in Sheffield, York, Manchester, Middlesex, and many more places. Yet to my utter amazement, because I'm a real 'doubting Thomas' - the portraits I'd drawn and sent, were actually *of* their girls and boys in Spirit. The real proof came after they'd received their drawings. The parents would send photographs of their beloved children in Spirit, and I was amazed at the likenesses.

Eventually it became too difficult for me to produce lots of drawings, for I was in such terrible pain with the arthritis in my shoulders. This has since progressed over time, so at the moment I'm unable do any drawing at all, because of the continuous pain. Though I have to live this Earthly life, so I must be practical about it.

One day, before things got too painful, I felt Russell had inspired me to do a portrait of himself, as a grown-up. When I started the drawing it was of Russell as a child, before he died. So out loud I said, *'oh come on Russell ! You said you wanted a grown-up one of you. This is not funny !'*

Mind you this is typical, because both Alan and Russell often played games with us. However, I proceeded to mess about with my portrait and to my amazement the face began to alter. What had begun as the portrait of a chubby little child, slowly turned into the face of a grown-up young man.

The day that Frank and I took the drawing to Gwen and Alfie's, was also the day of their ruby wedding anniversary. The timing ! I'd had no idea, but after seeing Gwen's reaction, it was obviously a special portrait for her. Gwen has more to say about this in another chapter.

I gradually became less and less able to do as many drawings for Spirit as I wanted, so I was starting to feel quite despondent. Then Spirit gave me another Spiritual gift - I became inspired to write poetry. Many of these have been included here in Gwen's book.

This new Spiritual avenue quite satisfied me at the time. I knew the poems certainly didn't come from my own mind, because they were far more lovely and eloquent than anything I might produce. Not that I have a dozy mind or anything, but I certainly didn't know anything about what was coming through in the writing, regarding the Spirit World !

The poetry started very simply. I was sitting at the bottom of my garden one day, when a beautiful Red Admiral butterfly came and settled on my leg. It stayed there for a while, then went up to my arm. Believe it or not, it stayed there for the next hour and a half. I was absolutely stunned - not to mention stiff-armed by the end of it ! Then a voice spoke to me, inside my head. It was little Russell, with the words, *'Today I Saw A Butterfly'* and that was the start of the first poem.

After this, poems began to come to me quite often, which was wonderful. This was during the early 1990s and whenever they came, I would quickly write them down. Gwen and I certainly had some great fun with them.

One day we realised that one of the poems was from a musical Spirit friend of Gwen's, who she recognised from the wonderful séances a few years before. The poem contained the line, *'Buddy can you spare a dime ?'*

'Oh, that's a song' Gwen said to me. Now Gwen does know an *awful lot* of songs ! *'I'll bring the lyrics for you, next time I come over'* she said.

The following week Gwen brought the lyrics with her and began to read them out to me. Suddenly she stopped part-way and stared at me. After a moment, Gwen said, *'oh look at the next line in the song, Frankie ! It says, 'say don't you remember, they called me Al ? It was Al all the time...'*

We were amazed at this, because my son in Spirit never communicates as Alan, only Al. Yet we only found it because we'd been inspired to look a little deeper.

Since then, Gwen has told me that for her, it was this moment that she realised how important song lyrics can be. I think, when we are inspired with a tune, we should always look to the lyrics - as they can often contain a message from a loved one in Spirit. I mean, at the time I didn't even know the song. Apparently it was written in the 1930s, way before my time and is all about a railroad. But how clever our Spirit friends are !

Now I'd like to relate one strange incident. I suggested to Gwen one day, that she record herself reading out some of my poems, with some lovely music in the background. Poor Gwen spent days sorting through all her music for me, but the finished recordings really seemed to bring my poems to life. Gwen left one recording with me, so I could let her know what I thought of it and because it was such a lovely day - and me being a sun worshipper - I thought I'd listen to it whilst out in my garden.

I pressed 'play' on the machine and could hear Gwen reading the poem, *'Today I Saw A Butterfly.'* Her voice was clear and quite normal. Then very quickly I realised that there was something wrong with the backing music, which she had chosen so carefully to speak over. It was making the most horrible noise and going far too slowly. Well this didn't seem possible. Gwen's voice was at normal speed, but the music wasn't ! This was a real mystery to me.

That evening, Frank was home from work and I was busy doing other things. I'd quite forgotten about the tape until out of the blue, Frank said, *'what does 'adagio' mean ?'*

'I don't know, Frank.' I said. *'I'll look it up in the dictionary.'*

When I found that 'adagio' was a musical term meaning 'to be played slowly' it suddenly dawned on me about the tape. It seemed that Spirit were clearly prompting Frank here, so I found the tape and played it for him to hear. Then I rang Gwen and let her listen to it down the phone. Gwen could hear her recorded voice, which was quite normal, but the background music was still going so slowly.

'The little b.....'s. I spent two days recording those tapes.' Gwen said. *'I'll kill them !'*

Gwen assured me that when she'd made the recording, the music was playing quite normally.

Now I'd heard that Spirit can mess about with electrics, so later that evening, when a friend came round to give me some Spiritual Healing, I said, *'Terry, will you listen to this tape ?'*

I explained to him what had happened, then pressed the 'play' button for him, then went into the kitchen. After a few minutes, I heard Terry calling, *'there's nothing wrong with this tape Frankie.'*

I came back and said, *'of course there is, just listen to it...'*

But then I couldn't believe what I was hearing. I felt such a fool. The tape sounded perfectly okay. Gwen's voice *and* the background music were now completely normal.

After Terry had left, both Frank and I thought this was so strange. We listened to the tape one more time and yet again, it had reverted back to the slow monotonous music, with Gwen speaking perfectly normally over the top of it. We were amazed, but thought there must be something wrong with the tape or the player. Otherwise there was no real explanation for this phenomena. The mystery deepened the following day, because when we listen to the tape once more, it was playing normally again !

Over time, I began to notice my psychic faculties were really developing - all with the help of a Spirit friend. I could literally 'hear' him dictating words to me for instrumental classical music, like that of George Frideric Handel. One day, after a meditation, I began hearing some words for the very beautiful Intermezzo, from Mascagni's opera *'Cavalleria Rusticana.'*

I was merrily 'composing' to myself with help of my Spirit composer friend, when Gwen arrived for a visit and she was singing something to herself from the same opera ! But then, she has such a lovely voice and knows so many tunes. This particular one was Mascagni's *'Regina Coeli'* sometimes called the *'Easter Hymn'* which is about love in the world. It is often sung at many a Spiritual seminar, where there are floods of tears from the people listening, because the words and music are so beautiful.

I feel so very lucky that we have these gifts of the Spirit, yet our two boys in Spirit can often play such tricks ! There are numerous times I can recall they have tried to lift our spirits in this way. Though sometimes it has been the simplest of messages, which has often heralded something absolutely wonderful. One time, Frank and I were using the board and glass to try and communicate with our Spirit loved ones, when a message came through from my son, Alan. He said,
'Mum, you are going to Crete next week.'

I replied, *'oh no, there's fat chance of that Alan. We've only got about a hundred pounds each and that won't get us far!'*

Alan came back saying,
'it will be this time next week, Mum.'

I said to Frank, *'he's having a game with us. There's no way that we could go to Crete for a hundred pounds each.'*

However, the next day I had a shock, because I found an advertisement which said, *'Special Offer - Crete - Two weeks - £99.'* I was amazed, because that made it just forty-five pounds a week each. So I phoned Frank at his workplace and he booked it straight away. Then the next week, off we went for a fantastic two week holiday on the Greek island of Crete!

When we arrived at Crete airport, we had to smile to ourselves because we noticed the tour company was called 'Summerland Tours' - *and* the plane was half empty, so I could really stretch out in my seat too. We had a taxi arranged, which took us all the way to the little fishing village that we'd chosen. It was beautiful and so remote and all for forty-five pounds a week. It was unbelievable. I think this was very clever of Russell and Alan, and the fact it was so remote is important for what happened next.

We were walking the quayside one day, when I told Frank that I'd like to take a gift home for Gwen. So we went into a little shop, where I bought Gwen and myself some Greek 'worry beads' - which the assistant duly wrapped up for me. After some lunch on the quayside, Frank and I went back to our apartment and I put my gifts away indoors, while we sat outside in the glorious sunshine.

After a while, I just *had* to go and look at the beads again. So I brought them outside and saw they'd been placed in a plastic bag and wrapped in some gift paper. As I took the small parcel from the bag, I couldn't believe my eyes. The paper that the assistant had wrapped them in, was printed with lots of Pink Panthers - who were all dancing and dressed in top hats. Perfect for Gwen and typical of Russell!

Now this was a tiny fishing village in a remote part of Crete, where you would expect their gift paper to be printed with Grecian urns or vines. So what were the chances of buying something for Gwen, for it to be wrapped in paper covered with Pink Panther's? We were both astonished and I think this was really clever, even for Russell!

Back home, not long after our holiday, we had lots of little Buddleia coming up all around the garden. We'd never had them grow before and I don't know much about flowers and plants, but Gwen told me the Buddleia was also called the butterfly bush and for her, this linked very closely with Russell. They grow so fast and really attract the butterflies. At the same time, I began to take lots of photos which had Spirit 'extras' on them.

I took one of my mother, while she was in our conservatory and when you look at it, you can see an image of Russell on one side of her and a Native American on the other. I never dared tell her, because if I did she'd have jumped ten feet in the air, but I thought it was quite funny myself! Another picture I took had on it the faces of Margaret Prentice's two sons, Richard and Simon and quite a few other little extras too. More recently we'd had some Spirit contact with some highly evolved souls and in one of my photos, one of them can be seen, but I will come back to these higher Spirits later on.

My partner Frank had developed quite a gift for communication with Spirit, using the glass and letters. Together, we would often have quite lengthy conversations using this method, with my son Alan and others. The evidence they give us can often be quite mind blowing. I remember one occasion when Alan came through. At first we thought he was having a joke with us, but he obviously knew better than we did, when he said, *'Andy's Dad wears women's clothes.'*

I was shocked! I said, *'Alan! That's not a very nice thing to say and it's not funny. Is this really you?'*

Alan replied, *'yes Mum. It's like Christmas every day of the year up here!'*

We were puzzled, but later that evening we discovered what Alan meant.

This was the mid-1980s and at that time we had a regular movie delivery service. That evening, the video delivery man arrived and Frank answered the door. The man recommended a movie and because it was dark and Frank wasn't wearing his glasses, he just accepted the tape and paid the man. We put the tape in the player and found it starred Vanessa Redgrave in a serious movie - about a man who regularly wore women's clothes and whose son was called Andy!

Later Frank went to bed and was channel hopping on his TV. I was doing exactly the same, downstairs in the lounge. We both stopped at the same channel at the same time and found a Monty Python movie. At that moment in the film, the cast were all singing, *'It's Christmas in heaven, every day of the year!'*

Frank and I very often had numerous bits of evidence, come through the glass and letters, when we'd sit together. Sometimes we had some of Gwen's RPPS Mums visit us for messages from *their* children in Spirit.

This was often a good exercise, because the messages were more evidential that way, especially when we knew nothing about them beforehand. We have had some wonderfully serious messages about life in the Spirit World *and* all it's wonders, but we've also had lots of fun and laughs too. I asked Alan one time, if it was difficult for him to communicate with us this in way. I expected a really long, detailed reply - when he answered,
'no Mum, only if you can't spell !'

Frank has a recollection of his own, that he'd like me to share here.

'One evening, I was giving Frankie some healing, when we began to notice a lovely perfumed scent, which very slowly started to envelop the room. We tried to figure it out, but couldn't understand where it could be coming from. Once we'd finished the healing, I went over to the fireplace thinking the scent might be coming from that part of the room. We had a Capodimonte rose there, so I leant down towards it and took a sniff. It seemed to be where the scent was coming from, but I couldn't believe it. I told Frankie and she didn't believe me at all. So I picked up the porcelain rose and the smell just stopped.

I put it back down and sniffed at it again - and the scent returned. I told Frankie to go over and do the same, which she did. When she'd put it down again, the scent got stronger and stronger. Frankie said that she didn't believe this was possible !

It turned out that this piece of porcelain was a special rose that had come from her mother-in-law. However, Frankie was convinced that what we could smell was simply the scent of a nearby air-freshener. So we both went up to it for a good sniff, but the air-freshener had it's lid on tight and there was no smell coming from it at all.

Then we noticed that Frankie's photograph of Alan was next to the rose and this same perfume seemed to be coming from it's frame. At this point, Frankie's other son Steve, came home from work. We didn't say anything at first, but then we asked him if he could smell anything. He said he could and asked us what it was. I said, 'believe it or not, it's coming from that porcelain rose.' Steve didn't believe us, but he went over to see for himself. He was surprised to find that it was true and he was amazed. We'd been hoping that the scent would last long enough for when Steve came home and it did. But honestly, we were all bewildered and astonished by it.

After about an hour, the smell gradually faded from the room and never returned. There was no way that it had come from the sealed air-freshener. So we didn't know what to think.'

* * *

Personally, I think some mental Mediums are extremely good, I also think some Mediums *are* mental !

One day, Frank and I were heading out to see a particular Medium for some healing. As soon as I had stepped out of our car, I could feel that my son Alan was close to me. Alan always had a very unusual bouncy step and I could just 'feel him' close by, walking along with me.

We went inside and found a seat in the healing room and I noticed there were some wonderful and lovely plants dotted all around. The Medium explained to us that Spirit helped the plants to grow to the size they were and that sometimes, while he was giving healing, the plants actually moved around the room !

All I said was, *'that's wonderful'* but then my turn came for the healing, so I took my place. As the Medium began, he said to me, *'I must tell you this, did you know that I was John the Baptist, in a previous life ?'*

I thought to myself, *'oh my God, we've got a right nutter here.'*

Then said, *'well if you're John the Baptist, I must be Doubting Thomas.'*

Quite seriously, he replied, *'no, I've already met him.'*

In the half hour or so that I'd been waiting to see this 'John the Baptist' character, I'd been looking at one of the plants in the room. It was a Prayer Plant, which had closed up its leaves for the night. In my mind, I said to Alan, *'if you're there Al, could you move this prayer plant ?'*

Nothing happened while I waited there, but during my healing, while the Medium talked of his 'past life' existence, I turned to look at Frank with raised eyebrows. As I did, to my utter amazement, I saw one of the leaves on the sleeping plant suddenly open up, shake, and then close again.

'Did you see that ?' I said to Frank, as I ignored the Medium and pointed to the plant.

Frank said he hadn't see anything, but two other women who were also waiting their turn, said they did. Later, they both said that they were absolutely stunned and had never seen anything like it. Personally, I'm inclined to think that it was Alan, who'd perhaps been listening in ? All in all, the whole visit has remained quite memorable !

More recently, Gwen and I have been very fortunate, as we seem to have been having some quite highly advanced Spirits coming through to us. I don't mean to be frivolous, but it's absolutely true. We are not the sort of people to get carried away with our own importance.

Around the same time, I'd felt impressed to do a painting for Gwen in oils. The picture was Egyptian in style. In the centre I painted the wings of an eagle in gold and inside that, I put two wonderful, navy coloured eyes. In the foreground was an Egyptian maiden, not unlike Gwen herself and a man coming towards her in a boat. When I'd finished the painting I was amazed that I could have created anything like it. I thought it was really great. Then these highly advanced Spirits began coming through for Gwen and me. They gave us such messages, poems and teachings - which actually connected with the painting. We were so impressed, I actually felt the we weren't worthy !

Gwen kept all the notes we made at the time, so could probably explain these things better than me, but I remember the first Spirit was an Egyptian. He called himself Raymar and he explained to us in detail, all the different elements of the painting. Russell also joined us at this time and whenever a high Spirit came through, there he was singing,
'High, High, High, Society ! All together now... '
The beautiful 'crystal' lady, who I'd seen holding a light, also made an appearance. She became known to us as Daphne and told us that we'd receive further details on the painting, but a little at a time, so we'd need to be patient. Gwen and I will add a joint account of Raymar's first visit, at the end of my chapter.

Spirit had been having some fun with us by giving us our own 'Spirit names !' I was named the *'Oracle'* and Gwen was given the name *'Psyche'* while our friend B- the Medium, was named *'Aurora.'* Gwen and B- both quite like their Spirit names, but when I found out that the mythical Oracle's real name was Sybil, I wasn't so keen ! Good job I've got a sense of humour. Yet the messages we we getting were really wonderful and many were about reincarnation. Now this is a subject that I didn't really wish to know too much about at the time. I was more concerned with this life and whether we do actually get to 'the other side' or not. Of course, now I realise that we *all* do !

Our Egyptian friend's second visit came when Gwen and I were together at my home. He was so powerful, but he needed to tone down his energy or vibrations for us. Raymar suggested that Gwen sing something that would help, so she sang, *'Softly Awakes My Heart'* from the opera Samson and Delilah. Earlier, Raymar had requested that Gwen should sing this song in an amphitheatre, which she would find on a forthcoming trip to Cyprus. Poor old Gwen ! We learned later that Raymar was good at making requests like this, but as usual we found there was always a good reason for it. The song was originally written in French, but as Gwen began to sing through the microphone that we'd rigged up to my music system, she said, *'oh I'll sing it in English. I can't recall all the French now.'*

Because I was in so much pain, I just lay on my bed and listened. The sound of Gwen's voice was wonderful. It was so vibrant and powerful that I truly felt I was *in* an amphitheatre ! The echoes and the atmosphere - I really don't have the words to do it justice. The sound was too beautiful to describe, as it seemed to float around the room like a tinkling bell. It truly touched my inner soul. As Gwen's voice soared up and up, like waves around the room, it was no wonder that I wept.

To crown it all, one of the lyrics was *'to Aurora's tender zephyr'* - Aurora being our friend B-'s Spirit name ! I knew that Raymar was there with us and through the music, he had given me an amazing experience, with Gwen's help of course. If only I could have bottled those wonderful healing moments and put a lid on them. For the times when I'm in great pain, I could just take the lid off and I'm sure I'd get well ! This was Raymar's doing and I can say that it was one of the most beautiful experiences I'd ever had in my home. I shall always be grateful to Gwen, Raymar and the Spirit people for this happening. The experience stays with me forever. I know I was privileged !

Gwen and B- both went to Cyprus and Gwen *did* sing the same piece in an amphitheatre there. How I wished I could have been there with them, but Raymar knew that I wouldn't be able to go, so he arranged this 'command performance' just for me !

Yet we have to keep our feet on the ground. When Raymar and the others came through my mind, I dictated their words to Gwen. They were telling us all about our 'past lives' together and for me, this really goes against the grain.

However, on another occasion when Raymar paid us a visit, we could feel his energy and power. He was awesome !
Through me, he said to Gwen that she mustn't be subservient to him, as that side of her life was over. At first we could only feel his presence, but then Gwen said she could physically see him. He was so powerful as he stood in front of her. I too could feel his power and all around us the whole of my conservatory started to crackle - with what I can only describe as electricity. We heard bangs and cracks, like the sound of a whip all over the room. I began to fear for my new conservatory as I said to Gwen, *'oh my God Gwen. This is a new conservatory. All the windows are going to fall in, in a minute !'*

The experience was so powerful and we sat there as though we were frozen in time. Raymar stayed for a while and I dictated to Gwen what he was saying.
At this point, I have asked Gwen to come in and relate *her* version of this experience...

'I went to visit Frankie on this particular day, to see how she was and to have a chat and a laugh. Frankie does have her own special brand of humour and we get on so well. I was certainly not expecting to meet a huge Egyptian !

Whenever Frankie and I sat together in the presence of Spirit, we often heard their knocks and bangs in the room. However, today they were even louder than ever and reminded us of the sound of a whip cracking. Frankie was in good spirits and made a joke about her new conservatory windows breaking. It did seem as though the room was almost shaking, yet we carried on regardless.

Frankie was to my left and sitting on her bed, which was about four feet away from me. When Frankie said, *'Raymar's here'* we could feel his presence in the room. Next I saw him objectively with my physical eyes. I could see that he wore the 'white crown' of Upper Egypt, which I later had to look for in a book. The material of his crown shone so much that I was astonished, almost dazzled and I just gazed in wonder. He was surrounded by the most wondrous turquoise blue colour, which seemed to shine all around him to at least eighteen inches distance. The electricity or energy I felt was so powerful, that I felt quite faint.

Most surprising were his eyes, for they were the *bluest* eyes I'd ever seen and he was looking straight at me. He also had the brightest smile with the most beautiful white teeth you could imagine. He was devastating to look at, yet there was such a wonderful feeling with him. He was truly wondrous and so solid. I wouldn't have been surprised to find that he had left footprints behind !

It seemed to me as though he'd been *filtered* down to us, almost as though he'd arrived on the end of a parachute ! I have no idea how long he stayed with us, because time just seemed to stand still and I can only recall how we felt. Frankie and I were totally blown away and wondered how on Earth it could have happened.

Now I would like to say that I really have no idea who he is, we only know that his name is *'Raymar.'* Perhaps he could be described as one of the 'Shining Ones' ?

However, I had to leave Frankie's quite soon after, as I wanted to avoid the rush-hour traffic on the A127. On the way home I still felt as if I was in a state of shock, although my concentration was doubled after a near-miss with another car ! The busy traffic did extend my journey but I arrived home safely, just as Frankie telephoned.

She had recorded our session with Spirit that day and said that she wanted me to hear part of it. Frankie played the audio to me down the phone and I remember her saying that she'd needed to speed the tape up a little. Listening to what sounded like our 'chipmunk' chatter on the tape, I suddenly heard an enormous sound. We hadn't heard anything at the time of the recording, but here on the tape was the huge, booming voice of a man. Over our chatter I heard him very clearly say, *'ladies delectable'* !

The voice was so loud that it drowned out mine and Frankie's voices completely. We both guessed that this was Raymar, but I thought it was an odd thing for an Egyptian to say. Then again, I'd never met an Egyptian before ! Though say it he did and I have it on tape as proof.

In the days that followed I became very preoccupied as to who Raymar was. He'd felt and sounded so powerful, but had not strained my belief one bit. I knew what I had seen and I didn't need to feel isolated with this happening either, since many people throughout history have heard such voices. Many illustrious people have heard a guiding voice from the ether, people like Emerson, Da Vinci, Socrates, George Washington, Tesla and Swedenborg. Even Saint Bernadette had claimed she had met the 'Queen of Heaven' and conversed with her.

I told a few selected friends about Raymar and various explanations to his identity were offered in return.
'Perhaps he comes from Sirius ?'
'Maybe he's an Atlantean ?'
'He might be a space traveller ?'
Someone suggested that, *'perhaps it was Horus, of the blue eyes ?'*

Now I have very limited knowledge of these things so said very little about them. I do *know* that I'd seen something wonderful, but was he one of those 'Higher Beings' that people all over the world are longing to communicate with ? I don't know.

To me Raymar is simply a friend. Now Russell's here, bringing me back to Earth by singing the Louis Armstrong calypso, *'High, High, High Society'* ! So I'll pass this chapter back to Frankie...'

I couldn't walk much after I'd had my back surgery. The doctors had advised me not to drive, but one day I felt determined to go shopping.

Going out to the car on my crutches I found one of my tyres looked flat. I was undeterred, so got into my car to start the engine. As I turned the key in the ignition, nothing happened and after a few attempts I decided the battery was flat. There seemed to be no life in it whatsoever, it was just dead.

Just then, I spotted three strong-looking young lads coming down the road towards me, so I thought I'd ask them to give my car a push. In the past I'd been a driving instructor and even a taxi driver, so I knew that a jump start could help. Even if the battery was as flat as a pancake, the engine can sometimes fire and you can get it going. This time however, it didn't work, so I reluctantly had to abandon the idea and the three lads kindly pushed my car to the roadside for me.

I went back indoors on my crutches and phoned my brother, who later came out to put a new tyre on the car for me. Then I asked my son Steve if he'd put the battery on charge as it was flat. So he went out to the car and turned the keys in the ignition and the car started straight away. I couldn't believe it ! Then in my head I heard the voice of my son Alan. Really clearly he said, *'that stopped you from driving the car didn't it Mum ?'*

* * *

I can relate numerous incidents where Spirit stepped in directly and I am grateful for all of them - many were even very funny. Although by far the most memorable experience I ever had, was at a séance.

Frank and I had the good fortune to be invited to the home of the author and Spiritualist Alan Crossley, where we were to take part in a séance with the Physical Medium, Stewart Alexander.

The following account of this séance also appeared in part, in the Noah's Ark Society newsletter of November 28th, 1992.

With mounting excitement Frank and I were ushered into Alan's tiny séance room. Alan lived in a mobile home, so how he got eleven of us in there still amazes me ! However, in the centre of the room was a table on which some wooden drumsticks and a couple of small hand bells had been placed and standing upright on the floor, were two séance trumpets.

Alan Crossley had asked us to sit very still and try not to move our arms or legs during the séance. This was so that we wouldn't disturb any 'ectoplasmic rods' and thereby harm the Medium.

Stewart Alexander was bound to his chair and each of his hands were held by a sitter throughout the séance. We opened proceedings with a prayer and some music was played. Stewart went very quickly into the required trance state and the Spirit of White Feather came through to speak first. He welcomed us all and said that he hoped those in Spirit could be of service to us that night.

Then young Christopher came through to speak to us, he was the Spirit of a little boy whom the group had nicknamed 'shuffle bottom'!
He made a joke and then asked to be introduced to us all. Alan told him that some of us had travelled a long way to be there and Christopher replied, *'not as far as I have!'*

Christopher spoke to me and instead of asking if I was a Cockney, in his own way he asked, *'are you a cockaney?'* which made me smile. Then he said he wanted to hear my voice, because he thought I sounded and looked like Lila Josephs, a lady Medium who was now in Spirit and helps behind the scenes. In the room we were sitting, on the wall Alan had a psychic portrait of Lila and the amazing thing is, I *do* look like her.

Christopher then told us we had a gentleman Spirit present, named Ted. Now Ted was my cousin who had only passed away a few months earlier. Ted wasn't able to speak to us directly, so Christopher passed on his message for us. He said Ted was talking about a 'pump' and laughing about it, which was was very evidential to us. Because it wasn't that long ago that we'd had some trouble with an old car tyre pump, after lending our brand new one to Ted's son.

Then suddenly Christopher said to Frank,
'do you know someone here with the letter A?'

Thinking of my son Alan, Frank said yes. Then Christopher spoke to me asking, *'do ten years mean something to you?'*
'Yes, it means a lot!' I said. We'd been told not to say too much, so that the information would be more evidential.

It had been ten years since I lost my young son Alan in suspicious circumstances and aside from Frank and myself, nobody in the room knew any of this - including the Medium. Then Christopher spoke to me again saying, *'just a minute. I've got something very serious now. There's a young man coming in who is very emotional. He says he passed in very suspicious circumstances.'*

To my utter amazement, Christopher said he was going to try and help this young man to come through by himself.

A moment later I heard my own dear son's voice - we all heard him. Although he seemed to have quite a struggle, because he was sobbing with

emotion and he'd clearly never done this kind of thing before. For the first time in ten years I heard my darling son speak to me,
'I want to speak to my Mum. It's Alan.' He said.
I've tried for so long. I love you. I'm alright...bye Mum.'

The emotion I felt was electrifying ! A deep feeling of love tore through me towards Alan and bounced right back to me. I <u>know</u> it was Alan who had spoken to me, but before we could even get our breath back, a different voice came through asking for Frank,
'Frank, it's Bob. I say...bloody hell, I don't know if I can do this.
The boy's with me, we're together.
Take care. So pleased to have the opportunity to see you here.
It's put a smile on your face ! All my love.'

Now this was most evidential to Frank and myself, as the Medium and all the sitters had assumed that Frank and I were married. Because we'd been told to say nothing about ourselves, they all thought that Alan was mine and Frank's son. I suppose they must have wondered why Alan only spoke to me and not to Frank. The voice we'd just heard was Frank's father-in-law Bob and he'd not spoken to me, only to Frank. Now we both felt that this was more evidential, because at church Bob always came through in messages for Frank.
To be honest, by this point we were both stunned !

Christopher took over once more and asked to speak to the both of us. He said, *'the young man here, who died in suspicious circumstances, has so much love, you could cut it with a knife. You're his Mum ? He wants you to know that he wouldn't want to come back at all, because he is so happy over here. He is only sad if you are sad. Now that you know he is okay, you must not cry anymore.'*

Now I'd always thought that Alan would be angry because he'd been robbed of his life at such a young age, so I felt this was quite evidential. Even though I've had lots of evidence of Alan's survival and even developed the gift of psychic art for myself, I still hadn't been certain until *that* night. Every mother knows her own son and I'd seen many Mediums by this point. A few had even purported to have had Alan speaking through them in Trance - but <u>not so</u> ! However on this magical night I knew, without a shadow of a doubt, that this was Alan I'd heard.

Christopher continued, by telling us that Alan tries to let us know when he's around at home. This was true, because we often heard 'Spirit knocks' all over the house. I thanked Christopher and he replied,
'that's alright, I'm only doing my job !'

He then said he was going away for a while, so Alan Crossley asked if he wanted us all to sing again. Christopher popped back and said, *'not bloody likely !'*
This made us all laugh which eased the tension in the room once more.

Next we heard from Jack, who is a another regular member of the Mediums Spirit team. He told us that since there were so many people wishing to come through that night, that we'd have to watch the time. He then went on to give a personal message to Alan Crossley about the progress of the group. Then Christopher returned and explained how they were going to take a little power from all of us in the room and we should all take a five-minute cigarette break ! Well he called it that, but it made us laugh.

After we'd all had a stretch, we soon reconvened. Then straight away Frank and I heard from a soul named Peter. We felt awful, because at the time we didn't recognise him. We were so stunned at everything we'd experienced so far, that it was two days later before we realised that we did actually know him - sorry Peter !

Next Alan Crossley conversed with the Spirit of an old friend. It was a Medium he knew by the name of Ronald Strong who was active during the 1940s and 50s. Alan didn't know it, but two of the other sitters had been discussing Ronald on their way to the séance. Another sitter named Brenda, received evidence about her dog in Spirit. Christopher said that he had christened the dog 'Wednesday' because the dog had come over to the Spirit World on a Wednesday !

For the next part of the séance Christopher asked another sitter named Ray to play the music loud, as this would help to raise the vibrations. He asked everyone to sit very still with their palms face upwards on their laps. Christopher said that what we were about to witness were not party tricks, but was being done to show us how close the two worlds were to one another.

Stewart the Medium was still bound to his chair and we could see where he was in the darkened room, because on his knees had been placed some luminous tape. What happened next was mind blowing.

First one of the séance trumpets lifted up into the air, then the other. Whilst this was going on, the table in the centre of the room moved towards one lady and pressed itself to her leg. People began to feel unseen hands patting them on their hands and on top of their heads. The bells which had been sitting on the table began to ring and the two drumsticks started tapping out a tune on the table. The control of the two séance trumpets was phenomenal. They shot upwards from the floor at tremendous speed and came right up to our faces, then shot away again. At one point, they came up to *my* face and what control ! They both went up to the ceiling and began to tap on it. Then at once they shot off in different directions and were about ten feet away from each other. They came down towards Frank and one of them gently stroked his hand then both went sailing up to the ceiling again, where they swayed and danced to the music in completely simultaneous control.

One of the trumpets then came down to the middle of the room, where it hung completely still for a moment. We were waiting for something to happen, when very quietly we began to hear a voice speaking through it.

This phenomena is known as the Direct Voice. The Spirit creates a miniature voice box in the narrow end of the trumpet, which allows us to hear them speak directly to us. The sound became clearer as we listened and I was told later that we were hearing the voice of the Reverend George Vale Owen. I learned that in the 1900s he had been friends with Sir Arthur Conan Doyle. Many Spiritualists know of him and his books on Mediumship.

Next we heard a lady speak through the trumpet and she was calling my name. She said her name was Alice, but had great difficulty in speaking, so young Christopher took over. He told me that this lady wanted to speak to me, but I said I didn't know an Alice. Afterwards I was telling my mother about the séance and she told me that Alice was my great grandmother's name. She had originally came to England from Ireland, when my grandmother was a child. My Mum told me that Alice's family were Irish Romany Rovers. Of course I knew nothing of this because we'd never spoken about it before. I was fascinated and so grateful that she had tried to speak to me !

After some evidence for others, Christopher came back and asked me to find a particular book on my shelves at home. He said that it would be the fourth book along the top shelf and it was blue. He said that on the tenth line, where the sentence ended on the eleventh line, on either page 102 or 104, was something about a lady and I should read it !

When we got home we looked at my books on the top shelf. The fourth book along had a green and blue cover. I looked at page 102 of this book and on the tenth line, I found the words,
'overwrought, overworked housewife...'

The rest of the text went on to explain how the mind affects the body in a trauma, with aches, pains and palpitations, etc. Now I suffer from all of these ailments and the text further explained that when the mind is clear of

searching for a personal relationship, the mind begins to heal the body. I thought this was very apt !
What *was* strange though, was that these three words were underlined in blue ink. Now I bought this book second-hand and hadn't marked these words myself, so was it Spirit or a coincidence ?

At the end of the séance, poor Stewart the Medium came out of Trance and said he was *freezing* cold, although we were all quite warm. There was another surprise however, because as the lights were turned back on we saw that Stewart - who had been bound to his chair the whole time - was no longer wearing his pullover. I don't see how he couldn't have removed it by himself. Alan Crossley told us later, that this was the first time it had happened to Stewart in a séance.

Now, I don't believe anyone can put a price on such wonderful experiences. Imagine the grieving parent who thought her child had gone forever, but who actually speaks to them again after so many years. For me this séance had been a priceless experience - but it wasn't my last !

Some time later at home, Frank was communicating with Spirit via the glass and letters. Alan came through and promised that the next time I went to a séance, we would be able to feel him. He said he would try and hold my hand and kiss me on the cheek !

The next time Frank and I did attend a séance, was later that year when Stewart Alexander was the guest Medium of the Noah's Ark Society. At that time, the N.A.S. were holding their séances at the home of Robin and Sandra Foy in Scole village, on the Norfolk/Suffolk border. Robin and Sandra had kindly set aside a room in their home specifically for séances. I later learned that when Alan Crossley, Robin and the rest of the N.A.S. had their first séance in this special room, Stewart's Spirit guide White Feather, came through to give the room a special blessing.

I was so pleased to find that my son Alan was able to come through and more strongly this time. As the séance got under way, the trumpets moved all around the room and even seemed to go into the floor. We also got the impression that the Spirit team were trying somehow, to 'lock' the trumpets together. One of them began floating around Frank's upturned hand and started to push. Frank laughed saying, *'my arm's being pushed back !'*

There were some drumsticks which started banging on the floor and then began to playfully tap the sitters on their shins. At this point, some of us also felt unseen hands touching us. Then Stewart's Spirit guide Jack said, *'we are going to try something different tonight.'*

He then asked the ladies who were either side of Stewart, to gently place a foot each on top of Stewart's feet and a hand each on his arms.

As we waited, the two ladies said they could feel Spirit hands touching their faces and arms. This was to show that it was impossible that Stewart was taking part in the proceedings. After this, we heard some shuffling and we began to see the luminous tabs on Stewart's knees, begin to disappear. We realised that Stewart and the heavy chair he was sitting in, were being moved. We found later that it had been turned right around, so that now he was actually facing the corner of the room.

Christopher came through and told us that he had a lot to do tonight. He said, *'my mates have come as well !'* Then he said, *'we've all been talking over here about the work that Frankie and Frank do, with the tapes and to help all the parents.'*

I said, *'thank you Christopher. They've all been uplifted.'*

'We are going to do something special tonight.' Christopher said. *'It's something we haven't done before. Normally, when people come through in the circle, they come to speak to the people sitting. Well I've got a lot of boys and girls here tonight and they want Frankie and Frank to pass on their love to their Mums and Dads.'*

'How wonderful !' I replied.

Christopher said, *'now we haven't done this before and it might be a bit confusing, but we'll try our best, because it will help some parents. It's impossible to bring all their Mums and Dads here, so we'll do the next best thing. Then it's up to Frankie and Frank to pass these messages on.'*

Many children spoke to us that evening and thanks to our use of a tape recorder, their parents received their children's messages. They also went on to share them with other bereaved parents. I am sure that the children we didn't know will eventually succeed somehow, in telling their parents that they are indeed *alive.*

I feel this was truly is a wonderful thing that our Spirit friends had done.

Christopher popped back during the recording and said to us, *'listen, we've all got our handkerchiefs out over here !'*

After this my Uncle Bill came through, with the usual type of humour he had on Earth saying, *'bloody hell, can you hear me ? It's old Bill here.'*

This was typical of him, so I said, *'you haven't changed Uncle Bill.'*

Then he said, *'I'm here with Alan. I tried to get through last time, but was unsuccessful.'*

Then very, very clearly, Frank's father-in-law Bob came through saying, *'it's Bob here, I'm here with Bill and Alan. We're all together.'*

Next, he made us laugh when he said, *'I made such an effort to speak to you last time, that afterwards I wasn't able to talk for a whole week !'*

Bob said how very pleased he was that Frank had found so much happiness, since before Frank had met me, his life had been very unhappy. Frank agreed, then Bob said, *'Life isn't about material things, it's about happiness. It's no good having money if you're not happy. Frank, now you have a million pounds worth of happiness !'*

We both thought this was a beautiful thing to say. Then Bob went on to say, *'I'm not idle over here you know, I'm working all the time. I didn't help anybody when I was on Earth, but I'm making up for it now.'*

Frank told me that this was very true of his father-in-law.
'Life is all about helping people,' Bob said.

Then he said he had to go now because he'd used up his time, so he said his goodbyes for now.

Then we heard the voice of a young boy, who said, *'I want to speak to Mrs Brown. You know my Mum !'*

I said, *'hello there, what's your Mum's name darling ?'*

'I'm John.' he said, *'and my Mum's name is June. Can you please tell my Mum I've been here ?'*

We all agreed and I said, *'we will John and she will be over the moon.'*

Now Frank and I sit in a Spiritual group of our own for Physical Phenomena and John is the son in Spirit, of our Medium. So naturally, we told her about this and gave her a tape recording of her son's voice.

John had got quite emotional before he was able to say anymore, so we reassured him that we would pass on his message. Then Christopher popped in saying, *'yep, yep, I'm getting very emotional myself. It's very emotional here. You've got to understand that they're all filled with emotion, but they're trying their best. Hang on...there's somebody else.'*

Then a young girl's voice came through saying, *'where's my Mum ? Somebody said my Mum is here.'*

Ray, one of the other sitters, asked, *'what's your Mummy's name darling ?'*

The young girl said, *'Dot, Dottie.'*

'What's your name ?' I asked her.

'Anna' the girl replied.

Frank said, *'do you have another name Anna?*

'Marie. Anna-Marie,' she said.

'That's right.' said Frank. *'Oh that's wonderful.'*

Now this was excellent evidence for us, as we both knew who Anna-Marie was, because we knew her mother Dorothy Wheatley. (See Chapter 14)

Anna-Marie said, *'the lady - will she tell my Mummy?'*

I said, *'yes of course I will darling.'*

Afterwards we dutifully sent a tape of Anne Marie's voice to her Mum, Dorothy.

White Feather then returned and gave us his greetings. He gave Frank and I a message for our own Spiritual group, then we came to the end of another wonderful evening. I have since sent tape recordings to all those Mums and Dads whose children spoke to us, with the love of White Feather and company. I know many of them have been comforted by the knowledge that was given on that magical evening.

A give a great big thank you to Stewart Alexander for sitting as our Medium and allowing his body to be used. I also thank Christopher, White Feather, Jack and the many unseen and unheard helpers, who made it possible for all those children to come through in such a way. I would like to thank Alan Crossley and his circle for their love, for without them the children couldn't have communicated. I also thank Alan Crossley for his dedication, help and knowledge in helping me to help others. I thank all for bringing our children back.

As I completed writing this story, I put down my pen and made myself a cup of tea. I walked into my lounge and on the back of my sofa found a white feather. This is White Feather's calling card, so I thank him too and I thank goodness this is all still going on.

I suppose in the next book, I'll be described as reincarnated from some old Greek woman, who for years has been carrying a water jug on her head. At least that would explain why I have all this pain in my neck now!

* * *

Gwen: This chapter has been Frankie Brown's story. Now since Frankie has written of our Egyptian Spirit friend Raymar, I feel I should add the following.

The publication of the first book *'Russell'* had left me so emotionally drained, it made me physically ill. So in May 1996, my friend B- and I arranged that we would go on a trip. We travelled to Cyprus and then went on a cruise to Israel and Egypt. Our friend Raymar knew that we were going, so he issued us with a few requests !

Raymar asked us to find a lighthouse in Cyprus, near an Amphitheatre, to coincide with my birthday which fell while we were away. I was also requested to wear a long dress and wear an Hibiscus flower in my hair, for the occasion to come ! I was asked to perform some songs, so some requests were given. None of this was a problem except, *'what about an audience ?'* I asked.

'We will all be there.' Raymar said. *'Please do this on May 20th.'*

Never one to argue with our Spirit friends, we actually did all of it and it was quite an experience. We had taken a portable tape player with us and had a recording of my accompaniments. We found the Amphitheatre by the lighthouse and that evening at around seven, we waited until the place was empty. While we were preparing for my 'gig' some people wandered in and must have wondered what on Earth we were doing, but they just sat down to watch and listen. Well they were welcome.

B- became my musical Director, in her shorts and saucy little red cap and I was decked out as instructed by Raymar. As the 'artiste' I was not happy with all the little lizards hanging about, because I'm sure they were all going to hop under my skirt. What a carry on !

However, it was quite an experience and I have to say, that one part of me was astonished by the natural acoustics of the place. I could only listen in wonder, but the other part of me felt like a right plonker ! However, soon enough the wonder of it all took me over and we had recorded the whole 'concert.'

In the middle of the recording while I was singing along to *'Musetta's Waltz Song'* from Puccini's *'La Boheme'* - quite clearly Russell can be heard on the tape in his little boy voice shouting, *'hello Mum it's me, I'm here.'*

What else can I say ? It's on the tape.

After Cyprus we went on to Egypt, travelling by coach from Port Said to Giza. On the coach I was frantically writing notes when B- said to me, *'Gwen do you have a pen I can borrow, I can't find mine ?'*

I handed her a purple pen with the name *'Russell'* on it.

Then somewhat hot and harassed we arrived at Giza and what a sight met our eyes. There in front of us stood the Pyramids and Sphinx. We gazed in wonder ! Though whilst gazing, we declined an offer to ride a camel. Well, we had the heat to contend with, plus all the young local boys who had gathered around us two 'tourists.'

We finally found ourselves at the foot of some wooden steps, which allows access into the Great Pyramid, the largest of the pyramids. With feelings of trepidation, nothing in this world could stop us going through the doorway in front of us. As we reached the door, there stood an Egyptian policeman looking quite stern. Then all of a sudden he pointed to B- and said excitedly, *'please give me your pen. I like, please give to me.'*

'Gwen, he wants your pen' B- said.

'Okay' I said *'just give it to him.'* So she did !

He smiled and looked at this purple pen, then just popped into his jacket pocket. It certainly didn't go with the rest of his uniform, but we had to grin to ourselves, as we headed straight into this giant pyramid.

Of course I was wearing a big, daft sun hat and it was getting in the way of those people who had suddenly chickened out. They were rushing out of the pyramid before they'd hardly got into it.

I won't try to explain my feelings, as we travelled deeper and deeper into the pyramid. They're something I hold close to my heart, but the experience literally 'blew us away.' Then on the way out, we saw the same purple pen with the name Russell on it, sticking out of the policeman's pocket. How could we not be amused ?

So much of our trip was rush, rush, rush ! On and off the coach we went and in what seemed like no time at all, we found ourselves at the 'Elvis Café' ! There were Elvis Presley statues and pictures everywhere, even his face was on the cups. I felt I had time travelled and somehow landed in Hollywood !

By now we were in Israel and I had replaced my big sun hat with an Arab-style head dress. Though we had to laugh at the photos later, for I looked like an Arab who had been cooked alive !

However, a photo B- had taken of me going into the Great Pyramid in Egypt, was very intriguing. It shows only my face and 'that' hat, the rest is a great blob of white energy or as some may call it 'Ectoplasm.' Now I wonder who was responsible for that ? No prizes for guessing !

After we'd returned home to England, I visited Frankie who naturally wanted to hear all about our trip, in fact she was agog !

I showed her the following poem, which was written on the day I sang at the Amphitheatre in Cyprus.

> *'On the Isle of Aphrodite,*
> *there's a mystery that I must explain.*
>
> *Because now you're mixing with 'High Society'*
> *the answer will become very plain.*
>
> *There's a road to the Troodos Mountains you see,*
> *Where stands, outstretched and full of blue blossom, a tree.*
>
> *That's where I want B- and you,*
> *and there by silent meditation, I will come through,*
>
> *I vow that Raymond, Richard and Alan will be with me,*
> *and together we can unravel more of the mystery.*
>
> *That's all for now,*
> *I really must go,*
>
> *For it's hard work you know*
> *and I'm losing the flow...'*
>
> ~ Russell

I told Frankie how we did go up the Troodos Mountains and do these things. I explained that we even sat under a blue tree. This did actually happen ! I also told Frankie that B- and I visited *'Petra tou Romiou'* - the name for the site of Aphrodite's birth place - which was so, so beautiful.

While I'd been away Frankie had communicated with our lovely Egyptian Spirit friend, Raymar and he'd given Frankie some new lyrics to a well known song by Andrew Lloyd Webber ! So it seems to me that Raymar is equally passionate about his music.

I include those words here, as I think they are excellent. I don't know what it is he is trying to say, but the tune is from the song *'With One Look'* from the musical *'Sunset Boulevard.'*

> *'With one note I'll take your Soul apart,*
> *With one song I'll mend broken hearts,*
> *Let me help your Soul to fly,*
> *With one note, all your fears will go.*
>
> *With my song I'll build a golden lake.*
> *With golden boats for you all to partake,*
> *My colour vibrations in the sky,*
> *They can raise you high.*

> *'Tis your chance you know, for you all to go.*
> *Take a chance with me - I can set you free.*
> *To your world of Love, come now rise above.*
> *I'm the great Raymar, I will not go far.*
>
> *So come my friends on this golden note,*
> *Take my hands and with me you'll float.*
> *A chance to leave this world behind,*
> *Earthly trappings of mankind.*
>
> *You will never know the one who loves you so,*
> *Cast off this shell, let your Spirit flow.*
> *I can set you free, Bands of Gold streak through the sky.*
> *With one note you'll know, that it's time to go.*
>
> *Here it comes, the Golden Gate,*
> *Leading you to the Crystal Estate.*
> *They'll say 'Now you're home at last'*
>
> *This time you're staying, you're staying for good.*
> *You'll be back where you all should be,*
> *follow my notes and you're free'*

Well, I wonder what Mr Webber would make of that ?

I still wonder what it's all about, but I say a big *'thank you'* to Raymar, for whoever he really is, he's certainly a very special friend.

Raymar told Frankie that I am his *'Songstress'* and that when I go over to the Spirit World, there are many souls waiting for me - to say thank you ! Raymar also told Frankie, *'Gwen has known greatness before, with me'*

All I can say to that is *'Crumbs !'*

Apparently he loves my own personal way of singing and when I get to meet him, he has my clothes and shoes all ready. He's even asked if I want a flying carpet...well of course I do !

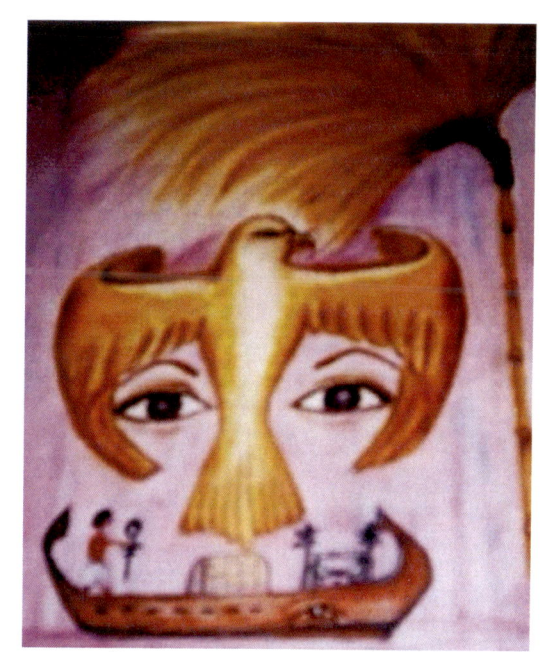

Gwen's 'Golden Bird of Isis'
painted by Frankie Brown

Gwen in Egypt

Twenty Four

My Field of Dreams

*A hundred years from now,
it will not matter what my bank account was,
the sort of house I lived in or the kind of car I drove.
But the world may be a little different,
Because I was important in the life of child.'*

~ Forest E. Witcraft

March 1990 was our Ruby Wedding Anniversary and Mothers Day too. I'd been out on the Friday to buy a gift for my son Gary, as his birthday coincided with our anniversary. Wandering through a market, I discovered a lovely waistcoat covered in Egyptian Hieroglyphics and just had to buy it. So, nearly forgetting my gift for Gary that I'd come out for, I went back home very pleased with myself. I had no idea then why I'd bought the waistcoat and back home, I just put it on a hanger and forgot all about it !

The Sunday of our anniversary was spent quietly and being Mothers Day too, naturally my thoughts went back to our Mothers. It was a quiet, lovely day - the evening however, was somewhat different.

At around seven the phone rang and it was Frankie Brown, who said, *'Can I pop over this evening Gwen, I've got something for you ?'*
'Okay' I replied, *'we'll see you at about eight then.'*

I hadn't a clue what was coming, but later when I saw Frankie walking up the drive to my door, she was with Frank and I saw he was carrying a large framed picture - and I mean large ! The reason I recall the time is because of another incident, which I'll also describe.

To be perfectly honest I am having difficulty with this chapter, because I remember how I felt with what happened next...

On answering the door, our friends Frankie and Frank came into the house. When Frankie handed me this huge colour picture, I just froze on the spot and I swear my heart stopped beating !

I began to function in an odd sort of way, I think the modern term for it is 'automatic pilot', but I was definitely in shock.

Here in front of me, was a portrait of my son Russell and I was thrilled with it, but it was a colour portrait of Russell the MAN ! I stared at it blinking my eyes, in case I was dreaming. I thanked Frankie profusely, but somehow I felt drained and my legs felt strangely wobbly, so I had to rush out of the room. I left Alfie chatting with our visitors and I think no one seemed to notice, as I went to our bedroom and just fell on the bed.

I would have thought that by now, every emotional button had been pressed, but I'd noticed it was eight fifty-five, which was the time Spirit would always send a 'knock'. As I lay back in the darkened room, in a kind of stunned excitement, so came the eight-fifty-five knock. Not only that, but I also saw a light coming towards me. Glowing beautifully in the dark was a ruby red Spirit light, at least one and a half inches in diameter. I just lay there and stared at it, still pinching myself.
'Oh my God', I thought, *'oh my God.'* Over and over again I said it and I lost track of time.

I sat up after what had been only a few minutes and took a hold of myself. I left our bedroom and walked back into the lounge, but said nothing for I was still in a time warp. In my mind, I was taken back to that beautiful day on September 20th, seven years earlier when my car had broken down on the motorway. (see Chapter 3)

Thanks to my friend Frankie, here was a pastel drawing of the same young man who'd come to help on that day. Indeed, he was like a Knight in shining armour who'd come my aid - and he helped save my friend Rose's life at the same time ! I knew him instantly and I loved him instantly ! For isn't a child at the root of a mother's heart ?

I told no one of this for months. I hugged the picture to myself and didn't want to share it with anyone. If I close my eyes now I can still see that figure in his brown leather jacket, as he came towards the group of us by the car. I can still hear his voice saying, *'can I help you ?'*
I can recall every moment when he stood shoulder to shoulder with me, helping to push the car. Each moment of that event is etched on my soul. It touched places that I never knew I had. I know now that,
'yes, I had seen an Angel !' I can recall it all with such clarity. The gorgeous tall, dark, handsome man. His words as he stood there, his smile. Even the walk across the road, our *thank-you's* and his parting call of, *'Cheerio !'*

I do not care at all if people ridicule me and I can wish all sorts of things now, years later - it's no use. But memories can stay with us always.

Sometimes I truly feel that I should never have shared this experience, but then that would be wrong.

I know that my friend Rose, who was with me at the time, knew who this beautiful man was. She's a Physical Medium, so I guess that would have helped to make this 'miracle' happen, though I do not use the word 'miracle' lightly, believe me. I know that people have seen Angels before, were they Spirit ? Call them what you will, I don't mind.

From *'The Little Prince'* Antoine de Saint-Exupéry writes,
'It is only with the heart that one can see rightly. What is essential, is invisible to the eye.'

I know I've been so blessed and a thousand times I have asked why ? Why ? Sometimes I just think, *'how did he do that ?'*

My son Gary saw an Angel when he was six. It was his brother Russell, as a child of ten. I believe that *'all God's angels come to us disguised'* as written by James Russell Lowell in his poem,
'On the Death of a Friend's Child.'

So if this is true, how many of us have *'entertained Angels unawares ?'* This is another favourite Angel quote of mine, from Hebrews 13:2 in the New Testament.

Later I received a message from Russell, the man. He said, *'Fancy you meeting me on the motorway and not knowing me - face to face and not knowing who I was, Mother !'*

'Alright' I thought, *'don't rub it in.'*

I know that he was having his usual joke with me. He knows that for me, that incident was so amazing. He also knew that on that day, I'd functioned purely on another level and that I kept the experience so close to my heart and told no one ! The whole incident defies explanation to this day. I even suspect very strongly that Russell has been beside me while I've written this chapter.

It's been so hard to try and put into words, it has distressed me so much. As I write, the same question comes to mind over and over again,
'how could I have not known him ?'

Yet I had only ever known him as a child, for nine and three quarter years. So if I had recognised him and thrown my arms around him, what would have happened ? It brings up many questions that I'm not prepared to answer and maybe never will. He'd once said to me in a song,
'Like a bolt out of the blue, Mum I'll be there' and he was.

I'm very aware that the whole incident has left its mark upon me, in such a way that I could not and would not speak of it for years. Even years later, I find it hard to speak of.

I once told my son Kevin about it and he listened intently, as he looked into my eyes. He never scoffed, for he knew I wouldn't have lied about it. Yet as he looked at me, his eyes resembled the eyes of his tall, dark, handsome brother, Russell. There is a similarity, except that Kevin's eyes are paler like his father's, whereas Russell's eyes are navy blue.
His appearance that day was as natural as the other, Earthly young man, who also came to our aid.

Speaking of his beloved brother Kevin, Russell once said,
'we've been together before Kev, we remember and then we let it go. You will not forget and neither will I. One day you may share your knowledge with the world, if you chose to. Think about it mate !'

I'm unable to write much more on this happening, for I am fast in need of my tissues. So I will end this short chapter with big thanks to Russell the man. May God bless you and keep you until we meet again one day.

A few lines of a song have just come to mind...

> *'I miss the hungry years, the once upon a time,*
> *The lovely long ago, we didn't have a dime,*
> *The days of you and me, we lost along the way.*
>
> *How could I be so blind not to see the door,*
> *Closing on the world, I now hunger for.*
>
> *Looking through my tears,*
> *I miss the hungry years...*

~ words by Neil Sedaka

Yes, I'm listening son ! Thank you, Russell.

Twenty Five

When A Child Is Born

December 12th 1994

> *'For unto us a child is born, unto us a son is given,
> and the government will be upon his shoulder,
> and he will be called Wonderful Councillor, Mighty God,
> Everlasting Father, Prince Of Peace.'*
>
> ~ Isaiah 9:6

We are here at the time when we celebrate the birth of the baby Jesus and this year seems to have flown ! It's been a year of both joy and sadness - the sadness this year came with the passing of Simon Prentice, my friend Margaret's eldest son. (See Chapter 21)

How cruel life can be, I thought. To lose one beloved boy is tragic enough, yet to lose two seems all too much. The news soon went round our group of Mothers and of course if you've walked that path, you can relate to it and speak quiet words. Words, which in themselves may not mean a lot, but you understand.

For Simon's funeral service, Alfie and I had a large pink wreath made, with a Pink Panther on the front. We knew Margaret wouldn't have been offended, but her bewildered look in the church and that of her husband Roy, made my heart ache. Standing near them both was their third son Matthew who had now 'lost' both of his brothers, within six years. I'm not ashamed to say that I wept for them all.

As time went on, we watched Margaret's bravery and were filled with pride to know such a lady of character. Here is a woman that, in spite of all her pain, can still reach out and help others. That is bravery indeed !

Of course the Summer came and went, as it does and gradually the number of Mothers in the RPPS increased. Since my first book *'Russell'* was published in 1994, we'd had some quite hectic times. On the whole it was fun, especially when a delightful young man came from *'Woman's*

Own' magazine to take some photographs, for an article they were doing on the book.

The lounge was full of cameras - talk about TV studio ! It all raised a laugh anyway especially for me, when the young man told me, *'my name is David Russell, but my Dad liked Russell best, so that's what he calls me.'*

I just had to grin to myself, because I knew there was another 'unseen' Russell watching the proceedings and also grinning !

Naturally, the article in *'Woman's Own'* and columns in some other local newspapers, raised a few eyebrows but who cares ! Most of the feedback was very kind.

We appeared on a chat show for ITV entitled *'Is There Life After Death ?'* It was a very eye opening experience for us. At the time, as was usual for this type of programme, sitting there in the front row was a certain gentleman named Chris French. He has seemed to earn a very good living taking part in such programmes over the year. But of course he 'knew it all' or so he thought. However, he hadn't got so much to say when we met him away from the cameras, face to face. These people used to call themselves 'Researchers' yet for some reason they are now called 'Parapsychologists.' To me, this just means they think they can destroy anyone's Truth !

Still never mind, they'll all find out for themselves some day, when they eventually go 'Home' to the Spirit World !

Next we had a visit from a TV producer, who wanted us to take part in his programme. Although he was pleasant enough and spoke excitedly about the show, he explained how they would find an actress that looked like me when I was younger, to tell the story of Russell.

Well, I'd seen this particular programme before and while I'm sure they meant well, I felt it was wrong to do it. They always seemed to give the usual 'spooky' treatment to all of their stories and I recall Russell saying to me at one of the séances in the 80s, *'I'm not a spook Mum, I'm Russell.'*

My son's words echoed back to me and so we declined the offer with a polite *'no thank you.'*

Spooks indeed !

Now we were nearing the end of 1994 and my thoughts went back to the Christmas of 1993. My son Kevin and his wife Chris, had asked us up to their home in Yorkshire and we were having a lovely, quiet time. Then on December 26th, I received a phone call from my sister Eileen.

I hadn't been in touch with her for years, but she'd rang to say that our other sister Doreen, was about to pass to Spirit. We were too far away and it was too late for us to head back home. Thankfully, my sister Doreen's passing was so peaceful for her. I knew that she had left her awful illness behind her and now, she could find peace with those she loved.

Doreen had truly adored Russell and she used to laugh so much at his antics. Now, I imagined her meeting up with him as I thought,
'well, he's still the same as he was Doreen - and he can be nine and three quarters whenever he wants !'
I was sure Russell would have a lovely welcome for his Auntie Doreen.

Returning to Christmas 1994 and we were fortunate to be able to have a seasonal chat with our Spirit friends.

Raymond Lodge told us,
'how quickly Yuletide comes round and passes like a dream, though for so many people on your Earth it is a nightmare. I wish people would give of their souls, instead of gifts. It is a festival of Love, Peace, Understanding and Joy, so don't grieve for us, we share your Yuletide.'

Raymond also said,
'I would like to extend my thanks to Frankie Brown for noting down my own lyrics, recently dictated to her for my favourite piece of music, the Intermezzo from 'Cavalleria Rusticana.'
My thanks also go to you, my dearest friend Gwen, for singing my words to that piece of music. I have enjoyed it so much.'

Then we heard from one of B-'s Spirit helpers, who wanted to share some stark words of his own.

John: *'I realise it is customary on Earth to celebrate December 25th as the birth of that Great Teacher you call Jesus. We cannot celebrate this day as Jesus's Birthday because he was not born on December 25th. Jesus was born in September, at the stroke of midnight between the 20th and the 21st. You only celebrate Christmas on December 25th because it replaces a Pagan Festival - for which the Church founders exchanged key Pagan dates, for key Christian festival dates. By this time they had elevated the man Jesus into a God and they believed he was a God.*
Jesus is simply an evolved soul who is capable of joining and being at one with the Godhead and that is the truth. So whilst you celebrate Christmas as the birthday of a child, we celebrate it as a festival of Love.

It is very appropriate that your world and ours should join together at this time, since we are trying to help people in your world to understand

Love. The birth of a child should fill the world with joy and it is right that it should. For each child is a unique gift to the world. So whether you approve or disapprove of the child's arrival, is not important. The reality is that the child is a blessing, whatever the circumstances of the birth may be. For there is no doubt that the birth of a child teaches the human soul how to love.

We have no room in our philosophy for any kind of abuse. I wish that it were so for all Religious and Spiritual organisations. Make no mistake about this, abuse of any kind has no connection with God. The physical and mental abuse of a child is one of the worst forms of abuse that any human soul can choose to inflict upon another. I warn all abusers that you will answer to God for any abuse that you inflict upon any other living soul, whether it walks on two legs or four.
It will be no good when you meet the Angels, call them what you will, to try to hide behind any uniform, regimentation or ritual - you will answer to the abuser.'

* * *

We had another chance to hear from our friends in Spirit, beginning with Raymond who refers to a second visit I made, with B- and her daughter, to his family's home of Wiltshire.

Raymond: *'At last dear lady I can speak to you about your Amesbury and Avebury tour. We guided you back to places that meant something to us, to let you know we were there by your side, did we not ? Were you happily surprised ? I can imagine your answer.'*

Gwen: *'Oh Raymond it was a wonderful day for all of us.'*

Raymond: *'The photographic evidence you received that day was to show how near we are to you and how we can interact and link with you. If we are determined, we can produce miracles, but only if the love link is good ! Of course I favour Direct Voice, but we have problems with that right now, so we communicate in this way.*

It is no accident that on August 14th we drew close and inspired you to go to Avebury and Amesbury, where my father lived. Most of my family are buried there, although as you know, I am not. Avebury has a lovely vibration and a nurturing energy. I know that you enjoyed it.

It was we who led you to the Medium Rita, who gave us those wonderful evenings we shared. Do enjoy the memory, but don't live for the memory. We go on, it is good that we try all things. One day, I hope the Medium's true story will be told.'

Gwen: *'It should be, Raymond.'*

Raymond: *'Yes but we do not wish you to worry, we know that there were problems. We hope that the work we do in the future will help you to understand the problems more deeply and how it all began. With understanding and enlightenment comes a greater wisdom. It is hard to believe that such wonderful things did happened, but they did and we are glad. I made such wonderful pals in you and Alf. It has been a long time since I have been able to come through and thank you!'*

How are you my friend Alf?

Alfie: *'I'm very well thanks Raymond.'*

Raymond: *'It is very odd that we all meet again like this and yet it was planned, but you know that!'*

Gwen: *'Raymond, it's even more odd that we find your ancestors live only about a mile away from us in Rayleigh!'*

Raymond: *'Yes my dear lady, what a coincidence. But then we don't believe in coincidences do we Gwen? It is very hard for me to believe that I have ancestors at all, but I do!'*

Gwen: *'Raymond, are they interested and aware of all this?'*

Raymond: *'Yes, but they are reluctant to become too deeply involved at this moment in time. They began by being a little ashamed by my father for his books and deliberations later in life. Everyone thought he was crazy with grief for me you know, but this wasn't true. That's silly, because he already knew there was an Afterlife. He recorded it on the airwaves dear lady. Valves! I didn't know he was involved in these experiments as it's not widely known, but it is true. Spirit energies and Spirit people can be picked up on the airwaves.*

There was one extraordinary instance late one night, when he picked something up. He really didn't know what it was and it quite alarmed him. No, he didn't write about it - I know you were going to ask this Gwen...'

Then our son Russell came in to speak to us and he referred to my work, then gave us an illuminating talk...

Russell: *'It has taken many years of your life Mum hasn't it?'*

Gwen: *'Well I've had to be patient Russell.'*

Russell: *'Yes Mum you are patient, you've had to be haven't you? I love you for it!*

Now I want to talk a little about positivity and negativity.

This book alone may cause a certain amount of negativity from some people, but the whole purpose of Spirit communication is to enrich and help people on the Earth plane. Anyone who follows this path of communication is equal and not one contributor mentioned in this book, is in any way more important or any different to another. It is the whole that makes it so powerful and true.

This book wouldn't have been possible without a great deal of loving co-operation. It is very important that the balance of that co-operation is maintained, because if one believes that they are greater than another or they have better links than another, then the whole thing becomes unbalanced and the momentum of the whole will be lost.

I'm sorry to have to talk like this, but it's very important. When all this knowledge is coming together you will encounter people along the way on this quest, who have said they are Spiritual people - but it takes far more than words to be Spiritual. They can <u>say</u> they're Spiritual but they have to <u>be</u> Spiritual !

In some relationships upon the Earth plane, we tend to think that the person who loves us most or treats us the best, will teach us the most. This is not true, for those people who treat us unkindly and unjustly, with great negativity are often our best teachers. Those who love and care for us and give positive encouragement in our lives, show us positivity and love. This is how it should be, but the others show us how it should <u>not</u> be and we have to thank these people.

We have to thank God for those that love us, but we also have to thank God for the others, for they teach us a great deal.

I have to say to anyone who reads this, it is folly to hate. There is no point in it. All jealousy is folly, all hate is folly and it will destroy the person who harbours those emotions - much more than the person they hate or despise. If you dislike a person, just leave them alone. Do them no disservice and just keep away from them, but those that inspire the very best in you, that is a different matter altogether. You can experience only positivity and encouragement from that relationship...'

John: *It is with great joy that we gather tonight to finish the tape for the ending of 'When A Child Is Born' - more so because Gwen is here to enjoy it with us. It is John who speaks to you now and I wish to tell you, that we of the White Brotherhood are very grateful for the work you have done for the books. We realise that it has taken up such a lot of your time - to transcribe these tapes and make them ready for publication. As it has also* taken many hours gathering all the various stories and putting them in order. Your work will bring its own rewards. We have been very pleased with the way the second book has been going and the way it has been compiled. When you work upon it, know that I am beside you.'

Russell: 'Mum, we are about to start on a new venture, if you want to work with us. I've previously explained about a book on reincarnation and we hope it will become more clear to you.

I hope you like the lovely Egyptian ring I gave you through B-'s kindness. It marks the beginning of the next stage. We do like to do things in stages and we thought it would be a good idea to give you a symbol to focus on. Raymond wants to talk to you now Mum...'

Raymond: 'Well dear lady, we are doing our best ! I guided you both on your recent excursion, working through this Medium. I guided you to the house where you found the horses, then I took you to a church where there were even more - for I knew that these animals uplift our Medium.

It was no accident that we found Rita the Medium, who provided the right circumstances for those most wonderful circles we used to have. She is linked with all of us. We hope in time, to help you understand why things happened the way they did. It is very easy to judge and to condemn, but it is very hard to forgive. In time you will see and understand that those involved were only doing what they had to do, to complete a certain set of circumstances that began many, many centuries ago.

Our Torch Bearers are lighting the 'Book Of Truth' Gwen. You wrote the first book with our help and now others are joining you to help with the second. The purpose of your books, is to teach the world how to love. For your world has almost forgotten how - and through that forgetfulness, they are destroying themselves and the civilisation in which you live...'

For a few moments here, we sat quietly. Then we heard an unidentified voice speaking very slowly. It said only one word. The word *'LOVE'* - but it was spoken with such a deep wealth of feeling, it's hard to describe.

When I asked who it was, we were told,

'It matters not my children, it matters not. We are drawing close to you to open your awareness to the endless possibilities of love. That is the sole purpose of our work and it is important this is understood. Many people tend to use us for their abilities - to further their own ends. This is not the way forward. This is not communication. It is very important to know that Higher Beings do not come to one individual person for the whole story.'

Russell: *'Mum we are lucky with the Mediums we are working with, they do understand and it is best that we all understand. It is very hard to learn through humility.'*

(Russell amuses us then, by saying this next bit in a real Cockney accent !)
'I try to be 'umble....but I have a lot of trouble and I have to go on courses.'

At this point I'm reminded of a poem that Russell gave us, through Frankie Brown. I think it's quite appropriate to include it here.
It's sung to the tune of *'I'm Always Chasing Rainbows'* which was actually adapted in 1917 from an 1834 piano piece by Chopin !

*'I'm always chasing Mediums,
Trying to find the one I love,*

*All my life's tied up with Mediums,
To help 'The Pink Panther Club'*

*Sometimes I get exasperated,
Cos some of them are really quite a pain,*

*Sometimes I get to feel elated,
Then they go and get it wrong again,*

It's hard work !

*I'm always chasing Mediums,
Hoping to reunite the loved ones up above.'*

Russell: *'We all get carried away sometimes, yet we are all on this journey and I'm no different to the other children mentioned in this book. All those mentioned are on this pathway, all have achieved wonders and one day they will draw even closer to you, but at this moment in time I'm telling my story. It takes time to find the right Medium and just because I'm coming through here to tell my story, doesn't make me any more important than the others.*

We all have a wonderful fellowship here and I know you all have the same too. It's very important that this fellowship is mentioned, because through that we can truly work to our best and work miracles. We all have to work on our humility and I have to work on mine, because of my name. I'm not more important - we are all working together.

My friend Al is doing pretty well. Rainbow's coming along great. Si's making progress now and Rich - well he's basically a 'Mr Man !' He always does well and has great abilities. I think Margaret will hear more from him in the future. He doesn't have to work on his humility as much as the rest of us and Steven and the girls and all the others too. They may not be so directly involved but they are just as important.

Now I know Raymond has already spoken of your trips to Avebury and Amesbury and how he took you all on a tour, when you sort of got lost ! We gave B- a flash of inspiration to find the cemetery and it was exactly right wasn't it Mum ? You went down that lane and there it was.
That's how we can work with you, we can take you to specific places at specific moments - that's how close the interaction is. Some people call it giving a link, so we 'link' with humility and love and it's like an enormous adventure open to all. It's there, if only you reach out for it.

The greatest adventure lies within yourself, in your own personal quest. This book is the story of you, who went on that personal quest. We just had to reach out to you. We are as near as a breath, so guard against negativity. Mum do you have a question ?'

'Yes !' I said. But before I could ask, the answer was given.

Russell: *'I know Mum !*

When B- and you sat together and the tape never came out right, we were experimenting. B- needed a coffee so she went downstairs. As you sat there waiting Mum, I picked up your thoughts. You looked at the poster B- had on her wall, the one of Kevin Costner from the 'Field of Dreams' where he is wearing a brown leather jacket.

Mum, that jacket's just like mine isn't it ? The one that I wore when I appeared to you in the Motorway incident. Then you thought, 'it would be nice Russ if you could mention it.' Well now I have ! I've let you know that I picked up your thoughts. I <u>know</u> it meant a lot to you Mother. You all have to have your 'Field of Dreams.'

So now, goodnight Father and goodnight my darling Mother. Don't forget to write of B-'s first visit to my old Earthly home in Rayleigh. I will be with you all the way...'

* * *

My next recollection is painful in more ways than one, but pain comes in many guises and I have wept a lot - but I have laughed a lot too.
So we need to fast-forward briefly to September 1995.

Alfie and I visited Thorpe Bay in Southend-On-Sea with the family and some friends. B- and her children stayed with us too, until my son Kev and his wife Chris had gone home, then the rest of us all returned to Rayleigh.

We spent time taking local walks. We went over tracks that I hadn't seen since the early Sixties. I didn't know where we were headed, because I just followed B- and her children ! We ended up at Hockley bluebell woods, where my grandsons - young Russell and his brother Brett - joined us for a picnic. We thought it would be a good idea if they had some old fashioned fun. So they climbed trees and rushed about the way children do !

In Southend my memory began doing summersaults, because we found ourselves at 'Never, Never Land' amusement park. Such was the interaction here between the two worlds, that as we climbed the cliffside paths, the recall was clear. This was the very place that Alfie, me and little Kevin and Gary had visited thirty-two years before, on Russell's first birthday after his passing. It was September 1963. We were struggling then to cope with the emptiness we all felt without Russell. Yet here I was, all these years later and I half expected him to pop up in front of me - especially when we came to the huge model of Merlin the magician ! I remember that dismal day back in 1963, was also the day that the sea front lights were switched on - which was quite a big event for Southend !

However, the influence of Spirit was so complete this time around in 1995, that as we all came down the cliff steps, we literally bumped into a group of people that B- and her children knew from Wiltshire. After our greetings, they said they were also waiting for the annual sea front light switch on. So here was I, on the same spot as thirty-two years before, but how could I express my deep feelings at such a time ? The only way I knew how, by giving Russell a song !

'No tears, no fuss,
Hooray for us !
Thanks for the memory...'

Every emotional button was pressed for me on that return visit. Yet I knew Spirit were guiding me along that particular memory lane, now they are my treasured memories.

My friend Margaret Prentice had also joined us for the day, although she had declined the climb up and up - bless her ! Yet here she was with a smile and so soon after 'losing' Simon. So don't let anyone try to tell me that *knowing,* not just believing in survival, doesn't help. Just ask Margaret.

We all had a good laugh and a good cry, then waved goodbye to a very tired family ! My God, you can forget just how much hard work children can be. Yet would we like to be without them ? Honestly now, would we ?

Twenty Six
Reincarnation ~ The Cycle of Souls

Summerland Tape 4
November 28th-29th 1994

'I think immortality is the passing of a soul through many lives and experiences, and such as are truly lived, used and learned, help on to the next, each growing richer, happier and higher, carrying with it only the real memories of what has gone before.'

~ Louisa May Alcott

Raymond: 'As is now customary, I would like to begin here with a short piece of prose entitled 'The Cycle of Souls.'

*On it goes, round it goes the Cycle of Souls,
Lifetime after lifetime the Cycle of Souls,*

*Once it was known by all living beings,
Once it was believed and once it was told,
the Cycle of Souls is the Cycle of Life,
But now people do not understand,*

*I promised I would return to your world,
to clear up the misunderstanding of the Cycle of Souls,
Some say we don't - some say we do,
there is even confusion in our world !
I will deal with this.*

*Why do souls in our world not believe it ?
Our world is on seven levels.
Yours is the eighth.
The ninth level is the oneness, the Greatness, the Whole !
Controversial as this may seem to your world below,*

(but to quote my lovely boy Russell)
'it's True - so there !'

The Cycle of Souls is only truly understood,
by souls who live on the higher levels,
it is not understood in your world because it does not fit in,
with the religions in the Western world,
They deny Reincarnation Truths,

the Eastern religions have retained a particle of this Truth,
but none have retained all of its knowledge.
We now come forward, my lovely boy and I,
to fill some of the spaces, some of the gaps,
let go of your egos my dear friends,

open up your minds to the concept of the Immortal soul,
engaged on a quest to bring Truth, Love and Peace.
For souls are what you are and group souls,
regroup to continue the quest.

All of us who took part in this book,
our group souls united on this great quest,
to bring knowledge and truth to people who seek
the Truth and Wisdom that governs us all.

We have regrouped to teach everyone,
how to love and to rediscover once more
the philosophy of life.
God is the truth, and love is the key,
Love is the power that makes us link with thee,

Through love we write this book,
Love for you the reader, whoever you may be,
are you trapped in a vortex, trapped in a hole ?
the way out is forward and onward we must go.
Free flow is important, onwards and upwards to release all souls.

So here we are and on it goes,
round and round - the Cycle of Life,
which joins the Cycle of Souls and goes on,
No one learning much, lifetime after lifetime
in this Cycle of Souls'

Russell: *'Hello Mum and Dad !*
Mum, I like the new tape of your singing, it's wonderful ! So my little

possum, you made it at last. Well done Mum ! People will get a great deal of comfort and joy from it and like I've said before, your voice heals at a deep and a Divine level. I think it will help many people.

Tonight, I want to talk about the 'concept of reincarnation' and there's no doubt about it, this is a controversial issue. It's widely misunderstood and it's hard to know where to start, but I'll begin at the beginning.

As Raymond has said, 'there's a great deal of confusion about reincarnation in your world and in ours.' Not everyone in our world believes in reincarnation either - this may sound extremely strange to you but it's true. You may know of some Mediums who link with helpers who deny the reality of reincarnation, but why do they deny this great reality ?

Well, first I must emphasise that reincarnation is not a Divine law of life. It is something that is chosen by the individual soul.

On occasions the 'White Brotherhood' and other 'Higher Orders' have asked souls to reincarnate upon the Earth plane for a special journey, but it is rare. There are souls on the Earth at this moment who have been asked to return, to try to lighten the darkness that lives there. The darkness is basically the refusal of the human race to love - and learn the total concept of love.

On the whole, it's true that the majority of souls will reincarnate because it is their choice, but they're not compelled to return by God. This is very important to understand, for you as it is for us here. This is why - or the beginning of why - there is so much confusion over the issue of reincarnation.

Mum, B- has told you of her Spirit helper John. He is her Spirit Teacher and through him she has learned some beginnings in the great laws of life. This is why they have written in this book, because their work together is to share the Divine laws with the whole. John is of a High Order, he is a Teacher and Master and the only one suitable who is truly able to teach the Divine laws of life. I am unable to do this as I've not yet reached that level of qualification. All I can share with you is that which I've learned, as I learn it. So at the moment, I'm able to share with you that reincarnation is not a Divine law of life !

Reincarnation is a choice !

Some people believe that when a soul dies on this Earth that reincarnation is automatic. They believe they will live in this world for maybe 40, 50 or 100 years and then automatically reincarnate back on the

Earth plane. Reincarnation doesn't work like that ! Reincarnation is always a choice. It is one of those choices that souls can make, in an all over quest to evolve their own Spirituality and oneness to God - but there are other roads open to them. It is up to them what they choose.

Some people believe that if they've lost a child, their child automatically comes back into another body. They believe that their child's soul goes back to Heaven, then reincarnates as soon as possible, to be with their family again. Now, this is not true !

A soul cannot reincarnate quickly in your time, after they've lived on the Earth plane. As a general rule, no one after living on the Earth plane, automatically returns at the first opportunity.

Now there are exceptions to this rule, but for a very good reason. For example, it's possible for the soul of an unborn child to reincarnate back to its parents, if it never lived on the Earth. So the child may return to the world again, to its parents, but it does not happen automatically. There does have to be a very strong and specific reason for this to happen of course. It could be that there's some urgent quest that this particular group of souls are engaged in and the newborn soul simply wishes to be involved.

I'll go into Group Souls later on, but souls usually come directly from the Spirit World where they may have spent eons of time. You see, this is why we can be so confused about Earth time - but you are not. You see time in seconds, minutes, hours, days, weeks, months and years, but the way you measure time has no relevance to us whatsoever in our world.

We operate upon a totally different level of time. This is often where the confusion is caused - especially if a Medium links with our world and tries to give times and dates to people on the Earth. It's very difficult for us to give specific times, simply because we operate on a different level to you. I'll try and speak of this on another tape, because I can't get involved with time, on a tape about reincarnation. It's a confusing enough issue as it is !

So if we accept that reincarnation is ultimately the choice of the person wishing to return, they can also be advised by the Guardian Souls who work with them. Now we all have Guardian Souls, all of us and it is through the advice of these Guardian Souls - combined with their own knowledge - whether people choose to reincarnate upon Earth or not.

There are other ways to evolve your Spirituality, aside from coming back to the Earth, lifetime after lifetime. Although since God gave them free will, many souls do choose to Reincarnate on the Earth. Some choose to do it for the wrong reasons, so then you get the unhappy situation with *souls reincarnating time and time again, yet learning very little from each lifetime. This causes problems, because in this way, so many people learn nothing of their own Spirituality.*

So if there are so many old souls on the Earth, why is it in such a bad state ? Well, if so many returning souls do not learn a great deal by the experience, they tend to make the same mistakes as they made before. They do not evolve their own Spirituality. It is sad, but it is true.

There are souls that come forward to reincarnate on your Earth, for the very first time. They want the experience of Life upon this unique and wondrous planet.

All life forms continually evolve, nothing stands still - it cant ! Life cannot stand still and retain the rhythm of its own life force. So all of us, everyone of us and everything that lives upon the Earth, is evolving its own Spirituality. This may be seem controversial and hard to conceive from one viewpoint - and all those on the Earth have only one viewpoint at this moment in time.

Yet the truth is, <u>they are Earthed</u> by their own physical bodies. Earthed by the demands that life makes upon them and they are Earthed by their commitments. As yet, so many people have no link to the Divine laws of Life. The whole concept can be very hard to grasp.

On the Earth plane you have a mixture of souls at different levels of growth and at different levels of evolvement. They all have their own Spirituality. You have souls that are new to the problems and demands of living on the Earth and souls that have done it all before, yet learned little from their experiences. Thank God you do have old souls that return by choice ! Some return to light the way for others to see, some return to help or encourage others to get back in touch with their own Spirituality. This is why we have such a chaotic state upon the Earth at this time.

The Traditional View

It does not help when religious organisations choose to ignore a belief or understanding of thought, because it doesn't fit in with the narrow view they teach. I am sorry to have to say this, but once again I must point out that religion is man-made.

I am not getting at any particular denomination, but sadly all religions are man-made ! At best, they are simply men and women in search of the truth, but they can be wrong and they can be misguided. Sadly, there are people that work from our world who can be wrong and misguided too. They can

*give misguided and wrong information to people on the Earth plane. It is the same with us, so be careful. Be careful who you listen to.
Listen to the philosophy they teach and only if they teach a philosophy of a purely positive nature, can they really worth listening to.*

All Spiritual leaders upon the Earth plane who teach a negative concept or a negative philosophy, are not aligned with God. Only positivity can come from God. God is the ultimate and God is the great creative power in the Universe. All creativity comes from God. It can only come from that one Source, it cannot come from any other. If a thing is creative and enriching and wondrous, then it comes from God. Anything negative and derisive, which in any way belittles anyone, does not come from God. Of course negativity exists, but God is the ultimate power and he allows negativity to exist to give us the ability to choose.

There are many who create negative concepts and sadly, there are many in our world who create them in yours, but again, anything that is not of the positive, cannot be of God.

I think it's good to realise there are seven levels in our world. Your world has one level, then we have the ninth. This is where, when a soul is ready and has evolved their own Spirituality enough, they can go and be at one with God.

In your Universe you find things called 'black holes' through which it is believed you can enter into another Universe. Well reaching the Godhead is not unlike moving through some kind of 'white hole' - one of pure love and light. Once a soul travels to the Godhead and they unite with that Source or God, they cannot come back to work at this or any other level.

Now there are few souls on the ninth level, who are sufficiently evolved to go back and link with the One God. The teacher, healer and wondrous mystic known as Jesus, is on the ninth level and he is able to form a Oneness with God. He chooses not to join the Source or God, because he knows he would not be able to return. Instead, he stays on the eighth level in our world and chooses to work as the leader of the 'White Brotherhood' - so this is Jesus.

Those souls who exist on the levels below Jesus and the 'White Brotherhood' can communicate with people on the Earth plane. They are wise souls and they are old souls, but they are not necessarily Masters. It is only a Master who can teach the true concept of reincarnation.

I am simply an apprentice, I'm not a Master, but John is. Now B- has been his pupil, so that through him we can have the knowledge that we have. John has never spoken much to B- about reincarnation, but he has taught me a little of the concept. So this is what I share with you now - with the permission of John and the Brotherhood.

There are souls who live on levels lower than the Brotherhood who deny all knowledge of reincarnation. They don't lie, they simply don't have knowledge of it, for it isn't a path that they have chosen to walk. There are many in our world, as in yours, who unless they have experienced it for themselves, give no thought to the concept of reincarnation, so for them it has no reality !

This is why there is a great deal of confusion about reincarnation in the Spiritualist movement – and many other movements. Many do not give it a place in their 'Philosophy of Life' because it's beyond their concept of understanding, but this does not mean it isn't a reality.

When Jesus walked the Earth plane two thousand years ago, the concept of reincarnation was understood and accepted by many people. During his lifetime, these people asked him whether or not he was the reincarnation of many of the Prophets, which is actually recorded in your New Testament. This just proves that reincarnation is a belief that is as old as time itself and when something has been believed for that long, there is usually a grain of Truth or several grains of Truth, in it.

Many orthodox beliefs - without being too specific, for we can get into confrontations which solve nothing and people just go round and round achieving very little understanding - many of them denied the concept of reincarnation, because it did not fit in with the philosophy they were teaching. They couldn't fit reincarnation into their interpretation of the teachings of Jesus, so it was banned ! They outlawed it saying that it didn't exist, since Jesus, who they call God, came to Earth to teach us something different.

Sadly, not all the teachings of this Great Master have been found. Many were not recorded and those that have been found have sometimes been genuinely misunderstood. Unfortunately a lot of them have been knowingly misinterpreted, to fit in with the way of life people wanted, even those people who spread the original doctrines. This was not always for a Spiritual reason either, since these Truths were sometimes interpreted in a way that safeguarded their interpreters ! These were the same people who built an empire on their version of the philosophy that Jesus taught, and that is such a great shame.

Far too much emphasis is put on _who_ Jesus was, rather than _what_ he was. Instead, more emphasis should have been put on his message. Sadly, this has been watered down, misinterpreted and edited so many times, that *what is left is only a pale reflection of his original message. This was such a wondrous Truth - he didn't just teach it, he lived it.*

The tragedy here is, that Western civilisation has lost the reality of reincarnation or the concept of its philosophy. This has just made the Truth even more unclear and the reason for living and the philosophy of life. We cannot leave out the bits that don't fit ! A philosophy or a religion cannot be made from those pieces of Truth that fit a concept or belief. Orthodox religion has done this and most of it has happened in the Western world.

It is the orthodoxy of the Western world which has vehemently denied reincarnation. The Eastern philosophies have retained their philosophy of reincarnation has been retained and that is to their credit. Although they have only retained particles of the Truth, they haven't kept the whole philosophy, which is vast.

I cannot tell you the whole concept of reincarnation in one sitting, It would take a greater Master than myself to do this. Reincarnation is a concept that is better understood from our world than yours. If you embark on a quest for knowledge of reincarnation, you would first have to ask yourself why you are doing it. Why would you want to know if you had lived before and what possible relevance would it have to your life today ?

Remembering Past Lives

This leads me onto something else which is very important - the reason why you don't remember your past lives.

Before you return to the Earth plane to incarnate into an Earth body, you go into a chamber where all past life memories are removed. The reason for this is straightforward. For life on the Earth is hard enough for the majority of people, without having all of the knowledge from many earlier lifetimes. People forget, that with each lifetime lived upon the Earth, you also have the trauma that goes with them. So if you were to retain all the memories of those earlier births, lives and deaths, how would you cope with the life you are living now ? The life you are currently living is the important one, not those you have lived before. You have incarnated on the Earth in this lifetime to specifically evolve your own Spirituality. It is what you do with this life that's the important issue - not what you did 50, 100, 200 or 1,000 years before.

Now, if you do feel moved to learn more about previous lifetimes, that is your choice. There must obviously be a reason you wish to do this, but you need to realise that you will learn things about previous lifetimes, that you will not like. Not all the memories you have, of all the lives you have gone through, are going to be pleasant ones. They could even be quite horrendous ! You have to decide whether you want the responsibility of that memory in your current life or not.

You have to ask, what good is it going to do and are you going to learn anything ? Are you going to use that legacy of Spirit in a positive way in this lifetime ? If you are, then its worth recalling and if not, then don't bother. For it will be a waste of time and time is precious and fleeting. Time is not for wasting.

So before everyone goes crazy over the idea of reincarnation, just think why. Why do you want to remember past lives ? What do you hope to do with it in the future, with this memory returned to you ? Will it enrich you or will it revile you ? Because ultimately one day, you <u>will</u> know how many past lives you've had and what you did with them. You will also learn the relevance of your past lives in relation to your current life. You'll discover it all when you return home to our world. You call it death, we call it coming home.

So if you want to explore it's up to you, it's your choice. You were born with free will, which is the first Divine law of life. Although you don't have to believe in reincarnation to be enlightened, because as you become more enlightened, reincarnation becomes less important.

If you have lived many lifetimes upon the Earth, then why do you keep coming back ? What lessons are there to learn here that you haven't already learnt ? Is it a good thing to keep coming back to the Earth ? Don't you think perhaps it is time you moved on from endless repeated lifetimes ? This doesn't mean you should opt out of life, because that is like opting out of your soul quest, if you like. If you did that, when you come over here, you may find that you'd probably have start that particular learning experience again. It is easy to give up in your world when you are in it, especially if you have no concept of all that is beyond. So keep going with your life on Earth - press on, because believe me, there's far more to come.

One myth that people have about reincarnation is that people who have lived a life together in years gone by, should automatically be involved again somehow. This is not necessarily true. Although if the interaction between the two souls was a very positive one in a previous incarnation, there could be a great deal of merit in those two souls finding one another again.

However, if the interaction between the two was negative from lifetime to lifetime, then there would be no point in them linking together, in this *lifetime. You might just be continuing on in an eternal battle between yourselves and that's not good - unless it achieves something positive or unless, one or both souls have evolved to the extent that they can eventually reduce the negative interaction between themselves.*

So simply because you knew someone as your husband or wife, two or three hundred years ago in another lifetime, does not mean they are right to be your husband or wife again, this time around.

Soul Groups and Soul Mates

Many people believe that certain souls return in groups, time after time. This is possible in some circumstances. In fact it's happening now with this book, because every person that's written in this book, is a member of a soul group or unit, who have returned to the Earth by choice to perform some work in aiding the philosophy and understanding of mankind.

While Soul Groups are a reality, there are also Spiritual families - which are quite different to our Earth families. If a group of souls spend a great deal of time together both in your world and in ours, it is possible for them to almost evolve together, to become a Spiritual family. Each member of a Spiritual family are linked, purely because their souls literally vibrate at a similar communicative level. However these are quite different to a regrouping of souls or Soul Group. Spiritual families are one thing and Soul Groups are another, this is one of the Divine laws of life.

However, it is possible for Soul Groups, over eons of time, to grow into Spiritual families, which are the highest form of Spiritual Life. They are in perfect harmony with one another and this is something you don't get with Soul Groups. Previous life experiences can dictate whom you choose as your mother, father, brother or sister, but evolved souls don't usually regroup in a family environment. An evolved soul will usually choose an Earthly family at a lower level of evolvement than their own, not always, but most of the time. An evolved soul is there to teach.

There are occasions, if there is special work to be done on the Earth, that evolved souls can choose to be born to other evolved souls, but it isn't often that you find many evolved souls in one family. Spiritual evolvement can also be handed on from generation to generation - for instance an evolved soul can choose to be born to a Spiritually evolved parent. So it may go on through the generations, although there is usually only one Spiritually evolved child in a family.

Spiritually evolved people do not always have Spiritually evolved

*children, but then a child can chose a Spiritually evolved parent, though the two rarely go together. Each help to evolve their own Spirituality - which can cause problems, but this is why the choices are made.
So just because someone was your mother in a previous life, doesn't necessarily mean you chose that person for your mother now. The same goes for fathers, brothers and sisters and all your Earthly family. Not all previous Earth life experiences are linked, but what does happen is that Spiritually evolved people are usually drawn together in some way or other. If you are meant to find your Spiritual family on this Earth, then you will find them or they will find you. Like attracts like - it's Divine law !*

    It can happen that two people can meet as strangers on the Earth and have a deep recognition and bond for one another, which goes soul deep. You may call this 'love at first sight' and it can bring feelings or emotions back from past lives experienced together - and not necessarily from a connection developed in our world. So recognition sometimes has its roots in reincarnation, but doesn't necessarily always have to. People can have friends and companions in our world, who haven't necessarily shared previous lives together.

    *Our beloved Medium has had such an experience with another person. They seemed to have met completely by chance, although of course there is no such thing as chance. We are very good at arranging meetings and creating coincidences !
When they met, something very deep and profound happened to them both - but this is her story not mine. She has felt this reality and I'm sure others have felt it too. So these experiences do have a basis in something real and sometimes they can be quite profound. They are a part of the philosophy of life, not just the heart ! That deep recognition on a soul level does happen.*

    People can meet under these circumstances for a specific purpose, which is what happened to our Medium. Although the reason is not yet clear to her, it will unfold in time. There is purpose behind these 'chance' meetings, so any of you reading this, who encounter or share this knowledge, must know that it is not imagination, it's real !

Russell and Gwen in Egypt

    *It would probably be disappointing for you Mother, if I didn't mention at least one life experience that you and I have shared together and although this tape is initially for you, I hope you can share it with others.
As readers will know, my mother is Gwen Byrne and we <u>have</u> shared more than one life experience together. I will not go into the reasons why, but I*

will say that it's a quest that we embarked upon, together. I will begin by going back to a lifetime we shared in Egypt.

There is a great deal of confusion about the timescales in Egyptian history. Many people believe that it had three stages. Well I say there were four, because the Egyptian culture and history was built upon a much older civilisation than the Egyptians you know. There have been many evolved civilisations throughout time and various disasters have befallen them all, so their knowledge or enlightenment has been hidden or lost ! Usually after such catastrophe, a very dark time follows when there is no light upon the Earth and only pure survival exists. When life is as basic as that, it is almost impossible to obtain any soul growth on the Earth plane.

In her Egyptian lifetime, my mother was a direct descendent of the civilisation that founded the Ancient Egyptian way of life. These were the people who built the Sphinx, long before the Ancient Egyptians. You see, the Sphinx is much older than is generally accepted and it contains information in the vaults beneath it, about the philosophy of life - secrets which have yet to be discovered. This information will be found, but it's for the future. It has direct relevance to your civilisation with many poignant messages for the Earth and society as it is today.

At that time, my mother had the looks and the abilities of these ancient people and a lot of knowledge, although my mother was Earthed in the ways of the world ! Today, my mother actually looks very similar to the way she looked then and it is no accident this is so. However, she was much taller then, since the women of that ancient civilisation were all 5'9" and 5'10" in height and the men were over 6'6", so I suppose you could say they were almost a race of giants !

They were a very Spiritually enlightened people, who loved and cherished the arts. Amongst them were the most wonderful writers, painters and singers and the most wonderful poets and musicians and it was from this line that my mother sprung !

During that lifetime, my mother came from a very ancient family line and one of the most prestigious things they could do, was produce a daughter capable of entering the 'Temple of Isis' to become a 'High Priestess.'

Not much has been written about these beliefs and philosophy, since so much has been lost through antiquity, although one day we hope to redress that balance, but that is for another time.

As a young girl in that lifetime, my mother was presented to live within the confines of the Temple by her family. Incidentally, my mother's mother at that time, was Rachael Hunt-High, her close friend in this lifetime.

The Temples were wondrously furnished with gold, silver and jewels. The young Priestesses all had to undergo rigorous training, with just one prerequisite, which was celibacy and because my mother was then a direct descendent of that ancient civilisation, she was gifted as a natural psychic.

In her lifetime today, my mother finds it very hard to believe that she was born with any psychic gift, but in this life as in the earlier one, she is Clairaudient, Clairsentient and Clairvoyant.

Then, she had been brought up with the heritage of her people and had learned a great knowledge of herbs and healing. She also had a beautiful singing voice, was a wonderful dancer and became quite a mystical lady. My mother has retained some of these gifts today, especially the love of singing. The chief characteristic of my mother's physical body at that time, were her navy blue eyes. My mother has the same navy blue eyes today. Most Egyptian's have dark brown eyes, but back then my mother's blue eyes marked her as a direct descendent of that founding civilisation.

These people were naturally gifted in the ways of the Spirit and had a knowledge of philosophy, but they assumed incorrectly that their genetic legacy brought a Spiritual legacy along with it. Well it didn't ! Everyone has to make their own journey to enlightenment, this was true then and it is true now. That quest continues throughout many lifetimes - if you choose reincarnation as your way.

My Birth

In that lifetime my mother pursued a celibate life and was channelling all her energies towards enlightenment. She was allowed to sing and dance with her sisters, though these were not her genetic sisters, they were more of a 'sisterhood' within the Isis Temple. My mother was very beautiful then, as she is now !

She and her 'sisters' used something called Kundalini energy, which was very strong in my mother. The whole of the Isis sisterhood were already becoming something of a myth rather than a truth, because of this.

My mother lived a wondrous life in the Temple, where she sang, danced and communicated directly to our world, through her psychic abilities. She also produced some stunning predictions of what was going to happen in the future of that land. This made her powerful within the community <u>and</u> with the rulers of the time.

Now I will say, that in those days, when wearing her ceremonial robes, my mother was a sight to behold. Dressed all in crystal and with the Temple lights and torches arranged so, that when she came in wearing her robes, she looked almost translucent. She was like a crystal lady or a lady of light and had undertook extensive training to achieve this status.

One of the rulers at the time became extremely fond of my mother and he fell under her spell. He did not love her as she was supposed to be loved as a Priestess, but as a woman. They became lovers and then I was conceived from that union - so once again I became my mother's son.

At the time, my mother was not yet a High Priestess, for she was still undergoing her training. Yet the the ruler who became my father, loved her deeply - both as a woman and a Priestess and because he had considerable influence, wealth and power, he managed to keep my birth a secret. I was born in the vaults of the Temple, which was situated near the Sphinx. My mother gave birth to me in this vault, then I was smuggled away. I was taken out into the city where my father at the time, knew a woman who could adopt me.
He was a very powerful man and the only person more powerful than him was the High Priestess herself. Now my mother was only an apprentice Priestess at the time, but together they soon became very powerful people.

This man knew the woman who he wanted to adopt and bring me up as her own, because she was in fact, his wife. Now this lady was Rita from <u>this</u> lifetime, the Medium who helped my parents find me again during the séances. Back then, she already had two daughters and one of them was B-, the Medium from <u>this</u> lifetime. Back then, B- was about six years old when I was first brought into the house as a little baby. At first, the man's wife resented me, but she grew to love me for she'd never had a son. At first, she took very little interest in me, so it was her young daughter who did all the nurturing.

However, once I'd reached a few years old my new adoptive mother began to love me as a son. Of course, because I was really <u>your</u> son, you could never let me go. So this powerful Egyptian ruler would smuggle you out of the Temple at night, so you could hold me in your arms. My little step-sister who cared for me, knew the truth about you Mother, so the Ruler, who was also her father, would sometimes take her along whenever we met. This went on and on for years.

While you were an apprentice Priestess within the Temple, you weren't able to acknowledge me. It was absolutely forbidden for the sisters to have carnal knowledge, let alone have a child. You would have been killed for it. However, my birth did not diminish your psychic powers and you arose to great ranks.

You eventually became the High Priestess of Isis, whilst all the time I was growing up outside of the Temple. Within the city walls we had our secret meetings, when you would walk with me along the Nile. You would teach me some of the secret Temple teachings, even though it was considered wrong for a male to know any of this. You taught me, then I shared this knowledge with my little step-sister, who showed great interest and natural ability.

Sometimes she would come along to our meetings and act as our lookout, to warn us if anyone was approaching. We did have a couple of narrow escapes, but we managed to hide in time.

Misuse of Power

Yet again the new was taking over from the old, as during this period of history, the Egyptian Dynasties were being formed.

In that lifetime Mother, within your family line were the remnants of an older civilisation, which had fallen. It had dispersed and disbanded a great deal of its power. Many secrets were lost, but you had the genetic link from that ancient culture, so you had a lot of knowledge within you. You had also learned a lot from your own Mother at the time and she was seen as a wise woman herself.

We are really going back to very ancient times here ! It is fair to say that back then, both woman and men had power but in different ways. They used Kundalini energy, which is very powerful and at its highest level, is unsurpassed as a way to link the two worlds and reach true Oneness. It is a God given gift, but when misused it is devastating and totally chaotic and negative.

That ancient civilisation which spawned the Egyptian Dynasties, understood Kundalini energy and the 'Oneness' that can be achieved through it. Therefore a man and a woman could reign as one at that time, <u>because</u> they had that true understanding. This was not only a physical oneness, but also Spiritual and mental oneness. Unfortunately, that ancient culture also abused and misused this power, which greatly contributed to its downfall. This power burned strongly within all the people at this time, including you Mother. Then you then passed it down the family line to me !

This ancient culture gave the newer Egyptian civilisation much, but things got lost and misinterpreted along the way. Even back then, there were souls upon the Earth using the Divine to gain Earthly power over the living. It was not long before you my dear Mother and the man who became my father, also became caught up in this power struggle and you were officially on opposite sides. Although love that you had for each *other would not die or give way, even under those circumstances and with his help, you still kept in close contact with me.*

My Death

When I was fourteen years old, a great famine came, but as the High Priestess, you hadn't foreseen this disaster Mother. So many believed this was because the whole culture of the Isis Temple was corrupt. You even believed that it was a kind of punishment and retribution, for loving a man and having his child.

The famine was brought on by freak weather conditions, so was simply an act of God. It was a climatic problem, which you had no control over, but you hadn't foreseen it. You misunderstood, because you were so tied up with Earthly things, when you should have been focused on more Spiritual ones. The famine was used as a tool to gain supremacy and power over many people and was used to undermine that civilisation's power. Things haven't changed much, because this kind of thing is still happening today !

Many people perished in this famine, but blamed the High Priestess and her sisters, for not helping the people be ready for it. That was you Mother.

As a direct descendent of the ancient civilisation, your characteristic navy blue eyes were passed on to me, at that time. This was noticed by many in the city, which caused much rumour and speculation. Nothing could be proved, but I was used as an excuse to plot your downfall. This made both my father and adoptive mother very frightened. My adoptive mother had grown to love me greatly and she became very frightened for my welfare, just as you were in the Temple.

My father had a plan to keep me safe, but my adoptive mother took matters into her own hands and smuggled me out of the city with her daughters. She took us to a very parched and deserted area, which was probably very safe, but not very good. We didn't have proper food, in fact we went very short of food and we began to starve.

I always had fragile health at that time and so the journey, travelling and lack of food took its toll. We were found by guards, of those who were trying to take over the Temple and we were brought back to the city in chains. Because I had the navy blue eyes and my adoptive mother and her daughters didn't, they were allowed to go free. However, they followed me back to the city. They didn't need to, but they did.

My adopted mother grew to hate you at that time, because you were my birth mother and I loved you. You had great power over my father, who was her husband and she resented this bitterly. She was also jealous of who you were and your power as High Priestess. She tried to protect me and so did my father, but I was kept in prison, incarcerated for some time. My step-sister chose to stay and look after me. In fact, she chose prison to be with me, but she didn't have to. She tried to smuggle in food for me, but it was not enough. My health failed and I starved to death in prison.

My step-sister looked for you at the Temple, where she told you and the people what had happened. Then without mercy, you turned your fury towards the city and you ordered an end to the growing disorder there. This grew into a conflict which accidentally caused the death of the Ruler, who was your lover, my father and my adopted mother's husband and she hated you for that. Strangely, my step-sister sought sanctuary with you. She had already put her life in danger because she had tried to protect me and she took refuge in the Temple, where you eventually nurtured her own interest in the Isis sisterhood.

The sisterhood continued and you were a very old lady when you died. My step-sister saw you Clairvoyantly when you passed away, as you met me in the Spirit World. She eventually took over as High Priestess and became the first who wasn't descended from the old civilisation.

Summing Up

This is what happened to us Mother, in just one lifetime. A lifetime in which you blamed yourself for my passing. You made judgement errors along the way and, combined with the strong Kundalini energy within you at the time, you created quite a stir amongst that civilisation. You were a powerful lady who, when dressed in your full crystal robes, were meant to represent the Goddess of Isis herself - whom you were believed to have a direct Spiritual link with.

This is why the 'Lady of the Light' walks with you still and one day, probably in the not too distant future, you may learn even more about this Egyptian life that we shared. As time and our work together progresses as I may be able to tell you more myself. That particular life was a very eventful one and sadly, there was much carnage and mayhem. Though not always, but they were very troubled times, with a great deal of change going on. There is always trouble and violence when an old civilisation spawns a new one. Power corrupts and there was a lot of turbulence, fighting and bloodshed as part of that story. Although there was much beauty and love and much tenderness too.

It would take six or seven tapes for me to tell you the whole story, but it isn't appropriate to include here in this book. I know you've always had a fascination for knowledge about your Egyptian life, so it's nice that you should know something of it. The only problem with this reincarnation story, is that I cannot prove any of it to you. I can't take you anywhere that will prove our existence there, but I may be able to in the future, although the time is not yet right, yet.

During that lifetime you were called 'Zara' and I was 'Ray-nier' - but these are just names and I can't prove any of it. I will leave it up to you dear Mother, to believe me or not - or whether it rings any 'bells' within your soul. It is no accident that you are linked together now with those from before. You were brought together to perform specific tasks on the Earth and to work together. It's no accident that the people working on this book, are linked with you.

There is a growing desire within the human race to discover the Truth about reincarnation. Some choose to regress under hypnosis and that is entirely their choice, but I will give a word of warning, since the mind is the most powerful of all Gods creations. No one on Earth truly understands how the mind functions so be very careful, because the mind can be influenced under hypnosis. It can be very dangerous to give your power to anyone in this way, which is exactly what happens under hypnosis. There are perfectly legitimate hypnotists, fraudulent hypnotists and others those who are not properly trained, so think carefully !

I don't believe the majority of hypnotists know what they are dealing with in the human mind. Even inadvertently and through ignorance, doors can be opened and thoughts can be channelled. So it's very important to think very carefully before you give over your power to another. It would also be very wise to have somebody with you, for any regression. It's important to have a third party present - for the sake of the person doing the regression and for one being regressed.

Yet you all have the power within you to press the key within your mind, to release those previous life experiences to you. It may be better to learn this, rather than rely on another person. Although all of this would only have relevance if something positive could be obtained from a past life and then used for a positive effect in <u>this</u> one.

Now this has been a very long tape, so I will conclude it now. I hope I've helped to clear up some confusion regarding reincarnation, which was my own choice of subject. I hope it has helped many of you.

*So thank you Mum for all the work you do for us. I hope this tape hasn't confused you totally and that it has helped or enlightened you !
Goodnight Mum and goodnight Dad. God Bless.'*

Gwen: At this point I thought this tape had ended, but to my surprise there was some more !

John: *'Almighty, everlasting and loving God. We ask for protection on our journey and our quest for knowledge...*

My beloved Gwen, this is John who is B-'s teacher and who has watched and worked with her all her life. I lived upon the Earth two and a half thousand years ago as a Jew and was a common working man and scribe. My name was John then, as it is now. I am a member of the 'White Brotherhood' and a teacher and healer.

My dear, I must congratulate you on the wonders you have achieved so far ! You may not be aware, but I have been in your life since you were a child, when you were born into such troubled times on the Earth. I have always been there. I accompanied you on your Spiritual quest to Caldey Island. I watched over you when your son was so very ill and dying. I heard you speak at the feet of your 'Spiritual guru' when you asked why this appalling tragedy should happen to your family.

I walked with you through your times of darkness, I searched with you through your pain and I have guided you to the greatest and the best, who have given you proof of human survival.

You were a quiet and withdrawn child, who tried to make sense of a reality you knew was not true. You chose your beloved Mother and Father, who were not on the same Spiritual level as yourself, but they 'earthed' you sufficiently to do the work you are doing now. It is a great blessing you were not brought up with any orthodox religious indoctrination ! This gave you a completely free mind to walk uncluttered and find the Truth.

You were married early in life to Arthur Alfred Byrne, which was no accident. He chose to walk with you through life as a Guardian Soul. He has helped to keep you safe from the rigours and realities of every day life, so you could embark on your Spiritual Quest. You have had a long and happy marriage.

You have re-learned so much in this lifetime, of that which you already knew. You were not born with any psychic or Spiritual abilities, so it was your quest in life to rediscover them. You could not have written of your journey, in the book 'Russell', if you already had any Spiritual knowledge.

You needed to go out and find your own Truth, which is exactly what you did. You chose to do so in this lifetime, to show others the way.

Your son passed with cancer at nine and three quarter years, because that was how he agreed to pass upon the Earth plane. You agreed to be his mother the same as Alfie agreed to be his father. Everything was interconnected and planned before you came. It was important for you to share your journey, for this knowledge was important and you had to start with nothing at all to find everything. Throughout your life you could have abandoned your quest and that was your choice, but you did not.

You were born with the gift of a wondrous singing voice, which you have nurtured and that gift will remain with you, to enrich and to heal the souls of others. Greater depth has been given to your gift because of all you have gone through, therefore the interpretation of the songs is greater than it otherwise would have been.

You have three sons in your world, two on the Earth and one with us and throughout the years, you have followed the progression of the two who remained with you on the Earth. One has chosen the academic life, which gives you great pleasure and honour in his achievements. The other has created a sound business that is run honestly and true and he has given you great pleasure in his endeavours. They have also produced and given you beautiful grandchildren and now a great-grandchild.

They have done much, but you did much for them. You reared them and brought them up in the world. However, you know little of the progress of your middle son Russell.

What you did not know, was that Russell embarked upon a training and a learning programme here with us. He told you of his passing in the ending of your first book, then he came home to us. Shortly afterwards I met Russell again, in my world. This was not our first meeting. I met him again and he was without doubt, one of the liveliest little souls I have ever encountered. Keeping Russell still and keeping him quiet was indeed a hard task, but Russell wanted to learn. He had a great feeling for knowledge and the philosophy of life.

It was not long afterwards that I realised he was quite an entertainer ! He takes after you and your line, as he is a born showman. Now to have a showman amongst us is a different way of working. This boy, with his natural talents and abilities was very well equipped to take our message forward. Now we look to the next century, for you have the means of mass communication, which is a wonderful way to get our message to the masses and very quickly.

In Russell, the Brotherhood now had a natural entertainer among its ranks and he wanted to learn more - this was his choice. So he became what you would call an 'apprentice' to the White Brotherhood and he was able to produce rare physical phenomena. This was wondrous but it had to end, because it was not leading where it should. Physical phenomena can lose its depth and relevance, for it has to take place within the knowledge and concept of the Philosophy of Life, before it has any meaning of a lasting nature. This may be controversial, but it is true. Physical phenomena in itself is pointless without the philosophy combined with it.

The best way to learn the Philosophy of Life is to work with a Spiritual channel and have that work transmitted to the written word. It is then available for people to return to, time and again, so they may decide for themselves. The closer the soul link between channel and communicating Spirit, the more clearly the concept is transmitted.

Your son Russell chose the role of teacher as well as healer, for his apprenticeship with us. He works with souls on the Earth and with those who have passed, to help heal them after their passing. Russell specialises in helping other children and wherever there has been any great disaster on the Earth involving children, Russell is there. He has gone forward in his chosen work and achieved much to join us.

To qualify as a teacher, Russell recently needed to work with a Medium on the Earth. He chose to speak on the healing power of music and since he is very theatrical, this was a very good choice - for the healing power of music is not truly understood on the Earth. We hope his information will enlighten people about the music they hear. Then he chose to speak about how the physical phenomena was produced and how it fits into the Philosophy of Life. His final choice was his own and typical of Russell. He chose one of the most difficult aspects of philosophy - reincarnation.

We are pleased with Russell's channelling work and through it, with help from you and B-, he has earned his seat around our table in the Halls of the White Brotherhood. Now he is able to meet and speak with the Masters and work with the Masters.

He wears a robe of blue and for important occasions he wears yellow - and the more he learns, the more golden it becomes. The more Spiritual knowledge he obtains, his robe will become white and edged with gold. So you have witnessed and taken part in the rare apprenticeship of a Master. I thought it would be good to share with you, Russell's moment of triumph in our world. We also acknowledge your work, dear Gwen and many,

many great souls who sit in the Halls of the White Brotherhood.

Your husband Alfie has a member of the White Brotherhood who walks with him, named 'White Eagle.' Remember that Alfie is 'Earthed' because to be your Guardian Soul, he has to be. His greatest attribute is that he is an honest man, a rare thing indeed ! He has born witness to the Truth you have both seen and he will continue to do so. Yet there is still much to do !

Also my Medium B- is someone who has grown very dear to us all in the Brotherhood and we feel that the work she and Russell have done together is good. We have learned much from them and continue to learn. We have enriched each other and they have our protection always - and when you work, my dear Gwen, the Angels themselves come down to protect and walk with you and if ever you falter, we will carry you.

God wants only the best for you. God wants you to be happy. Each of you who walks upon the Earth plane are on your own journey of Spirituality. That is why you are there. You are each a Divine manifestation of God. The only time that you become less than that, is when you <u>allow</u> yourself to become less than that. Only when you use and endorse negativity and treat others in a negative way, do you become less than you were created to be. You are the power of your lives.

Remember the first Divine law of life - God gave you free will. You have the right and the will to choose between negativity and positivity and the only person that can make you a lesser person than God created - is you. This is very important to understand. Do not simply blame Karma or your past lives. There is no Ancient Karmic Power that has control over your life. You must look to yourselves and your own Spirituality. That is the reason for the journey.

The most important thing to learn, is how to Love. This work of yours Gwen - and of Russell's and all the other children and their Mothers - is designed simply to teach all of you how to Love. The love of a parent is unselfish and unconditional. The highest form of Love that can be found anywhere, is the power that binds you, that guides you and guards you all.

I am greatly blessed to be able to share this with you. My good wishes to you, your family to all the mothers who have contributed to this book and all parents who grieve. We understand your pain and we work constantly in the White Brotherhood, to try to help you realise that ultimately, there is no death and each one of you will be reunited with your children.

God's Blessing to you all. Good Night.

May the blessings of the Great Spirit go forward and may the healing energies be interwoven with the Souls and minds of all who listen and all who may read these words.'

Gwen: Well now I'm speechless ! What can be said after that ?

It's now the early hours of the morning and this double ninety-minute recording has taken me forty hours to put onto paper. This may seem a long time to those of you who can type miraculously fast, but for me it is a true labour of Love. So whilst trying to shake my right hand back into life, since now it's almost seized up on me ! I'm thinking so deeply on these amazing revelations.

As I finally rest my pen, I can hear Russell singing to me,

> *'See the Pyramids along the Nile,*
> *Watch the sunrise on a tropic Isle,*
> *Just remember darling all the while,*
> *You belong to me...'*

Okay Russell, I get your drift !

Thank you and goodnight my lovely son. x

Twenty Seven
A Chapter of Mysteries to Solve !

*When you realise life is magical,
only then can you practice magic'*

~ The Seven Arrows

Whilst writing this book, I've experienced many surprises. Some of these have created puzzles for me to solve, requiring so much research. Although in the beginning, I had no idea what I was letting myself in for, I was led to dozens of books in different libraries and made hours and hours of notes !

Who is John ?

My first mystery, was who is the Spirit who identifies himself as John ? I knew he was B-'s Spiritual teacher who she's known all her life, but I was only introduced to him during the creation of the channelled tapes. Yet he seemed to know me and I wondered why I felt that I didn't know him, on *any* level. Well I didn't have to wonder long, because he introduced himself to me in the most beautiful way !

When I had the opportunity to ask, first of all he said, *'but I have spoken to you and you have heard me. Think my child.'*

So I did think about it and then I realised. Of course ! His was the voice I'd heard in the kitchen at Grail Haven, on the morning we took Alfie to the Hospital. I'd stood there looking out of the window and heard a strong male voice say, *'out of weakness, she was made strong.'*

At the time I knew nothing of John and I hadn't even met B- then. When we did meet in 1991/92, she never mentioned him, but why should she ?

However, during one difficult time at home in 1993, my mind was doing somersaults and I got up in the night because I couldn't sleep. I was just heading back to bed when I heard the same deep, gentle tones as before, *'in my Fathers house are many Mansions, if it were not true I would have told you.'*

This stopped me dead in my tracks and I hoped he would say something more, but he didn't. So in the middle of the night I went looking for my Bible and found this quote was from John 14:2. As I sat in my lounge reading, a feeling of peace came over me that was indescribable. No wonder then, that when I returned to bed and my head hit the pillow, I went straight back to sleep ! Yet more was to come...

The next time I heard from 'John' was at home and in relaxed frame of mind, simply knitting. Suddenly I had the strongest feeling of his presence and it was such an amazing feeling ! I could sense exactly where he was in the room and as I turned my head in that direction, I wouldn't have been surprised to actually have seen him standing there !

The feeling from him was so powerful, it seemed to almost lift me out of my armchair. My brain seemed to have been switched from its Earthly groove into a Spiritual groove ! I lost track of time, but had no idea how long this feeling lasted. I realised then that somehow I did *know* this man. He didn't speak this time, but his presence had been so very strong that my feet didn't touch the ground for the rest of the day !

I felt such a sense of peace now, knowing that somewhere we *had* met before. It was pretty clear to me too that he was from some Higher Realm, where there are much higher and wiser powers.

My next experience of John came during a quite a detailed dream, in January 1994. Although perhaps I should call it a dream *experience* ?

I was with a man who was just like Ron, my brother-in-law the ex-monk. He wore a long robe in the most wonderful purple colour. I felt someone behind me place an identical robe around my own shoulders, then I heard Ron say, *'Gwen, come and meet John.'*

As I looked, I saw an older man coming towards me, but my eyes were almost blinded by the great light around him. His hair was white and quite long and wild and he wore a cape which was almost white, yet silvery grey.

I heard Ron say *'Gwen dreams...'* Then the older man spoke saying, *'dream Gwen - but interpret'* then he just walked away.

Next, my brother-in-law Ron, who I've never heard sing before, began to sing the most wonderful tune. It had about six lines, with each one alternating between a beautiful castrato voice, to that of a man's voice. It's impossible for me to find the words to say how truly beautiful this tune sounded to me. Ron and I then began to walk and we chatted as we'd done many times before and I remember saying to him that I had no money or overnight bag or clothes - only this purple cloak. Then a car appeared and Ron asked the driver to take me to Caldey Island - which is where he'd lived as a Monk.

Suddenly, a loud knock on the door woke me...

This made me quite cross, because it was only the postman delivering a parcel, but in a daze I opened the door and signed for the delivery. It turned out that I'd been sent a tape of a televised interview that Alfie and I had recently done. It was called 'The Science of Eternity' by Summerland Videos and it's free to watch online these days, if you ever want to find it.

However, I was still feeling groggy as I headed for the kitchen to make some tea, but the phone rang before I'd even switched on the kettle. It was my friend Rachael from Grail Haven and she seemed to sense my disorientation, but out of nowhere she just said,
'Gwen you've been with the Masters. Your work is beginning !'
'Huh...they're a bit late !' I said, but Rachael replied, *'the rose that blooms later in the snow, is no less beautiful than the rose that blooms in June.'*

I spent the morning trying to interpret my dream, as I caught up with my ironing and chores. Then I heard Russell singing the Paul McCartney song, *'It's Just Another Day.'*

He was right of course, but I felt so elated thinking of John being in my dream, until Russell sang the Beatles tune, *'Try To See It My Way'* - which made me laugh and I realised he was right !

Eventually I came down to Earth and mentally I thanked John and Russell, then thought they must be friends ! Yet this dream experience had been so beautiful - it was one of those rare times when we *know* we are dreaming, which can bring a joy greater than any experienced before. Perhaps it was because it was so vivid and colourful, but I felt so refreshed from it, like I'd just arrived back from a wonderful holiday !

A Wonderful Sighting

In March 1994 shortly before '*Russell*' was published, I'd been writing letters to bereaved parents, which I often ask Russell to help me with. At around six-thirty next morning, I was awakened by a loud Spirit knock by my bed. When I opened my eyes, I saw the full materialisation of a most beautiful boy with Down's Syndrome. His face was so, so beautiful and I heard the words *'age 16 to 17 years'* then he just faded. I called out, *'please don't go'* and he came back. I was so stunned by his beauty, for he had the palest blue eyes and golden hair and he wore a kind of donkey jacket, zipped half way up.

As I stared at him, I realised who he was, but whether I could convince his father was another matter. I tried to draw the boy, although not very successfully. So I had another go later, then sent my story and the drawings to his father. I heard back from the man, although he didn't seem too impressed. This made me feel sad, for I knew Russell had tried to help the boy by showing him how to materialise.

Finally the father got in touch once more and he sent me some photos of his beautiful son. In one, he was wearing a blue-grey donkey jacket, just like the one I had seen him wear when he materialised in front of me.

The whole thing was a learning experience for me and a very beautiful one. I never knew the boy's name, but I will remember him always. It seems the boy's father had become very disillusioned with Mediums, for he was still waiting for one to give him his son's name. Yet both Russell and I had tried to help, but I don't know if we succeeded.

I'm sure many people would agree with me, that Down's children are very special, perhaps even more evolved souls. So God bless this dear, beautiful boy who I'm sure by now, will have grown to manhood and be doing some very special work in the Spirit World.

A Visit From Hermes ?

I found this next incident really amusing and laughed about it for ages.

March was the month I usually had a cold and sure enough, this year was no different. So I was in bed, sniffing, grumbling and totally surrounded by tissues. I'd put away my books and decided I'd lie down and relax. I was thoroughly fed up with myself as I lay there and began muttering to Spirit, *'oh why can't you cure colds ?'*

A few seconds later, Clairvoyantly I saw a funny little man just walk straight through my bedroom ! He came out of the wall on my left and was bustling along at a terrific pace. He seemed really busy, then he just went out through the wall on the right ! I was literally bowled over and thought, *'why on Earth was that funny little man rushing through my bedroom ?'*

He never looked at me, but in that brief instant I was able to take in his unusual appearance. He wore the strangest winged hat, in red and blue and had a short cape and some sort of leggings. His feet also had a pair of wings attached to them, just like his hat and he carried a golden staff with a kind of twirly bit on top. Now I'd forgotten my cold altogether, but I felt I recognised him from one of my Astrology books. After checking to be sure, I found that this odd little visitor seemed to resemble the Roman God, Mercury ! Now I *was* mystified, but told no one. Indeed, who could I tell ?

Later on I discovered that in Astrology, Mercury is connected with the sign of Gemini and he is the communicator. In Greek mythology he is known as Hermes. Still, I thought, *'whatever was he doing, passing through my bedroom?'*

After this, my friend Frankie Brown had gone to Greece for a holiday. She returned with a little gift for me of a dear little ornamental dish. Depicted on this dish was Hermes himself, yet I hadn't said a word about my odd visitor to Frankie or anyone. I think going further back in time, he was known in ancient Egypt as Thoth, but I had to learn this information for myself. I'd had no knowledge of it before.

I still don't know why he showed himself to me that day and I did keep it quiet. Perhaps it will come to light one day, but for now I just call him, *'the funny little man with wings on his feet!'*

A Mysterious Apport

On April 30th, 1994 just a few weeks before *'Russell'* was published, Alfie and I were at home watching television. We hadn't noticed anything unusual until I looked to my left and spotted something I hadn't seen earlier. *'Alfie'* I said, *'what's that on the sideboard?'*

We looked and found it was an unusual electrical adaptor that we couldn't account for. It was copper coloured and about three inches long. We both stared at it, then picked it up to look more closely. Alfie said he didn't know where it had come from, but then neither of us had set eyes on it before. There had been nobody in the lounge the whole time, except us.

Laying next to it was Alfie's decorative copper plate. This was something he'd brought back from Rhodesia in the 1960s. When we looked at that, we saw that it had somehow become damaged. It look as though someone had suddenly taken a hammer to it and bashed it in from the back. It was now bent upwards and quite out of shape.

Discussing this unusual find, we could only conclude that perhaps because Spirit had apported the adaptor, they needed so much energy that it affected the copper plate, although we hadn't heard or felt a thing.

We sat looking at this bent, solid copper plate in amazement - but I don't really know why, because lots of strange things tend to happen in our home anyway. We should have been a bit miffed because the plate was now bent, but having been to so many séances and witnessed the things that Spirit energy can do, we weren't all that bothered.

I did take the adaptor to different electrical shops, but none of them could clearly identify it. So I ended up just keeping it at home. I placed it back where it came from, next to Alfie's copper dish which remains bent and out of shape to this day !

The Real Christmas ?

In one of the channelled tapes, the Spirit teacher John had said that Jesus was born at midnight on September 20th. This led me to want to know more, so I began to research whatever I could.

Now my interest here may raise some eyebrows, but it was sheer curiosity that sent me on this search and certainly <u>not</u> because I think there may be any connection between Russell and Jesus. It was purely the birthdate that intrigued me. In fact I was amazed how much information there was on this subject *and* the books just 'came' to me, either as gifts or they'd just turn up at a charity shop.

I believe that Love is a sacred mystery and so is the birth of Jesus. I have always been fascinated by his story and now my curiosity wanted to examine other views, so my search was a simple labour of love. I also wanted to find any evidence of B-'s Spirit teacher John, but found it almost impossible, since there are five Johns in the New Testament alone. Perhaps the name 'John' was a favourite in the days of Jesus and maybe just as common then as it is now - anyway what's in a name ?
So although it went against the grain, reluctantly I gave up on the idea of finding John.

I once received a message from Russell regarding my beliefs. He said, *'Mum, don't worry if the Church attacks you. If they don't accept you, let them go. We can smile and dream and exclaim at the wonder of it all !'*
So be it Russell, I thought.

Now one particular author does fascinate me, so I don't understand why anyone would want to give his books away to charity, they are far too wonderful ! Yet I came home with one such book. It was a bargain copy of *'The Story Of Jesus'* by Edgar Cayce. His work is amazing reading and this book is such a treasure to me.

Cayce says that at the birth of Jesus, *'all were in awe at the brightness of his star when it appeared and shone, as the music of the spheres bought forth a joyful choir 'peace on Earth, good will to men of good faith'*
Cayce explains that the vibrations and great light were felt by all, including the shepherds and those at the Inn. Of course, *'those conditions*

were later dispelled by doubters', who said the people were simply *'overcome with wine'* !

However, when I read the next sentence in Cayce's account, it stopped me in my tracks. Cayce says that, *'just as the <u>midnight hour</u> came, there was the birth of the Master.'*

Now this agrees perfectly with what 'John A' had said in the channelled tapes, so I was stunned to find it here. Throughout his career Cayce gave many thousands of psychic 'readings' on many different subjects, but I discovered different dates were given for the for the precise month. One suggested March 19th, while another says we should keep Christmas to around December 24th-25th *'as ye have your time now'* - so for me the mystery deepened.

I refer now to a newspaper cutting from the *'Daily Mail'* from December 22nd 1993 - I always keep anything I can lay my hands on relating to the real birthday of Jesus. The newspaper had asked the author of *'The Star of Bethlehem Mystery'* David Hughes, if he believed that the Biblical dates were accurate. This was his reply.

'There was a superb Astrological event between September 15th and 17th B.C. - which is very close to the time when many historians now regard to be the real birthday of Jesus. The event was a triple conjunction of Jupiter and Saturn in the Constellation of Pisces. This would have made a perfect 'Star of Bethlehem' - but how do the dates fit ? Errors in calculations by Roman and early Christian scholars means that the date for the Nativity, of which <u>we</u> have only one calendar, is way off the mark.'

Yet another argument tells us that the shepherds were present during the time of the birth to *'watch their flocks by night'*, but in December ? The shepherds would have already rounded up their flocks for the oncoming Winter, surely ? So if Jesus had been born in December, there wouldn't be any shepherds outdoors to watch their flocks at all.

In his 1994 book *'A Search for the Historical Jesus'* Professor Fida Hassnain agrees with this view, saying that on December 25th Palestine is freezing cold, so there wouldn't be any sheep in the fields.

There is so much conflicting evidence on this subject and the more I read, the more I found. In yet another book, I learned that the Romans already celebrated December 25th, but as the birthday of Mithra - their own saviour of mankind. Then when the Romans adopted Christianity they turned their festival of Mithra into a Christian festival !

Even the official year Jesus was born was apparently changed - by a Sixth Century monk named Dionysius Exiguus, who lived over five hundred years after Jesus died. Before this, Jesus' birthday was celebrated as January 6th and it still is, in some European and South American churches. My question is why have the dates changed ? I mean, even in the Gospels, Luke says that Jesus was born in the Summer and not the Winter...

This whole mystery is purely a personal interest, but I hope readers can understand my curiosity. As I think on these things, now I can hear Russell singing George Harrison's '*My Sweet Lord...I really want to see you*'

Well thank you Russell, so do I !

The Great White Brotherhood

In the early seventies Alfie and I were at Stansted Hall for a course on Spiritual Healing. It was a subject that Alfie was very much interested in, but the long hours he spent at work, kept him from becoming a full time healer.

We were in the the Hall's main Sanctuary, when a friend beckoned to Alfie asking, '*will you please come and give me some healing ?*'

Alfie did so and it seemed he was a natural. We were accompanied that week by another friend, Margaret Rycroft. She was there with her husband John and they were two very dear people and wonderful healers in their own right. We were new friends to them at the time, but many years later we remain very close friends.

As we watched Alfie at work, I noticed Margaret was seeing something else and I wondered whether she could see a Spirit helper or guide. Well I'd guessed right, because afterwards Margaret spoke to Alfie and told him, '*you have a wonderful Native American helper with you Alf and he wears a huge head-dress, right down to the ground ! He's a member of the White Brotherhood.*'

As Alfie thanked Margaret, I realised that this was the first time I'd heard anyone mention the White Brotherhood, but in the years that followed, I kept every bit of information about them that I could find. I really just wanted to know more.

We discovered that this Spirit helper of Alfie's was named '*White Eagle*' and later on at the séances, he once spoke to Alfie via Direct Voice. I remember his words were indeed beautiful and spoken in a way that only our Native American friends can. He told us, '*I am a member of the Great White Brotherhood.*'

'*Well,*' I thought,'*you can't get much clearer than that, can you ?*'

Years later, when we received the channelled material explaining how Russell was an apprentice to the White Brotherhood, I admit that I did smile to myself. I remembered how he was a good boy when he was on Earth and always did well at school, but his sense of humour and his constant need to sing and dance - just like his mother - made me wonder how they would control those creative outbursts. But however he fared, I knew that he would do well.

On Earth Russell always wanted to know the finer details of everything - and I mean everything. Just like his mother did as a child ! He was always naturally comical and gets this humour from the Byrne's side of the family. He still has it and just can't help himself ! Yet, I know Russell will always do whatever Spiritual work he is called on to do, so his serious side is always there when it's needed and he has proved that to me.

I realise that if Russell and John are friends, there surely must be others in Spirit like him, with such humour and a love of music - after all, they *are* people just like us.

In his wonderful book *'The Story Of Jesus'*, Edgar Cayce speaks so much of the White Brotherhood and says that 'John the Beloved' is a member. I think this is truly an amazing book and I'm very grateful to whoever had left it to the charity shop for me to find !

I was also surprised to discover within it's pages, Cayce talking in depth about Mercury - or should I say Hermes 'the funny little man with wings on his feet' ! Though I think I'll save that to study another time, as it seems very involved.

Now I must mention here, something of the work of Mrs Grace Cooke. Before the 1920s, Grace Cooke became inspired by Spiritual Healing after becoming the Medium for the Spirit named White Eagle. Through Mrs Cooke's Mediumship, White Eagle explained that he was a member of the White Brotherhood and soon his teachings began inspiring many people.

In 1936, the first two White Eagle Lodges were opened in London and Edinburgh and today the wonderful teachings of White Eagle can found in many books and in various Lodges around the world.

Grace Cooke believed she had reincarnated to work as a Medium for the White Brotherhood and explains how she was once instructed by a Master called the 'Wise Knight' who appears with a purple cloak around his shoulders ! In her own words she explains,

'I show that the work of the Great White Brotherhood continues behind the veil, to spread the white carpet of Peace and Brotherhood over the world.'

A Rare Message

One afternoon, our friend Don Galloway invited us over to his home for tea. I remember that we sat in his delightful little cottage in Lincoln and out of the blue came a message. Don lit up a cigarette then crossed his legs, he smiled and asked Alfie a question,
'Have you been doing healing Alf?'
'Yes' Alf said, nodding.
Don said, *'you do know that Russell helps you, don't you?'*
Alf nodded again, as I sat there listening intently. Then Don said, *'you know, don't you Gwen, that Russell comes back as a man?'*
Alfie and I both nodded saying, *'oh yes!'*
Then Don looked at me and smiling his familiar smile, asked me,
'what is it Gwen?'
'Well Russell's certainly gone up in the world.' I said. *'I mean, he's climbed higher and higher up the ladder and is very learned...'*

We carried on enjoying our tea and cake as I thought to myself, *'in the twenty or so years I've known Don, he's only given us one message.'*
That was in a church demonstration once in London and of course it was accurate, but since then there'd been none at all. I remember saying to Don's secretary, the darling Gee Sumeray, who's now in the Spirit World, *'I'd love a sitting with Don.'*
Only, whenever I mentioned it I always got a straightforward *'No.'*
Although Gee did suggest,
'Gwen, if you book one in London, then he'll have to do it.'

Now I really didn't think that was a very fair thing to do to a Medium, so I went without. Yet Don's surprise message about Russell coming back as a man, was repeated for me in the sitting from April 1992 with my friend Shirley West. (See Chapter 7)
This was again confirmed, in the channelled tapes which came later - so what more could I ask?

Vicky and Paul

After hearing Russell's description of our incarnation together in Egypt from the channelled tapes, I began to have odd feelings of loneliness. These feelings were similar to the ones I'd experienced after Alfie and I had attended the physical séances. I felt sure that others might share these feelings, yet there was no mention of them amongst the amazing amount of mail I received.

Although I was being told about a former life, which felt so accurate and mirrored my current life in so many ways, I wondered how many others had experienced this before. I searched through many books which contained plenty of fictional tales, but found none written as fact. I was hoping to find someone, somewhere, who I could compare my experiences with, but it was not to be. I'd mentally called out to Spirit for help so many times - but then one day help arrived.

Out of the blue, I received two audio tapes in the post and was told that these recordings would interest me and the other RPPS mothers. Well the timing of their arrival couldn't have been better and this proved to me that Spirit really do understand our needs.

I was astonished to find that these tapes were of some séance sittings from the 1960s with a Medium called Florence Derbyshire. Her sitter was Doctor Ian Pearce, who had begun a quest of his own after the 'death' of his ten year old daughter Vicky. During the 1970s I do recall briefly meeting Dr. Pearce and his wife Ruth, whilst at Stansted Hall. As I chatted with them both, I remember thinking what a beautifully Spiritual couple they were. I was there that week to attend Dr. Pearce's lecture on healing, but I discovered that he was one of the country's foremost specialists in treating cancer.

He was best known for his pioneering work and alternative treatments, but was also a co-founder of the charity *'New Approaches to Cancer.'* At that time I was totally unaware that he and his wife had 'lost' a daughter to cancer, because it was something he never mentioned during the lecture.

As I began listening to these séance recordings, I discovered that the Pearce family had experienced a similar situation to my own. These tapes were so clear and enthralling as I heard Dr. Pearce actually being reunited with his beloved daughter, but there was more. Vicky herself presented details to her father of a former life she had experienced in Egypt !

Finally it seemed, I'd found someone I could relate to and at that particular time, that was exactly what I'd been seeking so desperately.

To support his recordings, Dr. Pearce had also written of his discoveries in Mediumship, in his most wonderful book, *'One Man's Odyssey'* published in 1986 by C.W. Daniel. His book, along with these tapes, have touched me on an extremely deep level. Of course I realise how difficult it must be for professionals to speak openly of these experiences. So I suppose in my case it helps to be ordinary ! I can speak my Truth without worrying about what people think or say - either bad or mad, I don't care !

Drawing on Dr Pearce's beautiful book myself, he describes the joy of first speaking to his daughter Vicky in the séance room, which is a thing so few have experienced and so few understand, yet his chats with her were so natural !

Dr Pearce had spent all his life fighting illness on behalf of others, but tragically he could do nothing to save his own daughter. He was brought up as a Christian but his beliefs gave him no comfort. He knew that Vicky had gone somewhere, he just didn't know where. Such was his pain that it seemed to him that God was not all powerful after all. So Dr Pearce began a Spiritual quest, which in the beginning he was wary of because of his faith, but it wasn't long before he began to have some success in his search.

During his early investigations, Dr Pearce began sitting with the Medium Florence Derbyshire, whose Spirit helper was nicknamed 'Snowdrop'. At one point, via the entranced Medium, Snowdrop suddenly tells Dr Pearce, *'we are going to try an experiment. Please try to be still !'*

Dr Pearce says, that as he observed the Medium her face began to change. He describes how her eyes and her cheeks altered and how her mouth took on a completely different shape. Before his eyes, this middle-aged woman had taken on the appearance of a small girl. Very slowly and hesitantly and clearly with great effort, the young girl spoke.

'Daddy, she said, *'I do love you !'*

Dr Pearce asked,
'Vicky - is this your Medium ?'

As soon as Vicky had responded with a 'yes' she began to fade away, due to of a lack of power - but at least she had managed to get through !

I find the audio conversations between Vicky and her beloved 'Daddy' so beautiful. Yet they seem so personal and to me it would seem like prying if I reproduced them in full, so I include just a little here to help make my point. I have spoken to many who agree, that Vicky is an amazing communicator, along the lines of Russell and he and I also had our poignant conversations. Some I have never written about, but I have them on tape and share them with a only limited few.

I love the following interaction between Vicky and her father Dr Pearce.

Vicky: *'Daddy ! I've seen <u>Him</u>.'*
Dr Pearce: *'Seen him ? Who ?'*
Vicky: (spoken very simply) *'Jesus.'*

Dr Pearce: (in awe-struck tones) *'You've seen...Jesus ? How wonderful !'*
Vicky: *'Daddy it's true ! People don't believe you do they ?'*
Dr Pearce: *'No, they don't darling. They think it is all a wonderful story.'*
Vicky: *'But it isn't a story, it's true. You know Daddy, if you want to help someone, then <u>He</u> knows. He really does know.'*
Dr Pearce: *'Even one little person like me ?'*
Vicky: *'Everyone ! No one is too little. No one ! When He comes, you know Daddy it is all so wonderful. I always hoped we would be able to talk again and you would see how I have grown. I have so many things to talk about, so many wonderful things...'*

Well how right Vicky is !
Her philosophy on Jesus touched me so much, but then I find any child speaking on Jesus, can be far superior than any priest.

There are so many parallels between Vicky's story and Russell's - including the time of her passing, her age and illness and the swiftness of it all. The similarities between their two stories become clear as it unfolds, though I also recall that in the early days of Dr Pearce's investigations, he'd also received a special apport - in the shape of a lock of Vicky's hair !

Dr Pearce's sittings with Mrs Derbyshire continued on a regular basis and once Vicky told him, *'I knew I was going to leave you - leave the Earth. But I knew it would be alright because Jesus said that He would prepare a place for us. I didn't know what it meant, but I know now.'*

To me, these words are like an echo of Russell's or maybe Russell's words are an echo of Vicky's ? Whichever it is, I think we should listen more to our children's wisdom.

Vicky gave her father some unusual evidence of her Egyptian incarnation in one sitting, yet I think Dr Pearce had trouble accepting this information as true in the beginning. From his book, Dr Pearce's says,

'I had previously been inclined to accept the concept of reincarnation...as being the only way...to reconcile the varying conditions of Earthly life... The idea that my darling daughter had once been anyone other than <u>my</u> daughter alone - that she was in fact 'another soul' - with quite separate and different experiences...was something that at this stage, I found totally repellent.'

Dr Pearce did come to terms with this Truth eventually, but I guess that he saw the whole subject in a different light to me. I think perhaps Russell only took it further with me, because I accepted it all in a more relaxed manner. Dr Pearce showed concern that Vicky might reincarnate again, but she soon assured him that she would not - especially since there was a new grandchild due to be born into the family a few months later.

Vicky's explanation seemed to ease her father's mind, yet there again I saw similarities. There have been many ask me whether my grandson, young Russell, was perhaps the reincarnation of my son Russell and he had returned to the family once more. However, I knew different because my Russell had explained it to me. Some people think that just because the two Russell's birth dates were the same, this proved reincarnation ! But this is not proof, it is a theory.

After listening to Vicky's sweet voice on tape and reading her father's book many times, I feel I know Vicky, but now I want to tell you a little about Paul, where even here I notice similarities.

The Spirit known as Paul came with Vicky to the Trance sittings and spent many hours chatting to Dr Pearce. When I first heard his voice on the tapes, I literally felt my hair stand on end ! His phraseology and his knowledge just seemed limitless. To me, it seemed that Paul was clearly part of the 'Big Plan' - as indeed I believe all things are planned. To appreciate their full beauty and intelligence, I recommend reading Paul's words as they are transcribed in Dr Pearce's book. Here is what Dr Pearce has to say of him,

'After many long conversations with Paul, I was [becoming] quite convinced that this was indeed he, whom we had known as St Paul the Apostle - one of the great Spiritual Masters, the great 'Lion of God' who had done so much to promote the spread of the Master's message throughout the world. Yet, he had deigned to come and talk with me, a humble Neophyte upon the path with everything to learn.

We ordinary citizens of the 20th Century were sitting and talking to one who had lived and worked in the times of the Master.

Words still fail me when I recall my feelings upon this occasion ! I know the difficulties in accepting this view, but <u>I was there.</u> I felt the force of his personality.'

As Paul dramatically put it himself during the sittings, *'we cannot escape the consequences of our deeds. We reap precisely whatever it is that we have sown ! Tomorrow we shall stand in the shadow of today.'*

Of his experiences, Dr Pearce said,
'one's pathway does not become easier.'

My own thoughts here, are that our pathway actually becomes harder, yet

I know Dr Pearce experienced something wonderful too. While listening to the recordings of Paul speaking with Vicky, I was reminded so much of B-'s Spiritual teacher John. I saw similarities in his personality, his humour and his wondrous way of putting anyone who was out of order, back in their place. For he does so with such great Love. I think Saint Paul came as part of the plan for Dr Pearce. So why shouldn't 'John the Beloved' also come as part of this Great Plan ? I know the ways of God are truly wonderful...

My 'plan' is to finish here, for I have had my say and can only gasp at the wonder of it all ! I end this chapter with a lovely little prayer from Vicky Pearce herself, which I feel is echoed by all the children in this book.

'Dear God, we have given to you all our love, which is so little for what you have done for us. We wish to do thy will. Help us in our union that we may be about thy business and whatever our hands find to do, we do so with all our heart and all our soul. Give us wisdom not to ask for that which we want, but to surrender to thee in thy wisdom and understanding to the things which we need.
God bless Mummy and Daddy, though we know you have blessed them, because you have helped us to talk together !
Dear God I am so happy ! Help me to make other people happy too.
Amen.
Bye bye Daddy.'

* * *

I have tried my best to keep this chapter simple and concise and hope I have succeeded. Though even as I write, I am experience daily Spiritual happenings, which I always record and keep until needed. I'm told it will all come out in a third book, so all I can say is 'watch this space' !

Often when these things happen around me, Russell pops in with his own version of the 'Herman's Hermits' tune,

'Something is happening,
and it's started happening,
and I know why I, I !'

Yes Russell, I bet you do...
But you won't tell me until you're ready, will you ?

Twenty Eight

Sunrise, Sunset

Summerland Tape 5
August 9th 1995

*'I am a little pencil in the hands of God,
who is sending a love letter to the World'*

~ Mother Teresa of Calcutta

B: *'It is approaching midnight on 8th August, 1995 and is a gloriously clear and bright night. Russell seems to like these tapes to coincide with anniversaries and this one is no exception, as it's close to the anniversary of his passing on August 14th.*

Softly playing in the background I have the 'Angel of Music' from Phantom of the Opera' so I will now hand over to our friends from the other realms.

Raymond: 'Hello my dear lady.
The hour may be late, but the time is always bright between us. It is with great joy that I join you and say God bless you and Alf. My dearest Gwen, we are so near...

The year 1963 had such an ending for you both, but there is another beginning yet to come ! My dear lady, you will receive something from me shortly, something of a material nature that was very important to me when I was upon the Earth plane. I know that it will mean a lot to you.

I must say, that I have grown very fond of the lady who allows me to speak through her and it is my dearest wish, that in the not too distant future, I will be able to talk to you by Direct Voice. I look forward to it.

We have decided to call this tape 'Sunrise, Sunset' and dear Gwen knows the reason why. As the sun rises, the sun sets and day by day becomes week by week, then month by month becomes year by year. One minute we are a child, the next we are adults. Then we are in our middle age and the next, we're in the sunset of our lives.

Some of us did not make it through our youth, some had it taken away by Earthly conflict, but our lives continue in this world. You know we are not governed by your time, but we are aware of it. Life on Earth is so fleeting, ours is everlasting. You have the Sunrise and the Sunset, we have the Sun.'

Russell: *'A short while ago Mum and Dad, you were together with B- for a joint birthday celebration.*

You celebrated the first evening by going to the Opera, then you all went to the opening ceremony of the Youth Olympics in Bath. This was the first time the Olympic flame had been lit in England since 1948, yet Mum and Dad were together even back then ! You were in London to attend the Olympic Games while you were courting in 1948 - and in Bath, you shared in the lighting of the flame once more !

The Youth Olympics is all about children and it is children who give us hope, for they are the future. Only adults create barriers, but children cross frontiers because they are not afraid, they are only taught to be afraid. Neither are children prejudiced or judgemental, they have to be taught these too. Your children all come straight from Spirit, direct from the God force and it is God who gave them their innocence. This is where you often find the greatest wisdom or profound Truth.

There were many instances Mum, during your visit to Bath which will remain memorable for you. For the Opera in the park, you were impressed to wear something with large camellias on it - although you had no idea why. Yet at the Opera, Montserrat Caballé sang something from 'La Traviata' which you are very familiar with - but what you didn't know, is that this opera is adapted from 'The Lady of the Camellias' by Alexandre Dumas, so you see how it ties in.

You were clearly enchanted Mother and by the Grand Finalé, the tears were flowing. There was the Grand March from Verdi's 'Aida' with trumpeters and a huge choir, who sang their hearts out. Your face was a picture and in between dabbing your eyes you were mentally thanking us ! I really think you were rendered speechless...'

Gwen: I've been asked to write of my experiences here, some of which were so special. In Bath, I always like to go to the Pump Room restaurant to enjoy atmosphere and music. Well I was still in an enchanted state after the Opera the night before, as B- and I sat there like a couple of Duchesses, enjoying Earl Grey tea and pastries.

After feeding our faces with cake, we were relaxing to the live music in the restaurant, when a lady came to play the the piano. Her selection was from the musical *'Carousel'* and she started by playing beautifully, one of Russell's favourite tunes called *'If I Loved You.'*

The trouble is, whenever I'm there I'm inclined to sing along with the music. Yet from my right hand side, half way through the song, I heard the voice of another lady duetting along with me ! It was a perfect moment and a magical experience. Afterwards the lady introduced herself as Betty Gould from America. Now I don't imagine for one moment that she'll ever read this, but we shared a lovely musical interaction. What are the chances of me being seated right next to a lovely mezzo singing voice ? It's all magic to me !

Next the lady pianist began to play *'The Rustle Of Spring'* by Christian Sinding. This piece of music has often used over the years by Russell, so that Mediums could get his name through correctly. Then there was a selection from *'Oliver !'* which is always Russell's favourite musical, followed a rendition of *'Over the Rainbow'* which I think brought B-'s lovely daughter in Spirit a little bit closer to us.

I really couldn't stop myself from singing along to these wonderful songs, but at least we didn't get thrown out of the restaurant because of it !

This experience just shows me how Spirit can interact with us in thought, through music. At times their influence can be very subtle, but the two worlds do work together, bound by love - which is the greatest magic of all. Love is the greatest healer and the greatest inspiration and as with all creative work 'Love is the key' and it will see you through...

Russell: *'In all the mothers stories in this book, you can see how their children draw close to communicate. So if we children can do it, then I am certain that you will eventually be able to sense their presence and their love. Indeed, anyone who has lost someone they love, if your mind opens to those endless possibilities of Love, then you will find your own awareness. Then with that awareness, you will truly find that just about <u>anything</u> is possible ! There <u>is</u> only life, there is no death.*

My mother and the other ladies in this book are witnesses to the honest testimony of Truth. My mother was the original 'Torch Bearer' and has been joined by others to help light the way for others. Hopefully that torch will burn as brightly as the Olympic flame and continue to be carried as a Torch of Love !

This knowledge inevitably leads to wisdom and the opening up of limitless possibilities for the one Love. Though perhaps there are several aspects of love - yes I know that's a song title by Andrew Lloyd-Webber - but it's the Truth ! I am talking of Spiritual Love...'

Gwen: While there's a pause here in the recording, I'll just mention our visit to the Youth Olympics opening ceremony and how our Spirit friends seemed to help us get there ! This was just part of a wonderful musical weekend in Bath that Alfie, B- and I had enjoyed.

Alfie knows how I love dancing, so while he'd volunteered to babysit, B- and I went to an exciting barn dance ! We had a fun evening dancing up and down the floor of this barn and leaping about all over the place. Yet the interaction of Spirit was already beginning, for our 'friends upstairs' were already at work.

During the evening B- had met some friends from the city, who she hadn't seen for a couple of years and after a chat about our weekend plans, we went off to enjoy some more dancing. At the end of the night I offered to drive B-'s large car back home, although trying to find my way out of the field which had doubled as a car park, was no fun at 2 in the morning !

On the day of the Youth Olympics opening ceremony, Alfie, B- and I drove round Bath looking for a good parking spot in the city. B- had told Alfie about the two friends she'd met at the barn dance, but unfortunately Bath is a big city and without proper directions, we got lost !

Thankfully we spotted a helpful looking policeman who was standing on the corner of an almost deserted road. We gave him the basic details we had, then after giving us some directions he said, *'you'll have to be quick - because the Royal carriage is coming this way shortly.'*

No wonder the road was clear ! But within minutes we'd found the address of B-'s old friends and there they were, waiting for us with our parking space all ready too. Imagine our surprise when we discovered that the main entrance to the Youth Olympics arena was just a short twenty metres walk from their house ! Now how's that for Spirit interaction ? Thanks to our Spirit friends, we secured a spot which was perfect for us.

We left the car and happily handed over our tickets, as we walked into the Olympic arena and into an amazing sight. We even had front row seats and felt that our Spirit friends were enjoying the occasion along with us.

It was like nothing I had ever seen before. There were clowns and dancers of every kind and B-'s children were beside themselves with excitement. In fact we were all in awe of the entire spectacle. The atmosphere was electric and for me felt truly magical. All the young athletes came in waving their flags, in fact I think their smiles were as huge as their flags ! One young lad received such a cheer, after travelling from his troubled home of Bosnia for the occasion. I already felt quite emotional and excited, when next the Royal carriage came rolling in, to an almighty cheer from the thousands of assembled spectators.

I'd never seen a Royal carriage before, in fact there was lot I did that day that I'd never done before. It was a crazy, magical day. The crazy part was when we all kept doing the Mexican wave - I began to feel about eighteen years old again and it felt great ! Of course, we were all still waiting on the arrival of the Olympic flame, to be carried in by Sir Roger Bannister then handed over to the athlete, Linford Christie.

Now Russell has already explained that Alfie and I were at Wembley for the London Games in 1948. We were very young and hadn't yet married, but we were selling programmes at five shillings each and we enjoyed the games too. It seemed quite odd to be watching those very same athletes again that we'd seen back in 1948, but now on a huge TV screen. Then when we saw the Olympic flame lit again after 40 years, well it was quite emotional for me, so of course I cried !

Some more 'crazy' came for me when the evening's programme began. We had the gorgeous singer Michael Ball and apart from looking like a Greek God, he can actually sing. He arrived on stage and burst into a rendition of *'Love Changes Everything'* and I thought, *'gosh, he might just bring the house down !'*

Before I knew what was happening, loads of female fans began running towards the stage yelling, *'Michael, Michael !'* at the tops of their voices.

Then B- grabbed me and said, *'come on Gwennie'* and off we went. We did the 100 yard dash and came to stand around the singer while he belted out the lovely *'Olympic Hymn.'* By the time the applause began, quite a few ladies were already up on the stage, while the rest of us tried to throw flowers at him. Some were even throwing their hats towards him, but I hung on to mine - well, it *was* my favourite sun hat all decorated with sunflowers ! The flowers we threw came from a huge display in front of the stage, nobody seemed to notice until some officials began appealing for calm saying, *'please ladies, please !'*

Eventually though we dispersed, as the lovely Michael left the stage with flowers in his hair and I thought,
'oh dear, what ever would my sons think of me, acting like a teenager ?'

Although I know one son who would have thought it was wonderful. I can just imagine him laughing about the whole thing !

This really was the kind of thing I should have done when I was eighteen years old, but back then we didn't do these kind of things - it just wasn't done. Yet I'd joined in without even thinking about it, so did I just get carried away ? I don't know - but it was fun !

Russell once referred to B- and I as *'two Daffy old ducks'* and I think that would be a good description of us that evening. By the end, we were all completely shattered and arrived home with the children sound asleep. All I can say is, our evening had been a bit dreamlike for me and perhaps even like a shift in consciousness ? After all it was a once in a lifetime event !

Right, now I'll pass the 'baton' back to Russell...

Russell: *'Mum, I was talking about the importance of children, wasn't I ? They are the future and very important to your dreams. They have the right to grow true, straight and strong, but the only way a child can grow is through love. Not only from their parents but from their environment, a love which seeks to nurture and protect them.*

In our world we cherish our children in a safe and protective environment and cannot allow them near anyone we have any doubts about. At this moment your world is a dangerous place for children and we are saddened by the conditions in which some of your children have to live. We are talking about a society which seems to take advantage of the weak and the vulnerable. It is the greatest mistake of society to allow the abuse or destruction of its children. Indeed, any society which embarks on this course of action sows the seeds of his own destruction. The truth is, that God only gives us what we need, not what we want...

Children have rights and they all need Love, Truth and Wisdom. Please cherish your children and cherish the older members of society. They are the link with your past and throughout their lives they may have gained great wisdom. Please do not dismiss them too casually, take time to listen to them, for they have their own Truth to share.

Oh Mum the tape is running out now, so goodnight and God bless.'

Gwen: Now I just want to share one final happening from our weekend in Bath. That morning I'd awoken with the tune *'Trotting to the Fair'* - which I believe is an traditional Irish air. I remember telling B- about it and was surprised at her response, when she told me that she couldn't have any secrets ! I had no idea what she meant and by the time we'd arrived in Bath I'd completely forgotten about the song.

We took a leisurely walk around Bath during the day, then the children asked if they could have their ears pierced. We finally found a suitable shop and in no time at all, the whole family were wearing gold studs in their ears ! Later I noticed that B- seemed to be hurrying which puzzled me slightly. Even the children seemed to be in a rush to get somewhere. Then we stopped to wait somewhere on a corner, but for what I had no clue. Just then, there arrived the most beautiful horse and buggy !

Now I'm a bit nervous of horses really, but we all climbed into the buggy and enjoyed a lovely trot around Bath city centre. It was a lovely experience and another first for me. It was a lovely surprise gift from B- for August 14th, Russell's anniversary, so now I realised what she'd meant about keeping secrets ! Although I think Russell had been trying to tell me about it that morning with his song...

Next we took the children to the fancy Pump Room restaurant, but they were a little too boisterous for us to relax. Then B- was looking for an ashtray without success, so I suggested that she ought to have one of those small portable ones to carry round in her handbag.

We were almost at the end of another super day, but as we went our separate ways home I headed back to a 'magic and joke shop' that we'd seen earlier. I wanted to buy some jokes and magic tricks for my two grandsons, Brett and young Russell. Inside, I found some fake fried eggs and jam tarts made from plastic, so put them in a little pile on the counter. Wandering around the shop some more, I looked at the other items on display and saw all kinds of things, like magic hats and goggle glasses. Then I began thinking just how much my Russell would love it all. I recalled his last ever Christmas gift from Alfie and me. We'd bought him a big box of magic tricks, which he loved and I still keep his magic wand to this day.

I could see the shop owner was moving about at the back of the shop, so realised he was must getting ready to close up for the day. I was his last customer and there was no one else around, so I returned to the counter to pay for my pile of plastic eggs and jam tarts for the boys.

To my astonishment, sitting on top of them I saw a small package. At first I just stared at it and wondered what it was. The shop was empty and the man hadn't come out from the back of the shop once. I picked up the little parcel and began to open it, it was one bag inside another. By now I was looking around the shop almost expecting someone to appear and claim it. Inside the bag I find a little ashtray, the kind you carry around with you.

At this point I was amazed and again felt the experience that comes with a slight shift in consciousness. I called to the shop owner and asked, *'is this yours ?'* He didn't have a clue and told me he didn't sell ashtrays with 'made in Indonesia' stamped underneath. So I paid for my jokes and left the shop with the ashtray in my hand, yet still felt quite odd at this point. Once outside I pulled myself together and looked at a leaflet the man had also given me. In big letters across the top it read, 'Boggle' - which really made me smile, because my mind was boggled indeed !

When I next saw B- I waited until she was on her own, then told her all about the mysterious ashtray. Once I'd explained, she was amazed and thrilled and we agreed that it was clearly Spirit interaction once again. Though perhaps it was a just a different kind of magic ? I bet Russell must be having lessons from Merlin himself !

It may seem unbelievable to some, but it happened. So thanks Russell !

Twenty Nine

The Heart Is Slow To Learn...

Summerland Tape 6
February/March 1992

*'I'll never love,
as I have loved you.'*

~ Don Black

B-: 'Divine and loving Spirit, we ask that you draw close and in the name of Love we ask for a vibration of healing for those who may hear or read this.'

Russell: *'Hello Mum. Hello Dad ! This is our final channelled tape for you and you know that I like to begin with a song. So we asked our friend B- to play the song 'My Heart Will Go On' because it has relevance to us and the work we are doing.*

The song is from the film 'Titanic' - a dramatic story which stays in the mind. The writer was inspired to create the film as a love story, against the backdrop of a disaster where few survived. One of the main symbols in the film is a jewelled heart, which the heroine drops into the dark void of the ocean. Then the old lady passes into the Spirit Realms and is reunited with the love she met aboard Titanic. That final, inspirational scene was placed into the mind of the writer by us, although he was quite unaware of it - yet it has been seen by millions !

  You may wonder why I refer to this film. Well firstly I can say that of those on the Earth who have 'lost' a child, there are very few who actually 'survive' the experience. When parents lose a child the whole fabric of their lives breaks up and the only way they can try to find them again is to cast their hearts into the void. They try to reach out in the darkness and sometimes, through their awareness and that simple act of Love, they are rewarded.

  So why are so many people drawn to the film Titanic ? It can't be because they don't know how the story ends and it's not a particularly *happy film. So perhaps it is because of the central thread ? That the love story <u>survives</u> the disaster. Maybe the story opens the mind up to the possibility that there's more to life than death ? I think it certainly brings hope, but then love stories have always been popular - but why is this ?*

We need to think about the heart itself - which is indeed 'slow to learn.' We all know that the physical heart is just pump that moves the the blood around the body, but why has the heart shape adorned every love token for centuries ?

Well, the physical heart occupies the space in your body which connects directly with a large Spiritual energy receptor. Your body has nine main Spiritual energy receptors, sometimes called chakras. The heart chakra is the one that communicates the things that you feel and learn in your life. It connects and leads you to higher knowledge and can activate other receptors in the body. So perhaps this makes the heart chakra the most powerful and important one of all ? Many early civilisations had knowledge of the heart chakra and its importance, although it was very much wrapped up in symbolism. These receptors are located in the body and connect directly with your soul.

Each of you are three in one, a combination of the mind, the body and the soul and although the physical body doesn't survive death, the mind and the soul do. When your body dies and you arrive over here, the mind, which contains all the memories of your latest life, connects with the higher soul energy.

Now I know that you are educated to think with your mind and you depend on it to dictate your life actions and your life's progress, but unless you work through the heart, you will never understand what is truly important in life. It is only when you can listen with your heart that you truly realise all that is, all that was and all that can be.

So many people are mocked for listening to or following their hearts, but so many more yearn to do this - to follow the simple yearning in their soul. Your heart chakra, that Spiritual energy receptor, can pump love into your life, into the cosmos and into your physical body for healing. If you love something enough it <u>can</u> be attained, but when listening with our hearts we must engage the mind. We must realise that the heart is the seat of Love and it is very powerful...

Gwen: Around the time this tape was being channelled, an interesting little incident happened.

I'd finally finished making a recording of some of my favourite songs. It was something I'd been working on for sometime and I called it *'One Hand, One Heart.'* The company producing the CD asked me how I wanted the cover to look, so I told them *'oh just my photo'* and I suggested they use a pale blue colour with a few yellow stars and crescent moons. I said, *'you can put on some fluffy clouds, if you like !'* I received the finished discs in the post and was highly amused to find they'd also included a little yellow heart symbol on the cover, situated just by my hand. On the phone, the man told me he'd thought it would be nice to have a little heart there too ! Now I wonder who put that idea in his head ?

So for a bit of fun, from now on in this chapter whenever Russell uses the word heart, I'll spell it with the ♥ symbol. I know he'd be amused !

Russell: *'Today's world is dominated by technology, but it's amazing and brilliant technology and has the capacity to make peoples lives better - but it is no substitute for God !*

There are those experimenting with the building blocks of life and you have cloned animals and cloned food, but within each of these discoveries lies the responsibility attached to them. We need to be very sure that we understand the full course of what we are doing. Because by interfering with the complexity of life, without understanding, there can be disasters. Those who think with the ♥ understand on a soul level that the tools of technology can also destroy. They know that the action of releasing a weapon can have terrible additional consequences and they know in their ♥ it is wrong.

There is so much fear in the world today and until you find love, the fear will remain. People need to understand that there is something bigger and better and finer to save them from disasters, we already know there is no death, but there is also Love ! Many people believe that the only power to save them is Love and they are right, but this isn't a new Truth, it is as old as time.

The gradual transition between the last Millennium and this one will be a lively one ! There will be many changes and many concepts will alter. Perceptions will shift, but this is progress and this is how we grow. The only way to shift your perception is to return to Love, because it's the only thing that will sustain you. To accept Love is to open up the ♥ chakra and obtain Divine inspiration from the mass creative consciousness, which is God. You can then help others to do the same.

The most negative thing on the Earth today is fear. So many people are trapped in a web of fear. Fear of the unknown, fear of loss, fear of change. Yet not all change is negative and neither is all loss. Some of these things can be very positive or they at least can be turned around to become positive. The problem comes when fear stops you living, but it's even more of a tragedy when fear stops you from loving. We need to help people to fear less and to love more ! Perhaps here, it may be beneficial for me to ask anyone who suffers with ♥ problems, the question - who was it that broke their ♥ ?

The symbol of the ♥ empowers people, but alas the ♥ is slow to learn ! We can spend our lives not even loving ourselves enough and it can take many lifetimes to learn this one basic Truth.

* * *

Throughout the channelled material in this book I have used music and lyrics to reveal messages. Although you may just think, 'oh well, he's very theatrical and it amuses his mother' this is not the reason. Music has a vibration and you have a vibration - all living things resonate to a particular vibration. So music is guaranteed to affect your vibration and when it is teamed with the right lyrics it becomes even more powerful. So how do we channel our messages through to people who are not Mediums ? Well we use inspiration directed to their creative side, just like the songwriter is inspired to give you lyrics about the ♥.

Creativity is not encouraged enough amongst your children. Children are naturally creative and should be allowed to explore their creativity, but so many people consider creativity a waste of time.
They say, 'they'll never earn any money from it.' or 'they'll never make a living !' This is purely fear-based thinking and very negative.

If society doesn't value its creative people then it loses its soul. So one of the best ways to empower yourself and strengthen your link with God, is to explore your own creativity. You could sing, dance or just listen to beautiful music or maybe even try to play some yourself. You might look at a beautiful painting and be inspired to create one or perhaps read some beautiful literature and be inspired to write. You don't need to be an expert, you can explore your own creativity simply for the love of it. If you give yourself the time, you could create something which might become a gift to the world.

You might try to play a musical instrument to express your creativity and in that love you will heal yourself as well as others. You could write your ideas down on paper or write of your pain. It's such a wonderful therapy and who knows, it could be of value to others. The trouble is, if you don't give yourself the time to try these things, you'll never know what creative avenues or levels you might achieve.

The arts are the gateway to the soul. Through them you open up your ♥ to the vastness of the cosmos and Divine inspiration. It is a wonderful way to develop communication with a power greater than yourself and deepen your connection with God. If you use your creativity, you begin to get some personal insights into who and what you are and this brings you into closer alignment with God, the Great Creator.

There are creative messages from God everywhere on your planet and to find them, you only need to open up your ♥. In turn this will open up your intuition and awaken that 'still, small voice' which acts as your personal guide throughout life. So if you wish your world was a better place, you need to open up your ♥ to the endless possibilities of creativity and Love.

We all have our creative aspects and by activating our creative energy we are tapping into our feminine side. Now I know that some people will find that hard to grasp but it is the Truth. Every man, woman and child that walks the Earth and every individual in our world, has a masculine and feminine side. Now many men believe that in order to access their feminine side, they have to lose their masculinity. This is not true and never will be. It takes great strength to surrender or let go, especially if all those around you are calling you weak. If a man chooses to work on his feminine or creative side, it is not a sign of weakness, it is a sign of strength.

When we stifle one side of ourselves we become unbalanced. So if we only work with our male energy we lose our sense of balance and perspective, then we become loud, aggressive, unpredictable and violent. Now does that ring any bells for you?

When we look at the state of the Earth we see there is a great deal of restlessness, animosity and violence. This is because your world is operating on a great deal of male energy and a life lived without the correct balance of male and female energies can often be violent, painful and unpredictable.

Now this doesn't only apply to the men in your world, this imbalance affects a great deal of women too. Some who decided they had the same rights as men in society, took things one step further. They began to emulate the worst masculine characteristics, then call it equality and liberation. We think this is very sad, for they are buying into an illusion.

To live with an imbalance of both male and female energies can be dangerous. It is best for everyone to develop the male and female aspects within themselves to create a positive balance. This balance begins with the self. So many have problems within their relationships, because some men don't know what to do anymore and some ladies are behaving like men - yet they believe this is the right way to be. The right way is to be balanced, with the two energies working in harmony. You shouldn't be trying to score points off each other, because one is more female and one is more male. You should try and learn from these insecurities. Individuals should not only try to serve their own needs but the needs of the other. This does not mean subservience or dominance, it means harmony and order !

If you are born male in this lifetime, you need to learn about female energy and how to find a balance between the two. If you are born female you need to learn about male energy and also find it's balance. This is one of the main lessons of life. The survival of the human race depends on the male and female species working in harmony. Not only does physical survival depend on it, but so does your emotional and mental survival. You cannot have one without the other, because both male and female are intrinsically linked.

It would not be right to have a purely male dominated world, the same as it wouldn't be right to have a purely female dominated world. Balance is always needed, with partnerships of equal measure. Though you may spend many lifetimes learning about balance, because of course the ♥ is slow to learn !

The ♥ is the seat of the soul and the soul knows that anything is possible. However, the mind can prevent us from being the person that we know we can be. Unfortunately we are conditioned in life to believe there are many limitations upon us. For instance you may say to yourself with all your ♥ that you are an Infinite being and everything you need to survive will be given to you, but then your mind can interrupt and tell you it's not true ! Remember that the conditioning you are up against may originate from this lifetime or other lifetimes and through this, we can undermine ourselves, our own importance and our own self worth.

There are many people who believe they are not worthy of life on this planet, so they go around and do their best to prove it all the time. If you don't believe you fall into this category, then you are indeed blessed but can you be absolutely sure that you do not ? How do you know whether your mind is not working against you and preventing you from expressing yourself as a part of the Divine ?

One has to know that there is enough good in the cosmos for everyone and just because one person has this knowledge, doesn't mean there isn't enough for you. This mistaken view is based on a fear of inadequacy which comes from the mind alone. At these times we must engage the ♥ and the soul and simply learn to Love.

* * *

Now Mum and Dad, I want to tell you of some important experiences I've had in the Spirit World recently...

I had just completed some difficult work with some people on the Earth and had become quite disappointed in the human condition. So many Mediums are hard work ! I was sitting in the Garden of Remembrance thinking about the interaction between those on the Earth and those of us here in Spirit, when my friend John came to talk to me...

I began to tell him of my disappointment and John said, 'oh dear my child, I think it's time you learned how to love !'

I told John that I didn't think that was really a problem and had no wish to learn anymore. Then being the wise and gentle master that he is, John said, 'very well my child, so be it' and he walked away. As I watched him disappear into the distance I wondered if I'd perhaps been a little hasty, but I wasn't going to admit it. Maybe I didn't know at all ?

Later, I was talking to my Mother on the Earth about what we might do in the future and I told her how I'd almost given up on Earthly people. Now my mother is a very good Medium but she doesn't know it, but then I realised how difficult it would be to get through to my Mum, without a Medium. I was wondering about this when John returned and he asked me how I was getting on. I told him that I wasn't doing so well really, but that I still wanted to work with people on the Earth. Once again John told me that first, I need to learn how to love.

I told him that I thought it was people on the Earth who needed to learn how to love, not me ! I told him I was just stuck on how I'd communicate with my Mother without a Medium, but that I knew how to love.

'Perhaps the people you speak of need some help.' John said to me. 'Since you know all about love, maybe you could devise a way to teach them ? Have you ever thought about parenting Russell ?'

Now I thought this was a silly thing to say. For John knew that at nine and three quarters, I'd not had the chance to learn that in my last lifetime. I thought he meant I'd need to go back through the records of my previous lifetimes, but he told me that wasn't necessary. He said there was a way I could learn about parenting over here and if I wished, I could become the guardian of a Spirit child. He said that this experience would teach me how to love, like no other.

At first I wasn't sure how this would help me, but John could see I was interested so we went to a place called the Baby Castle. This is a place where babies go when they first come to our world. This beautiful Baby Castle shone with a crystal light and I immediately fell in love with it. I wanted to go straight inside but John told me it was too soon. He knew there was a suitable child I could become guardian over, but she was still on the Earth, so I needed to wait.

Now I'm not very good at waiting and I wanted to start straight away, but John said I would have to wait.

He said, 'you see, this child's mother is a Medium so perhaps you could help them both - but you must wait for the child to arrive here first !'

John told me this experience could teach me more about love and the human condition and I'd only have a short time to wait. I really don't like waiting, but in the meantime we went back to the Garden of Remembrance.

Once there, John introduced me to a gentleman called Mr Alexander J. Potts. Mr Potts was an old man who still looked like an old man and I could see that he was sitting on some boxes. I asked Mr Potts what was in the boxes and he told me they contained all his money and jewels.

John explained that on Earth Mr Potts had been a very wealthy man, but he didn't want anyone else in his life costing him money, so he lived alone.

Mr Potts had locked himself into material thinking, so the only thing he believed in was his gold, silver and jewels. He once lived in a very fine house, but it had become neglected since he never spent anything on it, so Mr Potts died a very wealthy man, but he was alone. After he'd left his body, his mind refused to leave his wealth behind - he was so attached to it that he remained on the Earth for a very long time...

There were some souls from our world who tried to rescue him and bring him over here, but he wouldn't come without his boxes of money and jewels. Although other people on the Earth were now spending his money, he finally came over to the Spirit World - except he thought he could still hold onto his boxes of wealth, even though they were only imaginary.

In his mind, Mr Potts thought there were robbers everywhere, so he never left his boxes alone. He had sat on these boxes for a very long time and was oblivious to the beautiful gardens all around him. He really could have done anything he wanted to, but he just wanted to guard his money.

I was flabbergasted by this story, but couldn't understand why Mr Potts would guard these boxes that nobody wanted. There was no value within them to anyone here, but John explained to me that Mr Potts was a prisoner of his own mind. He really believed his own value was in the *things he owned or had bought. John said that people like this lose sight of the true reality of life and just spent all their time wishing to make more money. Then John said, 'now Russell, do you think you can help persuade Mr Potts to leave his boxes behind?' This surprised me, but I said I would have a go!*

Well I tried everything I could to shift him. First of all he didn't want to talk to me and when he did, he just told me to go away in a very nasty way indeed. Yet he wondered why I kept talking of love, then he said he had no thoughts of love and just wasn't interested.

Eventually Mr Potts became totally closed off to me and half the time he couldn't even hear me. I became extremely confused, but couldn't understand how someone on a Spiritual plane could be so obsessed with the material. I told John I'd made very little progress and I asked if he knew how long Mr Potts had been sitting here on his boxes of wealth. When John replied, 'oh, about a hundred years' I was amazed!

Then John said, 'it took us seventy-five years to get him off the Earth in the first place, so really we're doing quite well! You see, Mr Potts can't see the gardens all around him because he hasn't even lifted his vibrations above the material level enough, to be able to see them. He's not engaged his ♥.'

Well I couldn't believe that Mr Potts even had a ♥, but John explained that by keeping a tight hold on his possessions, Mr Potts thought he would survive, but now he had completely lost his perception of what was possible and impossible. John said that on Earth so many people still accept that it's okay to have lots of money, whilst still being employed in occupations they don't really want to do. He told me there is tremendous pressure put on people to obtain vast sums of money and material things, but so many believe this is all they need to obtain happiness and fulfilment.

I began to realise that with all these material pressures, life on Earth can't be very easy to maintain and it must certainly be so for Mediums, who live between the two worlds. Perhaps this was one of the hardest things to do, but I hadn't realised it during my own life on Earth. My parents would have also been trying to balance the demands of the material world, whilst trying to be the wonderful parents that they were to me and my brothers.

So I tried again to help Mr Potts, even though he was a sour old man and not a very easy person to love at all. He reminded me of Ebeneezer Scrooge, but I still wanted to help him. John assured me that Mr Potts had once been a lovely little boy, so I tried to visualise him this way and the more I engaged my ♥ the more clearly I began to see him. Then the more I saw, the more I realised that the little boy he had once been, was in a great deal of distress !

John suggested that I talk to Mr Potts as if he was a little boy once more. He said, 'if you can be a little boy in this world or any age you want, so can Mr Potts. Perhaps you could try and awaken the child within the man.' So that's exactly what I did.

   I approached Mr Potts as Russell the boy of nine and three quarters and since I had my football with me, I asked him to play a game with me. At first he told me to go away, but I took no notice and I began kicking my ball towards him and just talking to him. When I invited him to climb a tree with me, he said that was 'stuff and nonsense !' But I could sense a little bit of a thaw within him, so I kept talking to him and generally making a childish nuisance of myself. Then to my astonishment I actually began to feel as though Mr Potts rather liked it.

   One time I had other work to do, so when I next saw Mr Potts, do you know what he said to me ?
He said, 'where have you been and why haven't you been to see me ?'
For the first time I had a positive response from him. It seemed he had really missed me but I told him I'd been busy and 'anyway he wasn't much fun, because he wouldn't play football or anything.'

   Then something remarkable happened. Mr Potts got up off his boxes and kicked the ball back to me. So I just kicked it back - and he kicked to me again ! We did this for a fair while, until he suddenly realised that he was enjoying himself. Now he hadn't done this for years and feelings can be very strange, so he suddenly got back on his box again. However, I kept coming back to him again and again and did all manner of things to get his attention. Gradually he would get up off his boxes and stay off them for longer periods each time.

   Then Mr Potts began to laugh at my childish antics and this shifted his consciousness just enough, so that he could start to see things in the garden. He saw the trees for the first time and the grass, then he started to play with the football a little more. Next we started going for little walks and suddenly this lovely land that he was in, became totally visible to him.

As we talked, I learned that he had once been a fine little boy with a big ♥, though he never knew his father and his mother had died when he was young. He told me how he'd been evicted from his home and had to live rough for a while. As all this happened to him he gradually found it harder and harder to love and over time, it seemed he'd even forgotten how to love himself. Eventually he began to think there was something wrong with *him and that he wasn't even good enough for love at all !*

Sometime later, Alexander J. Potts was given the chance to review his life and he asked me to come along with him. Everything he'd told me was revealed, including how he <u>chose</u> to be alone and isolated in his life. We saw how he'd turned away every offer of help that was given to him and how he'd chosen material things over emotional and Spiritual ones. He explained to me that at least he knew where he was with money.

These days Alexander has re-evaluated his life and is learning a great deal. He no longer sits on his boxes of wealth and has developed an incredible liking for ice cream ! This is something I introduced him to while I helping him and he has loved it ever since. I can say now that I love him too, because Alexander J. Potts has been one of the best teachers I've ever had !

* * *

John told me that soon the time would come when I could meet the little baby I'd been told about, the one I could be a guardian for.

The little girl's Spirit name was 'Rainbow' and had been born on Earth and lived for just twelve days. She was then brought back to our land and spent her first year in the Baby Castle. When I went to obtain my Spiritual Guardianship of this little girl, I was asked why I wanted this special responsibility. My answers must have been satisfactory, because then I was able to collect this beautiful and lovely little girl called Rainbow.

Now Rainbow was told from the very beginning that her family lived on the Earth and that she would be forever loved by them. She was told that I would be there to help her grow and teach her how to love. I was so proud of Rainbow then and I still am, because she has a part of my ♥ and I think I have a part of her ♥ too !

I never expected to have a little girl to care for. I once thought of having a little boy, but then thought, well if I'm going to be involved in parenting I should have a little girl so I can learn about the female energy. Rainbow has now taught me a great deal and I hope I have managed to teach her something of value too.

Her mother on Earth is B- my Medium and I owe her Spirit daughter the care she deserves, especially for all the help she gives me and my parents on Earth. In fact I cannot imagine my life without her now. In the future I may care for other children or maybe they might choose me, I don't know, but Rainbow will always be very special.

Dear Mum and Dad, I wanted to share all this with you, to show how I got from the time of the séances, to where I am today. I think I've learnt some positive things and I hope this can help me draw closer to the Earth...'

B-: It's almost time to complete this channelled tape. It's December 22nd 1998 and Christmas time and my son and daughter have recently decorated our Christmas tree, so its parcels all round ! It's a very important time, a time of Love and Hope and Peace and the story of a child that would grow up and die far too young.

It's a time of giving and sharing and I believe it's a time that we should each look within ourselves to examine all that we have known and felt over the past year. I fully hope that early in the Spring we'll be ready for a greater Love. So now I leave the rest of this tape to our Spirit friends...

Russell: *'Well Mum and Dad, it looks like we're going for completion here ! It's Christmas time and some would say the most powerful time of the year. Why ? Well you'll just have to wait and see !*

You already know how B- and I spent time blending our energies, so we could do this work. This gave me a wonderful opportunity to witness more of life as it happens on Earth and I have learned so much. I've learned how to draw close to B- who, in her life experience has been savaged by some damaged people, so much so that she was in danger of closing her ♥ chakra altogether. She'd had quite enough pain in her life. Yet we knew there was even more to come and she would face a new challenge. We knew it would be very important for her and her family that she survived this challenge. Since we knew of her sensitivity and Mediumship, it was most important that she kept her ♥ chakra open, so we helped by bringing the right people into her life.

Many people, especially sensitives and Mediums, can completely close off their emotional receptors, including their ♥, after damaging life experiences. People may not do this on a conscious level, but many who suffer cannot bear their emotional pain any longer and the result can often be disease of the body. So if a person tells you that they suffer from a ♥ problem, it may be worth asking them who it was that broke their ♥.

I realise this is not an orthodox way of viewing the issue, but it's always worth examining the problem from a different perspective. Disease of the ♥ is one of the greatest killers on Earth today, especially in the Western world, so the question 'who broke your ♥' is always well worth asking.

Our wish is to not allow disorders of the ♥ to manifest in the first place. We prefer you to care for the ♥ chakra so these disorders can become a thing of the past. Try to open up your perception, to not only of what broke your ♥, but to what made you close it up in the first place. You may not find the answer immediately, but with time and application you will find the key. Of course, because you are endless and eternal souls, some problems of the ♥ may be the result of hurt from an earlier lifetime. As I always say: the ♥ is slow to learn.

Now before we close I wish to introduce someone who rarely ever speaks through a Medium. In fact he rarely speaks at all, since he is more of a listener. This Master of the White Brotherhood came into the B-'s life in August 1992. Initially, he simply came as a healer for B-'s son, after he'd been through a traumatic experience. He drew close to help him and B- had no idea he was with her also. She only knew he was helping her boy. He calls himself Wolf Dancer and is here now. Before he speaks my Mother wishes to just add something...'

Gwen: A few weeks before this tape was made, my friend Marion and I were together for one of our weekly automatic writing sessions. A communicator came through and told us that B- would soon have a great new Spiritual force come into her life. I never spoke of this to B- and at the time, she didn't appear to have a Spirit helper from the Native American race, as many Mediums do. Even after she told me that she'd seen a Native American in full head dress, I still said nothing.

Later she told me herself that he was there to work with her, only then did I say that I knew he was coming !

Wolf Dancer: 'I wish to speak because I wish to join this company. Much has been written here about the Mother's love for her child and it is right that this should be honoured. Now I wish to speak of the Love a Father has for his child. My name is Wolf Dancer and I lived on the Earth as one of the Choc-a-Towa people, many years ago. It is difficult to remember how long, when one sees many Summers. One season melts into the other and your Earth time has nothing to do with Spirit time.

I lived on the Plains of North America as a native when the white man just began to travel to our lands. I met a white man once and when he saw me, he saw a savage, but when I looked at him, I saw a savage ! It was not time for us to come together then. During that lifetime I had a wife and a daughter and I would watch and teach her plenty. We lived together. She is very special to me, a daughter of my heart. I taught her the sacred union between people and the Earth and how to honour other soul groups as brother and sister. I taught her to think in circles.

Many, many, years later my daughter incarnated between another man and woman and she walks the Earth again, as a white woman - but I am still a red man. My wish is not to offend your people of the Western culture who find reincarnation difficult to accept, but it is a reality. My daughter is now a white woman, but I still love her. I feel this in the heart, yet when I drew close to her I know she did not have an open mind for reincarnation.

I did not know how she felt about having another Papa from another time, but I did hear her say 'North American Indians are very Spiritual people' ! Not all people understand this, but it made my heart sing. I knew my daughter had not forgotten all of our life together. I knew she had some knowledge.

During her lifetime she has seen me watch over her son, who I call 'Little Brave.' She did not know that I came not only for her son, but for all of them, for they were all facing great sadness of the heart at that time. I speak to my daughter in dreams and send animals, for she has not forgotten the animals and loves them still. So I send animals to her in dreams.

One that came first was the Wolf. I know in your culture and tradition the wolf is bad, a monster. In our tradition and culture the wolf is the pathfinder and the teacher. I knew that if I sent the wolf to lead her through the green forest of meditation, if she followed, she would eventually find me. Also through the song of Russell's Mother, the song called 'Papa can you hear me,' she understands that in another lifetime I was her Papa.

She is my daughter and knowledge of this made her heart sing, for Father love can be as strong as Mother love ! It is different, but can be as strong. Often a man will not acknowledge the love of his child, not even to himself, this is a great shame for both man and child. For if they lose that child to death, the man can not grieve in the same way as the woman. This is very bad medicine. Man cannot grieve the same as a woman, for man is not the same as woman, but they should honour their grief and let it go. They should not dishonour the quest to find Truth so easily.

Men are frightened of love and frightened of the power of love. This does not mean that men have no courage, it means he does not understand. It takes a man many lifetimes to understand these things. I have a simple mind and my brothers are a simple people. We use our eyes and ears. We observe and we listen. We try to live in harmony with the planet. The main difference between the red man and the white man is, the red man thinks in circles, the white man thinks in straight lines. We all go to the same place and we all follow the same Truth, so we should honour the sacred spiral.

The white man goes in straight lines. You live in square houses, we live in round houses, we honour the circle. Your vehicles travel on the planet far too fast and are never of the circle, always the straight line. The tool you use for trade called money is mostly of the straight line. Only in worthless coin circles !

When you consider reincarnation you find it hard to understand, for you think in straight lines, as though you have one life, as though you just go to the land of your ancestor and stay there forever. The red man knows he lives one life, but that he returns to the Great Spirit, so it's a circle. If you think in circles you will understand how we incarnate many times, we have much to learn. We can live a life of the red man, one of the white man and another of the brown man. With knowledge of all of the races you might have been, doesn't that make your prejudices of colour seem to be of no consequence ?
Whatever race you may condemn today, you were probably one of that race yesterday or may be of that race tomorrow. So do not make it hard for yourself by condemning a race or colour. That is all I will say.'

Russell: *'Wolf Dancer would you answer a few questions which may interest my parents and some others ? We are approaching an important time, the Millennium...'*

Wolf Dancer: 'Yes, yes, Russell. I know of this. My people have long known of this, my people knew of this when I walked the Earth. This began a confusion for my people. It was written in prophecy that when the white man come with the circle, it would be time for us to work together. On the white man's cart we saw wheels so we believed the white man understood the circle ! It was not the right time. I believed it was not the right time, but others believed it was. So the history of my people happened.'

Russell: *'Was it a total tragedy for your people ?'*

Wolf Dancer: 'Well my people needed to evolve and to grow, but in order to grow, our beliefs and our teachings had to be true. We had to be sure in the heart and soul that this was so. Then the savage came to our land and questioned our belief. So we had to be sure what we believed, to then fight for it and find a peaceful solution.'

Russell: *'So are you saying that the history of your nation has been an exercise in Spiritual growth ?'*

Wolf Dancer: 'My heart has bled for my people and it has been very hard. It sounds easy to say, but yes."

Russell: *'Have you tried to help in dreams?'*

Wolf Dancer: 'The sweat lodges and animal lodges have tried to help, though it has not been easy. There comes a time when we must learn from past. We must know of the past and must examine the past - both the white man and the red man. Then decide the path for the future and whether to allow it ever to happen again. It is all about personal responsibility.'

Russell: *'What would be your message to the white man and the red man?'*

Wolf Dancer: 'To find peace, to find the way forward <u>together.</u> It is the only way. You cannot forever keep living in the past, for if you do not live in the present, you cannot make a future! That is the truth for all races on your planet today.'

Russell: *'Would you speak to us a little of the planet?'*

Wolf Dancer: 'Yes Russell, I can speak to you of this. Many believe the planet is a dead thing that you own, but this is the Mother planet which is on her own Spiritual journey. She shape-shifts and she grows, as we grow.

Many years ago there were stories among our people, there was a race that lived in harmony with the planet and would only tread lightly on the Earth. They looked into their future and they saw – nothing. They could see nothing, because they were no longer there. They were to disappear and leave no trace of themselves behind. They tried to change it, but they couldn't. So they sent people out over the Earth to leave a record of their existence. Some of these records reside on your Earth today and wait to be found.

Even in your time, other races take to the cosmos, a great star nation and other informants in different dimensions of time and space. Their legacies are all waiting to be uncovered when you are ready to understand, but if a calamity happens, the master race is finished - gone, with no one, not even a memory left behind.'

Russell: *'So if these people lived in such harmony and peace with the planet, why did this happen?'*

Wolf Dancer: 'Many reasons, but the planet allowed it to happen because she needed to grow. What people don't understand is that the planet has allowed the two-legged to abuse her. That way, she grows.'

Russell: *'You mean Spiritual growth?'*

Wolf Dancer: 'Yes. If Mother Earth did not want the two-legged to live on her surface, she would shake them off, just like a dog shakes off it's fleas.

She would drown them in the river, or roll on them in the river. She would get rid of them, but she needs the two-legged so she can learn from the experience and grow. Then she can shape-shift into another reality.'

Russell: *'So that gives us a bit of a different view, as far as the abuse of the planet.'*

Wolf Dancer: 'Always we think in a circle - you think in a straight line.'

Russell: *'Yes. So the Earth needs us ?'*

Wolf Dancer: 'A mother always needs it's child, the same as the Earth needs the two-legged. Is this book not all about 'Mother and Child ?' I speak of the same connection between the two-legged and the Earth. It is the same as mother and child.'

Russell: *'So what form will this time of change take ?'*

Wolf Dancer: 'I do not know, it is in the future. Time is not set, the future can be built. No one knows.'

Russell: *'Can you tell us anything else ?'*

Wolf Dancer: 'Only that people must listen to their heart ! What is the word in your language ? Develop...people must develop their intuitive link to know what is real and what is not real. It is very important for people all over the planet. They will find a way.'

Russell: *'Do you think the planet wants us to go into the next Millennium ?'*

Wolf Dancer: 'Yes, for she is the Mother. Tell me, what mother would turn on her child however ungrateful the child is ?'

Russell: *'Not many.'*

Wolf Dancer: 'Few mothers. Even a father may make a lot of noise, but very few turn on their child.'

Russell: *'So it's still a love story !'*

Wolf Dancer: 'It is always a love story Russell and though I am very old, I know these things !
I have a question Russell. Your Mother, will she listen to this tape ?'

Russell: *'Yes she will write it all down.'*

Wolf Dancer: 'So she will write down these words and they will be used to close the book. Mmm, this is good. Your mother is a lady who sings. I call her 'Painted Lady.' She thought for a time that I called her 'Dream Weaver' which is a thing we do in the lodge...'

Russell: *'So you call her 'Painted Lady ?'*

Wolf Dancer: 'Yes. Your father, will he also listen ?'

Russell: *'Yes, he'll read the words.'*

Wolf Dancer: 'I call your father 'Silver Fox' for he is strong in his council. Ha ! And Little Brave, the son of my daughter B-. He listens and watches like the Hawk !'

Russell: *'What about B-'s daughter ?'*

Wolf Dancer: 'I give the little girl the Buffalo and abundant prayers !'

Russell: *'...and your daughter B- ?'*

Wolf Dancer: 'Well she has to be the Blue Rose !'

Russell: *'Thank you very much for coming forward and sharing your thoughts.'*

Wolf Dancer: 'Thank you for inviting me to great meeting Russell.'

Russell: *'We will try to start thinking in circles, not straight lines. Thank you Wolf Dancer.'*

On the tape, a song is played here:

> *'No matter what they tell us,*
> *No matter what they do,*
> *No matter what they teach us,*
> *What we believe is true,*
>
> *No matter what they call us,*
> *However they attack,*
> *No matter where they take us,*
> *We'll find our own way back.'*
>
> ~ Andrew Lloyd Webber/Jim Steinman
> from the musical 'Whistle Down The Wind.'

Russell: *'Hello Mum and Dad, I hope you've enjoyed listening to Wolf Dancer and me talking ? I wanted this song at the end because many people attack our beliefs or ideas that threaten their beliefs. Sometimes belief systems need to change. I know that's hard but it is all growth.*

Now Mum and Dad, I'd like you to begin to understand something of the significance of symbols or symbology, but I want to explain why it's important. If it's understood properly, symbology can lead you to discover hidden Truths. Truths that were once considered to be dangerous, yet held in the conscious memory. Truths that were against the predominant belief system of the past. As such, these Truths became a great danger for those who knew them and in order to them to be preserved, they were wrapped up in symbology.

This is why, Mum and Dad, during my time, I've tried to prepare you to begin thinking about symbology. I want to remind you of the poem you received through another Mum, called 'The Butterfly and the Humble Bee' (see Chapter 22.)

The reason I gave you the bee as a symbol was because, according to science, it is aerodynamically impossible for a bee to fly. The trouble is nobody's told the bee that and he's been flying around for centuries ! The phenomena you both witnessed at our séances are also considered impossible, yet you saw them. You witnessed the impossible. So I think that a bee is a very good symbol of the impossible being possible.

Now in it's hive, the bee is part of a social network. One bee does one job and another bee does another job. So bees live and work together in harmony, for the good of the whole.
Remember the time at the séance, when I asked you to form a society for other parents and call it 'Russell's Pink Panther Society' - well any society can work for the good of the whole and just like bees, you have worked for the good of the whole.

Of course the beehive is dominated by the Queen bee and she is an aspect of the feminine, the Mother. Through her, new life comes to incarnate on the Earth. This book is a story of Mothers who brought life to incarnate on the Earth, but whose children 'left them' while they were still young. Your children came to our land, yet you searched for them and you all <u>found</u> them. This is the principle on which you have all worked. You searched for your children and you found them.

So many believe this is impossible and say, 'when you're dead, you're dead' - but you've all discovered that we <u>do</u> go on. So we are back to the humble bee, who makes the impossible become possible, as he flies around the garden every day. Just think about it !

To explain a little more my friend John wishes to come forward...'

John: 'Thank you Russell.
It is with great joy that I come to speak to you on symbology. Throughout your history women have often been associated with the rose. Roses are an aspect of the feminine and Russell has asked me to explain why. Well to observe the rose, we see how her roots go deep down into the ground. She is planted in the Autumn when the wind grows cold - but it is during this

time of harshness that the rose settles her roots into the earth. Once she has centred herself in the source of all life, only then can she bring forth life. She sends out new roots and shoots, with stems, leaves and thorns, which if you brush up against them they can make you bleed.

In the Summer when the temperature is kind and the sun is warm, the rose blooms to share her perfume and wonderful colour. The first rose appears and it is perfect and shows all of God's perfection in the sunshine. Then when skies grow dark once more and Winter comes, she sends her roots to grow more firmly into the ground. She waits for the Spring and the chance to bloom again in maturity and greater depth, when she will send forth new flowers. She is the symbol of the colour of life, of Love and of cold misfortune and harsh experience. Such is the cycle of the rose.

The times that ladies suffer loss, disenchantment, aridity and grief on the Earth plane, are the times she should grow deeper roots and return to the Source. By doing this she can find out who she really is ! Those of us in the Great White Brotherhood, know that any soul who chooses to incarnate in the female form, comes to Earth with knowledge from God.

Because the female form is capable of allowing new life to incarnate through her, she is born with great power, but with this power comes great responsibility. For if she faces the wondrous reality of aligning with the God force, to allow young souls and old souls to incarnate through her, then by that very act of creation, she knows that each must eventually die and return to our land of Light. It is in the heart and soul of every woman.

Any woman born on the Earth knows, that the moment of birth will lead to the inevitable moment of death - for all that are born on the Earth must one day die to leave it. This knowledge of life, death and rebirth, is carried at a soul level within every woman, though sometimes this awareness is too hard to bear. So despite the knowledge which brings the thorns to make us bleed, the bloom of the rose remains.'

Russell: *'Thank you very much John.*

Have you noticed Mother, that it has been men who have channelled the information for this tape, through a lady Medium. Perhaps you have wondered why ? Well this is to show you how good the balance between male and female energies can be. I hope the work we've done through this Medium has helped to open your mind a little, to the possibility of the balance that <u>can</u> be achieved between the male and female energies.

I do not mean to say that our lady Medium cannot channel a female energy, for she has done so before. In fact, her young daughter Rainbow is with me now and wishes to speak...'

Rainbow: *'Hello Mummy. I've waited a very, very long time to talk to you. Lots of people are here tonight, lots of people who want to talk to you and say lots of things through you, to others on the Earth. But I've come to say hello and to say I love you.*

Mummy, I know that my life and my death made you very, very sad and many, many times you wondered why it happened to us and why I only stayed with you for twelve days and then returned to Spirit ? Well Mummy, you and I have known each other before. We have lived upon the Earth before in different relationships. I know you may find that hard to believe Mummy but it's true - honestly.

Now Mummy, I wanted to come back down through the levels to work closely with people on the Earth. So before you came to Earth yourself for this life, you agreed with Daddy to allow me to incarnate on the Earth, through you. I needed to be born on Earth for a while, so I could come down through the levels in my world, to work with you and others now.

I am spending the rest of my childhood in the Land of Summer, but I incarnated on the Earth for a short time to be with you in this lifetime now.

The agreement you made, was taken away from your and Daddy's memory, so neither of you would fully understood that I was only coming here for a short time. But deep down in your soul you were expecting me. I knew you would be sad Mummy but I never left you. I am always with you. There was a purpose to my life and death on Earth !

Our friend John came to collect me from your world and take me into ours, though at first you were very, very angry with him about this. But you see, he agreed to do this for us long ago - at the very beginning. I have heard you say Mummy, that my life and my death changed your life. That's not something I did Mummy, that's something you did. Now you can help other parents open up their minds to the idea that they never lose their children - because every night in dream time, we are with them.

I love you very much and Daddy and my brother and sister. I will always love you all and always watch over you and try to help all you through.

I had a very easy journey Mummy, from your world to ours and I stayed with some lovely people in the Baby Castle. They looked after me until I was one year old, then Russ came to collect me and I made many, many friends over here. I have visited your grandparents here and many people who love you. Over here, I have lots of grandmothers and grandfathers and uncles and aunts all over the place ! I have Daddy now too and Poppa Russ of course, but I only have one Mummy and that's you !

I know you worry about whether I'm happy. Well yes I am happy and I go to school and on journeys with Poppa Russ and we try to help people who are ill or damaged. We help people with their journeys from your world into ours and I have lots of friends here. I have my own painted pony that I ride with Wolf Dancer, who was your Papa once. He is my Great, Great, Great GrandPapa, so he goes a long way back!

I am where I belong Mummy and you are where you belong and we will meet lots and lots of times. Mummy, I want to thank you for all the love you gave me when I was with you on Earth and for all the love you have given me since.

I love you with all my ♥.

Goodbye Mummy and I'll see you at dream time. Goodbye Mummy!'

Russell: *'Well I can't add any more to that can I?*

So we should finish this tape now. Goodnight Mum. Goodnight Dad and as I have said before Mum, just go out and build your own 'Field of Dreams.'

Goodnight and God bless you both. All my Love, Russell x.'

Oh, let's finish with a song:

> *'The ♥ is slow to learn,*
> *These feelings that we feel*
> *are foolish but they're real.*
>
> *I'm wise not to see this love could never be,*
> *Each day's like the last when living in the past.*
>
> *I know it's mad that you won't return.*
> *But then as I have said,*
> *The ♥ is slow to learn.'*

~ *Don Black/Andrew Lloyd Webber*

Thirty

Here Comes The Millennium !

January 2000

*'Shall we not then be glad
and rejoice in joy of our children ?'*
~ Henry Wadsworth Longfellow
from his 1847 poem 'Evangeline.'

My story began back in 1963, yet now we have now zoomed beyond the year 2000 ! Like many people we were glad when the Millennium finally did arrive, for so much had been written and said about it.

After our amazing adventures in the 1980s, the 1990s seemed quite tame in comparison. Yet we did have some truly wonderful times, which I'll never forget. However, the 90s also brought us a lot of trauma and like all families, we too experienced loss.

My own sister Doreen passed away, then Alfie's dear sister Stella and my brother-in-law Bill both passed away. We were all saddened of course, but we didn't grieve for them because we knew they'd all simply 'gone home'. Yet, I feel for all those in the family who don't share our understanding that nobody really dies. After all, they have their own beliefs and not everyone wants to know about life after death.

I saw Alfie's sister Stella, shortly before she passed and she whispered something to me. She said, *'Gwen, I've seen my Sean-y with his arms stretched out to me.'* (See Chapter 4)

So I said, *'Stella, he's your grandson and he's waiting to welcome you, so go. Go and gather him up in your arms.'*

Which is exactly what she did.

We experienced all the highs and lows of the 90s, but thankfully the highs often far outweigh the lows. I always find the 'Karmic stuff' the hardest to bear. Although there are often good reasons for certain events occurring, we can still find ourselves reeling for a time. We just have to lick our wounds and move on.

It's often said that 'as one door closes, another one opens' - so with the turn of the Millennium, I began to see that opening door and watch with great interest.

Our sadness continued for a time during the 1990s, because we lost touch with Alfie's brother Ron, the ex-monk. I think our religious differences did keep us apart, but I always wondered about him so much and dreamt of him many times. I'm not sorry for publishing *'Russell'* for it was a story that had to be written, but maybe I offended Ron with my views and for that I feel sad. Yet maybe there's a Karmic connection there too ? I'm sure my Spirit friends know all about it, but they've never let on.

My brother-in-law Ron, is one of the finest and dearest men you could meet, though maybe we must wait until we both arrive 'home' in the Spirit World, before we can find our compromise !

As the years roll by I feel sure that it's time people just Loved more. We must all respect each other's opinions with forgiveness and understanding - so instead of prejudice, let's have tolerance. We all know what's happening to planet Earth, which I feel is all down to imbalance. She is our Mother and the Earth can think and feel just as we do in our physical bodies. Just as there can be an imbalance in our own body and we feel ill, it is exactly the same with the planet. So what are we going to do about it ? We know we have to do something...

However, I've said enough about that and there are countless books out there full of advice. The trick is, to read the right ones of course ! There are also hundreds of songs about healing the world and love changing everything. As Russell says *'you've got to think with your ♥'* and it does work, for as the Beatles song goes, *'All You Need Is Love...'*

During 1999 I spent a lot of time in deep thought, which isn't difficult when day after day the media is full of such horrendous images.
I recently relived some of the last hundred years of history, after watching some riveting vintage newsreel pictures. The past 100 years have seen phenomenal changes, yet after seeing film of the dreadful battles in the fields of Flanders and Ypres, I think to myself, *'what have we learned ?'*

I have an old sepia photograph of my Dad's brother, Arthur. He was lost in action in 1917 - my God, what a waste ! Yet when I look at my photograph of his lovely face, he is the double of a grown up Russell. If you see the Spirit portrait of Russell as a man in this book, you would honestly think they were the same person.

After World War One, we endured even more horror with the Second

World War. Our own country was bombed and we heard children scream. There were hideous gas masks and everything was rationed. We had Anderson shelters in our gardens and there were battles in the skies, on the seas and on the land. So many of the soldiers and servicemen were little more than boys when they were torn away from their homes, to die abroad. Not to mention those who were sent to their deaths on pointless bombing raids. When I think of it and remember my own lovely cousin, another Russell, who was also lost in battle, how can one not be moved by it all ?

I don't need to speak of the horrors of the Holocaust. We all saw those devastating images of families and their children. Then when there's a new conflict, we see even more pictures - of sick mothers trying desperately to nurse their ill or dying babies and they are so innocent and helpless. It's so distressing. We seem to have outdone the Biblical Herod long ago and over and over again. So with all this in mind, the knowledge that *we don't die* is truly the most important knowledge we can ever have. Those who know it should really try and spread this knowledge now !

It occurs to me as I write this chapter, that I've gone round in a complete circle. I've come right back to the beginning of the book with my memories of war, without even realising it. Isn't life strange ?

Yet I must end this chapter on a happier note and in March 2000, Alfie and I celebrated our Golden Wedding Anniversary and three months before that, we were getting geared up for Christmas.

It was all go, go, go. Wrap the pressies, post the parcels, post the cards, decorate the house and dress the tree. The whole thing makes your head spin doesn't it ? My son Kevin and his wife Chris, had posted us an early Christmas gift, but the parcel had promptly vanished ! The post came and went and nothing - so where in the world had it gone ? Christmas came and went too, then the Millennium passed and still no parcel !

Then ten days into January, we returned from a shopping trip and on the back doorstep was the missing parcel ! It didn't even look creased and the brown paper was like new, so where had it been for the last four weeks ?

Once I opened it, I discovered a box containing three DVDs of some lovely musicals. There was *'My Fair Lady'*, *'The Sound Of Music'* and *'Me And My Gal.'* Now this last one took me back to my childhood, because the DVD cover described the original stage version. It opened at London's Victoria Palace Theatre in December 1938 and guess who had been there on opening night ? Me !

So no wonder young Mr Byrne had been singing it's songs down my ear all through Christmas !

> *'Me and my girl,*
> *Meant for each other,*
> *Sent for each other,*
> *And liking it so...*
> *Me and my girl,*
> *It's no use pretending,*
> *We knew the ending,*
> *a long time ago !'*

I had been puzzled with his timing of these songs though, because they're not very Christmassy are they ? However Russell knew all along what his beloved brother had sent me. So thanks Russell and Happy New Year !

Now I must finish this book, for something is calling me. No it's not Russell, it's my garden. It's still early January and the snowdrops are coming up beautifully, yet I still have to be ready for Spring. So tonight I'm going to bed to dream of flowers, although I'll probably wake up to 'his nibs' singing something like,

> *'Please, please don't eat the daisies,*
> *don't eat the daisies, please, please.*
> *Here I am waiting and anticipating,*
> *the kisses that I'll get from you..!'*

What more can I say ? Except, I love you Russell,

Mum x

Postscript

...& Russell Vernon Byrne has the last word!

   I want to share a few final thoughts before Russell has the last word. I know this is a long story, but it is Truth and that's all that matters in my world. I have grown Spiritually through it all and Russell has been the catalyst. Yet I couldn't have written this book with a cold detachment when it concerns my own child. It is the same for the other Mum's in this book.

   I feel sorry for anyone who remains unmoved after reading the other Mum's stories, especially since they have been told with such honesty. Yet we *are* all entitled to our own opinions, even though I believe that the evidence for Heaven is plentiful and Mother Love *is* a bridge.

   Now I am actually less concerned with whether my book *affects* readers, but more concerned that it contains *Truth*. For I have come to learn that there is always more to life than meets the eye, so all those 'experts' and science professors can keep silent. I don't mind what people think and although I really don't understand all the scientific stuff, I do know that I have a job to do within God's Plan - and do it I will!

   Even in the last few years I've learned so much and I must be true to myself and to Russell. I do believe that those who hurt us in life, are put there to teach us *how to love* and on another level, they simply teach us how *not* to be. All our certainties in life are hinged on uncertainties, so perhaps we should start to approach things in a more personal way. I really feel that everything happens for more than just one reason, so we must forever keep moving onwards and forwards.

   Happiness, when based on ignorance is delusion, so we must face facts, because giving lip service without behaviour has no value, love or charity. It's easy to talk, but - to use a Native American phrase - you have to *walk your talk*. This reminds me that many of our great leaders must be lonely people, for few dare to be different or unorthodox...

   I try not to let anything interfere with my inner peace now and even though I don't know what my future holds, I do know who holds it!

I look forward to the time when all my family and friends in the Spirit World can gather to greet me, with Russell and now my Alfie, at the front of the queue !

Sometimes I'm asked where the Spirit World actually is and I just say, *'it's no good asking me, I'm just a Mum.'*

Yet Russell did try very hard to explain it once when he said, *'you couldn't get there in a spaceship...but one day, perhaps you could just reach out your hand and we'll be there.'*

<u>Little People</u>
'from Les Misérables'

*'They laugh at me, these fellows just because I am so small,
They laugh at me, because I'm not a hundred foot tall,
I tell 'em there's a lot to learn, down here on the ground,
The world is big - but little people turn it around...*

*Little people know, when little people fight,
We may look easy pickings, but we got some bite.
So never kick a dog because it's just a pup,
You'd better run for cover when the pup grows up !
So we'll fight like twenty armies and we won't give up,
So be careful as you go, 'cos little people grow...*

~ Lyrics by Herbert Kretzmer 1980

Russell always said that *'by hook or by crook, I'll be last in this book'* and I know he wants to do his bit. So as promised, my son Russell Vernon Byrne finally has the last word...

Russell: *'Dear Mother, I send you roses and I send you music. You and I have shared many things as we have continued our life together, with me in my world and you in yours.*

This book is a testament, not just of my mother's love for me and my love for my mother and father, but also of the love between other children and their parents. It is primarily a story of children and parental love - it does not matter what these people become in life, because genuine love between a parent and child is completely unconditional. This is why we choose to work through that bond of love. Any of the mothers in this book will tell you, that the love they feel for their children in the Spirit World is equal to the love they feel for their children on Earth.

In any lifetime, some parents will come together to allow the children who have chosen them, to be born. They will contain the right balance for that new life to take root and incarnate into the world.

Those who experience loss through death, never actually lose those who they truly love. If two who are separated by death are truly one, in mind, Spirit and body on the Earth, then they will be one, in mind, body and Spirit in our world. Love survives the death experience and can even draw souls closer together. It is love that brings Spirit children back to their parents.

We hope that we have provided much for you to ponder on with this book, with the many possibilities about life, death and the effect of your interactions with others. If it has opened your mind even a little, then it will have served its purpose. My friends and I here in the Spirit realms, subscribe to the power of love, the power of truth and the most elusive of all things - wisdom. It is not for us or anyone else to tell you how to live your lives, you are here to choose that for yourselves. We can only hope to open your minds to the possible consequences of your actions. For every action we take has a consequence in this life, in our world and in other lifetimes.

If people knew how important they really were and how important their actions were in this life, they would understand so much more. People need to realise that it is much more important to be positive and constructive, rather than negative. For all beings that walk upon the Earth, either on two legs or four, or those that swim in the oceans or fly in the sky - each and every one has it's purpose.

We would also like to see come into reality, Mediumistic people working together on one project, without ego, jealousy or bitterness creeping into the equation ! During my time working with my Mother, Frankie Brown, Margaret Prentice and my channel B-, I have witnessed their comradeship, laughter and their tremendous interest, encouragement and enthusiasm. So to other Mediumistic people, I would say that it *is* possible to work that way, there is no need for ego or jealousy.

When a group of souls on the Earth gather to work with souls in our world, in one common cause and in the name of Love and Wisdom, then tremendous things can be achieved - and when you work in union and harmony, then tremendous information can be channelled. LOVE begins with the SOUL. You cannot feel love and comradeship with your associates on the Earth plane if you don't trust them - and if you really begin to think that any of us are greater or better or mightier than the Truth that is written, then we are already lost !

This book proves that it is possible for like-minded people to work together with decency, humour and with Love. Each and every one of those who have worked on this book, with your caring compassion and your complete faith and trust in each other, will not have the trust and love that you placed in us, betrayed.

I do want to say a word of thanks to my old mate 'frozen peas' Frankie ! My goodness we had some laughs and she really did open up - especially when those from the higher realms came to disturb her. Her wonderful efforts were a preparation for the great work to come, as she acted as a true co-operator with Spirit.

We wish others could share, not only the ability to communicate with us, but the ability to communicate with one another. The Earth would be a much better place if it were so.

I owe you all a great deal, but I must give special thanks to you Mum, for all the hard work and the many, many hours you spent transcribing these tapes into pages. I know it has been a labour of love and I love you for it.

God bless and thank you very much !

Love Russell x

Alfie & Russell

Printed by

id

ImprintDigital.com
Exeter